Modern DevOps Practices

Practices

Implement and secure DevOps in the public cloud with cutting-edge tools, tips, tricks, and techniques

Gaurav Agarwal

BIRMINGHAM—MUMBAI

Modern DevOps Practices

Group Product Manager: Wilson D'Souza

Publishing Product Manager: Vijin Boricha

Senior Editor: Arun Nadar

Content Development Editor: Mrudgandha Kulkarni

Technical Editor: Nithik Cheruvakodan

Copy Editor: Safis Editing

Project Coordinator: Ajesh Devavaram

Proofreader: Safis Editing

Indexer: Rekha Nair

Production Designer: Joshua Misquitta

First published: July 2021

Production reference: 2300821

Published by Packt Publishing Ltd.

Livery Place

35 Livery Street

Birmingham

B3 2PB, UK.

ISBN 978-1-80056-238-7

www.packt.com

I want to thank my wonderful wife, Deepti, for giving me the space and support I've needed to write this book. I'd also like to thank Vijin for granting me the opportunity to complete this journey and Ajesh for keeping me on track. Special thanks to Aniket for reviewing the book. The whole Packt editing team has helped this first-time author immensely, but I'd like to give special thanks to Mrudgandha and Arun, who edited most of my work.

Contributors

About the author

Gaurav Agarwal has a decade of experience as a **site reliability engineer (SRE)**, architect, tech influencer, trainer, mentor, and developer. Currently, Gaurav works as a cloud SRE at ThoughtSpot Inc. Prior to that, Gaurav worked as a cloud solutions architect at Capgemini and as a software developer at TCS. Gaurav has a B.Tech. in electronics and communication engineering, and he is a Certified Kubernetes Administrator, Certified Terraform Associate, and a Google Cloud Certified Professional Cloud Architect. When not working, Gaurav enjoys time with his wonderful wife, Deepti, and loves to read about history, human civilization, and the arts.

To the doctors, nurses, public health officials, and first responders who are protecting us from COVID-19.

About the reviewer

Aniket Mhala has more than 25 years of experience in solution architecture and implementing legacy and cloud-native systems. He heads a technology practice that mainly focuses on solution design, agile transformation, enterprise DevOps adoption, application modernization, and integration.

He is particularly experienced in microservices, modern DevOps, Kafka, cloud platforms, Docker, Kubernetes, and other open source frameworks. He has published the Anix framework for organization transformation and innovation.

Table of Contents

3

Creating and Managing Container Images

Section 2: Delivering Containers

6

Infrastructure as Code (IaC) with Terraform

7

Configuration Management with Ansible

8
IaC and Config Management in Action

9
Containers as a Service (CaaS) and Serverless Computing for Containers

10

Continuous Integration

11

Continuous Deployment/Delivery with Spinnaker

12
Securing the Deployment Pipeline

Section 3: Modern DevOps with GitOps

13
Understanding DevOps with GitOps

14

CI/CD Pipelines with GitOps

Other Books You May Enjoy

Index

Preface

This book goes beyond just the fundamentals of DevOps tools and their deployments. It covers practical examples to get you up to speed with containers, infrastructure automation, serverless container services, continuous integration and delivery, automated deployments, deployment pipeline security, GitOps, and more.

Who this book is for

If you are a software engineer, system administrator, or operations engineer looking to step into the world of DevOps within public cloud platforms, this book is for you. Current DevOps engineers will also find this book useful as it covers best practices, tips, and tricks to implement DevOps with a cloud-native mindset. Although no containerization experience is necessary, a basic understanding of the software development life cycle and delivery will help you get the most out of the book.

What this book covers

Chapter 1, *The Move to Containers*, introduces containers. Containers are in vogue lately, and though the concept is well understood, it is worth introducing to you the book's scope and how containers are changing the current IT landscape. As containers are a relatively new concept, it is imperative that we understand the best practices and techniques surrounding the building, deploying, and securing of container-based applications.

Chapter 2, *Containerization with Docker*, will introduce Docker and cover installing Docker, configuring Docker storage drivers, running our first Docker container, and monitoring Docker with journald and Splunk.

Chapter 3, *Creating and Managing Container Images*, covers Docker images. Docker images are one of the key components when working with Docker. In this chapter, we will learn about Docker images, the layered model, Dockerfile directives, how to flatten images, building images, and the best practices surrounding image building. We will also look at distroless images and how they are good from a DevSecOps perspective.

Chapter 4, Container Orchestration with Kubernetes – Part I, introduces Kubernetes. We will install Kubernetes using Minikube and KinD, talk a bit about Kubernetes' architecture, and then move on to the fundamental building blocks of Kubernetes, which include Pods, containers, ConfigMaps, secrets, and multi-container Pods.

Chapter 5, Container Orchestration with Kubernetes – Part II, moves on to the advanced concepts of Kubernetes, including networking, DNS, Services, Deployments, Horizontal Pod Autoscaler, and StatefulSets.

Chapter 6, Infrastructure as Code (IaC) with Terraform, introduces IaC with Terraform and explains the core concepts of IaC. We will then move on to a hands-on example where we will be building a resource group and a virtual machine from scratch on Azure using Terraform while understanding the core Terraform concepts.

Chapter 7, Configuration Management with Ansible, introduces configuration management with Ansible and explains its core concepts. We will then learn about the core Ansible concepts when configuring a MySQL and Apache application on Azure Virtual Machines.

Chapter 8, IaC and Config Management in Action, talks about immutable infrastructure using Packer and uses this, along with the concepts of *Chapter 5, Container Orchestration with Kubernetes – Part II*, and *Chapter 6, Infrastructure as Code (IaC) with Terraform*, to boot up an IaaS-based **Linux**, **Apache**, **MySQL**, and **PHP (LAMP)** stack on Azure.

Chapter 9, Containers as a Service (CaaS) and Serverless Computing for Containers, looks at how Kubernetes forms a hybrid between IaaS and PaaS approaches. But when we don't want to manage infrastructure and want something lightweight to host our container, we can look at serverless container services such as AWS ECS. We will also briefly discuss alternatives such as Google Cloud Run and Azure Container Instances. We will then discuss Knative, which is an open source, cloud-native, serverless technology.

Chapter 10, Continuous Integration, looks at continuous integration from a container perspective and talks about various tools and techniques for continuously building a container-based application. We will look at tools such as GitHub Actions, Jenkins, and AWS Cloud Build and discuss how and when to use each of them.

Chapter 11, Continuous Deployment/Delivery with Spinnaker, looks into continuous deployment/delivery using Spinnaker. Spinnaker is a modern continuous delivery tool that helps you deploy and manage your container application seamlessly.

Chapter 12, Securing the Deployment Pipeline, explores multiple ways of securing a container deployment pipeline, including managing secrets, storing secrets, container image analysis, vulnerability scanning, and binary authorization.

Chapter 13, Understanding DevOps with GitOps, looks at the GitOps approach for doing DevOps and how it is expanding in popularity.

Chapter 14, CI/CD Pipeline with GitOps, gets hands-on and sees you create a complete CI/CD pipeline using the GitOps approach. We will look at tools such as GitHub Actions and Flux CD.

To get the most out of this book

For this book, you will need the following:

- An Azure subscription to perform some of the exercises. Currently, Azure offers a free trial for 30 days with $200 worth of free credits; sign up at `https://azure.microsoft.com/en-in/free`.

- An AWS subscription. Currently, AWS offers a free tier for some products. You can sign up at `https://aws.amazon.com/free`. The book uses some paid services, but we will try to minimize how many we use as much as possible during the exercises.

- A Google Cloud Platform subscription. Currently, Google Cloud Platform provides a free $300 trial for 90 days, which you can go ahead and sign up for at `https://console.cloud.google.com/`.

Software/hardware covered in the book	OS requirements
Google Cloud Platform	Windows, macOS, or Linux
Azure	Windows, macOS, or Linux
AWS	Windows, macOS, or Linux
A Linux machine (physical or virtual)	Ubuntu 16.04 Xenial LTS

For some chapters, you will need to clone the following GitHub repository to proceed with the exercises:

`https://github.com/PacktPublishing/Modern-DevOps-Practices`

Download the color images

We also provide a PDF file that has color images of the screenshots/diagrams used in this book. You can download it here: `http://www.packtpub.com/sites/default/files/downloads/9781800562387_ColorImages.pdf`.

Conventions used

There are a number of text conventions used throughout this book.

`Code in text`: Indicates code words in text, database table names, folder names, filenames, file extensions, pathnames, dummy URLs, user input, and Twitter handles. Here is an example: "We're doing two things in this command – first, we are running `gcloud secrets versions access latest --secret=flask-app-secret` to access the contents of the secret, and then we are piping it directly to `kubectl apply -f -`."

A block of code is set as follows:

```
...
    spec:
      containers:
        - image: '<your_docker_user>/flask-app-secret:1'
          name: flask-app
          ports:
            - containerPort: 5000
          env:
            - name: SECRET
              valueFrom:
                secretKeyRef:
                  name: flask-app-secret
                  key: SECRET
```

Bold: Indicates a new term, an important word, or words that you see onscreen. For example, words in menus or dialog boxes appear in the text like this. Here is an example: "Click **Flash** from Etcher to write the image."

Any command-line input or output is written as follows:

```
$ git clone https://github.com/PacktPublishing/Modern-DevOps-\
Practices.git modern-devops
$ cd modern-devops/ch7
```

> **Tips or important notes**
> Appear like this.

Get in touch

Feedback from our readers is always welcome.

General feedback: If you have questions about any aspect of this book, mention the book title in the subject of your message and email us at customercare@packtpub.com.

Errata: Although we have taken every care to ensure the accuracy of our content, mistakes do happen. If you have found a mistake in this book, we would be grateful if you would report this to us. Please visit www.packtpub.com/support/errata, selecting your book, clicking on the Errata Submission Form link, and entering the details.

Piracy: If you come across any illegal copies of our works in any form on the Internet, we would be grateful if you would provide us with the location address or website name. Please contact us at copyright@packt.com with a link to the material.

If you are interested in becoming an author: If there is a topic that you have expertise in and you are interested in either writing or contributing to a book, please visit authors.packtpub.com.

Share Your Thoughts

Once you've read *Modern DevOps Practices*, we'd love to hear your thoughts! Scan the QR code below to go straight to the Amazon review page for this book and share your feedback.

https://packt.link/r/1-800-56238-1

Your review is important to us and the tech community and will help us make sure we're delivering excellent quality content.

Section 1: Container Fundamentals and Best Practices

This section will introduce you to the world of containers and build a strong foundation of knowledge regarding containers and container orchestration technologies. In this section, you will learn how containers help organizations build distributed, scalable, and reliable systems in the cloud.

This section comprises the following chapters:

- *Chapter 1, The Move to Containers*
- *Chapter 2, Containerization with Docker*
- *Chapter 3, Creating and Managing Container Images*
- *Chapter 4, Container Orchestration with Kubernetes – Part I*
- *Chapter 5, Container Orchestration with Kubernetes – Part II*

1
The Move to Containers

This first chapter will provide you with background knowledge of containers and how they change the entire IT landscape. While we understand that most DevOps practitioners will already be familiar with this, it is worth providing a refresher to build the rest of this book's base. While this book does not entirely focus on containers and their orchestration, modern DevOps practices heavily emphasize it.

In this chapter, we're going to cover the following main topics:

- The need for containers
- Container architecture
- Containers and modern DevOps practices
- Migrating to containers from virtual machines

By the end of this chapter, you should be able to do the following:

- Understand and appreciate why we need containers in the first place and what problems they solve.
- Understand the container architecture and how it works.

- Understand how containers contribute to modern DevOps practices.

- Understand the high-level steps of moving from a Virtual Machine-based architecture to containers.

The need for containers

Containers are in vogue lately and for excellent reason. They solve the computer architecture's most critical problem – *running reliable, distributed software with near-infinite scalability in any computing environment.*

They have enabled an entirely new discipline in software engineering – microservices. They have also introduced the *package once deploy anywhere* concept in technology. Combined with the cloud and distributed applications, containers with container orchestration technology has lead to a new buzzword in the industry – **cloud-native** – changing the IT ecosystem like never before.

Before we delve into more technical details, let's understand containers in plain and simple words.

Containers derive their name from shipping containers. I will explain containers using a shipping container analogy for better understanding. Historically, because of transportation improvements, there was a lot of stuff moving across multiple geographies. With various goods being transported in different modes, loading and unloading goods was a massive issue at every transportation point. With rising labor costs, it was impractical for shipping companies to operate at scale while keeping the prices low.

Also, it resulted in frequent damage to items, and goods used to get misplaced or mixed up with other consignments because there was no isolation. There was a need for a standard way of transporting goods that provided the necessary isolation between consignments and allowed for easy loading and unloading of goods. The shipping industry came up with shipping containers as an elegant solution to this problem.

Now, shipping containers have simplified a lot of things in the shipping industry. With a standard container, we can ship goods from one place to another by only moving the container. The same container can be used on roads, loaded on trains, and transported via ships. The operators of these vehicles don't need to worry about what is inside the container most of the time.

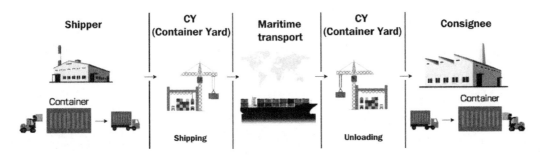

Figure 1.1 – Shipping container workflow

Similarly, there have been issues with software portability and compute resource management in the software industry. In a standard software development life cycle, a piece of software moves through multiple environments, and sometimes, numerous applications share the same operating system. There may be differences in the configuration between environments, so software that may have worked on a development environment may not work on a test environment. Something that worked on test may also not work on production.

Also, when you have multiple applications running within a single machine, there is no isolation between them. One application can drain compute resources from another application, and that may lead to runtime issues.

Repackaging and reconfiguring applications are required in every step of deployment, so it takes a lot of time and effort and is sometimes error-prone.

Containers in the software industry solve these problems by providing isolation between application and compute resource management, which provides an optimal solution to these issues.

The software industry's biggest challenge is to provide application isolation and manage external dependencies elegantly so that they can run on any platform, irrespective of the **operating system** (**OS**) or the infrastructure. Software is written in numerous programming languages and uses various dependencies and frameworks. This leads to a scenario called the matrix of hell.

The matrix of hell

Let's say you're preparing a server that will run multiple applications for multiple teams. Now, assume that you don't have a virtualized infrastructure and that you need to run everything on one physical machine, as shown in the following diagram:

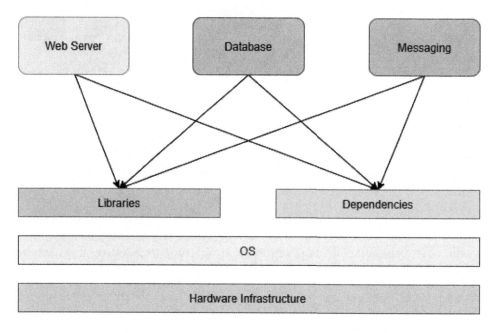

Figure 1.2 – Applications on a physical server

One application uses one particular version of a dependency while another application uses a different one, and you end up managing two versions of the same software in one system. When you scale your system to fit multiple applications, you will be managing hundreds of dependencies and various versions catering to different applications. It will slowly turn out to be unmanageable within one physical system. This scenario is known as the **matrix of hell** in popular computing nomenclature.

There are multiple solutions that come out of the matrix of hell, but there are two notable technology contributions – *virtual machines* and *containers*.

Virtual machines

A **virtual machine** emulates an operating system using a technology called a **Hypervisor**. A Hypervisor can run as software on a physical host OS or run as firmware on a bare-metal machine. Virtual machines run as a virtual guest OS on the Hypervisor. With this technology, you can subdivide a sizeable physical machine into multiple smaller virtual machines, each catering to a particular application. This revolutionized computing infrastructure for almost two decades and is still in use today. Some of the most popular Hypervisors on the market are VMWare and Oracle VirtualBox.

The following diagram shows the same stack on virtual machines. You can see that each application now contains a dedicated guest OS, each of which has its own libraries and dependencies:

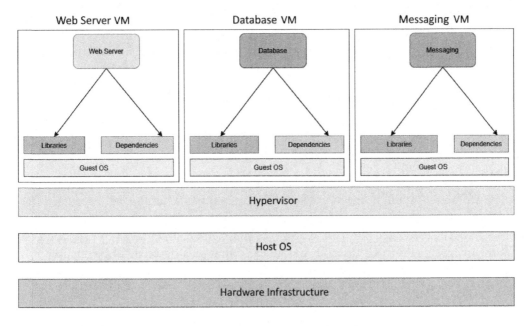

Figure 1.3 – Applications on Virtual Machines

Though the approach is acceptable, it is like using an entire ship for your goods rather than a simple container from the shipping container analogy. Virtual machines are heavy on resources as you need a heavy guest OS layer to isolate applications rather than something more lightweight. We need to allocate dedicated CPU and memory to a Virtual Machine; resource sharing is suboptimal since people tend to overprovision Virtual Machines to cater for peak load. They are also slower to start, and Virtual Machine scaling is traditionally more cumbersome as there are multiple moving parts and technologies involved. Therefore, automating horizontal scaling using virtual machines is not very straightforward. Also, sysadmins now have to deal with multiple servers rather than numerous libraries and dependencies in one. It is better than before, but it is not optimal from a compute resource point of view.

Containers

That is where containers come into the picture. Containers solve the matrix of hell without involving a heavy guest OS layer in-between them. Instead, they isolate the application runtime and dependencies by encapsulating them to create an abstraction called containers. Now, you have multiple containers that run on a single operating system. Numerous applications running on containers can share the same infrastructure. As a result, they do not waste your computing resources. You also do not have to worry about application libraries and dependencies as they are isolated from other applications – a win-win situation for everyone!

Containers run on container runtimes. While **Docker** is the most popular and more or less the de facto container runtime, other options are available on the market, such as **Rkt** and **Containerd**. All of them use the same Linux Kernel **cgroups** feature, whose basis comes from the combined efforts of Google, IBM, OpenVZ, and SGI to embed **OpenVZ** into the main Linux Kernel. OpenVZ was an early attempt at implementing features to provide virtual environments within a Linux Kernel without using a guest OS layer, something that we now call containers.

It works on my machine

You might have heard of this phrase many times within your career. It is a typical situation where you have erratic developers worrying your test team with *But, it works on my machine* answers and your testing team responding with *We are not going to deliver your machine to the client*. Containers use the *Build once, run anywhere* and the *Package once, deploy anywhere* concepts, and solve the *It works on my machine* syndrome. As containers need a container runtime, they can run on any machine in the same way. A standardized setup for applications also means that sysadmin's job has been reduced to just taking care of the container runtime and servers and delegating the application's responsibilities to the development team. This reduces the admin overhead from software delivery, and software development teams can now spearhead development without many external dependencies – a great power indeed!

Container architecture

You can visualize containers as mini virtual machines – at least, they seem like they are in most cases. In reality, they are just computer programs running within an operating system. Let's look at a high-level diagram of what an application stack within containers looks like:

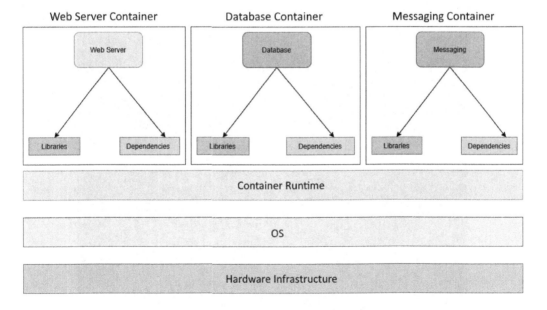

Figure 1.4 – Applications on containers

As we can see, we have the compute infrastructure right at the bottom forming the base, followed by the host operating system and a container runtime (in this case, Docker) running on top of it. We then have multiple containerized applications using the container runtime, running as separate processes over the host operating system using **namespaces** and cgroups.

As you may have noticed, we do not have a guest OS layer within it, which is something we have with virtual machines. Each container is a *software program* that runs on the Kernel userspace and shares the same operating system and associated runtime and other dependencies, with only the required libraries and dependencies within the container. Containers do not inherit the OS environment variables. You have to set them separately for each container.

Containers replicate the filesystem, and though they are present on disk, they are isolated from other containers. That makes containers run applications in a secure environment. A separate container filesystem means that containers don't have to communicate to and fro with the OS filesystem, which results in faster execution than Virtual Machines.

Containers were designed to use Linux namespaces to provide isolation and cgroups to offer restrictions on CPU, memory, and disk I/O consumption.

This means that if you list the OS processes, you will see the container process running along with other processes, as shown in the following screenshot:

```
$ pstree
systemd───NetworkManager───┬─{gdbus}
                           └─{gmain}
        ├─Thunar
        ├─Xtightvnc
        ├─accounts-daemon───┬─{gdbus}
                            └─{gmain}
        ├─acpid
        ├─2*[agetty]
        ├─amazon-ssm-agen───9*[{amazon-ssm-agen}]
        ├─2*[at-spi-bus-laun───┬─dbus-daemon]
                               ├─{dconf worker}]
                               ├─{gdbus}]
                               └─{gmain}]
        ├─2*[at-spi2-registr───┬─{gdbus}]
                               └─{gmain}]
        ├─atd
        ├─avahi-daemon───avahi-daemon
        ├─colord───┬─{gdbus}
                   └─{gmain}
        ├─containerd───┬─containerd-shim───┬─nginx───nginx
                       │                   └─9*[{containerd-shim}]
                       └─12*[{containerd}]
```

Figure 1.5 – OS processes

However, when you list the container's processes, you would only see the container process, as follows:

```
$ docker exec -it mynginx1 bash
root@4ee264d964f8:/# pstree
nginx---nginx
```

This is how namespaces provide a degree of isolation between containers.

Cgroups play a role in limiting the amount of computing resources a group of processes can use. If you add processes to a cgroup, you can limit the CPU, memory, and disk I/O that the processes can use. You can measure and monitor resource usage and stop a group of processes when an application goes astray. All these features form the core of containerization technology, which we will see later in this book.

Now, if we have independently running containers, we also need to understand how they interact. Therefore, we'll have a look at container networking in the next section.

Container networking

Containers are separate network entities within the operating system. Docker runtimes use network drivers to define networking between containers, and they are software-defined networks. Container networking works by using software to manipulate the *host iptables*, connect with external network interfaces, create tunnel networks, and perform other activities to allow connections to and from containers.

While there are various types of network configurations you can implement with containers, it is good to know about some widely used ones. Don't worry too much if the details are overwhelming, as you would understand them while doing the hands-on exercises later in the book, and it is not a hard requirement to know all of this for following the text. For now, let's list down various types of container networks that you can define, as follows:

- **None**: This is a fully isolated network, and your containers cannot communicate with the external world. They are assigned a loopback interface and cannot connect with an external network interface. You can use it if you want to test your containers, stage your container for future use, or run a container that does not require any external connection, such as batch processing.

- **Bridge**: The bridge network is the default network type in most container runtimes, including Docker, which uses the `docker0` interface for default containers. The bridge network manipulates IP tables to provide **Network Address Translation (NAT)** between the container and host network, allowing external network connectivity. It also does not result in port conflicts as it enables network isolation between containers running on a host. Therefore, you can run multiple applications that use the same container port within a single host. A bridge network allows containers within a single host to communicate using the container IP addresses. However, they don't permit communication to containers running on a different host. Therefore, you should not use the bridge network for clustered configuration.

- **Host**: Host networking uses the network namespace of the host machine for all the containers. It is similar to running multiple applications within your host. While a host network is simple to implement, visualize, and troubleshoot, it is prone to port-conflict issues. While containers use the host network for all communications, it does not have the power to manipulate the host network interfaces unless it is running in privileged mode. Host networking does not use NAT, so it is fast and communicates at bare metal speeds. You can use host networking to optimize performance. However, since it has no network isolation between containers, from a security and management point of view, in most cases, you should avoid using the host network.

- **Underlay**: Underlay exposes the host network interfaces directly to containers. This means you can choose to run your containers directly on the network interfaces instead of using a bridge network. There are several underlay networks – notably MACvlan and IPvlan. MACvlan allows you to assign a MAC address to every container so that your container now looks like a physical device. It is beneficial for migrating your existing stack to containers, especially when your application needs to run on a physical machine. MACvlan also provides complete isolation to your host networking, so you can use this mode if you have a strict security requirement. MACvlan has limitations in that it cannot work with network switches with a security policy to disallow MAC spoofing. It is also constrained to the MAC address ceiling of some network interface cards, such as Broadcom, which only allows 512 MAC addresses per interface.

- **Overlay**: Don't confuse overlay with underlay – even though they seem like antonyms, they are not. Overlay networks allow communication between containers running on different host machines via a networking tunnel. Therefore, from a container's perspective, it seems that they are interacting with containers on a single host, even when they are located elsewhere. It overcomes the bridge network's limitation and is especially useful for cluster configuration, especially when you're using a container orchestrator such as Kubernetes or Docker Swarm. Some popular overlay technologies that are used by container runtimes and orchestrators are **flannel**, **calico**, and **vxlan**.

Before we delve into the technicalities of different kinds of networks, let's understand the nuances of container networking. For this discussion, let's talk particularly about Docker.

Every Docker container running on a host is assigned a unique IP address. If you `exec` (open a shell session) into the container and run `hostname -I`, you should see something like the following:

```
$ docker exec -it mynginx1 bash
root@4ee264d964f8:/# hostname -I
172.17.0.2
```

This allows different containers to communicate with each other through a simple TCP/IP link. The Docker daemon does the DHCP server role for every container. You can define virtual networks for a group of containers and club them together so that you can provide network isolation if you so desire. You can also connect a container to multiple networks if you want to share it for two different roles.

Docker assigns every container a unique hostname that defaults to the container ID. However, this can be overridden easily, provided you use unique hostnames in a particular network. So, if you `exec` into a container and run `hostname`, you should see the container ID as the hostname, as follows:

```
$ docker exec -it mynginx1 bash
root@4ee264d964f8:/# hostname
4ee264d964f8
```

This allows containers to act as separate network entities rather than simple software programs, and you can easily visualize containers as mini virtual machines.

Containers also inherit the host OS's DNS settings, so you don't have to worry too much if you want all the containers to share the same DNS settings. If you're going to define a separate DNS configuration for your containers, you can easily do so by passing a few flags. Docker containers do not inherit entries in the `/etc/hosts` file, so you need to define them by declaring them while creating the container using the `docker run` command.

If your containers need a proxy server, you will have to set that either in the Docker container's environment variables or by adding the default proxy to the `~/.docker/config.json` file.

So far, we've been discussing containers and what they are. Now, let's discuss how containers are revolutionizing the world of DevOps and how it was necessary to spell this outright at the beginning.

But before we delve into containers and modern DevOps practices, let's understand modern DevOps practices and how it is different from traditional DevOps.

Modern DevOps versus traditional DevOps

DevOps is a set of principles and practices, as well as a philosophy, that encourage the participation of both the development and operations teams in the entire software development life cycle, software maintenance, and operations. To implement this, organizations manage several processes and tools that help automate the software delivery process to improve speed and agility, reduce the cycle time of code release through **continuous integration and delivery (CI/CD)** pipelines, and monitor the applications running in production.

DevOps' traditional approach would be to establish a DevOps team consisting of Dev, QA, and Ops members and work toward the common goal to create better software quicker. While there would be a focus on automating software delivery, the automating tools such as Jenkins, Git, and so on were installed and maintained manually. This led to another problem as we now had to manage another set of IT infrastructure. It finally boiled down to infrastructure and configuration, and the focus was to automate the automation process.

With the advent of containers and the recent boom in the public cloud landscape, DevOps' modern approach came into the picture, which involved automating everything. Right from provisioning infrastructure to configuring tools and processes, there is code for everything. Now, we have infrastructure as code, configuration as code, immutable infrastructure, and containers. I call this approach to DevOps modern DevOps, and it will be the entire focus of this book.

Containers help implement modern DevOps and form the core of the practice. We'll have a look at how in the next section.

Containers and modern DevOps practices

Containers follow DevOps practices right from the start. If you look at a typical container build and deployment workflow, this is what you get:

1.   First, code your app in whatever language you wish.

2.   Then, create a `Dockerfile` that contains a series of steps to install the application dependencies and environment configuration to run your app.

3.   Next, use the Dockerfile to create container images by doing the following:

     a) Build the container image

     b) Run the container image

     c) Unit test the app running on the container

4.   Then, push the image to a container registry such as **DockerHub**.

5.   Finally, create containers from container images and run them in a cluster.

You can embed these steps beautifully in the CI/CD pipeline example shown here:

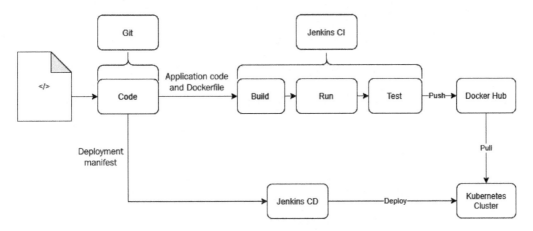

Figure 1.6 – Container CI/CD pipeline example

This means your application and its runtime dependencies are all defined in code. You are following configuration management from the very beginning, allowing developers to treat containers like ephemeral workloads (ephemeral workloads are temporary workloads that are dispensible, and if one disappears, you can spin up another one without it having any functional impact). You can replace them if they misbehave – something that was not very elegant with virtual machines.

Containers fit very well within modern CI/CD practices as you now have a standard way of building and deploying applications across, irrespective of what language you code in. You don't have to manage expensive build and deployment software as you get everything out of the box with containers.

Containers rarely run on their own, and it is a standard practice in the industry to plug them into a container orchestrator such as **Kubernetes** or use a **Container as a Service** (**CaaS**) platform such as AWS ECS and EKS, Google Cloud Run and Kubernetes Engine, Azure ACS and AKS, Oracle OCI and OKE, and others. Popular **Function as a Service** (**FaaS**) platforms such as AWS Lambda, Google Functions, Azure Functions, and Oracle Functions also run containers in the background. So, though they may have abstracted the underlying mechanism from you, you may already be using containers unknowingly.

As containers are lightweight, you can build smaller parts of applications into containers so that you can manage them independently. Combine that with a container orchestrator such as Kubernetes, and you get a distributed microservices architecture running with ease. These smaller parts can then scale, auto-heal, and get released independently of others, which means you can release them into production quicker than before and much more reliably.

You can also plug in a **service mesh** (infrastructure components that allow you to discover, list, manage, and allow communication between multiple components (services) of your microservices application) such as **Istio** on top, and you will get advanced Ops features such as traffic management, security, and observability with ease. You can then do cool stuff such as Blue/Green deployments and A/B testing, operational tests in production with traffic mirroring, geolocation-based routing, and much more.

As a result, large and small enterprises are embracing containers quicker than ever before, and the field is growing exponentially. According to businesswire.com, the application container market is showing a compounded growth of 31% per annum and will reach US$6.9 billion by 2025. The exponential growth of 30.3% per annum in the cloud, expected to reach over US$2.4 billion by 2025, has also contributed to this.

Therefore, modern DevOps engineers must understand containers and the relevant technologies to ship and deliver containerized applications effectively. This does not mean that Virtual Machines are not necessary, and we cannot completely ignore the role of **Infrastructure as a Service (IaaS)** based solutions in the market, so we will also cover a bit of config management in further chapters. Due to the advent of the cloud, **Infrastructure as code (IaC)** has been gaining a lot of momentum recently, so we will also cover Terraform as an IaC tool.

Migrating from virtual machines to containers

As we see the technology market moving toward containers, DevOps engineers have a crucial task–*migrating applications running on virtual machines so that they can run on containers*. Well, this is in most DevOps engineers' job descriptions at the moment and is one of the most critical things we do.

While, in theory, containerizing an application is simple as writing a few steps, practically speaking, it can be a complicated beast, especially if you are not using config management to set up your Virtual Machines. Virtual Machines running on current enterprises these days have been created by putting a lot of manual labor by toiling sysadmins, improving the servers piece by piece, and making it hard to reach out to the paper trail of hotfixes they might have made until now.

Since containers follow config management principles from the very beginning, it is not as simple as picking up the Virtual Machine image and using a converter to convert it into a Docker container. I wish there were such a software, but unfortunately, we will have to live without it for now.

Migrating a legacy application running on Virtual Machines requires numerous steps. Let's take a look at them in more detail.

Discovery

We first start with the discovery phase:

- Understand the different parts of your application.
- Assess what parts of the legacy application you can containerize and whether it is technically possible to do so.
- Define a migration scope and agree on the clear goals and benefits of the migration with timelines.

Application requirement assessment

Once the discovery is complete, we need to do the application requirement assessment.

- Assess if it is a better idea to break the application into smaller parts. If so, then what would the application parts be, and how will they interact with each other?

- Assess what aspects of the architecture, its performance, and its security you need to cater to regarding your application and think about the container world's equivalent.

- Understand the relevant risks and decide on mitigation approaches.

- Understand the migration principle and decide on a migration approach, such as what part of the application you should containerize first. Always start with the application with the least amount of external dependencies first.

Container infrastructure design

Once we've assessed all our requirements, architecture, and other aspects, we move on to container infrastructure design.

- Understand the current and future scale of operations when you make this decision. You can choose from a lot of options based on the complexity of your application. The right questions to ask include; how many containers do we need to run on the platform? What kind of dependencies do these containers have on each other? How frequently are we going to deploy changes to the components? What is the potential traffic the application can receive? What is the traffic pattern on the application?

- Based on the answers you get to the preceding questions, you need to understand what sort of infrastructure you will run your application on. Will it be on-premises or the cloud, and will you use a managed Kubernetes cluster or self-host and manage one? You can also look at options such as CaaS for lightweight applications.

- How would you monitor and operate your containers? Does it require installing specialist tools? Does it require integrating with the existing monitoring tool stack? Understand the feasibility and make an appropriate design decision.

- How would you secure your containers? Are there any regulatory and compliance requirements regarding security? Does the chosen solution cater to them?

Containerizing the application

When we've considered all aspects of the design, we can now start containerizing the application:

- This is where we look into the application and create a Dockerfile that contains the steps to create the container just the way it is currently. It requires a lot of brainstorming and assessment, mostly if config management tools don't build your application by running on a Virtual Machine such as Ansible. It can take a long time to figure out how the application was installed, and you need to write the exact steps for this.

- If you plan to break your application into smaller parts, you may need to build your application from scratch.

- Decide on a test suite that worked on your parallel Virtual Machine-based application and improve it with time.

Testing

Once we've containerized the application, the next step in the process is testing:

- To prove whether your containerized application works exactly like the one in the Virtual Machine, you need to do extensive testing to prove that you haven't missed any details or parts you should have considered previously. Run an existing test suite or the one you created for the container.

- Running an existing test suite can be the right approach, but you also need to consider the software's non-functional aspects. Benchmarking the original application is a good start, and you need to understand the overhead the container solution is putting in. You also need to fine-tune your application to fit the performance metrics.

- You also need to consider the importance of security and how you can bring it into the container world. Penetration testing will reveal a lot of security loopholes that you might not be aware of.

Deployment and rollout

Once we've tested our containers and are confident enough, we can roll out our application to production:

- Finally, we roll out our application to production and learn from there if further changes are needed. We then go back to the discovery process until we have perfected our application.

- Define and develop an automated runbook and a CI/CD pipeline to reduce cycle time and troubleshoot issues quickly.

- Doing A/B testing with the container applications running in parallel can help you realize any potential issues before you switch all the traffic to the new solution.

The following diagram summarizes these steps, and as you can see, this process is cyclic. This means you may have to revisit these steps from time to time, based on what you learned from the operating containers in production:

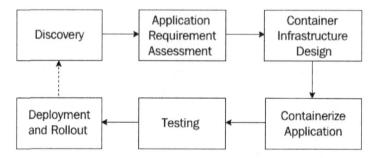

Figure 1.7 – Migrating from Virtual Machines to containers

Now let us understand what we need to do to ensure that we migrate from Virtual Machines to containers with the least friction and also attain the best possible outcome.

What applications should go in containers?

In our journey of moving from virtual machines to containers, you first need to assess what can and can't go in containers. Broadly speaking, there are two kinds of application workloads you can have – **stateless** and **stateful**. While stateless workloads do not store state and are computing powerhouses, such as APIs and functions, stateful applications such as databases require persistent storage to function.

Now, though it is possible to containerize any application that can run on a Linux Virtual Machine, stateless applications become the first low-hanging fruits you may want to look at. It is relatively easy to containerize these workloads because they don't have storage dependencies. The more storage dependencies you have, the more complex your application becomes in containers.

Secondly, you also need to assess the form of infrastructure you want to host your applications on. For example, if you plan to run your entire tech stack on Kubernetes, you would like to avoid a heterogeneous environment wherever possible. In that kind of scenario, you may also wish to containerize stateful applications. With web services and the middleware layer, most applications always rely on some form of state to function correctly. So, in any case, you would end up managing storage.

Though this might open up Pandora's box, there is no standard agreement within the industry regarding containerizing databases. While some experts are naysayers for its use in production, a sizeable population sees no issues. The primary reason behind this is because there is not enough data to support or disapprove of using a containerized database in production.

I would suggest that you proceed with caution regarding databases. While I am not opposed to containerizing databases, you need to consider various factors, such as allocating proper memory, CPU, disk, and every dependency you have in Virtual Machines. Also, it would help if you looked into the behavioral aspects within the team. If you have a team of DBAs managing the database within production, they might not be very comfortable dealing with another layer of complexity – containers.

We can summarize these high-level assessment steps using the following flowchart:

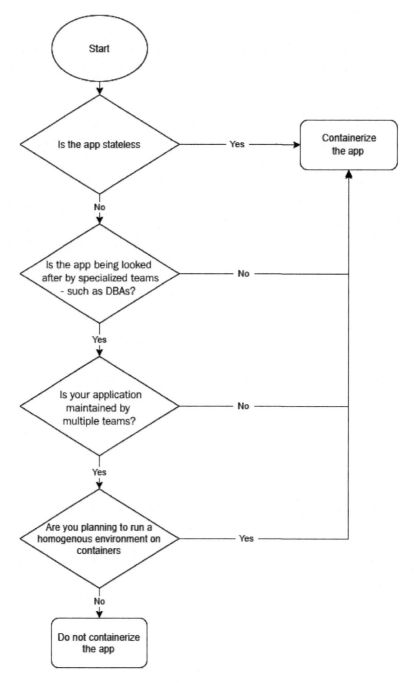

Figure 1.8 – Virtual Machine to container migration assessment

This flowchart accounts for the most common factors that are considered during the assessment. You would also need to factor in situations that might be unique to your organization. So, it is a good idea to take those into account as well before making any decisions.

Breaking the applications into smaller pieces

You get the most out of containers if you can run parts of your application independently of others.

This approach has numerous benefits, as follows:

- You can release your application more often as you can now change a part of your application without impacting the other; your deployments will also take less time to run as a result.

- Your application parts can scale independently of each other. For example, if you have a shopping app and your orders module is jam-packed, it can scale more than the reviews module, which may be far less busy. With a monolith, your entire application would scale with traffic, and this would not be the most optimized approach from a resource consumption point of view.

- Something that has an impact on one part of the application does not compromise your entire system. For example, if the reviews module is down, customers can still add items to their cart and checkout orders.

However, you should also not break your application into tiny components. This will result in considerable management overhead as you will not be able to distinguish between what is what. Going by the shopping website example, it is OK to have an order container, reviews container, shopping cart container, and a catalog container. However, it is not OK to have *create order*, *delete order*, and *update order* containers. That would be overkill. Breaking your application into logical components that fit your business is the right way to do it.

But should you bother with breaking your application into smaller parts as the very first step? Well, it depends. Most people would want to get a **return on investment** (**ROI**) out of your containerization work. Suppose you do a lift and shift from Virtual Machines to containers, even though you are dealing with very few variables and you can go into containers quickly. In that case, you don't get any benefits out of it – especially if your application is a massive monolith. Instead, you would be adding some application overhead on top because of the container layer. So, rearchitecting your application so that it fits in the container landscape is the key to going ahead.

Are we there yet?

So, you might be wondering, are we there yet? Not really! Virtual Machines are to stay for a very long time. They have a good reason to exist, and while containers solve most problems, not everything can be containerized. There are a lot of legacy systems running on Virtual Machines that cannot be migrated to containers.

With the advent of the cloud, *virtualized infrastructure* forms its base, and Virtual Machines are at its core. Most containers run on virtual machines within the cloud, and though you might be running containers in a cluster of nodes, these nodes would still be virtual machines.

However, the best thing about the container era is that it sees virtual machines as part of a standard setup. You install a container runtime on your Virtual Machines and then, you do not need to distinguish between them. You can run your applications within containers on any Virtual Machine you wish. With a container orchestrator such as Kubernetes, you also benefit from the orchestrator deciding where to run the containers while considering various factors – resource availability is one of the critical ones.

In this book, we will look at various aspects of modern DevOps practices, including managing cloud-based infrastructure, virtual machines, and containers. While we will mainly cover containers, we will also look at config management with equal importance using Ansible and how to spin up infrastructure with Terraform.

We will also look into modern CI/CD practices and learn how to deliver your application into production efficiently and error-free. For this, we will cover tools such as Jenkins and Spinnaker. This book will give you everything you need to perform a modern DevOps engineer role during the cloud and container era.

Summary

In this chapter, we looked at how the software industry is quickly moving toward containers and how, with the cloud, it is becoming more critical for a modern DevOps engineer to have the required skills to deal with both. Then, we took a peek at the container architecture and discussed some high-level steps in moving from a Virtual Machine-based architecture to a containerized one.

In the next chapter, we will install Docker and run and monitor our first container application.

Questions

1. Containers need a Hypervisor to run – true or false?

2. Which of the following statements regarding containers is NOT correct? (There may be multiple answers.)

   a. Containers are virtual machines within virtual machines

   b. Containers are simple OS processes

   c. Containers use cgroups to provide isolation

   d. Containers use a container runtime

   e. A container is an ephemeral workload

3. Can all applications be containerized? – true or false?

4. Which of the following is a container runtime? (There may be multiple answers.)

   a. Docker

   b. Kubernetes

   c. Containerd

   d. Docker Swarm

5. What kind of applications should you choose to containerize first?

   a. APIs

   b. Databases

   c. Mainframes

6. Containers follow CI/CD principles out of the box – true or false?

7. Which of the following is an advantage of breaking your applications into multiple parts? (There may be multiple answers.)

   a. Fault isolation

   b. Shorter release cycle time

   c. Independent, fine-grained scaling

   d. Application architecture simplicity

   e. Simpler infrastructure

8. While breaking an application into microservices, which aspect should you consider?

    a. Break applications into as many tiny components as possible

    b. Break applications into logical components

9. What kind of application should you containerize first?

    a. Stateless

    b. Stateful

10. Some examples of CaaS are what? (Pick more than one.)

    a. Azure Functions

    b. Google Cloud Run

    c. Amazon ECS

    d. Azure ACS

    e. Oracle Functions

Answers

1. False

2. a

3. False

4. a, c

5. a

6. True

7. a, b, c, e

8. b

9. a

10. b, c, d

2
Containerization with Docker

In the last chapter, we briefly covered containers, the history of containers, and how the technology has redefined the software ecosystem today. We also understood why it is vital for modern DevOps engineers to be familiar with containers and how containers follow config management principles right from the beginning.

In this chapter, we'll get hands-on and explore **Docker** – the de facto container runtime. By the end of this chapter, you should be able to install and configure Docker, run your first container, and then monitor it. This chapter will also form the basis for the following chapters, as we will use the same setup for the demos later.

In this chapter, we're going to cover the following main topics:

- Installing tools
- Installing Docker
- Introducing Docker storage drivers and volumes
- Running your first container
- Docker logging and logging drivers
- Docker monitoring with Prometheus
- Declarative container management with Docker Compose

Technical requirements

You will need a Linux machine running Ubuntu 16.04 Xenial LTS or later with `sudo` access for this chapter.

You will also need to clone the following GitHub repository for some of the exercises: `https://github.com/PacktPublishing/Modern-DevOps-Practices`

Installing tools

Before we deep dive into installing Docker, we need to install supporting tools for us to progress. So, let's first install Git and vim.

Git is the command-line tool that will help you clone code from Git repositories. We will use several repositories for our exercises in future chapters.

Vim is a popular text editor for Linux and Unix operating systems, and we will use it extensively in this and the coming chapters. There are alternatives to vim, such as the GNU nano editor, VS Code, and Sublime Text. Feel free to use whatever you are comfortable with.

Installing Git

Open your shell terminal and run the following command:

```
$ sudo apt update -y && sudo apt install -y git
```

> **Tip**
> If you get an output such as **E: Unable to acquire the dpkg frontend lock (/var/lib/dpkg/lock-frontend), is another process using it?**, that's because `apt update` is already running, so you should wait for 5 minutes and then retry.

To confirm that Git is installed, run the following:

```
$ git --version
```

It should give you the following output:

```
git version 2.7.4
```

Let's go ahead and install vim.

Installing vim

We will use `apt` to install vim as well, similar to Git:

```
$ sudo apt install -y vim
```

To verify whether vim is installed, try the following:

```
$ vim --version
```

It should output the following:

```
VIM - Vi IMproved 7.4 (2013 Aug 10, compiled Oct 13 2020
16:04:38)
Included patches: 1-1689
Extra patches: 8.0.0056
```

Now that we have installed Git and vim, let's move on to installing Docker on your machine.

Installing Docker

Install the supporting tools that Docker would need to run:

```
$ sudo apt install apt-transport-https ca-certificates curl \
gnupg-agent software-properties-common
```

Download the Docker gpg key and add it to the `apt` package manager:

```
$ curl -fsSL https://download.docker.com/linux/ubuntu/gpg | \
sudo gpg --dearmor -o /usr/share/keyrings/docker-archive-\
keyring.gpg
```

You then need to add the Docker repository to your apt config so that you can download packages from there:

```
$ echo "deb [arch=amd64 signed-by=/usr/share/\
  keyrings/docker-archive-keyring.gpg] \
  https://download.docker.com/linux/ubuntu \
  $(lsb_release -cs) stable" | sudo tee /etc/apt\
  /sources.list.d/docker.list > /dev/null
```

Now, finally, install the Docker engine by using the following commands:

```
$ sudo apt update -y
$ sudo apt install -y docker-ce docker-ce-cli containerd.io
```

To verify whether Docker is installed successfully, run the following:

```
$ sudo docker --version
```

You should expect a similar output to the following:

```
Docker version 20.10.7, build f0df350
```

Now, the next thing you might want to do is allow regular users to use Docker. You would not want your users to act as root for building and running containers. To do that, run the following command:

```
$ sudo usermod -a -G docker <username>
```

To apply the changes to your profile, you need to log out from your virtual machine and log back in.

So, now that Docker is fully set up on your machine, let's run a hello-world container to see for ourselves:

```
$ docker run hello-world
```

You should see the following output:

```
Unable to find image' hello-world:latest' locally
latest: Pulling from library/hello-world
0e03bdcc26d7: Pull complete
Digest:
sha256:e7c70bb24b462baa86c102610182e3efcb12a04854e8c582838d929
70a09f323
Status: Downloaded newer image for hello-world:latest
```

```
Hello from Docker!
```

Additionally, you would also receive the following message that tells you a lot of what has happened behind the scenes to print the **Hello from Docker!** message on your screen:

```
This message shows that your installation appears to be working
  correctly.

To generate this message, Docker took the following steps:
 1. The Docker client contacted the Docker daemon.
 2. The Docker daemon pulled the "hello-world" image from the
Docker Hub.
 3. The Docker daemon created a new container from that image
that runs the executable that produces the current reading
output.
 4. The Docker daemon streamed that output to the Docker
client,
which sent it to your terminal.

To try something more ambitious, you can run an Ubuntu
container
with:
 $ docker run -it ubuntu bash

Share images, automate workflows, and more with a free Docker
ID
: https://hub.docker.com/

For more examples and ideas, visit:
https://docs.docker.com/get-started/
```

Now, all this helpful information is self-explanatory. To explain Docker Hub a bit, it is a public Docker container registry that is used to host a ton of Docker images for people like you and me to consume.

As Docker works on a layered architecture, most Docker images are derived from one or more base images hosted on Docker Hub. So, please create a Docker Hub account for yourself to host your containers and share them with the rest of the world.

Suppose you are working for a client or customer. In that case, you might not want to share their images publicly, so you have the option of creating private repositories within Docker Hub. You can also host your own internal Docker registry, use a SaaS service such as **Google Container Registry (GCR)**, or install an artifact repository such as **Sonatype Nexus** or **JFrog Artifactory**. Whatever your choice of tool, the mechanism and how it works always remain the same.

Introducing Docker storage drivers and volumes

Docker containers are ephemeral workloads. That means whatever data you store on your container filesystem gets wiped out once the container is gone. The data lives on a disk during the container life cycle, but it does not persist beyond it. Pragmatically speaking, most applications in the real world are stateful. They need to store data beyond the container life cycle, and they want data to persist.

So, how do we go along with that? Docker provides several ways you can store data. By default, all data is stored on the writable container layer, which is ephemeral. The writable container layer interacts with the host filesystem via a storage driver. Because of the abstraction, writing files to the container layer is slower than writing directly to the host filesystem.

To solve that problem and also provide persistent storage, Docker provides volumes, bind mounts, and `tmpfs`. With them, you can interact directly with the host filesystem (and memory in the case of `tmpfs`) and save a ton on **I/O per second (IOps)**, hence improving performance. While this section focuses on storage drivers that cater to the container filesystem, it is worth discussing multiple data storage options within Docker to provide a background.

Docker data storage options

Every option has a use case and trade-off. Let's look at each option and where you should use which.

Volumes

Docker volumes store the data directly into the host's filesystem. They do not use the storage driver layer in between, and therefore writing to volumes is faster. They are the best way to persist data. Docker stores volumes in `/var/lib/docker/volumes` and assumes that no one apart from the Docker daemon can modify the data on them.

As a result, volumes provide the following features:

- Provide some isolation with the host filesystems. If you don't want other processes to interact with the data, then a volume should be your choice.

- You can share a volume with multiple containers as well.

- Volumes can either be named or anonymous. Docker stores anonymous volumes in a directory with a unique random name.

- Volumes also enable you to store data remotely or in a cloud provider by using volume drivers. That helps a lot if you have multiple containers sharing the same volume to provide a multi-instance active-active configuration.

- The data in the volume persists even when the containers are deleted.

Bind mounts

Bind mounts are very similar to volumes but with a significant difference. They allow you to mount an existing host directory as a filesystem on the container. That enables you to share important files with the Docker container, such as `/etc/resolv.conf`.

Bind mounts also allow multiple processes to modify data along with Docker. So, if you are sharing your container data with another application that is not running in Docker, bind mounts are the way to go.

tmpfs mounts

`tmpfs` mounts store data in memory. They do not store any data on disk – neither the container nor the host filesystem. You can use them to store sensitive information and the non-persistent state during the lifetime of your container.

Mounting volumes

If you mount a host directory that already contains files to an empty volume of the container, the container can see the files stored in the host. It is an excellent way to pre-populate files for your container(s) to use. If the directory does not exist in the host filesystem, though, Docker creates the directory automatically. If the volume is non-empty and the host filesystem already contains files, then Docker obscures the mount. That means while you won't be able to see the original files while the Docker volume is mounted to it, the files are not deleted, and you can recover them by unmounting the Docker volume.

Let's look at Docker storage drivers in the next section.

Docker storage drivers

There are numerous storage driver types. Some of the popular ones are as follows:

- `overlay2`: This is a production-ready and the preferred storage driver for Docker and works in most environments except CentOS and RHEL 7 and below.

- `aufs`: This was the preferred storage driver for Docker 18.04 and below running on Ubuntu 14.04 and kernel 13.3 and below as they did not support `overlay2`. It was a stable and production-ready driver, but `overlay2` has overtaken it.

- `devicemapper`: This is the preferred driver for devices running RHEL and CentOS 7 and below that do not support `overlay2`. You can use this driver if you have write-intensive activities in your containers.

- `btrfs` and `zfs`: These drivers are write-intensive and provide many features, such as allowing snapshots, and can only be used if you are using `btrfs` or `zfs` filesystems within your host.

- `vfs`: This storage driver should be used only if there is no copy-on-write filesystem available. It is extremely slow, and you should not use it in production.

Let's concentrate on two of the most popular ones – `overlay2` and `devicemapper`.

overlay2

`overlay2` is the default and the recommended storage driver in most operating systems except RHEL 7 and CentOS 7 and older. They use file-based storage and perform the best when subject to more reads than writes. If you are running Ubuntu or a Debian-based operating system, then this is also the recommended option.

devicemapper

`devicemapper` is block-based storage and performs the best when subject to more writes than reads. Though it is compatible and the default with CentOS 7, RHEL 7, and below, as they don't support `overlay2`, it is currently not recommended in the newer versions of these operating systems that do support `overlay2`.

> **Tip**
> Use `overlay2` where possible, but if you have a specific use case for not using it (such as too many write-intensive containers), `devicemapper` is a better choice.

Configuring a storage driver

For this discussion, we will configure `overlay2` as the storage driver, and though it is configured by default and you can skip the steps if you are following this book, it is worth a read just in case you may want to change it to something else.

Let's first list the existing storage driver:

```
$ docker info|grep 'Storage Driver'
  Storage Driver: overlay2
```

So, we see that the existing storage driver is already `overlay2`. Let's go through the steps on how to change it to `devicemapper` if we had to.

Edit the `/etc/docker/daemon.json` file using an editor of your choice. If you use vim, run the following command:

```
$ vim /etc/docker/daemon.json
```

Add the `storage-driver` entry to the `daemon.json` configuration file:

```
{
    "storage-driver": "devicemapper"
}
```

Then, restart the Docker service:

```
$ sudo systemctl restart docker
```

Check the status of the Docker service:

```
$ sudo systemctl status docker
```

Now, rerun `docker info` to see what we get:

```
$ docker info|grep 'Storage Driver'
  Storage Driver: devicemapper
WARNING: No swap limit support
WARNING: the devicemapper storage-driver is deprecated, and
will be removed in a future release.
```

We see the `devicemapper` storage driver. You also see several warnings with it that say that the `devicemapper` storage driver is deprecated and will be removed in a future version.

Therefore, we should stick with the defaults unless we have a particular requirement.

So, let's roll back our changes and set the storage driver to overlay2 again:

```
$ vim /etc/docker/daemon.json
```

Modify the storage-driver entry in the daemon.json configuration file to overlay2:

```
{
  "storage-driver": "overlay2"
}
```

Then, restart the Docker service and check its status:

```
$ sudo systemctl restart docker
$ sudo systemctl status docker
```

If you rerun docker info, you will see the storage driver as overlay2, and all the warnings will disappear:

```
$ docker info|grep 'Storage Driver'
  Storage Driver: overlay2
```

> **Tip**
> Changing the storage driver will wipe out existing containers from the disk, so exercise caution when you do so and take appropriate downtimes if done in production. You will also need to pull images again, as local images will fail to exist.

Right, so as we have installed Docker on our machine and have configured the right storage driver, it's time to run our first container.

Running your first container

You create Docker containers out of Docker container images. While we will discuss container images and their architecture in the following chapters, an excellent way to visualize it is as a copy of all files, application libraries, and dependencies that would comprise your application environment, similar to a virtual machine image.

To run a Docker container, we will use the `docker run` command, which has the following structure:

```
$ docker run [OPTIONS] IMAGE[:TAG|@DIGEST] [COMMAND] [ARG...]
```

Let's look at each of them using working examples.

In its simplest form, you can use `docker run` by simply typing the following:

```
$ docker run hello-world
Unable to find image 'hello-world:latest' locally
latest: Pulling from library/hello-world
0e03bdcc26d7: Pull complete
Digest: sha256:e7c70bb24b462baa86c102610182e3efcb12a04854e8c582
838d92970a09f323
Status: Downloaded newer image for hello-world:latest
Hello from Docker!
...
```

If you remember, we also used this command when we installed Docker. Here I have purposefully omitted `tag`, `options`, `command`, and `arguments`. We will cover it with multiple examples to show its real use cases.

As we didn't supply a `tag`, Docker automatically assumed the `tag` as `latest`, so if you look at the command output, you will see that Docker is pulling the `hello-world:latest` image from Docker Hub.

Now, let's look at an example with a specific version tag.

Running containers from versioned images

We can run `nginx:1.18.0` using the following command:

```
$ docker run nginx:1.18.0
Unable to find image 'nginx:1.18.0' locally
1.18.0: Pulling from library/nginx
852e50cd189d: Pull complete
48b8657f2521: Pull complete
b4f4d57f1a55: Pull complete
d8fbe49a7d55: Pull complete
04e4a40fabc9: Pull complete
Digest: sha256:2104430ec73de095df553d0c7c2593813e01716a48d66f
85a3dc439e050919b3
Status: Downloaded newer image for nginx:1.18.0
```

```
/docker-entrypoint.sh: /docker-entrypoint.d/ is not empty, will
attempt to perform configuration
/docker-entrypoint.sh: Looking for shell scripts in /docker-
entrypoint.d/
/docker-entrypoint.sh: Launching /docker-entrypoint.d/10-
listen-on-ipv6-by-default.sh
10-listen-on-ipv6-by-default.sh: Getting the checksum of /etc/
nginx/conf.d/default.conf
10-listen-on-ipv6-by-default.sh: Enabled listen on IPv6 in /
etc/nginx/conf.d/default.conf
/docker-entrypoint.sh: Launching /docker-entrypoint.d/20-
envsubst-on-templates.sh
/docker-entrypoint.sh: Configuration complete; ready for
start up
```

But then the prompt will be stuck after this. Well, there is a reason for that. That is because nginx is a long-running process, also known as a daemon. As NGINX is a web server that needs to listen to HTTP requests continuously, it should never stop. In the case of the hello-world application, its only job was to print the message and exit. NGINX has a different purpose altogether.

Now, no one would keep a Bash session open for a web server to run, so there has to be some way to run it in the background. You can run containers in detached mode for that. Let's have a look at that in the next section.

Running Docker containers in the background

To run a Docker container in the background as a daemon, you can use docker run in detached mode using the -d flag:

```
$ docker run -d nginx:1.18.0
beb5dfd529c9f001539c555a18e7b76ad5d73b95dc48e8a35aecd7471
ea938fc
```

As you see, it just prints a random ID and provides control back to the shell.

Troubleshooting containers

To see what's going on within the container, you can use the docker logs command. But before using that, we need to know the container ID or container name to see the container's logs.

To get a list of containers running within the host, run the following command:

```
$ docker ps
CONTAINER ID            IMAGE               COMMAND
CREATED                 STATUS              PORTS
NAMES
beb5dfd529c9            nginx:1.18.0         "/docker-
entrypoint.…."    2 minutes ago       Up 2 minutes            80/tcp
fervent_shockley
```

We see that it lists the NGINX container that we just started. Unless you specify a particular name to your container, Docker allocates a random name to it. In this case, it has called it `fervent_shockley`. It also assigns every container a unique container ID, such as `beb5dfd529c9`.

You can use either the container ID or the container name to interact with the container to list the logs. Let's use the container ID this time:

```
$ docker logs beb5dfd529c9
/docker-entrypoint.sh: /docker-entrypoint.d/ is not empty, will
attempt to perform configuration
...
/docker-entrypoint.sh: Configuration complete; ready for start
up
```

As you can see, it prints a similar log output as it did when we ran it in the foreground.

Practically speaking, you would be using `docker logs` 90% of the time unless you need to debug something with BusyBox. BusyBox is a lightweight shell container that can help you troubleshoot and debug issues with your container – mostly network issues.

Let's now make BusyBox echo `Hello World!` for us:

```
$ docker run busybox echo 'Hello World!'
Unable to find image 'busybox:latest' locally
latest: Pulling from library/busybox
9758c28807f2: Pull complete
Digest:
sha256:a9286defaba7b3a519d585ba0e37d0b2cbee74ebfe590960b0b1
d6a5e97d1e1d
Status: Downloaded newer image for busybox:latest
Hello World!
```

As we see, Docker pulls the latest `busybox` image from Docker Hub and runs the `echo 'Hello World'` command.

You can also use BusyBox in interactive mode by using the `-it` flag, which will help you run a series of commands on the BusyBox shell. It is also a good idea to add a `--rm` flag to it to tell Docker to clean up the containers once we have exited from the shell, something like this:

```
$ docker run -it --rm busybox /bin/sh
/ # echo 'Hello world!'
Hello world!
/ # wget http://example.com
Connecting to example.com (93.184.216.34:80)
saving to 'index.html'
index.html           100% |*********************************
****|  1256  0:00:00 ETA
'index.html' saved
/ # exit
```

When we list all the containers, we do not see the BusyBox container in there:

```
$ docker ps -a
CONTAINER ID          IMAGE               COMMAND
 CREATED              STATUS              PORTS
NAMES
beb5dfd529c9          nginx:1.18.0        "/docker-entrypoint.…"
 17 minutes ago       Up 17 minutes       80/tcp
fervent_shockley
```

There are various other flags that you can use with your containers, each serving a specific purpose. Let's look at a few common ones.

Putting it all together

The best setting for a highly available NGINX container should be something as follows:

```
$ docker run -d --name nginx --restart unless-stopped \
-p 80:80 --memory 1000M --memory-reservation 250M nginx:1.18.0
```

The following applies:

- `-d`: Run as a daemon in detached mode.

- `--name nginx`: Give the name `nginx`.

- `--restart unless-stopped`: Always automatically restart on failures unless explicitly stopped manually, and also start automatically on Docker daemon startup. Other options include `no`, `on_failure`, and `always`.

- `-p 80:80`: Forward traffic from host port `80` to container port `80`. That allows you to expose your container to your host network.

- `--memory 1000M`: Limit the container memory consumption to `1000M`. If the memory exceeds this limit, the container will stop and act according to the `--restart` flag.

- `--memory-reservation 250M`: Allocate a soft limit of `250M` memory to the container if the server runs out of memory.

There are other flags that we will look into in the subsequent sections as we get more hands-on.

> **Tip**
>
> Consider using `unless-stopped` instead of `always`, as it gives you control to stop the container manually if you want to do some maintenance.

Let's now list the containers and see what we get:

```
$ docker ps -a
CONTAINER ID          IMAGE               COMMAND
CREATED               STATUS              PORTS
NAMES
06fc749371b7          nginx               "/docker-entrypoint.…"
17 seconds ago        Up 16 seconds       0.0.0.0:80->80/tcp
nginx
beb5dfd529c9          nginx:1.18.0        "/docker-
entrypoint.…"    22 minutes ago    Up 22 minutes          80/tcp
fervent_shockley
```

If you look carefully, you'll see a container with the name `nginx` and a port forward from `0.0.0.0:80 -> 80`.

Let's now `curl` on `localhost:80` on the host to see what we get:

```
$ curl localhost:80
<!DOCTYPE html>
<html>
<head>
<title>Welcome to nginx!</title>
...
</html>
```

We get the NGINX welcome message. That means NGINX is running successfully, and we can access it from the machine. If you have exposed your machine's port 80 to the external world, you can also access this using your browser as follows:

Figure 2.1 – NGINX welcome page

You also might want to restart or remove your container from time to time. Let's look at ways to do that in the next section.

Restarting and removing containers

To restart your containers, you have to stop your container first and then start it.

To stop your container, run the following:

```
$ docker stop nginx
```

To start your container, run the following:

```
$ docker start nginx
```

If you want to get completely rid of your container, you need to stop your container first and then remove it, using the following command:

```
$ docker stop nginx && docker rm nginx
```

Alternatively, you can also use the following command to do it in one go:

```
$ docker rm -f nginx
```

Now, let's look at how we can monitor our containers with tools such as `journald` and Splunk in the next section.

Docker logging and logging drivers

Docker not only changed how applications are deployed but also the workflow for log management. Instead of writing logs to files, containers write logs to the console (`stdout/stderr`). Docker then uses a logging driver to export container logs to chosen destinations.

Container log management

Log management is an essential function within Docker, like any application. But, due to the transient nature of Docker workloads, it becomes more critical as we lose the filesystem and potentially logs as well when the container is deleted or faces any issue. So, we should use log drivers to export the logs into a particular place and store and persist it. If you have a log analytics solution, the best place for your logs to be is within it. Docker supports multiple log targets via logging drivers. Let's have a look.

Logging drivers

As of the time of writing this book, the following logging drivers are available:

- `none`: There are no logs available for the container, and therefore they are not stored anywhere.
- `local`: Logs are stored locally in a custom format and therefore minimizes overhead.
- `json-file`: The log files are stored in a JSON format, and this is the default Docker logging driver.
- `syslog`: Uses syslog for storing the Docker logs as well. This option makes sense when you use syslog as your default logging mechanism.

- `journald`: Uses `journald` to store Docker logs. You can use the `journald` command line to browse the container logs and the Docker daemon logs.

- `gelf`: Sends logs to a **Graylog Extended Log Format** (**GELF**) endpoint such as Graylog or Logstash.

- `fluentd`: Sends logs to Fluentd.

- `awslogs`: Sends logs to AWS CloudWatch.

- `splunk`: Sends logs to Splunk using the HTTP Event Collector.

- `etwlogs`: Sends logs to **Event Tracing for Windows** (**ETW**) events. You can use it only on Windows platforms.

- `gcplogs`: Sends logs to Google Cloud Logging.

- `logentries`: Sends logs to Rapid7 Logentries.

While all of these are viable options, we will look at `journald` and Splunk. While `journald` is a native operating system service monitoring option, Splunk is one of the most famous log analytics and monitoring tools available in the market. Now, let's understand how to configure a logging driver.

Configuring logging drivers

Let's start by finding the current logging driver:

```
$ docker info | grep "Logging Driver"
 Logging Driver: json-file
```

Right, so currently, the default logging driver is set to `json-file`. If we want to use `journald` or Splunk as the default logging driver, we must configure the default logging driver in the `daemon.json` file.

Edit the `/etc/docker/daemon.json` file using an editor of your choice. If you use vim, run the following command:

```
$ vim /etc/docker/daemon.json
```

Add the `log-driver` entry to the `daemon.json` configuration file:

```
{
  "log-driver": "journald"
}
```

Then, restart the Docker service:

```
$ sudo systemctl restart docker
```

Check the status of the Docker service:

```
$ sudo systemctl status docker
```

Now, rerun `docker info` to see what we get:

```
$ docker info | grep "Logging Driver"
 Logging Driver: journald
```

Right, as `journald` is now the default logging driver, let's launch a new NGINX container and visualize the logs:

```
$ docker run --name nginx-journald -d nginx
66d50cc11178b0dcdb66b114ccf4aa2186b510eb1fdb1e19d563566d2e
96140c
```

Let's now look at the `journald` logs to see what we get:

```
$ sudo journalctl CONTAINER_NAME=nginx-journald
-- Logs begin at Tue 2020-11-24 05:00:42 UTC, end at Tue
2020-11-24 06:00:47 UTC. -
Nov 24 05:58:37 localhost 66d50cc11178[4104]: /docker-
entrypoint
.sh: /docker-entrypoint.d/ is not empty, will attempt to
perform
 configuration
...
```

And we see the logs in the journal.

We can similarly configure the Splunk logging driver to send data to Splunk for analytics and visualization. Let's have a look now.

Edit the /etc/docker/daemon.json file using an editor of your choice. If you use vim, run the following command:

```
$ vim /etc/docker/daemon.json
```

Add the `log-driver` entry to the `daemon.json` configuration file:

```
{
  "log-driver": "splunk",
  "log-opts": {
    "splunk-token": "<Splunk HTTP Event Collector token>",
    "splunk-url": "<Splunk HTTP(S) url>"
  }
}
```

Then, restart the Docker service:

```
$ sudo systemctl restart docker
```

Check the status of the Docker service:

```
$ sudo systemctl status docker
```

Now, rerun `docker info` to see what we get:

```
$ docker info | grep "Logging Driver"
 Logging Driver: splunk
```

Right, as Splunk is now the default logging driver, let's launch a new NGINX container and visualize the logs:

```
$ docker run --name nginx-splunk -d nginx
dedde062feba33f64efd89ef9102c7c93afa854473cda3033745d35
d9065c9e5
```

Now, log in to your Splunk instance, and you will see the Docker logs streaming in. You can then analyze the logs and create visualizations out of them.

You can also have different logging drivers for different containers, and you can do so by overriding the defaults by passing the `log-driver` and `log-opts` flags from the command line. As our current configuration is Splunk, and we want to export data to a JSON file, we can specify `log-driver` as `json-file` while running the container. Let's have a look:

```
$ docker run --name nginx-json-file --log-driver json-file \
-d nginx
379eb8d0162d98614d53ae1c81ea1ad154745f9edbd2f64cffc22797721
98bb2
```

Right, so to visualize JSON logs, we need to look into the JSON log directory, that is, /var/lib/docker/containers/<container_id>/<container_id>-json.log.

For the `nginx-json-file` container, we can do the following:

```
$ cat /var/lib/docker/containers/379eb8d0162d98614d53ae1\
c81ea1ad154745f9edbd2f64cffc2279772198bb2379eb8d0162d9\
8614d53ae1c81ea1ad154745f9edbd2f64cffc2279772198bb2-json.log
{"log":"/docker-entrypoint.sh: /docker-entrypoint.d/ is not
empty, will attempt to perform configuration\n","stream":"
stdout","time":"2020-11-24T06:27:05.922950436Z"}
...
{"log":"/docker-entrypoint.sh: Configuration complete; ready
for start up\n","stream":"stdout","time":"2020-11-24T06:27:
05.937629749Z"}
```

We see that the logs are now streaming to the JSON file instead of Splunk. That is how we override the default log driver.

> **Tip**
> In most cases, it is best to stick with one default logging driver so that you have one place to analyze and visualize your logs.

Now, let's understand some of the challenges and best practices associated with Docker logging.

Typical challenges and best practices with Docker logging

Docker allows you to run multiple applications in a single machine or a cluster of machines. Most organizations run a mix of virtual machines and containers, and they have their logging and monitoring stack configured to support virtual machines.

Most teams struggle to try to fit the Docker logging to behave the way virtual machine logging works. So, most teams will send logs to the host filesystem, and the log analytics solution then consumes the data from there. That is not ideal, and you should not make that mistake. It might work if your container is static, but it becomes an issue if you have a cluster of servers, each running Docker, and you have the freedom of scheduling your container in any virtual machine you like.

So, treating a container as an application running on a virtual machine is a mistake from a logging point of view. Instead, you should visualize the container as an entity – just like a virtual machine. It would be best if you never associated containers with a virtual machine.

One solution can be to use the logging driver to forward the logs to a log analytics solution directly. But then the logging becomes heavily dependent on the availability of the log analytics solution. So, it might not be the best thing to do. People have faced issues when their services running on Docker went down because the log analytics solution was not available or there were some network issues.

Well, the best way to approach this problem is to use JSON files to store the logs temporarily in your virtual machine and use another container to push the logs to your chosen log analytics solution using the old-fashioned way. That way, you decouple dependency on an external service to run your application.

You can use the logging driver that exports log directly to your log analytics solution within the log forwarder container. There are many logging drivers available that support many log targets. Always mark the logs in such a way that the containers appear as an entity on their own. That will disassociate containers with virtual machines, and you can then make the best use of a distributed container-based architecture.

We've looked at the logging aspects of containers, but one of the essential elements of a DevOps engineer's role is monitoring. Let's have a look at the next section.

Docker monitoring with Prometheus

Monitoring Docker nodes and containers are an essential part of managing Docker. There are various tools available for monitoring Docker. While you can use traditional tools such as Nagios, Prometheus is gaining ground in cloud-native monitoring because of its simplicity and pluggable architecture.

Prometheus is a free, open source monitoring tool that provides a dimensional data model, efficient and straightforward querying using the **Prometheus query language** (**PromQL**), efficient time-series databases, and modern alerting capabilities.

It has several exporters available for exporting data from various sources and supports both virtual machines and containers. Before we delve into the details, let's look at some of the challenges with container monitoring.

Challenges with container monitoring

From a conceptual point of view, there is no difference between container monitoring and the traditional method. You would still need metrics, logs, health checks, and service discovery. These aren't things that are not known or explored before. The problem with containers is the abstraction that they bring with them; let's look at some of the problems:

- Containers behave like a mini virtual machine, but they are a process running on a server in reality. However, they still have everything to monitor that we would do in a virtual machine. A container process will have many metrics very similar to virtual machines to be treated as separate entities altogether. Most people make this mistake when dealing with containers when they map containers to a particular virtual machine.

- Containers are temporary, and most people don't realize that. When you have a container, and it is recreated, it has a new IP. That can confuse traditional monitoring systems.

- Containers running on clusters can move from one node(server) to another. That adds another layer of complexity as your monitoring tool needs to know where your containers are to scrape metrics from it. Well, it should not matter with the more modern, container-optimized tools.

Prometheus helps us address these challenges as it is built from a distributed application's point of view. To understand that, let's look at a hands-on example, but before that, let's install Prometheus on an Ubuntu 16.04 Linux machine.

Installing Prometheus

Installing Prometheus consists of several steps, and for simplicity, I've created a Bash script for installing and setting up Prometheus in an Ubuntu machine.

Use the following commands to set up Prometheus:

```
$ git clone https://github.com/PacktPublishing/Modern-DevOps-\
Practices.git modern-devops
$ cd modern-devops/ch2/prometheus/
$ sudo bash prometheus_setup.sh
```

To check whether Prometheus is installed and running, check the status of the Prometheus service using the following command:

```
$ sudo systemctl status prometheus
  prometheus.service - Prometheus
    Loaded: loaded (/etc/systemd/system/prometheus.service;
enabled; vendor preset: enabled)
    Active: active (running) since Tue 2021-01-12 09:26:57 UTC;
1min 22s ago
```

As the service is Active, we can conclude that Prometheus is installed and running successfully. The next step is to configure the Docker server to enable Prometheus to collect logs from it.

Configuring cAdvisor and the node exporter to expose metrics

Now, we'll launch a cAdvisor container on Docker to expose the metrics of the Docker containers. cAdvisor is a metrics collector that will scrape metrics from our containers. To launch the container, use the following command:

```
$ docker run -d --restart always --name cadvisor -p 8080:8080 \
-v "/:/rootfs:ro" -v "/var/run:/var/run:rw" -v "/sys:/sys:ro" \
-v "/var/lib/docker/:/var/lib/docker:ro" google/cadvisor:latest
```

OK, so as cAdvisor is running, we need to configure the node exporter to export node metrics. To do so, run the following commands:

```
$ cd ~/modern-devops/ch2/prometheus/
$ sudo bash node_exporter_setup.sh
```

As the node exporter is running, let's configure Prometheus to connect to cAdvisor and the node exporter and scrape metrics from there.

Configuring Prometheus to scrape metrics

We will now configure Prometheus so that it can scrape the metrics from cAdvisor. To do so, modify the /etc/prometheus/prometheus.yml file to include the following within the server running Prometheus:

```
$ sudo vim /etc/prometheus/prometheus.yml
  ...
  - job_name: 'node_exporter'
```

```
    scrape_interval: 5s
    static_configs:
      - targets: ['localhost:9100', '<Docker_IP>:9100']
  - job_name: 'Docker Containers'
    static_configs:
      - targets: ['<Docker_IP>:8080']
```

After changing this configuration, we need to restart the Prometheus service. Use the following command for that:

```
$ sudo systemctl restart prometheus
```

Now, let's launch a sample web application that we will monitor using Prometheus.

Launching a sample container application

Let's now run an NGINX container with the name web, that runs on port 8081 on the host system. To do so, use the following command:

```
$ docker run -d --name web -p 8081:80 nginx
f9b613d6bdf3d6aee0cb3a08cb55c99a7c4821341b058d8757579b52c
abbb0f5
```

Now that the setup of the Docker container is complete, let's go ahead and open the Prometheus UI by visiting https://<PROMETHEUS_SERVER_EXTERNAL_IP>:9090 and then running the following query by typing in the textbox:

```
container_memory_usage_bytes{name=~"web"}
```

It should show something like the following:

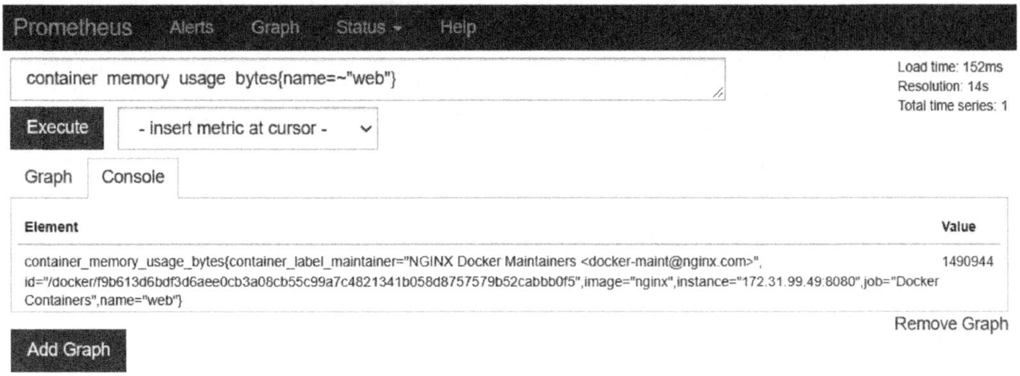

Figure 2.2 – Prometheus – container_memory_usage_bytes

We can also view the time series of this metric by clicking on the **Graph** tab, but before we do so, let's load our NGINX service by using the Apache Bench tool. Apache Bench is a load testing tool that will help us fire HTTP Requests to the NGINX endpoint using the command line.

On your Docker server, run the following command to start a load test:

```
$ ab -n 100000 http://localhost:8081/
```

It will hit the endpoint with 100,000 requests, and therefore it provides a fair amount of load to do a memory spike. Now, if you open the **Graph** tab, you should see something like the following:

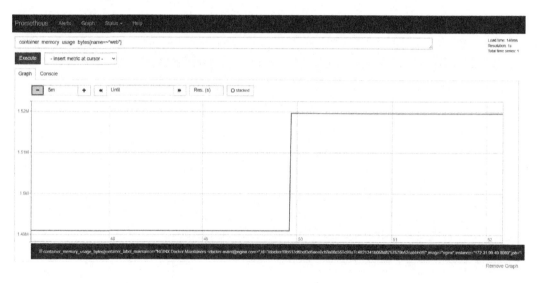

Figure 2.3 – Prometheus – container_memory_usage_bytes – Graph

To visualize node metrics, we can use the following PromQL statement to get the node_ cpu value of the Docker host:

```
node_cpu{instance="<Docker_IP>:9100",job="node_exporter"}
```

And as you can see in the following screenshot, it will provide us with the node_cpu metrics for multiple modes:

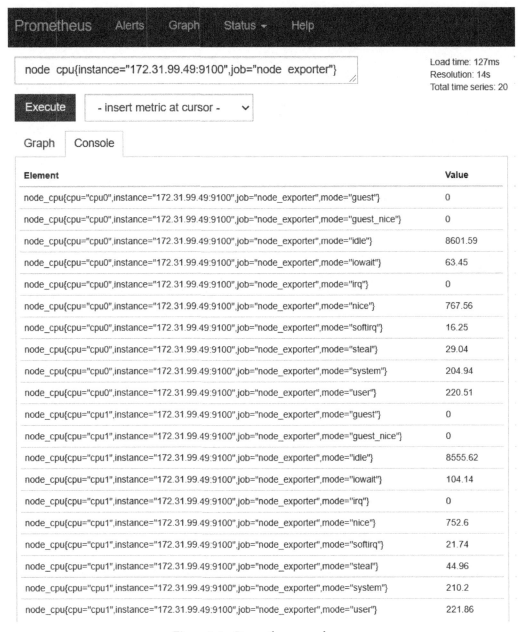

Figure 2.4 – Prometheus – node_cpu

There are a variety of other metrics that Prometheus gives you to visualize. Let's understand some of the metrics you can monitor.

Metrics to monitor

Monitoring metrics is a complex subject, and it would depend mostly on your use case. However, the following are some guidelines on what kind of metrics you might want to monitor.

Host metrics

You need to monitor your host metrics as your containers would run on them. Some of the metrics that you can watch are the following:

- **Host CPU**: It's good to know whether your host has sufficient CPU to run your containers. If not, it might terminate some of your containers to account for that. So, to ensure reliability, you need to keep this in check.

- **Host memory**: Like the host CPU, you need to watch the host memory to detect issues such as memory leaks and runaway memory.

- **Host disk space**: As Docker containers use the host filesystem to store the transient and persistent file, you need to monitor it.

Docker container metrics

Docker container metrics are the next thing and you should look at the following:

- **Container CPU**: This metric will provide the amount of CPU used by the Docker container. You should monitor it to understand the usability pattern and decide where to place your container effectively.

- **Throttled CPU time**: This metric allows us to understand the total time when the CPU was throttled for a container. That enables us to know whether a particular container needs more CPU time than others, and you can adjust the CPU share constraint accordingly.

- **Container memory fail counters**: This metric will provide the number of times the container requested more than the allocated memory. It will help you understand what containers required more than the allocated memory, and you can plan to run the container accordingly.

- **Container memory usage**: This metric will provide the amount of memory used by the Docker container, and you can set memory limits according to the usage.

- **Container swap**: This metric will tell what containers were using the swap instead of the RAM. It will help us identify memory-hungry containers.

- **Container disk I/O**: This is an important metric and will help us understand containers' disk profiles. Spikes can indicate a disk bottleneck, or you might want to revisit your storage driver configuration.

- **Container network metrics**: This metric will tell us how much network bandwidth the containers are using and help us understand traffic patterns. You can use these to detect an unexpected network spike or a denial of service attack.

> **Important tip**
>
> Profiling your application during the performance testing phase in the non-production environment will give you a rough idea of how the system will behave in production. The actual fine-tuning of your application begins when you deploy it to production. Therefore, monitoring is key for that, and fine-tuning is a continuous process.

Up until now, we have been running commands to do most of our work. That is the imperative way of doing this. But what if I tell you that instead of typing commands, you can simply declare what you want, and something can run all the required commands on your behalf? That is known as the declarative method of managing an application. Docker Compose is one of the popular tools to achieve that. Let's have a look in the next section.

Declarative container management with Docker Compose

Docker Compose helps you manage multiple containers in a declarative way. You create a YAML file and specify what you want to build, what containers you want to run, and how the containers interact with each other. You can define mounts, networks, port mapping, and many different configurations in the YAML file.

After that, you can simply run `docker-compose up` to get your entire containerized application running.

Declarative management is fast gaining ground because of the power and simplicity it offers. Now, sysadmins don't need to remember what commands they had run or write lengthy scripts or playbooks to manage containers. Instead, they can simply declare what they want in a YAML file, and `docker-compose` or other tools can help them achieve that state.

Installing Docker Compose

Installing Docker Compose is very simple. You download the `docker-compose` binary from its official repository, make it executable, and move it to your system's default binary path.

Download the `docker-compose` binary by running the following command:

```
$ sudo curl -L "https://github.com/docker/compose/releases/\
download/1.27.4/docker-compose-$(uname -s)-$(uname -m)" -o \
/usr/local/bin/docker-compose
```

Make `docker-compose` executable:

```
$ sudo chmod +x /usr/local/bin/docker-compose
```

That's it! Docker Compose is installed.

To verify whether the setup is correct, run the following command:

```
$ docker-compose –version
docker-compose version 1.27.4, build 40524192
```

As we installed Docker Compose successfully, let's see it in action with a sample application in the next section.

Deploying a sample application with Docker Compose

We have a Python Flask application that listens on port `5000`, which we will eventually map to the host port `80`. The application will connect with the Redis database running as a backend service on its default port `6379` and fetch the page's last visit time. We will not expose that port to the host system. That means the database is entirely out of bounds for any external party with access to the application.

The files are available in the GitHub repository of the book. Follow these steps to locate the files:

```
$ git clone https://github.com/PacktPublishing/Modern-DevOps-\
Practices.git modern-devops
$ cd modern-devops/ch2/docker-compose
$ ls -l
total 16
-rw-r--r-- 1 root root 681 Nov 25 06:11 app.py
-rw-r--r-- 1 root root 389 Nov 25 06:45 docker-compose.yaml
-rw-r--r-- 1 root root 238 Nov 25 05:27 Dockerfile
```

Declarative container management with Docker Compose   57

```
-rw-r--r-- 1 root root  12 Nov 25 05:26 requirements.txt
```

The app.py file looks as follows:

```python
import time
import redis
from flask import Flask
from datetime import datetime
app = Flask(__name__)
cache = redis.Redis(host='redis', port=6379)
def get_last_visited():
    try:
        last_visited = cache.getset('last_
visited',str(datetime.now().strftime("%Y-%m-%d, %H:%M:%S")))
        if last_visited is None:
            return cache.getset('last_visited',str(datetime.
now().strftime("%Y-%m-%d, %H:%M:%S")))
        return last_visited
    except redis.exceptions.ConnectionError as e:
        raise e


@app.route('/')
def index():
    last_visited = str(get_last_visited().decode('utf-8'))
    return 'Hi there! This page was last visited on {}.\n'.
format(last_visited)
```

The requirements.txt file is as follows:

```
flask
redis
```

I've already built the application for you, and the image is available on Docker Hub. We will cover how to build a Docker image in detail in the next chapter. For now, let's have a look at the docker-compose file in the next section.

Creating the docker-compose file

The next step in the process is to create a `docker-compose` file. A `docker-compose` file is a YAML file that contains a list of services, networks, volumes, and other associated configurations. Let's look at the following example `docker-compose.yaml` file to understand it better:

```yaml
version: "2.4"
services:
  flask:
    image: "bharamicrosystems/python-flask-redis:latest"
    ports:
      - "80:5000"
    networks:
      - flask-app-net
  redis:
    image: "redis:alpine"
    networks:
      - flask-app-net
    command: ["redis-server", "--appendonly", "yes"]
    volumes:
      - redis-data:/data

networks:
  flask-app-net:
    driver: bridge

volumes:
  redis-data:
```

The YAML file describes two services – Flask and Redis.

The Flask service uses the `python-flask-redis:latest` image – the image we built with the preceding code. It also maps host port `80` to container port `5000`, so this will expose this application to your host machine on port `80`, and you can access it via `http://localhost`.

The Redis service uses the official `redis:alpine` image and does not expose any port, as we don't want this service outside the container network's confines. However, it declares a persistent volume, `redis-data`, that comprises the `/data` directory. We would mount this volume on the host filesystem for persistence beyond the container life cycle.

There is also a `flask-app-net` network that uses the bridge driver, and both services share the same network. That means the services can call each other by using their service name. If you look at the `app.py` code, you will find that we establish a Redis service connection using the `redis` hostname.

To apply the configuration, simply run `docker-compose up -d`:

```
$ docker-compose up -d
Creating network "docker-compose_flask-app-net" with driver
"bridge"
Pulling redis (redis:alpine)...
alpine: Pulling from library/redis
188c0c94c7c5: Already exists
fb6015f7c791: Pull complete
f8890a096979: Pull complete
cd6e0c12d5bc: Pull complete
67b3665cee45: Pull complete
0705890dd1f7: Pull complete
Digest:
sha256:b0e84b6b92149194d99953e44f7d1fa1f470a769529bb05b4164
eae60d8aea6c
Status: Downloaded newer image for redis:alpine
Creating docker-compose_flask_1 ... done
Creating docker-compose_redis_1 ... done
```

Right, so let's list down Docker containers to see how we fare:

```
$ docker ps -a
CONTAINER ID          IMAGE
COMMAND                 CREATED               STATUS
PORTS                   NAMES
cb472d511fe0          bharamicrosystems/python-flask-redis:latest
"flask run"             About a minute ago   Up About a minute
0.0.0.0:80->5000/tcp   docker-compose_flask_1
8f80395d7790          redis:alpine
"docker-entrypoint.s…"   About a minute ago            Up About a
minute                  6379/tcp              docker-compose
_redis_1
```

We see two containers running for both services. We also see host port 80 forwarding connections to container port 5000 on the Flask service.

The Redis service is internal and, therefore, there is no port mapping.

Let's curl localhost and see what we get:

```
$ curl localhost
Hi there! This page was last visited on 2020-11-25, 06:35:24.
```

Right, so we get the last visited page from the Redis cache according to the sample Flask application code.

Let's run this a few times and see whether the time is changing:

```
$ curl localhost
Hi there! This page was last visited on 2020-11-25, 06:35:25.
$ curl localhost
Hi there! This page was last visited on 2020-11-25, 06:35:26.
$ curl localhost
Hi there! This page was last visited on 2020-11-25, 06:35:27.
```

We see that the last visited time is changing every time we curl. Since the volume is persistent, we should get similar last visited times even after a container restarts.

Let's first curl and get the last visited time and also the current date:

```
$ curl localhost && date
Hi there! This page was last visited on 2020-11-25, 06:46:35.
Wed Nov 25 06:52:15 UTC 2020
```

Now, next time we curl, we should get a date-time similar to 2020-11-25, 06:52:15. But before that, let's restart the container and see whether the data persists:

```
$ docker-compose restart redis
Restarting docker-compose_redis_1 ... done
```

Now, Redis has restarted. Let's curl again:

```
$ curl localhost
Hi there! This page was last visited on 2020-11-25, 06:52:15.
```

So, as we see, we get the correct last visited time, even after restarting the Redis service. That means data persistence is working correctly, and the volume is adequately mounted.

You can do many other configurations on docker-compose that you can readily get from the official documentation. However, you should now have a general idea about using docker-compose and what kinds of benefits it provides. Now let's look at some of the best practices associated with docker-compose.

Docker Compose best practices

Docker Compose provides a declarative way of managing Docker container configuration. That enables GitOps for your Docker workloads. While Docker Compose is mostly used in the development environment, you can use it in production very well, especially when Docker runs in production and does not use another container orchestrator such as Kubernetes.

Always use docker-compose.yml files alongside code

The YAML file defines how to run your containers. So, it becomes a useful tool for declarative building and deploying your containers from a single space. You can add all dependencies to your application and run related applications in a single network.

Separate multiple environment YAMLs by using overrides

Docker Compose YAML files allow us to both build and deploy Docker images. Docker has enabled the *build once, run anywhere* concept. Therefore, we would build once in the development environment and then use the created image in subsequent environments. So, the question arises of how we can achieve that. Docker Compose allows us to apply multiple YAML files in a sequence where the next configuration overrides the last. That way, we can have separate override files for various environments and manage multiple environments using a set of these files.

For example, say we have the following base `docker-compose.yaml` file:

```yaml
version: "2.4"
services:
  flask:
    image: "bharamicrosystems/python-flask-redis:latest"
    ports:
      - "80:5000"
    networks:
      - flask-app-net
  redis:
    image: "redis:alpine"
    networks:
      - flask-app-net
    command: ["redis-server", "--appendonly", "yes"]
    volumes:
      - redis-data:/data

networks:
```

```
  flask-app-net:
    driver: bridge

volumes:
  redis-data:
```

We've got to build the Flask application container image only in the development environment so that we can create an override file for the development environment – `docker-compose.override.yaml`:

```
web:
  build: .
  environment:
    DEBUG: 'true'
redis:
  ports:
    - 6379:6379
```

As we see, we've added a `build` parameter within the web service. That means the Python Flask application will be rebuilt and then deployed. We've also set the `DEBUG` environment variable within the web service and exposed the Redis port to the host filesystem. This makes sense in the development environment as we might want to directly debug Redis from the development machine. Still, we would not want something of that sort in the production environment. Therefore, the default `docker-compose.yaml` will work in the production environment, as we saw in the previous section.

Use a .env file to store sensitive variables

You might not want to store sensitive content such as passwords and secrets in version control. Instead, you can use a `.env` file that contains a list of variable names and values and keep it in a secret management system such as HashiCorp's Vault.

Be mindful about dependencies in production

When you change a particular container and want to redeploy the container, `docker-compose` also redeploys any dependencies. Now, this might not be something that you wish to do, and therefore, you can override this behavior by using the following command:

```
$ docker-compose up --no-deps -d <container_service_name>
```

Treat docker-compose files as code

Always version control your docker-compose files and keep them alongside code. That will allow you to track its version and use gating and Git features such as pull requests.

Summary

This chapter started with installing Docker, then running our first Docker container, looking at various modes of running a container, and understanding Docker volumes and storage drivers. We also learned how to select the right storage driver and volume options and some best practices. All these skills will help you set up a production-ready Docker server with ease. We also talked about the logging agent and how you can quickly ship Docker logs to multiple destinations, such as journald, Splunk, and JSON files, to help you monitor your containers. We looked at managing Docker containers declaratively using docker-compose and ran a complete composite container application.

In the following chapter, we will look at Docker images, creating and managing them, and some best practices.

Questions

1. You should use Overlay2 for CentOS and RHEL 7 and below – True or false?

2. Which of the following statements are true? (Multiple answers are possible)

   a. Volumes increase IOps.

   b. Volumes decrease IOps.

   c. tmpfs mounts use system memory.

   d. You can use bind mounts to mount host files to containers.

   e. You can use volume mounts for multi-instance active-active configuration.

3. Changing the storage driver removes existing containers from the host – True or false?

4. devicemapper is a better option than overlay2 for write-intensive containers – True or false?

5. Which one of the following logging drivers are supported by Docker? (Multiple answers are possible)

   a. journald

   b. Splunk

   c. JSON files

  d. Syslog

  e. Logstash

6. Docker Compose is an imperative approach for managing containers – True or false?

7. Which of the following `docker run` configurations are correct? (Multiple answers are possible)

  a. `docker run nginx`

  b. `docker run --name nginx nginx:1.17.3`

  c. `docker run -d --name nginx nginx`

  d. `docker run -d --name nginx nginx --restart never`

Answers

1. False – You should use devicemapper for CentOS and RHEL 7 and below as they do not support overlay2

2. b, c, d, e

3. True

4. True

5. a, b, c, d

6. False – Docker Compose is a declarative approach for container management.

7. a, b, c

3
Creating and Managing Container Images

In the previous chapter, we covered containerization with Docker, where we installed Docker and ran our first container. We also covered some core fundamentals, including Docker volumes, mounts, storage drivers, and logging drivers. We also covered Docker Compose as a declarative method of managing containers.

Now, we will discuss the core building blocks of containers; that is, container images. Container images also fulfill a core principle of modern DevOps practices – Config as Code. Therefore, understanding container images, how they work, and how to build an image effectively is very important for a modern DevOps engineer.

In this chapter, we're going to cover the following main topics:

- Docker architecture
- Understanding Docker images
- Understanding Dockerfiles, components, and directives
- Building and managing Docker images

- Flattening Docker images

- Optimizing containers with distroless images

- Understanding Docker registries

Technical requirements

For this chapter, we are assuming that you have Docker installed and running on a Linux machine running Ubuntu 16.04 Xenial LTS or later, with sudo access. You can follow *Chapter 2, Containerization with Docker,* for more details on how to do that.

You will also need to clone the following GitHub repository for some of the exercises in this chapter: `https://github.com/PacktPublishing/Modern-DevOps-Practices`. Also, you need a Docker Hub account for most of the exercises. To create one go to `https://hub.docker.com/`

Docker architecture

As we already know, Docker uses the *build once, run anywhere* concept. Docker packages applications into images. Docker images form the blueprint of containers, so a container is an instance of an image.

A container image packages applications and their dependencies, so they are a single mutable unit you can run in any machine that runs Docker. You can also visualize them as a snapshot of the container.

We can build and store Docker images in a Docker Registry such as **Docker Hub**, and then download and use those images in the system where we want to deploy them. Images comprise several layers, so it helps to break images into multiple parts. The layers tend to be reusable stages that other images can build upon. This also means that we don't have to transmit the entire image over a network when we change images and just transmit the delta, which saves a lot of network I/O. We will talk about the layered filesystem in detail later in this chapter.

The following diagram shows the components Docker uses to orchestrate the following activities:

- **Docker daemon**: This process runs on the servers where we want to run our containers. They deploy and run containers on the docker server.

- **Docker registries**: These store and distribute Docker images.

- **Docker client**: This is the command-line utility that we've been using to issue `docker` commands to the Docker daemon:

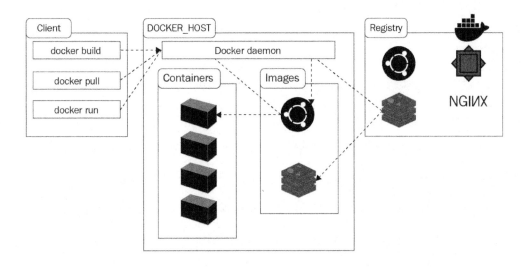

Figure 3.1 – Docker architecture

Now that we understand Docker architecture's key components and how Docker images play an essential role, let's understand Docker images and their components, directives, and registries in detail.

Understanding Docker images

Docker images form the blueprint of Docker containers. Just like you need a blueprint for a shipping container, such as its size and what goods it will contain, a Docker image specifies what packages, source code, dependencies, and libraries it needs to use. It also determines what it needs to do for the source code to run effectively.

Technically, it consists of a series of steps you would perform on a base OS image to get your application up and running. This may include installing packages and dependencies, copying the source code to the correct folder, building your code to generate a binary, and so on.

You can store Docker images in a container registry, a centralized location where your Docker machines can pull images from to create containers.

Docker images uses a layered filesystem. Instead of a huge monolithic block on the filesystem that comprises the template to run containers, we have many layers, one on top of the other. But what does this mean? What problem does this solve? Let's have a look in the next section.

The layered filesystem

Layers in Docker are intermediate Docker images. The idea is that every Dockerfile statement we execute on top of a layer changes something within the layer and builds a new one. The subsequent statement modifies the current one to generate the next one and so on. The final layer executes the Docker CMD or ENTRYPOINT command, and the resulting image comprises several layers arranged one on top of the other. Let's understand this by looking at a simple example.

If we pull the *Flask application* we built in the previous chapter, we will see the following:

```
$ docker pull bharamicrosystems/python-flask-redis
Using default tag: latest
latest: Pulling from bharamicrosystems/python-flask-redis
188c0c94c7c5: Pull complete
a2f4f20ac898: Pull complete
f8a5b284ee96: Pull complete
28e9c106bfa8: Pull complete
8fe1e74827bf: Pull complete
95618753462e: Pull complete
03392bfaa2ba: Pull complete
4de3b61e85ea: Pull complete
266ad40b3bdb: Pull complete
Digest: sha256:bb40a44422b8a7fea483a775fe985d4e05f7e5c59b0806a2
4f6cca50edadb824
Status: Downloaded newer image for bharamicrosystems/python-
flask-redis:latest
docker.io/bharamicrosystems/python-flask-redis:latest
```

As you can see, there are many **Pull complete** statements beside random IDs. These are called *layers*. The current layer contains just the differences between the previous layer and the current filesystem. A container image comprises several layers.

Containers contain an additional writable filesystem on top of the image layers. This is the layer where your containers make modifications to the filesystem to provide the expected functionality.

There are several advantages of using *layers* instead of merely copying the entire filesystem of the container. Since image layers are read-only, multiple containers that are created from an image share the same layered filesystem, which decreases the overall disk and network footprint. Layers also allow you to share filesystems between images. For example, if you have two images coming from a single base image, both images share the same base layer.

The following diagram shows a Python application that runs on an Ubuntu OS. At a high level, you will see a base layer (Ubuntu OS) and Python installed on top of it. On top of Python, we've installed the Python app. All these components form the image. When we create a container out of the image and run it, we get the writable filesystem on the top as the final layer:

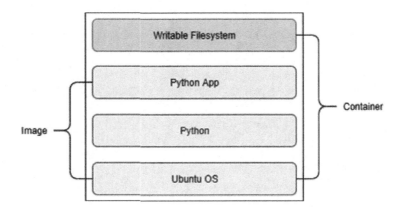

Figure 3.2 – Container layers

So, you can create multiple Python app images from the same base image and customize them according to your needs.

The writable filesystem is unique for every container you spin from container images, even if you create containers from the same image.

Image history

To get a sense of images and what layers they are comprised of, you can always inspect the image history.

Let's inspect the history of the last Docker image by running the following command:

```
$ docker history bharamicrosystems/python-flask-redis
IMAGE             CREATED            BY
SIZE              COMMENT
6d33489ce4d9      6 days ago         /bin/sh -c #(nop)    CMD
["flask" "run"]          0B
<missing>         6 days ago         /bin/sh -c #(nop) COPY
dir:61bb30c35fb351598…    1.2kB
<missing>         6 days ago         /bin/sh -c #(nop)
EXPOSE 5000               0B
<missing>         6 days ago         /bin/sh -c pip install
-r requirements.txt       11.2MB
```

```
<missing>              6 days ago        /bin/sh -c #(nop) COPY
file:4346cf08412270cb...    12B
<missing>              6 days ago        /bin/sh -c apk add
--no-cache gcc musl-dev 1...    143MB
<missing>              6 days ago        /bin/sh -c #(nop)    ENV
FLASK_RUN_HOST=0.0.0.0   0B
<missing>              6 days ago        /bin/sh -c #(nop)    ENV
FLASK_APP=app.py         0B
<missing>              6 days ago        /bin/sh -c #(nop)    CMD
["python3"]              0B
<missing>              6 days ago        /bin/sh -c set -ex;
wget -O get-pip.py "$P...    7.24MB
<missing>              6 days ago        /bin/sh -c #(nop)    ENV
PYTHON_GET_PIP_SHA256...    0B
<missing>              6 days ago        /bin/sh -c #(nop)    ENV
PYTHON_GET_PIP_URL=ht...    0B
<missing>              6 days ago        /bin/sh -c #(nop)    ENV
PYTHON_PIP_VERSION=20...    0B
<missing>              6 days ago        /bin/sh -c cd /usr/
local/bin && ln -s idle3...    32B
<missing>              6 days ago        /bin/sh -c set -ex  &&
apk add --no-cache --...    28.3MB
<missing>              6 days ago        /bin/sh -c #(nop)    ENV
PYTHON_VERSION=3.7.9     0B
<missing>              6 days ago        /bin/sh -c #(nop)    ENV
GPG_KEY=0D96DF4D4110E...    0B
<missing>              6 days ago        /bin/sh -c set -eux;
apk add --no-cache   c...    512kB
<missing>              5 weeks ago       /bin/sh -c #(nop)    ENV
LANG=C.UTF-8             0B
<missing>              5 weeks ago       /bin/sh -c #(nop)    ENV
PATH=/usr/local/bin:/...    0B
<missing>              5 weeks ago       /bin/sh -c #(nop)    CMD
["/bin/sh"]              0B
<missing>              5 weeks ago       /bin/sh -c #(nop)    ADD
file:f17f65714f703db90...    5.57MB
```

As you can see, there are several layers, and every layer has associated commands. You
can also see when the layers were created and the size of the disk space occupied by each.
Some layers do not occupy any disk space. This is because these layers haven't added
anything new to the filesystem, such as CMD and EXPOSE directives. These perform some
functions, but they do not write anything to the filesystem, while commands such as apk
add write to the filesystem, you can see them taking up disk space.

Every layer modifies the old layer in some way, so every layer is just a delta of the
filesystem configuration.

In the next section, we will deep dive into Dockerfiles and understand how we can build Docker images, and see what the layered architecture looks like.

Understanding Dockerfiles, components, and directives

A Dockerfile is a simple file that constitutes a series of steps needed to build a Docker image. Each step is known as a **directive**, and there are different kinds of directives. Let's look at a simple example to understand how it works.

We will create a simple NGINX container, but this time by building the image from scratch and not using the one available on Docker Hub.

So, start by creating a Dockerfile, as follows:

```
$ vim Dockerfile
FROM ubuntu:xenial
RUN apt update && apt install -y curl
RUN apt update && apt install -y nginx
CMD ["nginx", "-g", "daemon off;"]
```

Let's look at each line and directive one by one to understand how this Dockerfile works:

- The FROM directive specifies what the base image for this container should be. This means we are using another image as the base and will be building layers on top of it. We start by using the ubuntu:xenial package as the base image for this build, since we want to run NGINX on Ubuntu.

- The RUN directives specify commands that we need to run on a particular layer. You can run one or more commands separated by &&. We will want to run multiple commands in a single line if we're going to club dependent commands in a single layer. Every layer should meet a particular objective. In the preceding example, the first RUN directive is used to install curl, while the next RUN directive is used to install nginx.

- You might be wondering why we have an apt update before every installation. This is required as Docker builds images using layers. So, one layer should not have implicit dependencies on the previous one. In this example, if we omit apt update while installing nginx, and if we want to update the nginx version without changing anything in the directive containing apt update (that is, the line that installs curl), when we run the build, apt update will not run again, so your nginx installation might fail.

- The CMD directive specifies a list of commands that we need to run when the built image runs as a container. This is the default command that will be executed, and its output will end up in the container logs. Your container can contain one or more CMD directives. For a long-running process such as NGINX, the last CMD should contain something that will not pass control back to the shell and continue to run for the container's lifetime. In this case, we run `nginx -g daemon off;`, which is a standard way of running NGINX in the foreground.

Some directives can easily be confused with each other, such as using ENTRYPOINT instead of CMD or using CMD instead of RUN. These questions also test how solid your Docker fundamentals are, so let's look at both.

Can we use ENTRYPOINT instead of CMD?

Instead of CMD, you can also use ENTRYPOINT. While they serve a similar purpose, there is a difference, and they are two very different directives. Every Docker container has a default ENTRYPOINT – /bin/sh -c. Anything you add to CMD is appended post ENTRYPOINT and executed; for example, CMD ["nginx", "-g", "daemon off;"] will be generated as /bin/sh -c nginx -g daemon off;. Now, if you use a custom ENTRYPOINT instead, the commands you use while launching the container will be appended post it. So, if you define ENTRYPOINT ["nginx", "-g"] and use `docker run nginx daemon off;`, you will get a similar result.

To get a similar behavior without adding any CMD arguments while launching the container, you can also use ENTRYPOINT ["nginx", "-g", "daemon off;"].

> **Tip**
> Use ENTRYPOINT unless there is a need for a specific CMD requirement.
> Using ENTRYPOINT ensures that users cannot change the default behavior of your container, so it's a more secure alternative.

Now, let's look at RUN versus CMD.

Are RUN and CMD the same?

No, RUN and CMD are different and serve different purposes. While RUN is used to build the container and only modifies the filesystem while building it, CMD commands are only executed on the writable container layer, after the container is running.

While there can be several RUN statements in a Dockerfile, each modifying the existing layer and generating the next, if a Dockerfile contains more than one CMD command, all but the last one is ignored.

The RUN directives are used to execute statements within the container filesystem to build and customize the container image, thus modifying the image layers. The idea of using a CMD command is to provide the default command(s) with the container image that will be executed at runtime. This only changes the writeable container filesystem. You can also override the commands by passing a custom command in the docker run statement.

Now, let's go ahead and build our first container image.

Building our first container

Building a container image is very simple. It is actually a one-line command – docker build -t <image-name>:version <build_context>. While we will discuss building container images in detail in the *Building and managing container images* section, let's build the Dockerfile we created:

```
$ docker build -t <your_dockerhub_user>/nginx-hello-world .
Sending build context to Docker daemon  2.048kB
Step 1/d : FROM ubuntu:xenial
xenial: Pulling from library/ubuntu
be8ec4e48d7f: Pull complete
33b8b485aff0: Pull complete
d887158cc58c: Pull complete
05895bb28c18: Pull complete
Digest: sha256:3355b6e4ba1b12071ba5fe9742042a2f10b257c908fbdfac
81912a16eb463879
Status: Downloaded newer image for ubuntu:xenial

 ---> 9499db781771
Step 2/4 : RUN apt update && apt install -y curl
 ---> Running in f995ce5cb427
Get:1 http://archive.ubuntu.com/ubuntu xenial InRelease [247
kB]
Get:2 http://security.ubuntu.com/ubuntu xenial-security
InRelease [109 kB]
---
138 added, 0 removed; done.
Running hooks in /etc/ca-certificates/update.d...
done.
Removing intermediate container f995ce5cb427
 ---> 0857dcffcf6f
Step 3/4 : RUN apt update && apt install -y nginx
 ---> Running in 7b14980fdfe0
Hit:1 http://security.ubuntu.com/ubuntu xenial-security
```

```
InRelease
Hit:2 http://archive.ubuntu.com/ubuntu xenial InRelease
-----
Removing intermediate container 7b14980fdfe0
 ---> 5de3dfb4b18f
Step 4/4 : CMD ["nginx", "-g", "daemon off;"]
 ---> Running in e0e29edeb5dd
Removing intermediate container e0e29edeb5dd
 ---> 0f58eb98361f
Successfully built 0f58eb98361f
Successfully tagged <your_dockerhub_user>/nginx-hello-
world:latest
```

You might have noticed that the name of the container had a prefix in front of it. That is your Docker Hub account name. The name of the image has a structure of `<registry-url>/<account-name>/<container-image-name>:<version>`.

Here, we have the following:

- `registry-url`: The URL to the Docker Registry – defaults to `docker.io`
- `account-name`: The user or account that owns the image
- `container-image-name`: The container image's name
- `version`: The image version

Now, let's create a container out of the image using the following command:

```
$ docker run -d -p 80:80 <your_dockerhub_user>\
/nginx-hello-world
5f232f57afdfa2c28f4ead5ac643f61520eb937c70332a3858528d580c
552322
$ docker ps
CONTAINER ID          IMAGE
COMMAND                      CREATED              STATUS
        PORTS                      NAMES
5f232f57afdf          <your_dockerhub_user>/nginx-hello-world
"nginx -g 'daemon of…"   37 seconds ago        Up 36 seconds
0.0.0.0:80->80/tcp    wonderful_cori
```

Here, we can see that the container is up and running.

If we run `curl localhost`, we can get the default `nginx html` response, as follows:

```
$ curl localhost
<!DOCTYPE html>
<html>
<head>
<title>Welcome to nginx!</title>
...
</body>
</html>
```

That's great! We have built our first image using a Dockerfile.

What if we wanted to customize the image according to our requirements? Practically speaking, no one would want an NGINX container just responding with the default `Welcome to nginx!` message, so let's create an index page and use that instead:

```
$ vim index.html
Hello World! This is my first docker image!
```

This one outputs a custom message instead of the default NGINX HTML page.

We all know that the default NGINX directory containing the `index.html` file is `/var/www/html`. If we can somehow copy the `index.html` file into this directory, it should sort out our problem.

So, modify the Dockerfile so that it includes the following:

```
$ vim Dockerfile
FROM ubuntu:xenial
RUN apt update && apt install -y curl
RUN apt update && apt install -y nginx
WORKDIR /var/www/html/
ADD index.html ./
CMD ["nginx", "-g", "daemon off;"]
```

Here, we've added two directives to the file – WORKDIR and ADD. Let's understand what each one does:

- WORKDIR: This defines the current working directory, which is `/var/www/html` in this case. The last WORKDIR in the Dockerfile also specifies the working directory when the container is executed. So, if you exec into a running container, you will land in the last defined WORKDIR. WORKDIRs can be absolute as well as relative to the current working directory.

- ADD: This adds a local file to the container filesystem – the working directory, in this case. You can also use a COPY directive here instead of ADD, though ADD offers some more features, such as downloading files from a URL and using an archive such as a TAR or ZIP package.

When we build this file, we expect the index.html file to be copied to the /var/www/html directory within the container filesystem. Let's have a look:

```
$ docker build -t <your_dockerhub_user>/nginx-hello-world .
Sending build context to Docker daemon  3.072kB
Step 1/6 : FROM ubuntu:xenial
 ---> 9499db781771
Step 2/6 : RUN apt update && apt install -y curl
 ---> Using cache
 ---> 0857dcffcf6f
Step 3/6 : RUN apt update && apt install -y nginx
 ---> Using cache
 ---> 5de3dfb4b18f
Step 4/6 : WORKDIR /var/www/html/
 ---> Running in 38d87bda3b37
Removing intermediate container 38d87bda3b37
 ---> 59f22dca2cb0
Step 5/6 : ADD index.html ./
 ---> c8319580f297
Step 6/6 : CMD ["nginx", "-g", "daemon off;"]
 ---> Running in 7e4098ec3976
Removing intermediate container 7e4098ec3976
 ---> 410792102996
Successfully built 410792102996
Successfully tagged <your_dockerhub_user>/nginx-hello-world:latest
```

This time, the build was much faster! When we executed the Docker build, it used a lot of layers from the cache. That is one of the advantages of a layered architecture – you only build the part that is changing and use the existing one the way it is.

> **Tip**
> Always add source code after installing packages and dependencies. This is because the source code changes frequently, and the packages more or less remain the same. This will result in faster builds and save a lot of CI/CD time.

Let's rerun the container and see what we get. Note that you need to remove the old container before doing so:

```
$ docker ps
CONTAINER ID          IMAGE                    COMMAND
CREATED               STATUS                                   PORTS
NAMES
5f232f57afdf          0f58eb98361f              "nginx -g
'daemon of…"    18 minutes ago       Up 18 minutes
0.0.0.0:80->80/tcp   wonderful_cori
$ docker rm 5f232f57afdf -f
5f232f57afdf
```

At this point, we can't see the container anymore. Now, let's rerun the container using the following command:

```
$ docker run -d -p 80:80 <your_dockerhub_user>\
/nginx-hello-world
4fc39c745ffe074df32c1c7b15d00c6389f6bf5b7dac3fa318728d15a
8a20e3f
$ docker ps
CONTAINER ID          IMAGE
COMMAND                    CREATED          STATUS
 PORTS                NAMES
4fc39c745ffe          <your_dockerhub_user>/nginx-hello-world
"nginx -g 'daemon of…"    27 seconds ago       Up 25 seconds
0.0.0.0:80->80/tcp   sweet_dewdney
```

Here, we can see that the container is up and running. Let's use `curl localhost` to see what we get:

```
$ curl localhost
Hello World! This is my first docker image!
```

Here, we get the custom message instead of the default NGINX HTML response!

This looks good enough for now, but I will discuss a few more directives to make this image more reliable. First, we haven't explicitly documented what port this container should expose. This works perfectly fine as we know that NGINX runs on port 80, but what if someone wants to use your image and doesn't know the port? Well, in that scenario, it is a best practice to define the port explicitly. We will use the EXPOSE directive for that.

> **Tip**
>
> Always use the EXPOSE directive to give more clarity and meaning to your image.

We also need to define the action to the container process if someone sends a docker stop command. While most processes take the hint and kill the process, it makes sense to explicitly specify what STOPSIGNAL the container should send on a docker stop command. We will use the STOPSIGNAL directive for that.

Now, while Docker monitors the container process and keeps it running unless it receives a SIGTERM or a stop, what would happen if your container process hangs for some reason? So, while your application is in a hung state, Docker still thinks it is running as your process is still running. Therefore, it would make sense to monitor the application through an explicit health check. We will use the HEALTHCHECK directive for this.

Let's combine all these aspects and see what we get in the Dockerfile:

```
$ vim Dockerfile
FROM ubuntu:xenial
RUN apt update && apt install -y curl
RUN apt update && apt install -y nginx
WORKDIR /var/www/html/
ADD index.html ./
EXPOSE 80
CMD ["nginx", "-g", "daemon off;"]
STOPSIGNAL SIGTERM
HEALTHCHECK --interval=60s --timeout=10s --start-period=20s
--retries=3 CMD curl -f localhost
```

While EXPOSE and STOPSIGNAL are self-explanatory, let's look at the HEALTHCHECK directive. So, the HEALTHCHECK directive runs a command (hence CMD) called curl -f localhost. So, this container will report itself as healthy until the result of the curl command is a success.

The HEALTHCHECK directive also contains the following optional fields:

- --interval (default: 30s): The time interval between two subsequent health checks.

- --timeout (default: 30s): The health check probe timeout interval. If the health check times out, it implies a health check failure.

- `--start-period (default: 0s)`: The time lag between the container start and the first health check. This allows you to ensure that your container is up and running before a health check is performed.

- `--retries (default: 3)`: The number of times the probe will retry before declaring an unhealthy status.

Now, let's build this container:

```
$ docker build -t <your_dockerhub_user>/nginx-hello-world .
Sending build context to Docker daemon  3.072kB
Step 1/9 : FROM ubuntu:xenial
 ---> 9499db781771
Step 2/9 : RUN apt update && apt install -y curl
 ---> Using cache
 ---> 0857dcffcf6f
Step 3/9 : RUN apt update && apt install -y nginx
 ---> Using cache
 ---> 5de3dfb4b18f
Step 4/9 : WORKDIR /var/www/html/
 ---> Using cache
 ---> 59f22dca2cb0
Step 5/9 : ADD index.html ./
 ---> Using cache
 ---> c8319580f297
Step 6/9 : EXPOSE 80
 ---> Running in 0f8b8c20a150
Removing intermediate container 0f8b8c20a150
 ---> 3cb751f18ff3
Step 7/9 : CMD ["nginx", "-g", "daemon off;"]
 ---> Running in 6b42fe419917
Removing intermediate container 6b42fe419917
 ---> 8628203bb22a
Step 8/9 : STOPSIGNAL SIGTERM
 ---> Running in e1b1fbfa4918
Removing intermediate container e1b1fbfa4918
 ---> 8f3848c50a4f
Step 9/9 : HEALTHCHECK --interval=60s --timeout=10s --start-
period=20s --retries=3 CMD curl -f localhost
 ---> Running in 437b37698081
Removing intermediate container 437b37698081
 ---> d5fffc5610a7
Successfully built d5fffc5610a7
```

```
Successfully tagged <your_dockerhub_user>/nginx-hello-
world:latest
```

It's time to run it and see for ourselves:

```
$ docker run -d -p 80:80 <your_dockerhub_user>\
/nginx-hello-world
04e0cbe3487ad0e24df9f69a077ba17326c48b5e9fed6d8ad61239f5d0
840bcb
```

Now that we have successfully launched the container, let's try ps and see what we get:

```
$ docker ps
CONTAINER ID          IMAGE
COMMAND                    CREATED              STATUS
                PORTS                    NAMES
04e0cbe3487a          <your_dockerhub_user>/nginx-hello-world
"nginx -g 'daemon of..."   7 seconds ago        Up 5 seconds
(health: starting)    0.0.0.0:80->80/tcp    ecstatic_ellis
```

So, as we can see, the container shows health: starting, which means the health check hasn't been started yet, and we are waiting for the start time to expire.

Let's wait a while and do a docker ps again:

```
$ docker ps
CONTAINER ID          IMAGE
COMMAND                    CREATED              STATUS
          PORTS                    NAMES
04e0cbe3487a          <your_dockerhub_user>/nginx-hello-world
"nginx -g 'daemon of..."   3 minutes ago        Up 3 minutes
(healthy)    0.0.0.0:80->80/tcp    ecstatic_ellis
```

This time, it reports the container as healthy. So, our container is now more reliable as anyone monitoring it will know what part of the application is healthy and what part is not.

This health check only reports on the container's health status. It takes no action beyond that. It is your responsibility to monitor the containers periodically and write a script that can action unhealthy containers.

One way to manage this would be to create a script that checks for unhealthy containers and restarts them. You can schedule such a script in your cron. You can also create a long-running **systemd** script that continuously polls the container processes and checks for the health status.

> **Tip**
>
> While using `HEALTHCHECK` is a great option, you should avoid using it to run your containers on Kubernetes or a similar container orchestrator. You should make use of liveness and readiness probes instead. Similarly, you can define health checks on Docker Compose if you are using it, so use that instead of baking the health check into the container image.

Now, let's go ahead and understand how to build and manage Docker images.

Building and managing Docker images

We built some Docker images in the previous section, so by now, you should have some idea about how to write Dockerfiles and create Docker images from them. We've also covered a few best practices regarding it, which, in summary, are as follows:

- Always add the layers that do not change frequently first, followed by the layers that may change often. For example, install your packages and dependencies first and copy the source code later. Docker builds the Dockerfile from the part that you change until the end, so if you change a line that comes at a later stage, Docker takes all the existing layers from the cache. Adding more frequently changing parts later in the build helps reduce the build time and will result in a faster CI/CD experience.

- Combine multiple commands to create as few layers as possible. Avoid multiple consecutive `RUN` directives. Instead, try to combine them into a single `RUN` directive by using the `&&` clauses. This will help reduce the overall container footprint.

- Only add the required files within your container. Your container does not need the heavyweight package managers and the **Go** toolkit while running your containers if you have already compiled the code into a binary. We will discuss how to do this in detail in the following sections.

Docker images are traditionally built using a sequence of steps specified in the Dockerfile. But as we already know, Docker is DevOps compliant and uses config management practices from the beginning. Most people build their code within the Dockerfile. This means we will also need the programming language library in the build context. With a simple sequential Dockerfile, these programming language tools and libraries end up within the container image. These are known as single-stage builds, which we will cover next.

Single-stage builds

Let's containerize a simple Go application that prints `Hello, World!` on the screen. While I am using **Golang** in this application, this concept is applicable universally, irrespective of the programming language.

The respective files for this example are present in the `ch3/go-hello-world/single-stage` directory within this book's GitHub repository.

Let's look at the Go application file, `app.go`, first:

```
package main
import "fmt"
func main() {
    fmt.Println("Hello, World!")
}
```

The Dockerfile looks as follows:

```
FROM golang:1.12.4
WORKDIR /tmp
COPY app.go .
RUN GOOS=linux go build -a -installsuffix cgo -o app . && chmod
+x ./app
CMD ["./app"]
```

This is standard stuff. We take the `golang:1.12.4` base image, declare a `WORKDIR /tmp`, copy `app.go` from the host filesystem to the container, and build the Go application to generate a binary. Finally, we use the `CMD` directive with the generated binary to be executed when we run the container.

Let's build the Dockerfile:

```
$ docker build -t <your_dockerhub_user>\
/go-hello-world:single_stage .
Sending build context to Docker daemon  3.072kB
Step 1/5 : FROM golang:1.12.4
1.12.4: Pulling from library/golang
e79bb959ec00: Pull complete
d4b7902036fe: Pull complete
1b2a72d4e030: Pull complete
d54db43011fd: Pull complete
963c818ebafc: Pull complete
9eee6e7073aa: Pull complete
83e75b35417b: Pull complete
```

```
Digest:
sha256:83e8267be041b3ddf6a5792c7e464528408f75c446745642db08cfe4
e8d58d18
Status: Downloaded newer image for golang:1.12.4
 ---> b860ab44e93e
Step 2/5 : WORKDIR /tmp
 ---> Running in 4709e81236ff
Removing intermediate container 4709e81236ff
 ---> b75e5716e223
Step 3/5 : COPY app.go .
 ---> 75b2e26e6e7f
Step 4/5 : RUN GOOS=linux go build -a -installsuffix cgo -o app
. && chmod +x ./app
 ---> Running in e878ae4c92dc
Removing intermediate container e878ae4c92dc
 ---> 6d1ffeb5be7d
Step 5/5 : CMD ["./app"]
 ---> Running in bc0b12e67a97
Removing intermediate container bc0b12e67a97
 ---> 6d77e881a81d
Successfully built 6d77e881a81d
Successfully tagged <your_dockerhub_user>/go-hello-
world:single_
stage
```

Now, let's run the Docker image and see what we get:

```
$ docker run <your_dockerhub_user>/go-hello-world:single_stage
Hello, World!
```

We get the expected response back. Now, let's run the following command to list the image:

```
$ docker images
REPOSITORY                                      TAG
IMAGE ID             CREATED              SIZE
<your_dockerhub_user>/go-hello-world        single_stage
6d77e881a81d         6 minutes ago        784MB
```

This image is huge! It takes 784 MB just to print `Hello, World!` on the screen. This is not the most efficient way of building Docker images.

Before we look at the solution, let's understand why the image is so bloated in the first place. We are using the Golang base image, which contains the entire Go toolkit and generates a simple binary. For this application to run, we do not need the complete Go toolkit, and it can efficiently run in an Alpine Linux image.

Docker solves this problem by providing multi-stage builds. You can split your build into stages where you can build your code in one stage and then, in the second stage, export the built code to another context that begins with a different base image that is much lighter, and only contains those files and components that we need to run the code. We'll have a look at this in the next section.

Multi-stage builds

Now, let's modify the Dockerfile according to the multi-stage build process and see what we get.

The respective files for this example are present in the `ch3/go-hello-world/multi-stage` directory within this book's GitHub repository.

The following is the Dockerfile:

```
FROM golang:1.12.4 AS build
WORKDIR /tmp
COPY app.go .
RUN GOOS=linux go build -a -installsuffix cgo -o app . && chmod
+x ./app

FROM alpine:3.12.1
WORKDIR /tmp
COPY --from=build /tmp/app .
CMD ["./app"]
```

The Dockerfile contains two FROM directives – FROM golang:1.12.4 AS build and FROM alpine:3.12.1. The first FROM directive also includes an AS directive that declares the stage and names it build. Anything we do after this FROM directive can be accessed using the build term until we encounter another FROM directive, which would form the second stage. Since the second stage is the one where we want to run our image from, we are not using an AS directive.

In the first stage, we are building our Golang code to generate the binary, so we are using the golang base image.

In the second stage, we are using the `alpine` base image and copying the `/tmp/app` file from the build stage into our current stage. This is the only file we need to run in the container. The rest of the stuff was just required for the build and was bloating our container during runtime.

Let's build the image and see what we get:

```
$ docker build -t <your_dockerhub_user>\
/go-hello-world:multi_stage .
Sending build context to Docker daemon  3.072kB
Step 1/8 : FROM golang:1.12.4 AS build
 ---> b860ab44e93e
Step 2/8 : WORKDIR /tmp
 ---> Using cache
 ---> b75e5716e223
Step 3/8 : COPY app.go .
 ---> Using cache
 ---> 75b2e26e6e7f
Step 4/8 : RUN GOOS=linux go build -a -installsuffix cgo -o app
 . && chmod +x ./app
 ---> Using cache
 ---> 6d1ffeb5be7d
Step 5/8 : FROM alpine:3.12.1
3.12.1: Pulling from library/alpine
188c0c94c7c5: Pull complete
Digest: sha256:c0e9560cda118f9ec63ddefb4a173a2b2a0347082d7dff7
dc14272e7841a5b5a
Status: Downloaded newer image for alpine:3.12.1
 ---> d6e46aa2470d
Step 6/8 : WORKDIR /tmp
 ---> Running in 3332cd5a781d553
Removing intermediate container 2cd5a781d553
 ---> 2cb357f1744c
Step 7/8 : COPY --from=build /tmp/app .
 ---> 7ba4e00f4c94
Step 8/8 : CMD ["./app"]
 ---> Running in 772c593ed1ce
Removing intermediate container 772c593ed1ce
 ---> fdaedb6c84ab
Successfully built fdaedb6c84ab
Successfully tagged <your_dockerhub_user>/go-hello-world:multi_
stage
```

Now, let's run the container:

```
$ docker run <your_dockerhub_user>/go-hello-world:multi_stage
Hello, World!
```

We get the same output, but this time with a minimal footprint. Let's look at the image to confirm this:

```
$ docker images
REPOSITORY                                  TAG                    IMAGE
ID              CREATED             SIZE
<your_dockerhub_user>/go-hello-world        multi_stage
fdaedb6c84ab            2 minutes ago       7.57MB
```

This one is occupying just 7.57 MB instead of the huge 784 MB. This is a massive improvement! We have reduced the image size 100 times.

That is how we build efficiency within our container image. Building efficient images is the key to running production-ready containers, and most professional images you find on Docker Hub use multi-stage builds to create efficient images.

> **Tip**
> Use multi-stage builds where possible to just include the minimal amount of content within your image. Consider using an Alpine base image if possible.

In the next section, we will look at managing images within Docker, some best practices, and some of the most frequently used commands.

Managing Docker images

In modern DevOps practices, Docker images are primarily built either in a developer machine or a CI/CD pipeline. The images are stored in a container registry and then deployed to multiple staging environments and production machines. They might run Docker or a container orchestrator such as Kubernetes on top of them.

To efficiently use images, we need to understand how we can tag them.

Primarily, Docker pulls the image once when you do a docker run. This means that once an image with a particular version is present on the machine, Docker will not attempt to pull it on every run unless you explicitly pull.

To pull the image explicitly, you can use the `docker pull` command, as follows:

```
$ docker pull nginx
Using default tag: latest
latest: Pulling from library/nginx
852e50cd189d: Pull complete
571d7e852307: Pull complete
addb10abd9cb: Pull complete
d20aa7ccdb77: Pull complete
8b03f1e11359: Pull complete
Digest: sha256:6b1daa9462046581ac15be20277a7c75476283f969cb3a
61c8725ec38d3b01c3
Status: Downloaded newer image for nginx:latest
docker.io/library/nginx:latest
```

Now, if we attempt to launch a container using this image, it will instantly launch the container without pulling the image, as follows:

```
$ docker run nginx
/docker-entrypoint.sh: /docker-entrypoint.d/ is not empty,
will attempt to perform configuration
/docker-entrypoint.sh: Looking for shell scripts in /docker-
entrypoint.d/
/docker-entrypoint.sh: Launching /docker-entrypoint.d/10-
listen-
on-ipv6-by-default.sh
10-listen-on-ipv6-by-default.sh: Getting the checksum of /etc/
nginx/conf.d/default.conf
10-listen-on-ipv6-by-default.sh: Enabled listen on IPv6 in /
etc/
nginx/conf.d/default.conf
/docker-entrypoint.sh: Launching /docker-entrypoint.d/20-envsu
bst-on-templates.sh
/docker-entrypoint.sh: Configuration complete; ready for start
 up
```

So, it is a bad idea to use the latest tag on an image, and a best practice is to use semantic versions as your tag. There are two primary reasons for this:

- If you build the latest image every time, orchestrators such as Docker Compose and Kubernetes will assume the image is already present on your machine and will not pull your image by default. If you use an image pull policy such as `Always` on Kubernetes or use a script to pull the image, it is a waste of network bandwidth. It is also important to note that Docker limits the number of pulls you can make on open source images, so you need to ensure you limit your pulls to only when it is necessary.

- Docker tags allow you to quickly roll out or roll back your container deployment. If you always use the latest tag, the new build overrides the old one, so there is no way you can roll back a faulty container to the last known good version. It is also a good idea to use versioned images in production to ensure your container's stability. If, for some reason, you lose the local image and decide to rerun your container, you may not get the same version of the software you were already running as the latest tag changes frequently. So, it's best to use a particular version of the container in production for stability.

Images are comprised of multiple layers and most of the time, there is a relationship between various versions of containers that run on your server. With time and with new versions of images being rolled out in your production environment, it is best to remove the old images through some housekeeping. This will reclaim some valuable space the container images were occupying and results in a cleaner filesystem.

To remove a particular image, you can use the `docker rmi` command, as follows:

```
$ docker rmi nginx
Error response from daemon: conflict: unable to remove
repository reference "nginx" (must force) - container
dfb0f297237c is using its referenced image bc9a0695f571
```

Oh! We get an error, but why? Well, that's because we have a container that is running and using this image.

> **Tip**
> You cannot remove images that are currently being used by a running container.

First, you will have to stop and remove the container. Then, you can go ahead and remove the image using the preceding command. If you want to do everything at once, you can force removal by using the -f flag, which will stop the container, remove it, and then remove the image. So, unless you know what you are doing, do not use the -f flag:

```
$ docker rmi -f nginx
Untagged: nginx:latest
Untagged: nginx@sha256:6b1daa9462046581ac15be20277a7c75476283f
969cb3a61c8725ec38d3b01c3
Deleted: sha256:bc9a0695f5712dcaaa09a5adc415a3936ccba13fc2587d
fd76b1b8aeea3f221c
```

We built our container many times, but what should we do if we need to push to Docker Hub or other registries? But before we do that, we will have to authenticate with Docker Hub using the following command:

```
$ docker login
```

Now, you can push the image to Docker Hub using the following command:

```
$ docker push <your_dockerhub_user>/nginx-hello-world:latest
The push refers to repository [docker.io/<your_dockerhub_user>/
nginx-hello-world]
cacb663b40a4: Pushed
edb1aeb7d278: Pushed
267bd53b3a52: Pushed
1a1a19626b20: Mounted from library/ubuntu
5b7dc8292d9b: Mounted from library/ubuntu
bbc674332e2e: Mounted from library/ubuntu
da2785b7bb16: Mounted from library/ubuntu
latest: digest: sha256:62c2ccf0f0d1704f7e4a7e338d154c22cfac3b28
e22773d1db98f14b2583fa4b size: 1781
```

This has pushed three layers and mounted the rest from Ubuntu. This is because we used Ubuntu as the base image, which was already available on Docker Hub.

If you have multiple tags for the image and you want to push all of them, then you can simply omit the tag in the push command; this will push all the tags for that particular image, like the following:

```
$ docker push <your_dockerhub_user>/go-hello-world
The push refers to repository [docker.io/<your_dockerhub_user>/
go-hello-world]
a059162b3fbe: Pushed
ace0eda3e3be: Mounted from <your_dockerhub_user>/python-flask-
redis
multi_stage: digest: sha256:21290d4de7247a0d718a78e6da8c11c89
583f8c9961601ac107872dbad154489 size: 739
d97df0a335e4: Pushed
a2b5736da0cc: Pushed
39747431f79f: Mounted from library/golang
fcfab44ef5d3: Mounted from library/golang
f4907c4e3f89: Mounted from library/golang
b17cc31e431b: Mounted from library/golang
12cb127eee44: Mounted from library/golang
604829a174eb: Mounted from library/golang
fbb641a8b943: Mounted from library/golang
single_stage: digest:
sha256:8f9aa63570078265b014ed5669e4044a641
5e9daa8e85c47430cfefd5fa01157 size: 2214
```

When your build fails for some reason and you make changes to your Dockerfile, there are chances that old images' layers will remain dangling. Therefore, it is a best practice to prune the dangling images at regular intervals. You can use docker images prune for this, as follows:

```
$ docker images prune
REPOSITORY          TAG             IMAGE ID
CREATED             SIZE
```

In the next section, we'll look at another way to improve Docker image efficiency – by flattening Docker images.

Flattening Docker images

Docker inherently uses a layered filesystem, and we have already discussed why it is necessary and how it is beneficial in depth. However, in some particular use cases, Docker practitioners have observed that a Docker image consisting of fewer layers performs better. You can reduce layers in an image by flattening it. However, it is still not a best practice, and you need not do this unless you see a performance improvement because of this. You can live with filesystem overhead to compensate for this.

To flatten a Docker image, follow these series of steps:

1. Run a Docker container with the usual image.

2. Do a `docker export` of the running container to a `.tar` file.

3. Do a `docker import` of the `.tar` file into another image.

Let's use `nginx-hello-world` image to flatten it and export it to another image; that is, `<your_dockerhub_user>/nginx-hello-world:flat`.

Before we move on, let's get the history of the latest image:

```
$ docker history <your_dockerhub_user>/nginx-hello-world:latest
IMAGE                  CREATED          BY
SIZE                   COMMENT
d5fffc5610a7           5 days ago       /bin/sh -c #(nop)
HEALTHCHECK &{["CMD-SHELL...    0B
8f3848c50a4f           5 days ago       /bin/sh -c #(nop)
STOPSIGNAL SIGTERM             0B
8628203bb22a           5 days ago       /bin/sh -c #(nop)
CMD ["nginx" "-g" "daemon...   0B
3cb751f18ff3           5 days ago       /bin/sh -c #(nop)
EXPOSE 80                      0B
c8319580f297           5 days ago       /bin/sh -c #(nop) ADD
file:574b9ce515bfc9fd4...   44B
59f22dca2cb0           5 days ago       /bin/sh -c #(nop)
WORKDIR /var/www/html/         0B
5de3dfb4b18f           6 days ago       /bin/sh -c apt update
&& apt install -y nginx   54MB
0857dcffcf6f           6 days ago       /bin/sh -c apt update
&& apt install -y curl    46.5MB
9499db781771           12 days ago      /bin/sh -c #(nop)   CMD
["/bin/bash"]                  0B
<missing>              12 days ago      /bin/sh -c mkdir -p
/run/systemd && echo 'do...   7B
```

```
<missing>            12 days ago         /bin/sh -c rm -rf /var
/lib/apt/lists/*        0B
<missing>            12 days ago         /bin/sh -c set -xe
&& echo '#!/bin/sh' > /…   745B
<missing>            12 days ago         /bin/sh -c #(nop) ADD
file:8eef54430e581236e…   131MB
```

Now, let's run a Docker image with the latest image:

```
$ docker run -d --name nginx \
<your_dockerhub_user>/nginx-hello-world:latest
0523f28ae6b3824493170d1a3f451bf4a724892a8248244346651e545
8896199
```

Next, let's take an export out of the running container:

```
$ docker export nginx > nginx-hello-world-flat.tar
```

Import nginx-hello-world-flat.tar to a new image; that is, <your_
dockerhub_user>/nginx-hello-world:flat:

```
$ cat nginx-hello-world-flat.tar | docker import - \
<your_dockerhub_user>/nginx-hello-world:flat
sha256:71d52d9e074a5ea760df7ea023b3cf65ad64bf55f60739630790
b5b7dcc3a352
```

Now, let's list the images and see what we get:

```
REPOSITORY                                  TAG
IMAGE ID            CREATED                 SIZE
<your_dockerhub_user>/nginx-hello-world    flat
71d52d9e074a         44 seconds ago         184MB
<your_dockerhub_user>/nginx-hello-world    latest
d5fffc5610a7         5 days ago             231MB
```

Here, we can see that the flat image is present and that it occupies less space than the latest image. If we get the history out of it, we should see just a single layer:

```
$ docker history <your_dockerhub_user>/nginx-hello-world:flat
IMAGE               CREATED                 BY        SIZE
COMMENT
71d52d9e074a         2 minutes ago
184MB                Imported from -
```

So, it has flattened the image. But is it really a best practice to flatten Docker images? Well, it depends. Let's understand when and how to flatten Docker images and what you should consider:

- Are several applications using a similar base image? If that is the case, then flattening images will only increase the disk footprint as you won't be able to take advantage of a layered filesystem.

- Consider alternatives to flattening images by using a small base image such as Alpine.

- Multi-stage builds are helpful for most complied languages and can reduce your image size considerably.

- You can also slim down images by using as few layers as possible by combining multiple steps into a single RUN directive.

- Consider if the benefit of flattening the image outweighs the disadvantages, see if you get considerable performance improvements, and see whether performance is critical for your application needs.

These combinations will help you understand your container image footprint and help you manage container images. Remember that although reducing the size is ideal, flattening the Docker image should be a last resort.

So far, all the images we've used have been derived out of a Linux distribution and always used a distro as their base image. You can also run a container without using any Linux disto as the base image to make it more secure. We'll have a look at how in the next section.

Optimizing containers with distroless images

Distroless containers are one of the latest trends in the container world. They are promising in that they consider all the aspects of optimizing containers for the Enterprise environment. There are three important things you should consider while optimizing containers – performance, security, and cost.

Performance

You don't spin containers out of thin air. You must download images from your container registry and then run the container out of the image. Each step uses network and disk I/O. The bigger the image, the more resources it consumes, and the less performance you get out of it. Therefore, a smaller Docker image naturally performs better.

Security

Security is one of the most important aspects of the current IT landscape. Companies usually focus a lot on this aspect and invest a lot of money and time in it. Since containers are a relatively new technology, they are generally prone to hacking, so appropriately securing your containers is important. Standard Linux distributions have a lot of stuff that can allow hackers to access a lot more than just what they could have if you secured your container properly. Therefore, you need to ensure that you only have what you need within the container.

Cost

A smaller image also results in less costs. The lower your container footprint, the more containers you can pack within a machine, so there are fewer machines you would need to run your applications. This means you save a lot of money that accumulates over time.

As a modern DevOps engineer, you need to ensure that your images are optimized for all these aspects. Distroless images help take care of all of them. Therefore, let's understand what distroless images are and how to use them.

Distroless images are the most minimal of images and only contain your application, dependencies, and the necessary files for your container process to run. Most of the time, you do not need package managers such as apt or even a shell such as bash. Not having a shell has its advantages. For one, it will help you avoid any outside party gaining access to your container while it is running. Your container now has a small attack surface, which means it won't have many security vulnerabilities.

Google provides distroless images in their official GCR registry, which is available on their GitHub page at `https://github.com/GoogleContainerTools/distroless`. Now, let's get hands-on and see what we can do with them.

The required resources for this exercise are present in `ch3/go-hello-world/distroless` in this book's GitHub repository.

Let's start by creating a Dockerfile:

```
FROM golang:1.12.4 AS build
WORKDIR /tmp
COPY app.go .
RUN GOOS=linux go build -a -installsuffix cgo -o app . && chmod
+x ./app

FROM gcr.io/distroless/base
WORKDIR /tmp
COPY --from=build /tmp/app .
```

```
CMD ["./app"]
```

This Dockerfile is similar to the multi-stage build Dockerfile for the `go-hello-world` container, but instead of using `alpine`, it uses `gcr.io/distroless/base` as the base image. This image contains a minimalistic Linux glibc-enabled system and lacks a package manager or a shell. You can use it to run binaries compiled in a language such as Go, Rust, or D.

So, let's build this first using the following command:

```
$ docker build -t <your_dockerhub_user>/\
go-hello-world:distroless .
Sending build context to Docker daemon  3.072kB
Step 1/8 : FROM golang:1.12.4 AS build
 ---> b860ab44e93e
Step 2/8 : WORKDIR /tmp
 ---> Using cache
 ---> b75e5716e223
Step 3/8 : COPY app.go .
 ---> Using cache
 ---> 75b2e26e6e7f
Step 4/8 : RUN GOOS=linux go build -a -installsuffix cgo -o app
 . && chmod +x ./app
 ---> Using cache
 ---> 6d1ffeb5be7d
Step 5/8 : FROM gcr.io/distroless/base
latest: Pulling from distroless/base
e59bd8947ac7: Pull complete
31eb28996804: Pull complete
Digest: sha256:ca60828b628c3032b2e79bb8f20868ed5314ec5b8a92725
23a9d74cfba18192b
Status: Downloaded newer image for gcr.io/distroless/base:
latest
 ---> 972b93457774
Step 6/8 : WORKDIR /tmp
 ---> Running in 03cf9aaaf7fa
Removing intermediate container 03cf9aaaf7fa
 ---> 815a043db067
Step 7/8 : COPY --from=build /tmp/app .
 ---> 024a5af197be
Step 8/8 : CMD ["./app"]
 ---> Running in d859c7e46ecb
Removing intermediate container d859c7e46ecb
```

```
 ---> ef518cf9aad5
Successfully built ef518cf9aad5
Successfully tagged <your_dockerhub_user>/go-hello-
world:distroless
```

Now, let's run this image and see what we get:

```
$ docker run <your_dockerhub_user>/go-hello-world:distroless
Hello, World!
```

It works! Let's look at the size of the image:

```
$ docker images
REPOSITORY                                 TAG             IMAGE
ID              CREATED              SIZE
<your_dockerhub_user>/go-hello-world       distroless
ef518cf9aad5          3 minutes ago        18.9MB
```

It's just 18.9 MB. Yes, it's a tad bit more than the Alpine image, but it does not contain a shell, so it is more secure from that point of view. Also, there are distroless images available for interpreted programming languages such as Python and Java, so you can use them instead of the bloated image containing the toolkits.

Docker images are stored in Docker registries, and we have all been using Docker Hub for a while. In the next section, we'll understand what they are and the options we have for storing our images.

Understanding Docker registries

A **Docker Registry** is a stateless, highly scalable server-side application that stores and lets you distribute Docker images. The registry is open source under the permissive **Apache license**. It is a storage and distribution system where all your Docker servers can connect and upload and download images as and when needed. It acts as a distribution site for your images.

A Docker Registry contains several Docker repositories. A Docker repository holds several versions of a specific image. For example, all the versions of the nginx image are stored within a single repository within Docker Hub called nginx.

By default, Docker interacts with its public Docker Registry instance, called Docker Hub, which helps you distribute your images to the broader open source community.

Not all images can be public and open source, and many proprietary activities are going on. Docker provides an option to use a private Docker Registry for such a scenario that you can host within your infrastructure called **Docker Trusted Registry**. There are several online options available, such as using a SaaS service such as GCR or creating private repositories at Docker Hub.

While the SaaS option is readily available and intuitive, let's look at hosting our own private Docker Registry.

Hosting your private Docker registry

Docker provides an image that you can run on any server that has Docker installed. Once the container is up and running, you can simply use that as the Docker Registry. Let's have a look:

```
$ docker run -d -p 80:5000 --restart=always --name registry \
registry:2
Unable to find image 'registry:2' locally
2: Pulling from library/registry
cbdbe7a5bc2a: Pull complete
47112e65547d: Pull complete
46bcb632e506: Pull complete
c1cc712bcecd: Pull complete
3db6272dcbfa: Pull complete
Digest: sha256:8be26f81ffea54106bae012c6f349df70f4d5e7e2ec01
b143c46e2c03b9e551d
Status: Downloaded newer image for registry:2
90629823fa3b053678941910a1ad2bb13f68c74180b715123b2975f
0b57479c8
```

Since we know that the registry is running on localhost and listening on port 80, let's try to push an image to this registry. First, let's tag the image to specify localhost as the registry. We will add a registry location at the beginning of the Docker tag so that Docker knows where to push the image. We already know that the structure of a Docker tag is <registry_url>/<user>/<image_name>:<image_version>. We will use the docker tag command to give another name to an existing image, as shown in the following command:

```
$ docker tag <your_dockerhub_user>/nginx-hello-world:latest \
localhost/<your_dockerhub_user>/nginx-hello-world:latest
```

Now, we can go ahead and push the image to the local Docker Registry:

```
$ docker push localhost/<your_dockerhub_user>/\
nginx-hello-world:latest
The push refers to repository [localhost/<your_dockerhub_user>/
nginx-hello-world]
cacb663b40a4: Pushed
edb1aeb7d278: Pushed
267bd53b3a52: Pushed
1a1a19626b20: Pushed
5b7dc8292d9b: Pushed
bbc674332e2e: Pushed
da2785b7bb16: Pushed
latest: digest: sha256:62c2ccf0f0d1704f7e4a7e338d154c22cfac3b
28e22773d1db98f14b2583fa4b size: 1781
```

And that's it! It is as simple as that!

There are other considerations as well, since this is too simplistic. You will have to mount volumes as well; otherwise, you will lose all the images when you restart the registry container. Also, there is no authentication in place, so anyone who can access this server can push or pull images, but this is something we don't desire. Also, communication is insecure, and we want to encrypt the images during transit.

First, let's create the local directories that we will mount to the containers:

```
mkdir -p /mnt/registry/certs
mkdir -p /mnt/registry/auth
```

Now, let's generate an htpasswd file for adding authentication to the Registry. For this, we will run the htpasswd command from within a new Docker Registry container to create a file on our local directory:

```
$ docker run --entrypoint htpasswd registry:2.7.0 \
-Bbn user pass > /mnt/registry/auth/htpasswd
```

The next step is to generate some self-signed certificates for enabling TLS on the repository. Add your server name or IP when asked for a **fully qualified domain name** (**FQDN**). You can leave the other fields blank or add appropriate values for them:

```
$ openssl req \
-newkey rsa:4096 -nodes -sha256 -keyout \
/mnt/registry/certs/domain.key \
-x509 -days 365 -out /mnt/registry/certs/domain.crt
```

Before we proceed further, let's remove the existing registry:

```
$ docker rm -f registry
registry
```

Now, we are ready to launch our container with the required configuration:

```
$ docker run -d -p 443:443 --restart=always --name registry \
  -v /mnt/registry/certs:/certs \
  -v /mnt/registry/auth:/auth \
  -v /mnt/registry/registry:/var/lib/registry \
  -e REGISTRY_HTTP_ADDR=0.0.0.0:443 \
  -e REGISTRY_HTTP_TLS_CERTIFICATE=/certs/domain.crt \
  -e REGISTRY_HTTP_TLS_KEY=/certs/domain.key \
  -e REGISTRY_AUTH=htpasswd \
  -e "REGISTRY_AUTH_HTPASSWD_REALM=Registry Realm" \
  -e REGISTRY_AUTH_HTPASSWD_PATH=/auth/htpasswd \
  registry:2
9b45d5eeabdfc81ab3d624c4fffeab01865fccc7a6fb20ed91c9d678b373
293a
```

The container is now up and running. Let's use `https` this time, but before that, let's `docker login` to the registry. Add the username and password you set while creating the `htpasswd` file (in this case, `user` and `pass`):

```
$ docker login https://localhost
Username: user
Password:
WARNING! Your password will be stored unencrypted in /root/
.docker/config.json.
Configure a credential helper to remove this warning. See
https://docs.docker.com/engine/reference/commandline/login/
#credentials-store

Login Succeeded
```

Since the login succeeded, we can go ahead and push our image to the registry:

```
$ docker push localhost/<your_dockerhub_user>/nginx-hello-world
The push refers to repository [localhost/<your_dockerhub_user>/
nginx-hello-world]
cacb663b40a4: Pushed
edb1aeb7d278: Pushed
267bd53b3a52: Pushed
```

```
1a1a19626b20: Pushed
5b7dc8292d9b: Pushed
bbc674332e2e: Pushed
da2785b7bb16: Pushed
latest: digest: sha256:62c2ccf0f0d1704f7e4a7e338d154c22cfac3b2
8e22773d1db98f14b2583fa4b size: 1781
```

And this time, it works the way we want it to.

Other public registries

Apart from running your registry in a dedicated Docker server, there are other cloud and on-premises options.

Most public cloud providers offer paid online registries and container-hosting solutions that you can use with ease if you are running in the cloud. Some of them are as follows:

- **Amazon Elastic Container Registry (ECR)**: A popular **AWS** offering that you can use if you have your infrastructure running on AWS. It is a highly available, highly performant, fully managed solution. It can host both public and private registries, and you only pay for the amount of storage you consume and the amount of data that's transferred to the internet. The best part is that it integrates with AWS IAM.

- **Google Container Registry (GCR)**: Backed by **Google Cloud Storage** (**GCS**), GCR is one of the best choices if you run your infrastructure on GCP. It hosts both public and private repositories, and you only pay for the storage on GCS.

- **Azure Container Registry** (**ACR**): This is a fully managed, geo-replicated container registry and only supports a private registry. It is a good option when you are running your infrastructure on **Azure**. Besides storing container images, it also stores Helm charts and other artifacts that help you manage your containers well.

- **Oracle Cloud Infrastructure Registry**: Oracle Cloud Infrastructure Registry is an Oracle-managed, highly available container registry. It can host both public and private repositories.

- **CoreOS Quay**: This supports **OAuth** and **LDAP** authentication. It offers both (paid) private and (free) public repositories, automatic security scanning, and automated image builds via integration with **GitLab**, **GitHub**, and **Bitbucket**.

If you don't want to go with managed options in the cloud or run on-premises, you can also use distribution management software such as *Sonatype Nexus* or *JFrog Artifactory*. Both tools support Docker registries out of the box. You can simply create a Docker Registry there using fancy UIs, and then use `docker login` to connect to the registry.

Summary

In this chapter, we have covered a lot of ground. At this point, you should understand Docker from a hands-on perspective. We started with Docker images, how to use a Dockerfile to build Docker images, the components and directives of the Dockerfile, and how to create efficient images by following some best practices. We also discussed flattening Docker images and how to improve container security by using distroless images. Finally, we discussed Docker registries, how to run a private Docker Registry on a Docker server, and how to use other turnkey solutions such as Sonatype Nexus and JFrog Artifactory.

In the next chapter, we will delve into container orchestration using Kubernetes.

Questions

1. Docker images use a layered model – true or false?

2. You can delete an image from a server if a container using that image is already running – true or false?

3. How do you remove a running container from a server? (Multiple answers are possible)

   a. `docker rm <container_id>`

   b. `docker rm -f <container_id>`

   c. `docker stop <container_id> && docker rm <container_id>`

   d. `docker stop -f <container_id>`

4. Which of the following options are container build best practices? (Multiple answers are possible)

   a. Always add layers that don't frequently change at the beginning of the Dockerfile

   b. Combine multiple steps into a single directive to reduce layers

   c. Only use the required files in the container to keep it lightweight and reduce the attack surface

   d. Use semantic versioning in your Docker tags and avoid the latest version

   e. It is a best practice to include package managers and a shell within the container as it helps with troubleshooting a running container

   f. Only use an apt update at the start of your Dockerfile

5. You should always flatten Docker images to a single layer – true or false?

6. A distroless container contains a shell – true or false?

7. What are some of the ways to improve container efficiency? (Multiple answers are possible)

a. Try to use a smaller base image if possible, such as Alpine

b. Only use multi-stage builds to add the required libraries and dependencies to the container and omit heavyweight toolkits that are not necessary

c. Use distroless base images where possible

d. Flatten Docker Images

e. Use single-stage builds to include package managers and a shell as that will help in troubleshooting in production

8. It is a best practice to prune Docker images from time to time – true or false?

9. Health checks should always be baked into your Docker image – true or false?

Answers

1. True

2. False – You cannot delete an image that is being used by a running container

3. a. False

   b. True

   c. True

   d. False

4. a. True

   b. True

   c. True

   d. True

   e. False

   f. False

5. False – Only flatten Docker images if you benefit from better performance

6. False – Distroless containers do not contain a shell

7.   a. True

      b. True

      c. True

      d. True

      e. False

8.   a. True

9.   False – If you're using Kubernetes or Docker Compose, use the liveness probes or define health checks with a YAML file instead

4

Container Orchestration with Kubernetes – Part I

In the last chapter, we covered creating and managing container images, where we discussed container images, Dockerfile, its directives, and components. We also looked at the best practices of writing a Dockerfile and building and managing efficient images. We then looked at flattening Docker images and took a deep dive into distroless images to improve container security. Finally, we created a private Docker registry.

Now we will deep dive into container orchestration. We will learn how to schedule and run containers using the most popular container orchestrator – Kubernetes.

In this chapter, we're going to cover the following main topics:

- What is Kubernetes and why do I need it?
- Kubernetes architecture
- Installing Kubernetes (Minikube and KinD)
- Understanding Kubernetes pods

Technical requirements

For this chapter, we assume that you have Docker installed and running on a Linux machine running **Ubuntu 16.04 Xenial LTS** or later, with `sudo` access. You can follow *Chapter 2, Containerization with Docker,* for more details on how to do that.

You will also need to clone the following GitHub repository for some of the exercises: `https://github.com/PacktPublishing/Modern-DevOps-Practices`.

Run the following command to clone the repository into your home directory, and `cd` into the `ch4` directory to access the required resources:

```
$ git clone https://github.com/PacktPublishing/Modern-DevOps-\
Practices.git modern-devops
$ cd modern-devops/ch4
```

As the repository contains files with placeholders, you will have to replace the `<your_dockerhub_user>` string with the your actual Docker Hub user. Use the following commands to substitute the placeholders.

```
$ find ./ -type f -exec sed -i -e 's/\
<your_dockerhub_user>/<your actual docker hub user>/g' {} \;
```

What is Kubernetes and why do I need it?

By now, you should have a firm understanding of what containers are and how to build and run containers using Docker. However, the way we were running containers using Docker was not optimal from a production standpoint. Let me give you a few considerations to think about:

- As containers are portable, they can run on any machine that runs Docker just fine. Multiple containers also share server resources to optimize resource consumption. Now, think of a microservices application that comprises of hundreds of containers. How will you choose what machine to run the containers? What if you want to dynamically schedule the containers to another machine based on resource consumption?

- Containers provide horizontal scalability as you can create a copy of the container and use a **Load balancer** in front of a pool of containers. One way of doing this is to decide upfront and deploy the desired number of containers, but that isn't optimal resource utilization. What if I tell you that you need to horizontally scale your containers dynamically with traffic, in other words, by creating additional container instances to handle the extra load when there is more traffic, and reducing them when there is less?

- The container health check reports on the containers' health. What if the container is unhealthy and you want to auto-heal it? What would happen if an entire server goes down and you want to schedule all containers running on that server to another?

- As containers mostly run within a server and can see each other, how would I ensure that only the required containers can interact with the other, something we usually do with VMs? We cannot compromise on security.

- Modern cloud platforms allow us to run autoscaling VMs. How can we utilize that from the perspective of containers? For example, if I need just one VM for my containers during the night and five during the day, how can I ensure that the machines are dynamically allocated when we need them?

- How do you manage the networking between multiple containers if they are part of a more comprehensive service mesh?

The answer to all these questions is a container orchestrator, and the most popular and the *de facto* standard for that is Kubernetes.

Kubernetes is an open source container orchestrator. It was first developed by a bunch of Google engineers and then open sourced to the **Cloud Native Computing Foundation**. Since then, the buzz around Kubernetes has not subsided, and for an excellent reason – Kubernetes with containers have entirely changed the technology mindset and how we looked at infrastructure. Instead of treating servers as a dedicated machine to an application or as part of an application, Kubernetes has allowed visualizing servers as an entity with a container runtime installed. So, when we treat servers as a standard setup, we can virtually run anything in a cluster of servers. So, we don't have to plan **High Availability (HA)**, **Disaster Recovery (DR)**, and other operational aspects for every application on your tech stack. Instead, you can cluster all your servers into a single unit, a Kubernetes cluster, and containerize all your applications. You can then offload all container management functions to Kubernetes. You can run Kubernetes on bare-metal servers, VMs, and also as a managed service in the cloud through multiple Kubernetes as a service offerings.

Kubernetes solves these problems by providing HA, scalability, and zero downtime out of the box. It essentially performs the following functions to provide them:

- **Provides a centralized control plane for interacting with it**: The API server exposes a list of useful APIs that you can interact with to invoke many Kubernetes functions. It also provides a Kubernetes command line called `kubectl` to interact with the API using simple commands. The idea of having a centralized control plane is to ensure that Kubernetes makes the ultimate decision to schedule resources such as containers within your servers. That way, you offload that job to Kubernetes rather than self-managing it.

- **Interacts with the container runtime to schedule containers**: Kubernetes interacts with the container runtime installed on your server to schedule containers. When we send the request to schedule a container to `kube-apiserver`, Kubernetes decides what server it needs to schedule the container based on various factors and then interacts with the particular server's container runtime through the `kubelet` component.

- **Stores the expected configuration in a key-value data store**: Kubernetes applies the cluster's anticipated configuration and stores that in a key-value data store – `etcd`. That way, Kubernetes continuously ensures that the cluster remains in the desired state. If there is any deviation from the expected state, Kubernetes will take every action to bring it back to the desired configuration. So that way, Kubernetes makes sure that your containers are up and running and are healthy as well.

- **Provides a network abstraction layer and service discovery**: Kubernetes uses a network abstraction layer to allow communication between your containers. Therefore, every container is allocated a virtual IP, and Kubernetes ensures that a container is reachable from another container running on a different server. It provides the necessary networking by using an overlay network between the servers. From the container's perspective, all containers in the cluster behave as if they are running on the same server. Kubernetes also uses a DNS to allow communication between containers through a domain name. That way, containers can interact with each other by using a domain name instead of an IP address, as containers are ephemeral, and if they are recreated, you will get a different IP address.

- **Interacts with the cloud provider**: Kubernetes interacts with the cloud provider to commission objects such as load balancers and **persistent disks**. So, suppose you tell Kubernetes that your application needs to persist data and define a volume. In that case, Kubernetes will automatically request a disk from your cloud provider and mount it to your container wherever it runs. You can also expose your application on an external load balancer by telling Kubernetes about it. Kubernetes will interact with your cloud provider to spin up a load balancer and point it to your containers. So, that way, you can do everything related to containers by merely interacting with your Kubernetes API server.

Kubernetes comprises multiple moving parts that take over each function we discussed. Let's now look at Kubernetes architecture to understand each one of them.

Kubernetes architecture

Kubernetes is made of a cluster of nodes. There are two possible roles for nodes in Kubernetes – control plane and worker nodes. The control plane nodes control the Kubernetes cluster as a whole, scheduling the workloads, listening to requests, and other aspects that help run your workloads and make the cluster function. They typically form the brain of the cluster.

On the other hand, the worker nodes are the powerhouses of the Kubernetes cluster and provide raw compute for running your container workloads.

Kubernetes architecture follows the client-server model via an API server. Any interaction, including internal interactions between components, happens via the Kubernetes API server. Therefore, the Kubernetes API server is known as the brain of the Kubernetes control plane.

There are other components of Kubernetes as well, but before we delve into the details, let's look at the following diagram to understand the high-level Kubernetes architecture:

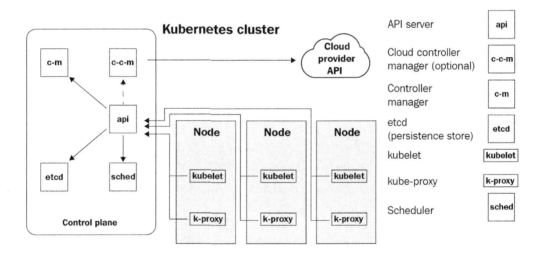

Figure 4.1 – Kubernetes cluster architecture

The control plane comprises the following components:

- **API server**: As discussed already, the API server exposes a set of APIs for external and internal actors to interact with Kubernetes. All interactions with Kubernetes happen via the API server, as evident from the image. If you visualize the Kubernetes cluster as a ship, the API server is the ship's captain.

- **Controller manager**: The controller manager is the Executive Officer of the ship and is tasked with ensuring that the captain's orders are followed in the cluster. From a technical perspective, the controller manager reads the current state and the desired state and takes all actions necessary to move the current state to the desired state. It contains a set of controllers that interact with the Kubernetes components via the API server as and when needed. Some of these are as follows:

  A. **Node-controller**: This watches when the node goes down and responds to that by interacting with the Kube scheduler via the Kube API server to schedule the pods to a healthy node.

  B. **Replication controller**: This ensures that the correct amount of container replicas defined by replication controller objects in the cluster exist.

  C. **Endpoints controller**: These assist in providing endpoints to your containers via services.

  D. **Service Account & Token Controllers**: These create default accounts and tokens for new namespaces.

- **Cloud controller manager**: This is an optional controller manager that you would run if you happen to run Kubernetes in a public cloud, such as AWS, Azure, or GCP. The cloud controller manager interacts with the cloud provider APIs to provision resources such as persistent disks and load balancers that you declare in your Kubernetes configuration.

- **etcd**: etcd is the log book of the ship. That is where all the details about the expected configuration exist. From a technical perspective, this is a key-value store where all the desired Kubernetes configuration is stored. The controller manager refers to the information on this database to action changes in the cluster.

- **Scheduler**: The schedulers are the boatswain of the ship. They are tasked with supervising the loading and unloading of containers on the ship. A Kubernetes scheduler schedules containers in a worker node it finds fit after considering the availability of resources to run it, the HA of your application, and other aspects.

- **kubelet**: kubelets are the seamen of the ship. They carry out the actual loading and unloading of containers from a ship. A kubelet interacts with the underlying container runtime to run containers on the scheduler's instruction from a technical perspective. While most components of Kubernetes can run as a container, the kubelet is the only component that runs as a systemd service instead. They usually run on worker nodes, but if you plan to run the control plane components as containers instead, the kubelet will also run on the control plane nodes.

- **kube-proxy**: `kube-proxy` runs on each worker node and provides the components for your containers to interact with the network components inside and outside your cluster. They are a vital component that facilitates the Kubernetes service concept.

Well, that's a lot of moving parts, but the good news is that there are tools available to set that up for you, and provisioning a Kubernetes cluster is very simple. If you are running on a public cloud, it is only a few clicks away, and you can use your cloud's web UI or CLI to provision it very quickly. If you have an on-premises installation, you can use `kubeadm` for the setup. The steps in this regard are well documented and understood, and it won't be too much of a hassle.

For development and your CI/CD environments, you can use **Minikube** or **KinD**. While Minikube is a single-node Kubernetes cluster that runs on your machine, KinD can run a multi-node Kubernetes cluster by running the nodes as containers. In both cases, all you need is a VM with the requisite resources and you are good to go.

In the next section, let's boot a single-node Kubernetes cluster with Minikube.

Installing Kubernetes (Minikube and KinD)

Let's now move on and install Kubernetes for your development environment. We will first begin with Minikube to get you started quickly, and then we will look into KinD. We will then use KinD for the rest of the chapter.

Installing Minikube

We will install Minikube in the same Linux machine we used to install Docker in *Chapter 2, Containerization with Docker*. So, if you haven't completed that, please go to *Chapter 2, Containerization with Docker*, and use the instructions to set up Docker on the machine.

We will first install `kubectl`. As described previously, `kubectl` is the command line utility that interacts with the Kubernetes API server. We will use `kubectl` multiple times in the book.

To download the latest release of `kubectl`, run the following command:

```
$ curl -LO "https://storage.googleapis.com/kubernetes-release/\
release/$(curl -s https://storage.googleapis.com/kubernetes-\
release/release/stable.txt)/bin/linux/amd64/kubectl"
```

You might also want to download a specific version on `kubectl`. To do so, use the following command:

```
$ curl -LO https://storage.googleapis.com/kubernetes-release/\
release/v<kubectl_version>/bin/linux/amd64/kubectl
```

We will stick with the latest release for this chapter. Let's now go ahead and make the binary executable and then move it to any directory in your system PATH:

```
$ chmod +x ./kubectl
$ sudo mv kubectl /usr/local/bin/
$ sudo ln -s /usr/local/bin/kubectl /usr/bin/kubectl
```

Now, let's check whether `kubectl` is successfully installed by running the following command:

```
$ kubectl version --client
Client Version: version.Info{Major:"1",
Minor:"20", GitVersion:"v1.20.0",
GitCommit:"af46c47ce925f4c4ad5cc8d1fca46c7b77d13b38",
GitTreeState:"clean", BuildDate:"2020-12-08T17:59:43Z",
GoVersion:"go1.15.5", Compiler:"gc", Platform:"linux/amd64"}
```

As `kubectl` is installed successfully, we will now download the `minikube` binary and then move it to your system path using the following commands:

```
$ curl -Lo minikube https://storage.googleapis.com/minikube/\
releases/latest/minikube-linux-amd64
$ chmod +x minikube
$ sudo mv minikube /usr/local/bin/
$ sudo ln -s /usr/local/bin/minikube /usr/bin/minikube
```

Now, let's install the packages required by Minikube to function correctly by running the following command:

```
$ sudo apt-get install -y conntrack
```

We also need to provide the appropriate permissions to the directory that will be used to store Minikube files using the following command:

```
$ sudo chown -R $USER $HOME/.minikube
$ chmod -R u+wrx $HOME/. minikube
$ sudo chown -R $USER $HOME/.kube
$ chmod 600 $HOME/.kube/config
```

We can then finally bootstrap a Minikube cluster using the following command:

```
$ minikube start --driver=docker
* minikube v1.15.1 on Ubuntu 16.04
* Using the docker driver based on user configuration
* Starting control plane node minikube in cluster minikube
* Pulling base image ...
* Downloading Kubernetes v1.19.4 preload ...
    > preloaded-images-k8s-v6-v1.19.4-docker-overlay2-amd64.
tar.lz4: 486.35 MiB
* Creating docker container (CPUs=2, Memory=1968MB) ...
* Preparing Kubernetes v1.19.4 on Docker 19.03.13 ...
* Verifying Kubernetes components...
* Enabled addons: default-storageclass, storage-provisioner
* Done! kubectl is now configured to use "minikube" cluster and
"default" namespace by default
```

As Minikube is now up and running, we will use the kubectl command-line utility to interact with the Kube API server to manage Kubernetes resources. The kubectl commands have a standard structure and are self-explanatory in most cases. They are structured as follows:

kubectl <verb> <resource type> <resource name> [--flags]

Where:

verb: Action to perform, like, get, apply, delete, list, patch, run, etc.

resource type: The Kubernetes resource to manage, such as node, pod, deployment, service, etc.

resource name: The name of the resource to manage.

Now let's use kubectl to get nodes and check whether our cluster is ready to run our containers

```
$ kubectl get nodes
NAME        STATUS    ROLES     AGE       VERSION
minikube    Ready     master    4m45s     v1.19.4
```

And we can see that it is a single-node Kubernetes cluster that is running version **v1.19.4**. Kubernetes is now up and running!

This setup is excellent for development machines where developers want to deploy and test a single component they are working on. However, to simulate a real environment, especially within a CI/CD pipeline, Minikube has its limitations. While Minikube does support multiple nodes, it is still an experimental feature not recommended in production or CI/CD pipelines.

To stop the Minikube cluster and delete it from the machine, you can use the following command:

```
$ minikube stop
```

As we have removed Minikube, let's look at an exciting tool for creating a multi-node Kubernetes cluster in the next section.

Installing KinD

Kubernetes in Docker or **KinD**, in short, allows you to run a multi-node Kubernetes cluster on a single server that runs Docker. We understand that a multi-node Kubernetes cluster requires multiple machines to run on, but how can we run a multi-node Kubernetes cluster on a single server? Well, the answer is simple – KinD uses a Docker container as a Kubernetes node. So, if we need a four-node Kubernetes cluster, KinD will spin up four containers that behave like four Kubernetes nodes. It is as simple as that.

While you need Docker to run KinD, KinD internally uses **containerd** as a container runtime instead of Docker. Containerd implements the container runtime interface, and therefore Kubernetes does not require any specialized components, such as **dockershim**, to interact with it. Therefore, KinD will still work on Docker in future versions of Kubernetes when Docker would be unsupported as a Kubernetes container runtime.

As KinD supports a multi-node Kubernetes cluster, you can use it for your development activities and also in your CI/CD pipelines. In fact, KinD redefines CI/CD pipelines as you don't require a static Kubernetes environment to test your build. KinD is swift to boot up, and therefore you can integrate the bootstrapping of the KinD cluster, running, and testing your container builds within the cluster, and then destroying it all within your CI/CD pipeline. It gives development teams immense power and speed.

Important

Never use KinD in production. Docker in Docker implementations is not very secure, and therefore KinD clusters should not exist beyond your Dev environments and CI/CD pipelines.

Bootstrapping KinD is just a few commands away. We first need to download KinD, make it executable, and then move it to the default `PATH` directory using the following commands:

```
$ curl -Lo kind https://kind.sigs.k8s.io/dl/v0.9.0/kind-linux-\
amd64
$ chmod +x kind
$ sudo mv kind /usr/local/bin/kind
```

To check whether KinD is installed, we can run the following command:

```
$ kind version
kind v0.9.0 go1.15.2 linux/amd64
```

Now, let's bootstrap a multi-node KinD cluster. We first need to create a KinD `config` file. The KinD `config` file is a simple yaml file where you can declare what sort of configuration we want for each node. If we need to bootstrap a single control plane and three worker node clusters, we can add the following configuration:

```
$ vim kind-config.yaml
kind: Cluster
apiVersion: kind.x-k8s.io/v1alpha4
nodes:
- role: control-plane
- role: worker
- role: worker
- role: worker
```

You can also have an HA configuration with multiple control planes using multiple node items with the control plane role. For now, let's stick with a single control plane, three worker node configuration.

To bootstrap your KinD cluster with the preceding configuration, run the following command:

```
$ kind create cluster --config kind-config.yaml
Creating cluster "kind" ...
  Ensuring node image (kindest/node:v1.19.1)
  Preparing nodes
  Writing configuration
  Starting control-plane
  Installing CNI
  Installing StorageClass
  Joining worker nodes
```

```
Set kubectl context to "kind-kind"
You can now use your cluster with:
kubectl cluster-info --context kind-kind
Have a nice day!
```

And our KinD cluster is up and running. Let's verify this by using the following command:

```
$ kubectl cluster-info --context kind-kind
Kubernetes control plane is running at https://127.0.0.1:36444
KubeDNS is running at https://127.0.0.1:36444/api/v1/
namespaces/kube-system/services/kube-dns:dns/proxy

To further debug and diagnose cluster problems, use 'kubectl
cluster-info dump'.
```

And it all looks good! Let's now list the nodes to see for certain by using the following command:

```
$ kubectl get nodes
NAME                  STATUS    ROLES      AGE       VERSION
kind-control-plane    Ready     master     4m3s      v1.19.1
kind-worker           Ready     <none>     3m29s     v1.19.1
kind-worker2          Ready     <none>     3m28s     v1.19.1
kind-worker3          Ready     <none>     3m28s     v1.19.1
```

And we see that there are four nodes in the cluster – one control plane and three workers. As the cluster is now up and running, let's deep dive into Kubernetes and look at some of the most frequently used Kubernetes resources in the next section.

Understanding Kubernetes pods

Kubernetes pods form the basic building block of a Kubernetes application. A pod contains one or more containers, and all containers within a pod are always scheduled in the same host. Usually, there is a single container within a pod, but there are use cases where you might want to schedule multiple containers in a single pod.

It takes a while to digest why Kubernetes started with the pod's concept in the first place instead of using containers, but there are reasons for that, and you will appreciate this as you gain more experience with the tool. For now, let's look at a simple example of a pod and how to schedule it in Kubernetes.

Running a pod

We will start by running an NGINX container in a pod using simple imperative commands. We will then look at how we can do it in a declarative fashion.

To access the resources for this section, `cd` into the following:

```
$ cd ~/modern-devops/ch4/pod/
```

To run a pod with a single NGINX container, execute the following command:

```
$ kubectl run nginx --image=nginx
```

To check whether the pod is running, run the following command:

```
$ kubectl get pod
NAME     READY     STATUS      RESTARTS     AGE
nginx    1/1       Running     0            26s
```

And that's it! As we see, the pod is now running.

The `kubectl run` command was the imperative way of creating pods, but there's another way of interacting with Kubernetes – by using declarative manifests. Kubernetes manifests are YAML or JSON files that you can use to declare the desired configuration instead of telling Kubernetes everything through a command line. The method is similar to docker-compose.

> **Tip**
> Always use the declarative method to create Kubernetes resources in staging and production environments. They allow you to store and version your Kubernetes configuration in a source code management tool such as Git and enable GitOps. You can use imperative methods during development, as commands have a quicker turnaround than using YAML files.

Let's look at an example pod manifest, `nginx-pod.yaml`:

```
apiVersion: v1
kind: Pod
metadata:
  labels:
    run: nginx
  name: nginx
spec:
  containers:
```

```
- image: nginx
  imagePullPolicy: Always
  name: nginx
  resources:
    limits:
      memory: "200Mi"
      cpu: "200m"
    requests:
      memory: "100Mi"
      cpu: "100m"
restartPolicy: Always
```

Let's understand the file first. The file contains the following:

- apiVersion: This defines the version of the resource we are trying to define. In this case, as it is a pod and it's a generally available (GA) resource, the version we're going to use is v1.

- kind: This defines the kind of resource we want to create, a pod in this case.

- metadata: The metadata section defines the name and labels surrounding this resource. It helps in uniquely identifying the resource as well as grouping multiple resources using labels.

- spec: This is the main section where we define the actual specifications for the resource.

- spec.containers: This section defines one or more containers that form the pod.

- spec.containers.name: The container name, nginx-container in this case.

- spec.containers.image: The container image, nginx in this case.

- spec.containers.imagePullPolicy: This can be Always, IfNotPresent, or Never. If set to Always, Kubernetes always pulls the image from the registry. If set to IfNotPresent, Kubernetes pulls the image only if the image is not found on the node where the pod is scheduled. If set to Never, Kubernetes will never attempt to pull images from the registry and rely completely on local images.

- spec.containers.resources: Defines the resource requests and limits.

- spec.containers.resources.limit: Defines the resource limits. This is the maximum amount of resources that the pod can allocate, and if the resource consumption increases beyond it, the pod is evicted.

- `spec.containers.resources.limit.memory`: Defines the memory limit.

- `spec.containers.resources.limit.cpu`: Defines the CPU limit.

- `spec.containers.resources.requests`: Defines the resource requests. This is the minimum amount of resources the pod would request during scheduling and will not be scheduled on a node that cannot allocate it.

- `spec.containers.resources.requests.memory`: Defines the amount of memory to be requested.

- `spec.containers.resources.requests.cpu`: Defines the amount of CPU cores to be requested.

- `spec.restartPolicy`: Defines the restart policy of containers – `Always`, `OnFailure`, or `Never`. This is similar to the restart policy on Docker.

There are other settings on the pod manifest, but we will explore these as and when we progress.

Important tips

Set `imagePullPolicy` to `IfNotPresent` unless you have a strong reason for using `Always` or `Never`. That will ensure that your containers boot up quickly and you don't download images unnecessarily.

Always use resource requests and limits while scheduling pods. These ensure that your pod is scheduled in an appropriate node and does not exhaust any existing resources. You can also apply a default resource policy at the cluster level to ensure that your developers don't cause any harm if they miss out on this section for some reason.

To apply the manifest, run the following command:

```
$ kubectl apply -f nginx-pod.yaml
```

The pod is entirely out of bounds from the host. It is running within the container network, and by default, Kubernetes does not allow any pod to be exposed to the host network unless we explicitly want to expose it.

There are two ways to access the pod – using port forwarding with `kubectl port-forward`, or exposing the pod through a `Service` resource.

Using port forwarding

Before we get into the service side of things, let's look at using the `port-forward` option.

To expose the pod using port forwarding, execute the following command:

```
$ kubectl port-forward nginx 8080:80
Forwarding from 127.0.0.1:8080 -> 80
Forwarding from [::1]:8080 -> 80
```

And the prompt is stuck at this. This means it has opened a port forwarding session and is listening on port 8080. It will automatically forward the request it receives on port 8080 to NGINX port 80.

Open a duplicate terminal session and then let's `curl` on the preceding address to see what we get:

```
$ curl 127.0.0.1:8080
<!DOCTYPE html>
<html>
<head>
<title>Welcome to nginx!</title>
...
</html>
```

We can see that it is working as we get the default NGINX response.

Now, a few things to remember:

When we use the HTTP port-forward, we are forwarding requests from the client machine running `kubectl` to the pod, something similar to the following diagram:

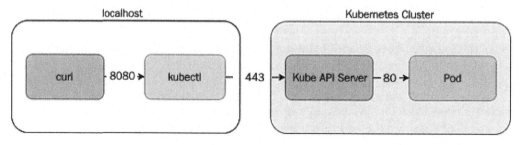

Figure 4.2 – kubectl port-foward

When you run a `kubectl port-forward`, the `kubectl` client opens up a TCP tunneling via the Kube API server, and the Kube API server then forwards the connection to the correct pod. As the connection between the `kubectl` client and the API server is encrypted, it is a very secure way of accessing your pod, but hold your horses before deciding to use the `kubectl port-forward` to expose pods to the outside world.

There are particular use cases for using `kubectl port-forward`:

- For troubleshooting any misbehaving pod.
- For accessing an internal Kubernetes service, such as the Kubernetes dashboard. That is when you don't want to expose the service to the external world, but only allow Kubernetes admins and users to log in to the dashboard. It is assumed that only these users will have access to the cluster via `kubectl`.

For anything else, you should be using `Service` resources to expose your pod, internally or externally. While we will cover the `Service` resource in the coming sections, let's look at a few operations we can perform with a pod.

Troubleshooting pods

As we can browse logs from a container using `docker logs`, we can browse logs from a container within a Kubernetes pod using the `kubectl logs` command. If more than one container runs within the pod, we can specify the container name using the `-c` flag.

To access the container logs, run the following command:

```
$ kubectl logs nginx -c nginx
...
127.0.0.1 - - [18/Dec/2020:05:38:01 +0000] "GET / HTTP/1.1" 200
612 "-" "curl/7.47.0" "-"
```

As the pod is running a single container, we need not specify the `-c` flag, so instead you can also use the following command:

```
$ kubectl logs nginx
```

There might be instances where you may want to get a shell to a running container and troubleshoot what's going on within that. We use `docker exec` for that in the Docker world. Similarly, we can use `kubectl exec` for that within Kubernetes.

Run the following command to open a shell session with the container:

```
$ kubectl exec -it nginx -- /bin/bash
root@nginx:/# cd /etc/nginx/ && ls
```

```
conf.d  fastcgi_params  koi-utf  koi-win  mime.types  modules
nginx.conf  scgi_params  uwsgi_params  win-utf
root@nginx:/etc/nginx# exit
```

You can even run specific commands without opening a shell session. For example, we can perform the preceding operation with a single line, something like the following:

```
$ kubectl exec nginx -- ls /etc/nginx
conf.d  fastcgi_params  koi-utf  koi-win  mime.types  modules
nginx.conf  scgi_params  uwsgi_params  win-utf
```

kubectl exec is an important command that helps us in troubleshooting containers.

> **Tip**
>
> If you modify files or download packages within the container in the exec mode, they will persist until the current pod is alive. Once the pod is gone, you will lose all changes. Therefore, it isn't a great way of fixing issues. You should only diagnose problems by using exec, bake the correct changes in a new image, and then redeploy it.

When we looked at distroless containers in the previous chapter, they did not allow exec into the container for security reasons. There are debug images available for distroless that will enable you to open a shell session for troubleshooting purposes if you wish to.

> **Tip**
>
> By default, a container runs as the root user if you haven't specified the user within the Dockerfile while building the image. You can set a runAsUser attribute within your pod's security context if you want to run your pod as a specific user, but this is not ideal. The best practice is to bake the user within the container image.

We've discussed troubleshooting running containers, but what if the containers fail to start for some reason?

Let's look at the following example:

```
$ kubectl run nginx-1 --image=nginx-1
```

Now, let's try to get the pod and see for ourselves:

```
$ kubectl get pod nginx-1
NAME        READY    STATUS           RESTARTS    AGE
nginx-1     0/1      ImagePullBackOff  0           25s
```

Oops! There is some error now, and the status is `ImagePullBackOff`. Well, it seems like there is some issue with the image. While we understand that the issue is with the image, we want to understand the real issue, so for further information on this, we can describe the pod using the following command:

```
$ kubectl describe pod nginx-1
```

Now, this gives us a wealth of information regarding the pod, and if you look at the events section, you will find a specific line that tells us what is wrong with the pod:

```
Warning  Failed      60s (x4 over 2m43s)   kubelet
Failed to pull image "nginx-1": rpc error: code = Unknown desc
= failed to pull and unpack image "docker.io/library/nginx-
1:latest": failed to resolve reference "docker.io/library/
nginx-1:latest": pull access denied, repository does not exist
or may require authorization: server message: insufficient_
scope: authorization failed
```

So, this one is telling us that either the repository does not exist, or the repository exists but it is private, and hence the authorization failed.

> **Tip**
> You can use `kubectl describe` for most Kubernetes resources, and it should be the first command you should use while troubleshooting issues.

So, as we all know that the image does not exist, let's change the image to a valid one. To do that, we have to delete the pod and then recreate it with the correct image.

To delete the pod, run the following command:

```
$ kubectl delete pod nginx-1
```

So, the next step would be to recreate the pod with the correct image.

To recreate the pod, run the following command:

```
$ kubectl run nginx-1 --image=nginx
```

Now, let's get the pod, and it should run:

```
$ kubectl get pod nginx-1
NAME       READY   STATUS    RESTARTS   AGE
nginx-1    1/1     Running   0          42s
```

And the pod is now running as we have fixed the image issue.

Till now, we've managed just to run containers using pods, but pods are very powerful resources and help you manage containers as well. Kubernetes pods provide a bunch of probes to ensure the reliability of your application. Let's have a look at that in the next section.

Ensuring pod reliability

We've talked about health checks in the chapter on Docker, and I also mentioned that you should not use it on the Docker level and instead use the ones provided by your container orchestrator. Kubernetes provides three **probes** to monitor your pod's health – the **Startup Probe**, **Liveness Probe**, and **Readiness Probe**.

The following diagram depicts all three probes graphically:

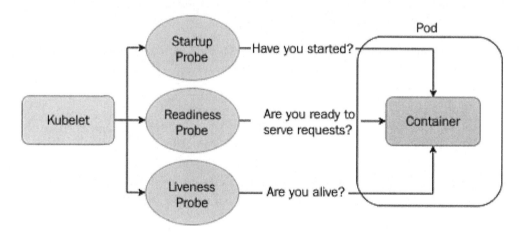

Figure 4.3 – Kubernetes probes

Let's now look at each one in turn and understand how and when to use them:

Startup probe

Kubernetes uses startup probes to check whether the application has started. You can use startup probes on applications that start slowly, or you don't know how long it might take to start. While the startup probe is active, it disables other probes to not interfere in its operation. As the application has not started until the startup probe reports it, there is no point in having any other probes active.

Readiness probe

Readiness probes are used to ascertain whether a container is ready to serve requests. They differ from startup probes because, unlike the startup probe that only checks whether the application has started, the readiness probe ensures that the container can begin to process requests. A pod is ready when all containers of the pod are ready. Readiness probes ensure that no traffic is sent to a pod if the pod is not ready. Therefore, it allows for a better user experience.

Liveness probe

Liveness probes are used to check whether a container is running and healthy. The probe checks the health of the containers periodically. If a container is found unhealthy, the liveness probe will kill the container. If you've set the `restartPolicy` of your pod to `Always` or `OnFailure`, Kubernetes will restart the container. Therefore, it improves the service's reliability by detecting deadlocks and ensuring that the containers are running instead of just reporting as running.

Now, let's have a look at an example to understand probes better.

Probes in action

Let's improve the last manifest and add some probes to that to create the following `nginx-probe.yaml` manifest file:

```
...
startupProbe:
  exec:
    command:
     - cat
     - /usr/share/nginx/html/index.html
  failureThreshold: 30
  periodSeconds: 10
readinessProbe:
  httpGet:
    path: /
    port: 80
  initialDelaySeconds: 5
  periodSeconds: 5
livenessProbe:
  httpGet:
    path: /
    port: 80
```

```
        initialDelaySeconds: 5
        periodSeconds: 3
   restartPolicy: Always
```

The manifest file contains all three probes:

- The startup probe checks whether the /usr/share/nginx/html/index.html file exists. It will continue checking it 30 times at an interval of 10 seconds until one of them succeeds. Once it detects the file, the startup probe will stop probing further.

- The readiness probe checks whether there is a listener on port 80 and responds with HTTP 2xx – 3xx on path /. It waits for 5 seconds initially, and then it checks the pod every 5 seconds. If it gets a 2xx – 3xx response, it will report the container as ready and accept requests.

- The liveness probe checks whether the pod responds with HTTP 2xx – 3xx on port 80 and path /. It waits for 5 seconds initially and probes the container every 3 seconds. Suppose, during a check, that it finds the pod not responding for failureThreshold times (defaults to 3). In that case, it will kill the container, and the kubelet will take appropriate action based on the pod's restartPolicy.

- Let's apply the YAML file using the following command and see what we get:

```
$ kubectl apply -f nginx-probe.yaml
```

Now, let's watch the pods come to life using the following command:

```
$ kubectl get pod -w
NAME       READY    STATUS              RESTARTS    AGE
nginx      0/1      ContainerCreating   0           8s
nginx      0/1      Running             0           14s
nginx      1/1      Running             0           23s
```

As we see, the pod is quickly ready from the running state. It takes approximately 10 seconds for that to happen. That is because the readiness probe kicks in 10 seconds after the pod started. The liveness probe then keeps monitoring the health of the pod.

Now, let's do something that will break the liveness check. Imagine a scenario when someone gets a shell to the container and deletes some important files from there. How do you think the liveness probe will react? Let's have a look.

Let's delete the `/usr/share/nginx/html/index.html` file from the container and then check how the container behaves using the following command:

```
$ kubectl exec -it nginx -- rm -rf /usr/share/nginx/\
html/index.html && kubectl get pod nginx -w
NAME     READY    STATUS      RESTARTS    AGE
nginx    1/1      Running     0           25s
nginx    0/1      Running     1           35s
nginx    0/1      Running     1           40s
nginx    1/1      Running     1           43s
```

So, while we are watching the pod, the initial delete is detected only after 10 seconds. That's because of the liveness probe. It tries for 9 seconds, that is, three times `periodSeconds`, as the `failureThreshold` defaults to 3, before declaring the pod as unhealthy and killing the container. No sooner does it kill the container than the kubelet restarts it as the pod's `restartPolicy` is set to `Always`. We then see the startup and readiness probes kicking in, and soon the pod gets ready.

Therefore, no matter what, your pods are reliable and will work even if a part of your application is faulty.

> **Tip**
> Using both the readiness and liveness probes will help provide a better user experience as no requests go to pods that are not ready to process any request. If your application does not respond appropriately, it will replace the container. If you have multiple pods running to serve the request, your service is exceptionally resilient.

As we discussed previously, a pod can contain one or more containers. Let's look at some of the use cases where you might want to use multiple containers instead of one.

Pod multi-container design patterns

You can run multiple containers in pods in two ways – running a container as an init container, or running a container as a helper container to the main container. Let's explore both approaches in the following subsections.

Init containers

Init containers are run before the main container is bootstrapped, and therefore you can use them to initialize your container environment before the main container takes over, for example:

- A directory might require a particular set of ownership or permissions before you want to start your container using the non-root user.

- You might want to clone a Git repository before spinning up the web server.

- You can add a start up delay.

- You can generate configuration dynamically, such as for containers that want to dynamically connect to some other pod that it is not aware of during build time, but should be during runtime.

> **Tip**
>
> Use `InitContainers` only as a last resort, as they hamper the start up time of your containers. Try to bake configuration within your container image or customize it if needed.

Let's now look at an example to see init containers in action.

To access the resources for this section, `cd` into the following:

```
$ cd ~/modern-devops/ch4/multi-container-pod/
```

Let's serve the `example.com` website from our `nginx` web server. We will get the `example.com` web page and save it as `index.html` in the `nginx` default HTML directory before starting `nginx`.

Access the manifest file, `nginx-init.yaml`, which should contain the following:

```
...
spec:
  containers:
  - name: nginx-container
    image: nginx
    volumeMounts:
    - mountPath: /usr/share/nginx/html
      name: html-volume
  initContainers:
  - name: init-nginx
    image: busybox:1.28
```

```
    command: ['sh', '-c', 'mkdir -p /usr/share/nginx/html &&
wget -O /usr/share/nginx/html/index.html http://example.com']
    volumeMounts:
    - mountPath: /usr/share/nginx/html
      name: html-volume
  volumes:
  - name: html-volume
    emptyDir: {}
```

If we look at the spec section of the manifest file, we see the following:

- `containers`: This section defines one or more containers that form the pod.

- `containers.name`: The container name, `nginx-container` in this case.

- `containers.image`: The container image, `nginx` in this case.

- `containers.volumeMounts`: This defines a list of volumes that should be mounted to the container. It is similar to the volumes we read about in *Chapter 3, Creating and Managing Container Images.*

- `containers.volumeMounts.mountPath`: This defines the path to mount the volume on, `/usr/share/nginx/html` in this case. We will share this volume with the init container so that when the init container downloads the index.html file from example.com, this directory would contain the same file.

- `containers.volumeMounts.name`: The name of the volume, `html-volume` in this case.

- `initContainers`: This section defines one or more init containers that run before the main containers.

- `initContainers.name`: The init container name, `init-nginx` in this case.

- `initContainers.image`: The init container image, `busybox:1.28` in this case.

- `initContainers.command`: The command that the busybox should execute. In this case, `'mkdir -p /usr/share/nginx/html && wget -O /usr/share/nginx/html/index.html http://example.com'` will download the content of `example.com` to the `/usr/share/nginx/html` directory.

- `initContainers.volumeMounts`: We will mount the same volume that we defined in `nginx-container` on this container. So, anything we save in this volume will automatically appear in `nginx-container`.

- `initContainers.volumeMounts.mountPath`: This defines the path to mount the volume on, `/usr/share/nginx/html` in this case.

- initContainers.volumeMounts.name: The name of the volume, html-volume in this case.

- volumes: This section defines one or more volumes associated with the containers of the pod.

- volumes.name: The volume name, html-volume in this case.

- volumes.emptyDir: This defines an emptyDir volume. It is similar to a tmpfs volume in Docker, and therefore is not persistent and lasts just for the container's lifetime.

So, let's go ahead and apply the manifest using the following command:

```
$ kubectl apply -f nginx-init.yaml
```

Now, as the pod is created, let's watch the pod and see what we get using the following command:

```
$ kubectl get pod nginx -w
NAME     READY    STATUS          RESTARTS    AGE
nginx    0/1      Init:0/1    0               6s
nginx    0/1      PodInitializing    0            7s
nginx    1/1      Running         0           17s
```

Initially, we see that the nginx pod shows the status of Init:0/1. This means that 0 out of 1 initContainers have started initializing. After some time, we see that the pod reports the status – PodInitializing, which means that the init containers have started running. Once the init containers have run successfully, the pod reports a status of running.

Now, once the pod starts to run, we can port-forward the container port 80 to host port 8080 using the following command:

```
$ kubectl port-forward nginx 8080:80
```

Open a duplicate terminal and try to curl the localhost on port 8080 by using the following command:

```
$ curl localhost:8080
<!doctype html>
<html>
<head>
    <title>Example Domain</title>
            ---
</html>
```

And we see the example domain response from our web server. This means that the init container worked perfectly fine.

Now, as you may have understood by now, the life cycle of init containers ends before the primary containers start, and a pod can contain one or more main containers. Therefore, let's look at a few design patterns that we can use in the main container.

Ambassador pattern

The **ambassador pattern** derives its name from ambassador, who is an envoy that represents a country overseas. You can also think of an ambassador as a proxy of a particular application. Let's say, for example, that you have migrated one of your existing Python Flask applications to containers, and one of your containers needs to communicate with a Redis database. The database always existed in the localhost of your system. Therefore, the database connection details within your application contain localhost everywhere.

Now, there are two approaches you can take:

- You can either change the application code and use config maps and secrets (more on these later) to inject the database connection details into the environment variable, or

- You can keep using the existing code and use a second container to act as a TCP proxy to the Redis database. The TCP proxy will link with the config map and secrets and contain the Redis database's connection details.

> **Tip**
> The ambassador pattern helps your developers focus on your application without worrying about the configuration details. Consider using it if you want to decouple application development with config management.

The second approach solves our problem if we wish to do a like-for-like migration. We can use config maps to define the environment-specific configuration without changing the application code. The following diagram shows the approach.

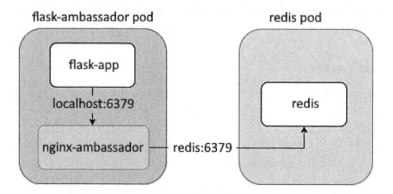

Figure 4.4 – Ambassador pattern

Before we delve into the technicalities, let's understand what a config map is.

Config map

A config map contains key-value pairs that we can use for various purposes, such as defining environment-specific properties or injecting an external variable at container startup or during runtime.

The idea of the config map is to decouple the application with configuration and to externalize configuration at a Kubernetes level. It is similar to using a Java properties file, for example, to define the environment-specific configuration.

The following diagram explains it beautifully:

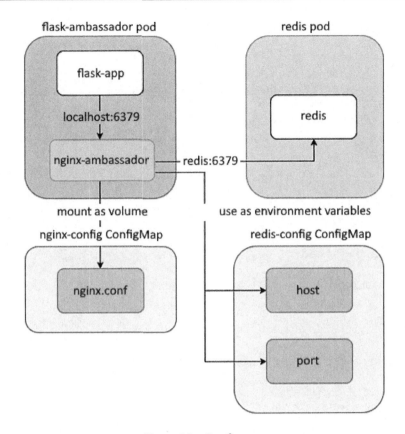

Figure 4.5 – Config maps

We will use `ConfigMap` to define the connection properties of the external Redis database within the ambassador container.

Example application

So, let's go ahead and look at the application code for this exercise.

The `app.py` file of the Flask application looks like the following:

```python
import time
import redis
from flask import Flask
from datetime import datetime

app = Flask(__name__)
cache = redis.Redis(host='localhost', port=6379)

def get_last_visited():
```

```
    try:
        last_visited = cache.getset('last_
visited',str(datetime.now().strftime("%Y-%m-%d, %H:%M:%S")))
        if last_visited is None:
            return cache.getset('last_visited',str(datetime.
now().strftime("%Y-%m-%d, %H:%M:%S")))
        return last_visited
    except redis.exceptions.ConnectionError as e:
        raise e


@app.route('/')
def index():
    last_visited = str(get_last_visited().decode('utf-8'))
    return 'Hi there! This page was last visited on {}.\n'.
format(last_visited)
```

And the `requirements.txt` file is the following:

```
flask
redis
```

We also need to create a `Dockerfile`, which is the following:

```
FROM python:3.7-alpine
ENV FLASK_APP=app.py
ENV FLASK_RUN_HOST=0.0.0.0
RUN apk add --no-cache gcc musl-dev linux-headers
COPY requirements.txt requirements.txt
RUN pip install -r requirements.txt
EXPOSE 5000
COPY . .
CMD ["flask", "run"]
```

Let's build the container using the following command:

```
$ docker build -t <your_dockerhub_user>/flask-redis .
```

Let's push it to our container registry using the following command:

```
$ docker push <your_dockerhub_user>/flask-redis
```

As you may have noticed, the app.py code defines the cache as localhost:6379. We will run an ambassador container on localhost:6379. The proxy will tunnel the connection to the redis pod running elsewhere.

Let's first create the `redis` pod using the following command:

```
$ kubectl run redis --image=redis
```

Now, let's expose the `redis` pod to the cluster resources via a `Service` resource. That will allow any pod within the cluster to communicate with the `redis` pod using the hostname `redis`. We will discuss Kubernetes `Service` resources in the next chapter in detail:

```
$ kubectl expose pod redis --port 6379
```

Cool, so as the pod and the `Service` resource are up and running, let's work on the ambassador pattern.

We need to define two config maps first. The first one describes the `redis` host and port details, and the second one defines the template `nginx.conf` file to work as a reverse proxy.

So, the `redis-config-map.yaml` file looks like the following:

```
apiVersion: v1
kind: ConfigMap
metadata:
  name: redis-config
data:
  host: "redis"
  port: "6379"
```

The preceding yaml file defines a config map called `redis-config`, which contains two properties – `host` and `port`. You can have multiple config maps, one for each environment.

The `nginx-config-map.yaml` file is the following:

```
apiVersion: v1
kind: ConfigMap
metadata:
  name: nginx-config
data:
  nginx.conf: |
    user nginx;
    worker_processes auto;
    error_log /var/log/nginx/error.log;
    pid /run/nginx.pid;
```

```
    include /usr/share/nginx/modules/*.conf;
events {
    worker_connections 1024;
}
stream {
    server {
        listen      6379;
        proxy_pass stream_redis_backend;
    }
    upstream stream_redis_backend {
        server REDIS_HOST:REDIS_PORT;
    }
}
```

This config map injects the `nginx.conf` template as a config map value. We can mount this file to a volume and then manipulate it according to the environment. We will use an `initContainer` to initialize the proxy with the correct configuration.

Let's now have a look at the pod configuration manifest `flask-ambassador.yaml`. There are multiple parts of this YAML file. Let's look at the containers section first:

```
...
spec:
  containers:
  - name: flask-app
    image: <your_dockerhub_user>/flask-redis
  - name: nginx-ambassador
    image: nginx
    volumeMounts:
    - mountPath: /etc/nginx
      name: nginx-volume
  ...
```

It contains a container called `flask-app` that uses the `<your_dockerhub_user>/flask-redis` image that we built in the previous section. The second container is the `nginx-ambassador` container; this is the container that will act as the proxy to `redis`. Therefore, we have mounted the `/etc/nginx` directory on a volume. The volume is also mounted on the init container to generate the required configuration before `nginx` boots up.

The following is the `initContainers` section:

```
initContainers:
- name: init-nginx
  image: busybox:1.28
  command: ['sh', '-c', 'cp -L /config/nginx.conf /etc/nginx/
nginx.conf && sed -i "s/REDIS_HOST/${REDIS_HOST}/g" /etc/nginx/
nginx.conf']
  env:
    - name: REDIS_HOST
      valueFrom:
        configMapKeyRef:
          name: redis-config
          key: host
    - name: REDIS_PORT
      valueFrom:
        configMapKeyRef:
          name: redis-config
          key: port
  volumeMounts:
  - mountPath: /etc/nginx
    name: nginx-volume
  - mountPath: /config
    name: config
```

It defines a busybox container – `init-nginx`. The container needs to generate the `nginx-ambassador` proxy configuration to communicate with Redis, and therefore there are two environment variables present. Both environment variables are sourced from the `redis-config` config map. Apart from that, we have also mounted the `nginx.conf` file from the `nginx-config` config map. The command section within the init container is using the environment variables to replace placeholders within the `nginx.conf` file, and we finally get a TCP proxy to the Redis backend.

The volumes section defines `nginx-volume` as an `emptyDir` volume, and `config` volume is mounted from `nginx.conf` present in the `nginx-config` config map:

```
volumes:
- name: nginx-volume
  emptyDir: {}
- name: config
  configMap:
    name: nginx-config
    items:
```

```
        - key: "nginx.conf"
          path: "nginx.conf"
```

So, now let's start applying the yaml files in steps.

Apply both the config maps first using the following commands:

```
$ kubectl apply -f redis-config-map.yaml
$ kubectl apply -f nginx-config-map.yaml
```

Let's apply the pod configuration using the following command:

```
$ kubectl apply -f flask-ambassador.yaml
```

Get the pod to see whether the configuration is correct using the following command:

```
$ kubectl get pod/flask-ambassador
NAME                 READY    STATUS     RESTARTS    AGE
flask-ambassador     2/2      Running    0           10s
```

As the pod is running successfully now, let's port-forward 5000 to the localhost for some tests using the following command:

```
$ kubectl port-forward flask-ambassador 5000:5000
```

Now, open a duplicate terminal and try to curl on localhost:5000 using the following command:

```
$ curl localhost:5000
Hi there! This page was last visited on 2020-12-22, 06:52:28.
$ curl localhost:5000
Hi there! This page was last visited on 2020-12-22, 06:52:28.
$ curl localhost:5000
Hi there! This page was last visited on 2020-12-22, 06:52:32.
```

And as we see, every time we curl the application, we get the last visited time on our screen. The ambassador pattern is working.

That was a simple example of the ambassador pattern. There are advanced configurations you can do to add fine-grain control on how your application should interact with the outside world. You can use the ambassador pattern to secure traffic that moves from your containers. It also simplifies application development for your dev team, as they need not worry about these nuances. In contrast, the ops team can use these containers to manage your environment in a better way, without stepping on each other's toes.

> **Tip**
> As the ambassador pattern adds some form of overhead as you tunnel
> connections via a proxy, you should use it only if the management benefits
> outweigh the extra cost you incur because of the ambassador container.

Now, let's look at another multi-container pod pattern – sidecars.

Sidecar pattern

Sidecars derive their names from motorcycle sidecars. The sidecar, though, does not
change the bike's core functionality, and it can work perfectly fine without it. Instead,
it adds an extra seat, a functionality that helps you give an additional person a ride.
Similarly, sidecars in a pod are helper containers that provide different functionalities
unrelated to the main container's core functionality, but enhance it instead. Examples
include logging and monitoring containers. Keeping a separate container for logging will
help decouple the logging responsibilities from your main container, which would help
monitor your application even when the main container goes down for some reason.

It also helps if there is some issue with the logging code, and instead of the entire
application going down, only the logging container is impacted. You can also use sidecars
to keep helper or related containers together with the main container, as we know that
containers within the pod share the same machine.

> **Tip**
> Use multi-container pods only if two containers are functionally related and
> work as a unit.

You can also use sidecars to segregate your application with secrets. For example, if you are running a web application that needs to have access to specific passwords to operate, it would be best to mount the secrets to a sidecar and let the sidecar provide the passwords to the web application via a link. That is because, if someone gains access to your application container's filesystem, they cannot get hold of your passwords as another container is responsible for sourcing it, something like the following diagram:

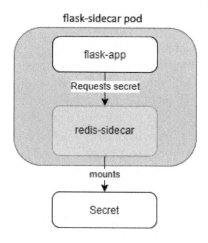

Figure 4.6 – Sidecar pattern

Let's implement the preceding pattern to understand a sidecar better. So, we have a Flask application that interacts with a Redis sidecar. We will pre-populate the Redis sidecar with a secret, `foobar`, and we are going to do that by using the Kubernetes secret resource.

Secrets

Secrets are very similar to config maps, with the difference that the secret values are `base64`-encoded instead of `plaintext`. While `base64` encoding does not make any difference, and it is as bad as `plaintext` from a security standpoint, you should use secrets for sensitive information such as passwords. That is because the Kubernetes community will develop a solution to tighten the security around secrets in future releases. If you use secrets, you will directly benefit from it.

> **Tip**
> As a rule of thumb, always use secrets for confidential data such as API keys and passwords and config maps for non-sensitive configuration data.

Let's now move on to the example Flask application.

Example application

The Flask application queries a Redis sidecar for the secret and sends that as a response. That is not ideal as you won't send secrets back as a response, but for the demo, let's go ahead with that.

So, let's first design our sidecar to pre-populate data within the container after it starts.

We need to create a secret named `secret` with the value `foobar`. Now `base64` encode the Redis command to set the secret into the cache by running the following command:

```
$ echo 'SET secret foobar' | base64
U0VUIHNlY3JldCBmb29iYXIK
```

As we now have the `base64`-encoded secret, we can create a `redis-secret.yaml` manifest with the string as follows:

```
apiVersion: v1
kind: Secret
metadata:
  name: redis-secret
data:
  redis-secret: U0VUIHNlY3JldCBmb29iYXIK
```

We then need to build the Redis container such that this secret is created at startup. To do so, we create an `entrypoint.sh` file as follows:

```
redis-server --daemonize yes && sleep 5
redis-cli < /redis-master/init.redis
redis-cli save
redis-cli shutdown
redis-server
```

The shell script looks for a file, `init.redis`, within the `/redis-master` directory and runs the `redis-cli` command on it. This means that the cache will be pre-populated with the values we have defined in our secret, provided we mount the secret as `/redis-master/init.redis`.

We then create a `Dockerfile` that will use this `entrypoint.sh` script as follows:

```
FROM redis
COPY entrypoint.sh /tmp/
CMD ["sh", "/tmp/entrypoint.sh"]
```

OK, now that we are ready, we can build and push the code to Docker Hub:

```
$ docker build -t <your_dockerhub_user>/redis-secret .
$ docker push <your_dockerhub_user>/redis-secret
```

Now that we are ready with the Redis image, we need to build the application image.

Let's look at the app.py file first:

```python
import time
import redis
from flask import Flask
from datetime import datetime

app = Flask(__name__)
cache = redis.Redis(host='localhost', port=6379)

def get_secret():
    try:
        secret = cache.get('secret')
        return secret
    except redis.exceptions.ConnectionError as e:
        raise e

@app.route('/')
def index():
    secret = str(get_secret().decode('utf-8'))
    return 'Hi there! The secret is {}.\n'.format(secret)
```

This is similar to the previous example, with the difference being that it is getting the secret from the cache this time and returning that in the response.

The requirements.txt file is the following:

```
flask
redis
```

We then create the following Dockerfile:

```dockerfile
FROM python:3.7-alpine
ENV FLASK_APP=app.py
ENV FLASK_RUN_HOST=0.0.0.0
RUN apk add --no-cache gcc musl-dev linux-headers
COPY requirements.txt requirements.txt
```

```
RUN pip install -r requirements.txt
EXPOSE 5000
COPY . .
CMD ["flask", "run"]
```

So, let's build and push the container image to Docker Hub:

```
$ docker build -t <your_dockerhub_user>/flask-redis-secret .
$ docker push <your_dockerhub_user>/flask-redis-secret
```

OK, so as our images are now ready, let's look at the pod manifest – flask-sidecar. yaml:

```
...
spec:
  containers:
  - name: flask-app
    image: <your_dockerhub_user>/flask-redis-secret
  - name: redis-sidecar
    image: <your_dockerhub_user>/redis-secret
    volumeMounts:
    - mountPath: /redis-master
      name: secret
  volumes:
  - name: secret
    secret:
      secretName: redis-secret
      items:
      - key: redis-secret
        path: init.redis
```

The pod defines two containers – flask-app and redis-sidecar. The flask-app runs the Flask application that would interact with redis-sidecar for the secret. The redis-sidecar has mounted the secret volume on /redis-master. The pod definition also contains a single volume called secret, and the volume points to the redis-secret secret and mounts that as a file, init.redis.

So, in the end, we have a file, /redis-master/init.redis, and as we know, the entrypoint.sh script looks for this file and runs the redis-cli command to pre-populate the Redis cache with the secret data.

Let's apply the secret first using the following command:

```
$ kubectl apply -f redis-secret.yaml
```

And then apply the `flask-sidecar.yaml` file using the following command:

```
$ kubectl apply -f flask-sidecar.yaml
```

Now, let's get the pods using the following command:

```
$ kubectl get pod flask-sidecar
NAME             READY    STATUS          RESTARTS    AGE
flask-sidecar    2/2      Running         0           11s
```

And as the pod is running, it's time to port-forward it to the host using the following command:

```
$ kubectl port-forward flask-sidecar 5000:5000
```

Now, let's open a duplicate terminal, run the `curl localhost:5000` command, and see what we get:

```
$ curl localhost:5000
Hi there! The secret is foobar.
```

And as we see, we get the secret, `foobar`, in the response. The sidecar is working correctly!

Let's now look at another popular multi-container pod pattern – the adapter pattern.

Adapter pattern

As the name suggests, the adapter pattern helps change something to fit a standard, similar to the cellphone and laptop adapters that convert our mains power supply to something our devices can digest. A great example of an adapter pattern is transforming log files to fit an enterprise standard to feed your log analytics solution:

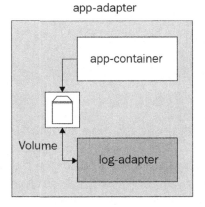

Figure 4.7 – Adapter pattern

It helps when you have a heterogeneous solution outputting log files in several formats, but a single log analytics solution that accepts messages in a particular format only. There would be two ways of doing it – either change the code for outputting log files in a standard format, or use an adapter container to execute the transformation.

Let's look at the following scenario to understand it further.

We have an application that continuously outputs log files, but without having a date at the beginning. Our adapter should read the stream of logs and append the timestamp as soon as a log line is generated.

So, we use the following pod manifest, `app-adapter.yaml`:

```
...
spec:
  volumes:
  - name: logs
    emptyDir: {}
  containers:
  - name: app-container
    image: ubuntu
    command: ["/bin/bash"]
    args: ["-c", "while true; do echo 'This is a log line' >> /
var/log/app.log; sleep 2;done"]
    volumeMounts:
    - name: logs
      mountPath: /var/log
  - name: log-adapter
    image: ubuntu
```

```
   command: ["/bin/bash"]
   args: ["-c", "apt update -y && apt install -y moreutils &&
tail -f /var/log/app.log | ts '[%Y-%m-%d %H:%M:%S]' > /var/log/
out.log"]
   volumeMounts:
   - name: logs
     mountPath: /var/log
```

The pod contains two containers – the app container, which is a simple Ubuntu container that outputs This is a log line every 2 seconds, and the log adapter, which continuously tails the app.log file, adds a timestamp at the beginning of the line, and sends the resulting output to /var/log/out.log. Both containers share the /var/log volume that is mounted as an emptyDir volume on both containers.

Now, let's apply this manifest using the following command:

```
$ kubectl apply -f app-adapter.yaml
```

Let's wait for some time and check whether the pod is running by using the following command:

```
$ kubectl get pod app-adapter
NAME            READY    STATUS      RESTARTS    AGE
app-adapter     2/2      Running     0           8s
```

As the pod is running, we can now get a shell into the log adapter container using the following command:

```
$ kubectl exec -it app-adapter -c log-adapter -- bash
```

When we get into the shell, we can cd into the /var/log directory and list its contents using the following command:

```
root@app-adapter:/# cd /var/log/ && ls
app.log apt/ dpkg.log out.log
```

And as we see, we get app.log and out.log as two files. Let's now use the cat command to print both of them to see what we get.

First, cat the app.log file using the following command:

```
root@app-adapter:/var/log# cat app.log
This is a log line
This is a log line
This is a log line
```

```
This is a log line
This is a log line
This is a log line
```

And we see a series of log lines being printed.

Now, `cat` the `out.log` file to see what we get using the following command:

```
root@app-adapter:/var/log# cat out.log
[2020-12-28 06:35:25] This is a log line
[2020-12-28 06:35:27] This is a log line
[2020-12-28 06:35:29] This is a log line
[2020-12-28 06:35:31] This is a log line
[2020-12-28 06:35:33] This is a log line
[2020-12-28 06:35:35] This is a log line
```

And we see timestamps in front of the log line. This means that the adapter pattern is working correctly. You can then choose to export this log file to your log analytics tool.

Summary

We have reached the end of this critical chapter. We've covered enough ground to get you started with Kubernetes and understand and appreciate the best practices surrounding it.

We started with Kubernetes and why we need it, and then discussed bootstrapping a Kubernetes cluster using Minikube and KinD. We then looked at the pod resource and discussed creating and managing pods, troubleshooting them, ensuring your application's reliability using probes, and multi-container design patterns to appreciate why Kubernetes uses pods in the first place instead of containers.

In the next chapter, we will deep dive into the advanced aspects of Kubernetes, where we will cover controllers, services, ingresses, managing a stateful application, and Kubernetes command-line best practices.

Questions

1. All communication with Kubernetes happens via which one of the following?

   A. Kubelet

   B. API server

   C. Etcd

D. Controller Manager

E. Scheduler

2. Which one of the following is responsible for ensuring that the cluster is in the desired state?

    A. Kubelet

    B. API server

    C. Etcd

    D. Controller Manager

    E. Scheduler

3. Which one of the following is responsible for storing the desired state of the cluster?

    A. Kubelet

    B. API server

    C. Etcd

    D. Controller Manager

    E. Scheduler

4. A pod can contain more than one container (True/False).

5. You can use port-forwarding for which one of the following use cases (multiple answers are possible)?

    A. For troubleshooting a misbehaving pod

    B. For exposing a service to the internet

    C. For accessing a system service such as the Kubernetes dashboard

6. Using a combination of which two probes can you ensure that your application is reliable even when your application has some intermittent issues (choose two)?

    A. Startup probe

    B. Liveness probe

    C. Readiness probe

7. We may use KinD in production (True/False).

8. Which of the following multi-container patterns is used as a forward proxy?

   A. Ambassador

   B. Adapter

   C. Sidecar

   D. Init containers

Answers

1. B
2. D
3. C
4. True
5. A, C
6. B, C
7. False
8. A

5
Container Orchestration with Kubernetes – Part II

In the previous chapter, we covered Kubernetes and why we need it, and then discussed bootstrapping a Kubernetes cluster using minikube and KinD. We then looked at the `Pod` resource and discussed how to create and manage Pods, how to troubleshoot them, and how to ensure your application's reliability using probes, along with multi-container design patterns to appreciate why Kubernetes uses Pods in the first place instead of containers. We also looked at Secrets and ConfigMaps.

Now, we will deep dive into the advanced aspects of Kubernetes and Kubernetes command-line best practices.

In this chapter, we're going to cover the following main topics:

- Kubernetes Deployments
- Kubernetes Services and Ingresses
- Horizontal Pod autoscaling
- Managing stateful applications
- Kubernetes command-line best practices, tips, and tricks

Technical requirements

For this chapter, we will spin up a cloud-based Kubernetes cluster, **Google Kubernetes Engine (GKE)**, for the exercises. That is because you will not be able to spin up load balancers and persistent volumes within your local system, and therefore we cannot use KinD and minikube in this chapter. Currently, **Google Cloud Platform** provides a free $300 trial for 90 days, so you can go ahead and sign up for one at `https://console.cloud.google.com/`.

Spinning up Google Kubernetes Engine

Once you've signed up and logged into your console, you can open the Google Cloud Shell CLI to run the commands.

You need to enable the Kubernetes Engine API first using the following command:

```
$ gcloud services enable container.googleapis.com
```

To create a three-node GKE cluster, run the following command:

```
$ gcloud container clusters create cluster-1 --zone \
us-central1-a
Creating cluster cluster-1 in us-central1-a... Cluster is being
health-checked (master is healthy)...done.
Created [https://container.googleapis.com/v1/
projects/<project-id>/zones/us-central1-a/clusters/cluster-1].
To inspect the contents of your cluster, go to: https://
console.cloud.google.com/kubernetes/workload_/gcloud/
us-central1-a/cluster-1?project=<project-id>
kubeconfig entry generated for cluster-1.
NAME        LOCATION        MASTER_VERSION      MASTER_IP
MACHINE_TYPE    NODE_VERSION        NUM_NODES   STATUS
cluster-1  us-central1-a  1.16.15-gke.4901     35.225.159.183
n1-standard-1  1.16.15-gke.4901   3            RUNNING
```

And that's it! The cluster is up and running.

You will also need to clone the following GitHub repository for some of the exercises: `https://github.com/PacktPublishing/Modern-DevOps-Practices`.

Run the following command to clone the repository into your home directory, and cd into the ch5 directory to access the required resources:

```
$ git clone https://github.com/PacktPublishing/Modern-DevOps-\
Practices.git modern-devops
$ cd modern-devops/ch5
```

Now, let's start with Deployments in the next section.

Kubernetes Deployments

Container application deployments within Kubernetes are done through Deployment resources. Deployment resources employ **ReplicaSet resources** behind the scenes, so it would be good to look at ReplicaSet resources first before we move on to understand Deployment resources.

ReplicaSet resource

ReplicaSet resources are Kubernetes resources that help you run multiple replicas of a Pod at a given time. They provide horizontal scaling for your container workloads, and it forms the basic building block of a horizontal scale set for your containers, which is a group of similar containers tied together to run as a unit.

ReplicaSet resources define the number of replicas of a Pod to run at a given time. The Kubernetes controller then tries to maintain the replicas and recreates a Pod if it goes down.

You should never use ReplicaSet resources on its own, but instead, it should act as a backend to a Deployment resource.

For the sake of understanding, however, let's look at an example. To access the resources for this section, cd into the following:

```
$ cd ~/modern-devops/ch5/deployments/
```

The ReplicaSet resource manifest, nginx-replica-set.yaml, looks like the following:

```
apiVersion: apps/v1
kind: ReplicaSet
metadata:
  name: nginx
  labels:
    app: nginx
```

```
spec:
  replicas: 3
  selector:
    matchLabels:
      app: nginx
  template:
    metadata:
      labels:
        app: nginx
    spec:
      containers:
      - name: nginx
        image: nginx
```

The resource manifest includes `apiVersion` and `kind`, like any other resource. It also contains a `metadata` section that defines the resource's `name` and `labels` attributes, similar to any other Kubernetes resource.

The `spec` section contains the following attributes:

- `replicas`: Defines the number of replicas of the Pods matched by the selector to run at a given time.

- `selector`: Defines the basis on which the `ReplicaSet` resource will include Pods in it.

- `selector.matchLabels`: This section defines the labels and their values to select the Pods. Therefore, the `ReplicaSet` resource will select any `Pod` with the label `app:nginx`.

- `template`: This is an optional section that you can use to define the `Pod` template. This section's contents are very similar to defining a `Pod`, except that it lacks the name attribute as the `ReplicaSet` resource will generate dynamic names for the Pods.

Let's go ahead and apply this manifest to see what we get:

```
$ kubectl apply -f nginx-replica-set.yaml
```

Now, let's run the following to list the `ReplicaSet` resources:

```
$ kubectl get replicaset
NAME      DESIRED    CURRENT    READY     AGE
nginx     3          3          0         9s
```

Right, so we see that there are three desired replicas. Currently, three replicas are running, but 0 are ready. Let's wait for a while and then rerun the following command:

```
$ kubectl get replicaset
NAME      DESIRED    CURRENT    READY     AGE
nginx     3          3          3         1m10s
```

And now we see three ready Pods that are awaiting a connection. Now, let's list the Pods and see what the `ReplicaSet` resource has done behind the scenes using the following command:

```
$ kubectl get pod
NAME            READY    STATUS     RESTARTS    AGE
nginx-6qr9j     1/1      Running    0           1m32s
nginx-7hkqv     1/1      Running    0           1m32s
nginx-9kvkj     1/1      Running    0           1m32s
```

There are three `nginx` Pods, and each has a name that starts with `nginx` but ends with a random hash. Well, the `ReplicaSet` resource has appended a random hash at the end of the `ReplicaSet` resource name to generate unique Pods. Yes, the name of every resource of a particular kind in Kubernetes should be unique.

Let's go ahead and use the following command to delete one of the Pods from the `ReplicaSet` resource and see what we get:

```
$ kubectl delete pod nginx-9kvkj && kubectl get pod
pod "nginx-9kvkj" deleted
NAME            READY    STATUS     RESTARTS    AGE
nginx-6qr9j     1/1      Running    0           8m34s
nginx-7hkqv     1/1      Running    0           8m34s
nginx-9xbdf     1/1      Running    0           5s
```

And we see that even though we deleted the `nginx-9kvkj` Pod, the `ReplicaSet` resource has replaced it with a new Pod `nginx-9xbdf`. That is how `ReplicaSet` resources work.

You can delete a `ReplicaSet` resource just like any other Kubernetes resource. You can either run the `kubectl delete replicaset <ReplicaSet name>` command for an imperative approach or use `kubectl delete -f <manifest_file>` for a declarative approach.

Let's use the former approach and delete the `ReplicaSet` resource by using the following command:

```
$ kubectl delete replicaset nginx
```

Let's check whether the `ReplicaSet` resource has been deleted by running the following command:

```
$ kubectl get replicaset
No resources found in default namespace.
```

And we don't have anything in `default namespace`. This means that the `ReplicaSet` resource is gone.

As we discussed, `ReplicaSet` resources should not be used on their own, but should instead be the backend of `Deployment` resources. Let's now look at the Kubernetes `Deployment` resources.

Deployment resource

Kubernetes `Deployment` resources help to manage deployments for container applications. They are typically used for managing stateless workloads. You can still use them to manage stateful applications, but the recommended approach for stateful applications is using `StatefulSet` resources.

Kubernetes deployments use `ReplicaSet` resources as a backend, and the chain of resources looks like the following diagram:

Figure 5.1 – Deployment chain

Let's take the preceding example and create an NGINX `Deployment` resource manifest – `nginx-deployment.yaml`:

```yaml
apiVersion: apps/v1
kind: Deployment
metadata:
  name: nginx
  labels:
    app: nginx
spec:
  replicas: 3
  selector:
    matchLabels:
      app: nginx
  template:
    metadata:
      labels:
        app: nginx
    spec:
      containers:
      - name: nginx
        image: nginx
```

The manifest is very similar to the `ReplicaSet` resource, except for the `kind` attribute, which is `Deployment` in this case.

Let's apply the manifest by using the following command:

```
$ kubectl apply -f nginx-deployment.yaml
```

So, as the `Deployment` resource has been created, let's look at the chain of resources it created. Let's run `kubectl get` to list the `Deployment` resource using the following command:

```
$ kubectl get deployment
NAME     READY   UP-TO-DATE   AVAILABLE   AGE
nginx    3/3     3            3           6s
```

And we see there is one `Deployment` resource called `nginx`, with 3/3 ready Pods and three UP-TO-DATE Pods. As `Deployment` resources manage multiple versions, UP-TO-DATE therefore signifies whether the latest `Deployment` has rolled out successfully. We will look into the detail of this in the subsequent sections. It also shows three available Pods at that time.

As we know that `Deployment` resources create `ReplicaSet` resources in the background, let's get the `ReplicaSet` resources using the following command:

```
$ kubectl get replicaset
NAME                DESIRED    CURRENT    READY    AGE
nginx-6799fc88d8    3          3          3        11s
```

And we see that `Deployment` resource has created a `ReplicaSet` resource, which starts with `nginx` and ends with a random hash. That is required as a `Deployment` resource might contain one or more `ReplicaSet` resources. We will look at how in the subsequent sections.

Next in the chain are Pods, so let's get the `Pod` resources using the following command to see for ourselves:

```
$ kubectl get pod
NAME                        READY    STATUS     RESTARTS    AGE
nginx-6799fc88d8-d52mj      1/1      Running    0           15s
nginx-6799fc88d8-dmpbn      1/1      Running    0           15s
nginx-6799fc88d8-msvxw      1/1      Running    0           15s
```

And, as expected, we have three Pods. Each begins with the `ReplicaSet` resource name and ends with a random hash. That's why you see that there are two hashes in the `Pod` name.

Now, let's assume you have a new release and want to deploy a new version of your container image. So, let's update the `Deployment` resource with a new image and also record the command in the deployment history, using the following command:

```
$ kubectl set image deployment/nginx \
nginx=nginx:1.16.1 --record
deployment.apps/nginx image updated
```

To check the deployment status, run the following command:

```
$ kubectl rollout status deployment nginx
deployment "nginx" successfully rolled out
```

To check the deployment history, run the following command:

```
$ kubectl rollout history deployment nginx
deployment.apps/nginx
REVISION   CHANGE-CAUSE
1          <none>
2          kubectl set image deployment/nginx nginx=nginx:1.16.1
--record=true
```

As we can see, there are two revisions in the deployment history. Revision 1 was the initial deployment, and revision 2 was because of the kubectl set image command we ran, as evident from the CHANGE-CAUSE. Now, let's say you find an issue after your deployment and want to roll it back to the previous version. To do so, run the following command:

```
$ kubectl rollout undo deployment nginx
deployment.apps/nginx rolled back
```

Let's recheck the status of the deployment using the following command:

```
$ kubectl rollout status deployment nginx
Waiting for deployment "nginx" rollout to finish: 2 out of 3
new replicas have been updated...
Waiting for deployment "nginx" rollout to finish: 1 old
replicas are pending termination...
deployment "nginx" successfully rolled out
```

And finally, let's recheck the deployment history using the following command:

```
$ kubectl rollout history deployment nginx
deployment.apps/nginx
REVISION   CHANGE-CAUSE
2          kubectl set image deployment/nginx nginx=nginx:1.16.1
--record=true
3          <none>
```

And we get revision 3 with `change-cause <none>`. That is because we did not record the rollback using the `--record` flag in this case as we did in the last command.

Tip

Always record deployment updates as it becomes easier to peek into the history to see what got deployed.

Now, let's look at some common Kubernetes deployment strategies to make sense of how to use Deployments effectively.

Kubernetes Deployment strategies

Updating an existing Deployment requires you to specify a new container image. That is why we version container images in the first place so that you can roll out, and roll back, application changes as required. As we run everything in containers, and containers, by definition, are ephemeral, this enables a host of different deployment strategies that we can implement. There are several deployment strategies, and some of these are as follows:

- **Recreate**: This is the simplest of all. Delete the old `Pod` and deploy the new one.

- **Rolling Update**: Slowly roll out Pods of the new version while still running the old version, and slowly remove the old Pods as the new Pods get ready.

- **Blue/Green**: This is a derived deployment strategy where we keep both versions running simultaneously and switch the traffic to the newer version when we want.

- **Canary**: This is applicable to Blue/Green deployments where we switch a percentage of traffic to the newer version of the application before fully rolling out the release.

- **A/B testing**: A/B testing is more of a technique to apply to Blue/Green deployments. This is when you want to roll out the newer version to a subset of willing users and study the usage patterns before rolling out the newer version in general. You do not get A/B testing out of the box with Kubernetes but instead should rely on service mesh technologies that plug in well with Kubernetes, such as **Istio**, **Linkerd**, and **Traefik**.

Kubernetes provides two deployment strategies out of the box – `Recreate` and `RollingUpdate`.

Recreate

The **Recreate** strategy is the most straightforward deployment strategy. When you update the deployment with the `Recreate` strategy, Kubernetes immediately spins down the old `ReplicaSet` resource and creates a new one with the required number of replicas, along the lines of the following diagram:

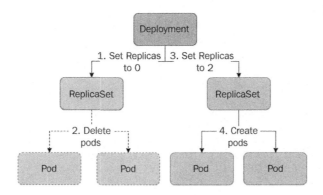

Figure 5.2 – Recreate strategy

Kubernetes does not delete the old `ReplicaSet` resource, but instead just sets the `replicas` to `0`. That is required if you need to quickly roll back to the new version. This approach results in downtime, and is not therefore something that you want to use every time unless you have a constraint. Thus, this strategy isn't the default deployment strategy in Kubernetes.

> **Tip**
>
> You can use the Recreate strategy if your application does not support multiple replicas, if it does not support more than a certain number of replicas, such as applications that need to maintain a quorum, or if it does not support multiple versions at once.

Let's update `nginx-deployment` with the `Recreate` strategy. Let's look at the `nginx-recreate.yaml` file:

```
apiVersion: apps/v1
kind: Deployment
metadata:
  name: nginx
```

```
    labels:
      app: nginx
 spec:
   replicas: 3
   selector:
     matchLabels:
        app: nginx
   strategy:
     type: Recreate
   template:
     metadata:
       labels:
          app: nginx
     spec:
       containers:
       - name: nginx
          image: nginx
```

The YAML file now contains a strategy section with type – Recreate. Now, let's apply the nginx-recreate.yaml file and watch the ReplicaSet resources using the following command:

```
$ kubectl apply -f nginx-recreate.yaml
$ kubectl get replicaset -w
deployment.apps/nginx configured
NAME                    DESIRED    CURRENT    READY    AGE
nginx-6799fc88d8        0          0          0        0s
nginx-6889dfccd5        0          3          3        7m42s
nginx-6889dfccd5        0          0          0        7m42s
nginx-6799fc88d8        3          0          0        1s
nginx-6799fc88d8        3          3          0        2s
nginx-6799fc88d8        3          3          3        6s
```

As we see, the Deployment resource creates a new ReplicaSet resource – nginx-6799fc88d8, with 0 desired replicas. It then sets 0 desired replicas to the old ReplicaSet resource, and waits for the old ReplicaSet resource to be completely evicted. It then starts rolling out the new ReplicaSet resource to the desired images immediately.

Rolling update

When you update the `Deployment` with a **RollingUpdate** strategy, Kubernetes creates a new `ReplicaSet` resource, and it simultaneously spins up the required number of Pods on the new `ReplicaSet` resource, while slowly spinning down the old `ReplicaSet` resource as evident from the following diagram:

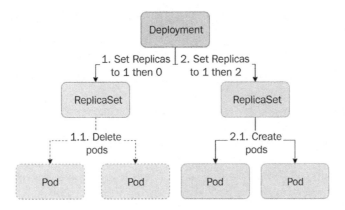

Figure 5.3 – Rolling update strategy

`RollingUpdate` is the default deployment strategy. You can use the `RollingUpdate` strategy in most applications, apart from ones that cannot tolerate more than one version of the application at a given time.

Let's update the nginx deployment using the `RollingUpdate` strategy. We will reuse the standard `nginx-deployment.yaml` file that we used before. Use the following command and see what happens to the `ReplicaSet` resources:

```
$ kubectl apply -f nginx-deployment.yaml
$ kubectl set image deployment nginx nginx=nginx:1.16.1
$ kubectl get replicaset -w
deployment.apps/nginx image updated
NAME                DESIRED    CURRENT    READY    AGE
nginx-6799fc88d8    3          3          3        49s
nginx-6889dfccd5    1          1          1        4s
nginx-6799fc88d8    2          2          2        53s
nginx-6889dfccd5    2          2          2        8s
nginx-6799fc88d8    1          1          1        57s
nginx-6889dfccd5    3          3          3        11s
nginx-6799fc88d8    0          0          0        60s
```

And as we see, the old `ReplicaSet` resource – `nginx-6799fc88d8`, is being *Rolled Down* and the new `ReplicaSet` resource – `nginx-6889dfccd5`, is being *Rolled Out* simultaneously.

The `RollingUpdate` strategy also has two options – `maxUnavailable` and `maxSurge`.

While `maxSurge` defines the maximum number of additional Pods we can have at a given time, `maxUnavailable` defines the maximum number of unavailable Pods we can have at a given time.

> **Tip**
>
> Set `maxSurge` to 0 if your application cannot tolerate more than a certain number of replicas. Set `maxUnavailable` to 0 if you don't want to compromise on reliability, and your application can tolerate more than the set replicas. You cannot specify both parameters to 0, as that will make any rollout attempts impossible. While setting `maxSurge`, always ensure that your cluster has spare capacity to spin up additional Pods, or the rollout will fail.

Using these settings, we can create some different kinds of custom rollout strategies – some of the popular ones are discussed in the following sections.

Ramped slow rollout

You may want to use this strategy if you have numerous replicas, but you don't want to roll out the new version all at once. Instead, you want to slowly roll out the release and observe the application, meanwhile, for any issues. If you encounter problems, you can roll your deployment back.

Let's create an `nginx` deployment, `nginx-ramped-slow-rollout.yaml`, using the **Ramped slow rollout** strategy:

```
apiVersion: apps/v1
kind: Deployment
metadata:
  labels:
    app: nginx
  name: nginx
spec:
  replicas: 10
  selector:
```

```
    matchLabels:
      app: nginx
  strategy:
    type: RollingUpdate
    rollingUpdate:
      maxSurge: 1
      maxUnavailable: 0
  template:
    metadata:
      labels:
        app: nginx
    spec:
      containers:
      - image: nginx
        name: nginx
```

The manifest is very similar to the generic deployment, except that it contains 10 replicas, and there is a `strategy` section.

The `strategy` section contains the following:

- `type`: `RollingUpdate`

- `rollingUpdate`: The section describing rolling update attributes

Now, let's apply the YAML file and wait for the deployment to completely rollout to 10 replicas using the following commands:

```
$ kubectl apply -f nginx-ramped-slow-rollout.yaml
deployment.apps/nginx created
$ kubectl rollout status deployment nginx
...
deployment "nginx" successfully rolled out
```

As, we see, the Pods have rolled out completely. Let's now update the `Deployment` resource with a different `nginx` image version and see what we get using the following command:

```
$ kubectl set image deployment nginx nginx=nginx:1.16.1
$ kubectl get replicaset -w
deployment.apps/nginx image updated
NAME                DESIRED    CURRENT    READY    AGE
nginx-6799fc88d8    10         10         10       3m51s
nginx-6889dfccd5    1          1          0        0s
nginx-6799fc88d8    9          10         10       4m
.  .  .  .  .  .  .  .  .  .  .  .  .  .  .
nginx-6889dfccd5    8          8          8        47s
nginx-6799fc88d8    2          3          3        4m38s
nginx-6889dfccd5    9          9          8        47s
nginx-6799fc88d8    2          2          2        4m38s
nginx-6889dfccd5    9          9          9        51s
nginx-6799fc88d8    1          2          2        4m42s
nginx-6889dfccd5    10         9          9        51s
nginx-6799fc88d8    1          2          2        4m42s
nginx-6889dfccd5    10         10         10       55s
nginx-6799fc88d8    0          1          1        4m46s
nginx-6799fc88d8    0          1          1        4m46s
nginx-6799fc88d8    0          0          0        4m46s
```

So, we see that there are two `ReplicaSet` resources here – `nginx-6799fc88d8` and `nginx-6889dfccd5`. While the `nginx-6799fc88d8` Pod is slowly rolling down from 10 Pods to 0, one at a time, simultaneously, the `nginx-6889dfccd5` Pod is slowly rolling up from 0 Pods to 10. At any given time, the number of Pods never exceeds 11. That is because `maxSurge` is set to 1, and `maxUnavailable` is 0. This is a slow rollout in action.

> **Tip**
>
> Ramped slow rollout is useful when we want to be cautious before we impact many users, but this strategy is extremely slow and may not suit all applications.

Let's look at the best effort-controlled rollout strategy for a faster rollout without compromising application availability.

Best effort controlled rollout

Best effort controlled rollout helps you roll out your deployment on the best effort basis, and you can use it to roll out your release faster and ensure that your application is available. It can also help with applications that do not tolerate more than a certain number of replicas at a given point.

We will set `maxSurge` to `0` and `maxUnavailable` to any percentage we find suitable for remaining unavailable at a given time for implementing this. It can be specified using the number of Pods or as a percentage.

> **Tip**
> Using a percentage is a better option since, with this, you don't have to recalculate your `maxUnavailable` parameter if the replicas change.

Let's look at the manifest – `nginx-best-effort-controlled-rollout.yaml`:

```yaml
apiVersion: apps/v1
kind: Deployment
metadata:
  labels:
    app: nginx
  name: nginx
spec:
  replicas: 10
  selector:
    matchLabels:
      app: nginx
  strategy:
    type: RollingUpdate
    rollingUpdate:
      maxSurge: 0
      maxUnavailable: 25%
  template:
    metadata:
      labels:
        app: nginx
    spec:
      containers:
```

```
        - image: nginx
          name: nginx
```

Let's now apply the YAML file and see what we get:

```
$ kubectl apply -f nginx-best-effort-controlled-rollout.yaml
$ kubectl get replicaset -w
deployment.apps/nginx configured
NAME                DESIRED      CURRENT      READY      AGE
nginx-6799fc88d8    2            0            0          20m
nginx-6889dfccd5    8            8            8          16m
nginx-6799fc88d8    2            2            1          20m
nginx-6889dfccd5    7            8            8          16m
nginx-6799fc88d8    3            2            1          20m
nginx-6889dfccd5    7            8            8          16m
nginx-6799fc88d8    3            3            1          20m
nginx-6889dfccd5    7            7            7          16m

.  .  .  .  .  .  .  .  .  .  .  .

nginx-6799fc88d8    9            8            7          20m
nginx-6889dfccd5    1            2            2          16m
nginx-6799fc88d8    9            9            7          20m
nginx-6889dfccd5    1            1            1          16m
nginx-6799fc88d8    9            9            8          20m
nginx-6889dfccd5    0            1            1          16m
nginx-6799fc88d8    10           9            8          20m
nginx-6889dfccd5    0            0            0          16m
nginx-6799fc88d8    10           10           10         20m
```

So, we see the `ReplicaSet` resource rolling out such that the total Pods do not exceed more than 10 at any point, and the total unavailable Pods are never more than 25%. You may also notice that instead of creating a new `ReplicaSet` resource, the deployment is using an old `ReplicaSet` resource that contained the `nginx:latest` image. Remember when I said that when you update a deployment, the old `ReplicaSet` resource is not deleted?

`Deployment` resources on their own are great ways of scheduling and managing Pods. However, we have overlooked an essential part of running containers in Kubernetes – exposing them to the internal or external world. Kubernetes provides several resources to help expose your workloads appropriately – primarily `Service` and `Ingress` resources. Let's have a look at these in the next section.

Kubernetes Services and Ingresses

The **Service** resource helps expose Kubernetes workloads to the internal or external world. As we know, Pods are ephemeral resources – they can come and go. Every Pod is allocated a unique IP address and hostname, but once a `Pod` is gone, the Pod's IP address and the hostname change. Consider a scenario where one of your Pods wants to interact with another. However, because of the transient nature, you cannot configure a proper endpoint. If you use the IP address or the hostname as the endpoint of a `Pod`, and the `Pod` is destroyed, you will no longer be able to connect to it. Therefore, exposing a `Pod` on its own is not a great idea.

Kubernetes provides the `Service` resource to provide a static IP address to a group of Pods. Apart from exposing the Pods on a single static IP address, it also provides load balancing of traffic between Pods in a round-robin configuration. It helps distribute traffic equally between the Pods and is therefore the default method of exposing your workloads.

`Service` resources are also allocated a static **Fully Qualified Domain Name (FQDN)** (based on the service name), and therefore, in order to make your endpoints fail-safe, you can use the `Service` resource FQDN instead of the IP address within your cluster.

Now, coming back to `Service` resources, there are multiple `Service` resource types – **ClusterIP**, **NodePort**, and **LoadBalancer**, each having their respective use cases:

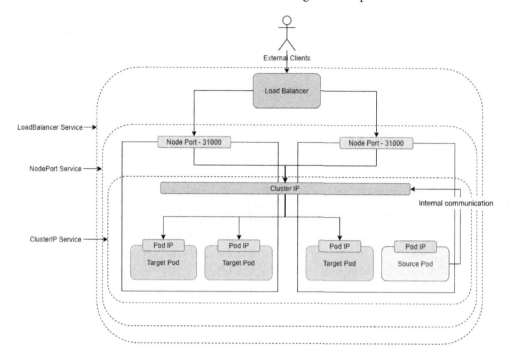

Figure 5.4 – Kubernetes Services

Let's understand each of these with the help of examples.

ClusterIP Services

`ClusterIP Service` resources expose Pods within the Kubernetes cluster and they are the default if you don't specify a type. It is not possible to access `ClusterIP Service` resources outside the cluster, and therefore it is never used to expose your Pods to the external world. `ClusterIP Service` resources are generally used to expose backend apps such as data stores and databases, especially the business layer and the data layer in a three-layer architecture.

> **Tip**
>
> When choosing between `Service` resource types, as a general rule of thumb, always start with the `ClusterIP Service` resource and change it if you need to later. This will ensure that the least amount of your workloads are exposed externally.

Let's create a `redis` **Deployment resource** first using the imperative method by using the following command:

```
$ kubectl create deployment redis --image=redis
deployment.apps/redis created
```

Check whether the deployment has rolled out successfully using the following command:

```
$ kubectl rollout status deployment redis
deployment "redis" successfully rolled out
```

As the deployment is rolled out successfully, let's try exposing the `Pod` on a `ClusterIP` `Service` resource. To access the resources for this section, `cd` into the following:

```
$ cd ~/modern-devops/ch5/services/
```

Let's look at the `Service` resource manifest, `redis-clusterip.yaml`, first:

```yaml
apiVersion: v1
kind: Service
metadata:
  labels:
    app: redis
  name: redis
spec:
  ports:
  - port: 6379
    protocol: TCP
    targetPort: 6379
  selector:
    app: redis
```

The `Service` resource manifest starts with `apiVersion` and `kind` as any other manifest. It has a `metadata` section that contains the name and labels.

The `spec` section contains the following:

- `ports`: This section includes a list of ports that we want to expose via the `Service` resource:

  A. `port`: The port we wish to expose.

  B. `protocol`: The protocol of the port we are exposing (TCP/UDP).

C. `targetPort`: The target container port where the exposed port will forward the connection. This allows us to have a port mapping similar to Docker.

- `selector`: This section contains labels based on which the `Pod` group is selected.

Let's apply the `Service` resource manifest using the following command and see what we get:

```
$ kubectl apply -f redis-clusterip.yaml
```

Let's run `kubectl get` to list the `Service` resource and get the cluster IP:

```
$ kubectl get service redis
NAME    TYPE        CLUSTER-IP      EXTERNAL-IP   PORT(S)    AGE
redis   ClusterIP   10.96.118.99    <none>        6379/TCP   8s
```

And we see a redis `Service` resource running with a `ClusterIP`. But as this `Pod` is not exposed externally, the only way to access it is through a second `Pod` running within the cluster.

Let's create a `busybox` Pod in interactive mode to inspect the `Service` resource and run some tests using the following command:

```
$ kubectl run busybox --rm --restart Never -it --image=busybox
/ #
```

And with this, we see a prompt. This means that we have launched the `busybox` container and are currently within that. We will use the `telnet` application to check the connectivity between Pods.

Let's `telnet` the cluster IP and port to see whether it's reachable using the following command:

```
/ # telnet 10.96.118.99 6379
Connected to 10.96.118.99
```

The IP/port pair is reachable from there. Kubernetes also provides an internal DNS to promote service discovery and connect to the `Service` resource. We can do a reverse `nslookup` on the cluster IP to get the `Service` resource's fully qualified domain name using the following command:

```
/ # nslookup 10.96.118.99
Server:         10.96.0.10
Address:        10.96.0.10:53
```

```
99.118.96.10.in-addr.arpa        name = redis.default.svc.
cluster.local
```

And as we see, the IP address is accessible from the FQDN – `redis.default.svc.cluster.local`. We can use the entire domain or parts of it based on where we are located. The FQDN is formed of these parts: `<service_name>.<namespace>.svc.<cluster-domain>.local`.

Kubernetes uses namespaces to segregate resources, You can visualize namespaces as multiple virtual clusters which exist within the same physical Kubernetes cluster. You can use them if you have many users working in multiple teams or projects. We have been working in the default namespace till now and will continue doing so. If your source `Pod` is located in the same namespace as the `Service` resource, you can simply use `service_name` to connect to your `Service` resource, something like the following example:

```
/ # telnet redis 6379
Connected to redis
```

If you want to call a `Service` resource from a `Pod` situated in a different namespace, you can use `<service_name>.<namespace>` instead, something like the following example:

```
/ # telnet redis.default 6379
Connected to redis.default
```

Some service meshes, like Istio, allow multi-cluster communication. In that situation, you can also use the cluster name for connecting to the `Service` resource, but as this is an advanced topic, it is beyond the scope of this discussion.

> **Tip**
> Always use the shortest domain name as possible for endpoints as it allows for more flexibility in moving your Kubernetes resources across your environments.

`ClusterIP` services work very well for exposing internal `Service` resources, but what if we want to expose our `Service` resource to the external world? Let's have a look at the `NodePort Service` resource for that.

NodePort services

NodePort Service resources are used to expose your Pods to the external world. When you create a NodePort Service resource, it spins up a ClusterIP Service resource and maps the ClusterIP port to a random high port number (default: 30000-32767) on all cluster nodes. You can also specify a static NodePort number if you so desire. So, with a NodePort Service resource, you can access your Pods using the IP address of any node within your cluster and the NodePort.

> **Tip**
>
> Though it is possible to specify a static NodePort number, you should avoid using it. That is because you might end up in port conflicts with other Service resources and put a high dependency on config and change management. Instead, keep things simple and use dynamic ports.

Going by the Flask application example, let's create the flask-app Pod with the redis Service resource we created before, acting as it's backend, and then we will expose the Pod on NodePort.

Use the following command to create a Pod imperatively:

```
$ kubectl run flask-app --image=<your_dockerhub_user>\
/python-flask-redis
```

Now, as we've created the flask-app Pod, let's check its status using the following command:

```
$ kubectl get pod flask-app
NAME         READY    STATUS      RESTARTS    AGE
flask-app    1/1      Running     0           19s
```

The flask-app Pod is running successfully and is ready to accept requests. It's time to understand the resource manifest for the NodePort Service, flask-nodeport.yaml:

```
apiVersion: v1
kind: Service
metadata:
  labels:
    run: flask-app
  name: flask-app
spec:
  ports:
```

```
  - port: 5000
    protocol: TCP
    targetPort: 5000
  selector:
    run: flask-app
  type: NodePort
```

The manifest is very similar to the `ClusterIP` manifest, but it also contains a `type` attribute that specifies the `Service` resource type – `NodePort` in this case.

Let's apply this manifest to see what we get using the following command:

```
$ kubectl apply -f flask-nodeport.yaml
```

Now, let's list the `Service` resource to get the `NodePort` using the following command:

```
$ kubectl get service flask-app
NAME           TYPE        CLUSTER-IP      EXTERNAL-IP     PORT(S)
AGE
flask-app      NodePort    10.3.240.246    <none>          5000:32618/
TCP     9s
```

And we see that the type now is `NodePort`, and that the container port `5000` is mapped to node port `32618`.

Now, if you are within the Kubernetes cluster, you can access the `Service` resource using `localhost:32618`. But as we are using Google Cloud Shell, we need to `ssh` into a Kubernetes node to access the `Service` resource.

Let's list the nodes first using the following command:

```
$ kubectl get nodes
NAME                                          STATUS    ROLES
AGE     VERSION
gke-cluster-1-default-pool-c30a0b48-1dhh      Ready     <none>
17m     v1.16.15-gke.4901
gke-cluster-1-default-pool-c30a0b48-71hl      Ready     <none>
17m     v1.16.15-gke.4901
gke-cluster-1-default-pool-c30a0b48-zwg1      Ready     <none>
17m     v1.16.15-gke.4901
```

And as we see, we have three nodes. Let's ssh into the gke-cluster-1-default-pool-c30a0b48-1dhh node using the following command:

```
$ gcloud compute ssh gke-cluster-1-default-pool-c30a0b48-1dhh
```

Now, as we are within the gke-cluster-1-default-pool-c30a0b48-1dhh node, let's curl localhost:32618 using the following command:

```
$ curl localhost:32618
Hi there! This page was last visited on 2020-12-30, 08:32:25.
```

And we get a response back! You can ssh into any node and curl the endpoint and should get a similar response.

To exit from the node, and get back to the Cloud Shell prompt, run the following command:

```
$ exit
Connection to 35.202.82.74 closed.
```

And you are back at the Cloud Shell prompt.

> **Tip**
>
> NodePort Services are an intermediate kind of resource. This means that while it forms an essential building block of providing external services, it is not used on its own most of the time. When you are running on the cloud, you can use LoadBalancer Service resources instead. Even for an on-premises setup, it makes sense not to use NodePort for every Service resource and instead use Ingress resources.

Now, let's look at the LoadBalancer Service resource used extensively to expose your Kubernetes workloads externally.

LoadBalancer services

LoadBalancer Service resources help expose your Pods on a single load-balanced endpoint. These Service resources can only be used within cloud platforms and platforms that provide Kubernetes controllers with access to spin up external network resources. A LoadBalancer Service practically spins up a NodePort Service resource and then requests the Cloud API to spin up a load balancer in front of the node ports. That way, it provides a single endpoint to access your Service resource from the external world.

Spinning up a LoadBalancer Service resource is simple – just set the type to LoadBalancer.

Let's expose the Flask application as a load balancer using the following manifest – flask-loadbalancer.yaml:

```
...
spec:
  ports:
  - port: 5000
    protocol: TCP
    targetPort: 5000
  selector:
    run: flask-app
  type: LoadBalancer
```

Now, let's apply the manifest using the following command:

```
$ kubectl apply -f flask-loadbalancer.yaml
```

And let's get the Service resource to notice the changes using the following command:

```
$ kubectl get svc flask-app
NAME           TYPE          CLUSTER-IP      EXTERNAL-IP    PORT(S)
AGE
flask-app      LoadBalancer  10.3.240.246    34.71.95.96
5000:32618/TCP    17m
```

And the Service resource type is now LoadBalancer. As you can see, it now contains an external IP along with the cluster IP.

You can then curl on the external IP on port 5000 using the following command:

```
$ curl 34.71.95.96:5000
Hi there! This page was last visited on 2020-12-30, 08:32:25.
```

And you get the same response as before. Your `Service` resource is now running externally.

> **Tip**
>
> `LoadBalancer Service` resources tend to be expensive as every new resource spins up a network load balancer within your cloud. If you have HTTP-based workloads, you should use `Ingress` resource instead of `LoadBalancer` to save on resource cost and optimize traffic.

While Kubernetes services form the basic building block of exposing your container applications internally and externally, Kubernetes also provides `Ingress` resources for additional fine-grain control over traffic. Let's have a look at this in the next section.

Ingress resources

Ingress resources act as reverse proxies into Kubernetes. You don't need a load balancer for every application you run within your estate. Load balancers normally just forward traffic, and they don't require high computing power. Therefore, it does not make sense to spin up a load balancer for everything.

Therefore, Kubernetes provides a way of routing external traffic into your cluster via `Ingress` resources. These resources help you subdivide traffic according to multiple conditions. Some of these are as follows:

- Based on the URL path
- Based on the hostname
- A combination of the two

The following diagram illustrates how `Ingress` resources work:

Figure 5.5 – Kubernetes Ingress

Ingress resources require an ingress controller to work. While most cloud providers have a controller installed, you will have to install an ingress controller on-premises or on a self-managed Kubernetes cluster. For more details on installing an ingress controller, refer to https://kubernetes.io/docs/concepts/services-networking/ ingress-controllers/. You can install more than one ingress controller, but you will have to annotate your manifests to denote explicitly which controller the Ingress resource should use.

The client connects to the ingress resource via an ingress-managed load balancer, and the traffic moves to the ingress controllers that act as the backend to the load balancer. The ingress controllers then route the traffic to the correct Service resource via routing rules defined on the Ingress resource.

Let's now expose the flask-app Service resource via an Ingress resource, but before we do that, we will have to expose the flask-app Service resource as a NodePort Service resource, so let's apply the relevant manifest using the following command:

```
$ kubectl apply -f flask-nodeport.yaml
```

The next step is to define an ingress resource. Remember that as GKE is running on a public cloud, it has the ingress controllers installed and running. So, we can simply go and create an ingress manifest – flask-basic-ingress.yaml:

```
apiVersion: networking.k8s.io/v1beta1
kind: Ingress
metadata:
  name: flask-app
spec:
  backend:
    serviceName: flask-app
    servicePort: 5000
```

This resource passes all traffic to the flask-app Pod, so it is counter-productive, but let's look at it for the sake of simplicity.

Apply the manifest using the following command:

```
$ kubectl apply -f flask-basic-ingress.yaml
```

Now, let's list the `Ingress` resource using the following command:

```
$ kubectl get ingress flask-app
NAME          HOSTS    ADDRESS          PORTS    AGE
flask-app     *        34.120.27.34     80       30s
```

We see an external IP allocated to it and that is's listening on port `80`.

> **Important note**
>
> Bear in mind that ingress rules take a while to propagate across the cluster, so if you receive a 404 error initially when you `curl` the endpoint, wait for 5 minutes, and you should get the response back.

Let's `curl` this IP and see what we get using the following command:

```
$ curl 34.120.27.34
Hi there! This page was last visited on 2020-12-30, 09:02:53.
```

Now, let's clean up the ingress resource using the following command:

```
$ kubectl delete ingress flask-app
```

As I said, the simple ingress rule is counterproductive as it is routing all traffic to a single `Service` resource. The idea of ingress is to use a single load balancer to route traffic to multiple targets. Let's look at two ways to do this – *path-based routing* and *name-based routing*.

Path-based routing

Let's consider an application with two versions, *v1* and *v2*, and you want both of them to co-exist on a single endpoint. You can use **path-based routing** for such a scenario.

Let's create the two application versions first using the imperative method by running the following commands:

```
$ kubectl run nginx-v1 --image=bharamicrosystems/nginx:v1
$ kubectl run nginx-v2 --image=bharamicrosystems/nginx:v2
```

Now, expose the two Pods as `NodePort Service` resources using the following commands:

```
$ kubectl expose pod nginx-v1 --port=80 --type=NodePort
$ kubectl expose pod nginx-v2 --port=80 --type=NodePort
```

We will then create an ingress resource using the following manifest file, app-path-ingress.yaml, that will expose two endpoints – <external-ip>/v1, which routes to the *v1* Service resource, and <external-ip>/v2, which routes to the *v2* Service resource:

```
...
spec:
  rules:
  - http:
      paths:
      - path: /v1/*
        backend:
          serviceName: nginx-v1
          servicePort: 80
      - path: /v2/*
        backend:
          serviceName: nginx-v2
          servicePort: 80
```

The ingress manifest contains several rules. The http rule has two paths – /v1 and /v2. Traffic arriving on /v1 is routed to the nginx-v1 Service resource on port 80, and traffic arriving on /v2 is routed to the nginx-v2 Service resource on port 80.

Let's apply the manifest by using the following command:

```
$ kubectl apply -f nginx-app-path-ingress.yaml
```

Now, let's list the Ingress resource by running the following command:

```
$ kubectl get ingress nginx-app -w
NAME          HOSTS     ADDRESS        PORTS     AGE
nginx-app     *         34.120.27.34   80          43s
```

And now that we have the external IP, we can curl both endpoints to see what we get using the following commands:

```
$ curl 34.120.27.34/v1/
This is version 1
$ curl 34.120.27.34/v2/
This is version 2
```

Sometimes, a path-based route is not always feasible, as you might not want your users to remember the path of multiple applications. However, you can still run multiple applications using a single ingress endpoint, that is, by using *name-based routing*.

Name-based routing

Name-based routing, or **FQDN-based routing**, relies on the host header that we pass while making an HTTP request. The `Ingress` resource can route based on the header. For example, if we want to access the *v1* `Service` resource, we can use `v1.example.com`, and for the *v2* `Service` resource, we can use the `v2.example.com` URL.

Let's now have a look at the `nginx-app-host-ingress.yaml` manifest to understand this concept further:

```
...
spec:
  rules:
  - host: v1.example.com
    http:
      paths:
      - path: /
        backend:
          serviceName: nginx-v1
          servicePort: 80
  - host: v2.example.com
    http:
      paths:
      - path: /
        backend:
          serviceName: nginx-v2
          servicePort: 80
```

The manifest now contains multiple hosts – `v1.example.com` routing to `nginx-v1`, and `v2.example.com`, routing to `nginx-v2`.

Now, let's apply this manifest and get the ingress using the following commands:

```
$ kubectl apply -f nginx-app-host-ingress.yaml
$ kubectl get ingress
NAME        HOSTS                            ADDRESS       PORTS
nginx-app   v1.example.com,v2.example.com    34.120.27.34  80
```

This time, we can see that there are two hosts defined, `v1.example.com` and `v2.example.com`, both running on the same address. Before we hit those endpoints, we need to make an entry on the `/etc/hosts` file to allow our machine to resolve `v1.example.com` and `v2.example.com` to the ingress address.

Edit the `/etc/hosts` file and add the following entry at the end:

```
34.120.27.34 v1.example.com v2.example.com
```

Now, let's `curl` both endpoints and see what we get:

```
$ curl v1.example.com
This is version 1
$ curl v2.example.com
This is version 2
```

And, as we can see, the name-based routing is working correctly! Combining multiple hosts and path-based routing, you can create a more dynamic setup.

`Service`, `Ingress`, `Pod`, `Deployment`, and `ReplicaSet` resources help us to maintain a set number of replicas within Kubernetes and help to serve them under a single endpoint. As you may have noticed, they are linked together using a combination of `labels` and `matchLabels` attributes. The following screenshot will help you to visualize this:

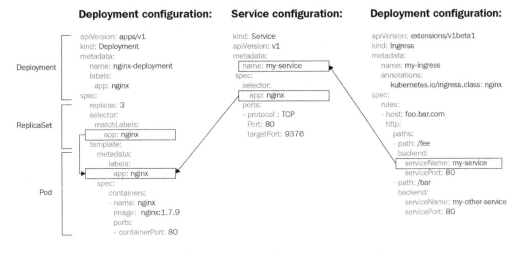

Figure 5.6 – Linking between Deployment, Service, and Ingress

Till now we were scaling our Pods manually, but a better way would be to autoscale the replicas based on resource utilization and traffic. Kubernetes provides a resource called `HorizontalPodAutoscaler` to handle that requirement.

Horizontal Pod autoscaling

`HorizontalPodAutoscaler` is a Kubernetes resource that helps you to update the replicas within your `ReplicaSet` resources based on defined factors, the most common being CPU and memory.

To understand this better, let's create an `nginx` deployment, and this time we will set the resource limits within the `Pod`. Resource limits are a vital element that enable `HorizontalPodAutoscaler` resource to function. It relies on the percentage utilization of the limits to decide when to spin up a new replica. We will use the following `nginx-autoscale-deployment.yaml` manifest for this exercise:

```yaml
apiVersion: apps/v1
kind: Deployment
metadata:
  name: nginx
  labels:
    app: nginx
spec:
  replicas: 1
  selector:
    matchLabels:
      app: nginx
  template:
    metadata:
      labels:
        app: nginx
    spec:
      containers:
      - name: nginx
        image: nginx
        resources:
          limits:
            cpu: 200m
            memory: 200Mi
```

Use the following command to spin up a new deployment:

```
$ kubectl apply -f nginx-autoscale-deployment.yaml
```

Let's expose this deployment with a `LoadBalancer Service` resource and get the external IP:

```
$ kubectl expose deployment nginx --port 80 --type LoadBalancer
$ kubectl get svc nginx
NAME      TYPE            CLUSTER-IP      EXTERNAL-IP      PORT(S)
AGE
nginx     LoadBalancer    10.3.243.225    34.123.234.57    80:30099/
TCP    41s
```

Now, let's autoscale this deployment. The `Deployment` resource needs to have at least one `Pod` replica and can have a maximum of five Pod replicas while maintaining an average CPU utilization of 25%. Use the following command to create a `HorizontalPodAutoscaler` resource:

```
$ kubectl autoscale deployment nginx \
--cpu-percent=25 --min=1 --max=5
```

Now that we have the `HorizontalPodAutoscaler` resource created, we can load test the application using the `hey` load testing utility preinstalled in Google Cloud Shell. But before you fire the load test, open a duplicate shell session, and watch the `Deployment` resource using the following command:

```
$ kubectl get deployment nginx -w
```

Open another duplicate shell session and watch the `HorizontalPodAutoscaler` resource using the following command:

```
$ kubectl get hpa nginx -w
```

Now, in the original window, run the following command to fire a load test:

```
$ hey -z 120s -c 10 http://34.123.234.57
```

It will start a load test for 2 minutes, with 10 concurrent users continuously hammering the `Service` resource. If you open the window where you're watching the `HorizontalPodAutoscaler` resource, you will see the following output. As soon as we start firing the load test, we see that the average utilization reaches 46%. The `HorizontalPodAutoscaler` waits for some time, and then it starts to increase the replicas, first to 2, then to 4, and finally to 5. When the test is complete, the utilization drops quickly to 27%, 25%, and finally, 0%. When the utilization goes to 0%, the `HorizontalPodAutoscaler` spins down the replicas from 5 to 1 gradually:

```
$ kubectl get hpa nginx -w
NAME      REFERENCE          TARGETS          MINPODS    MAXPODS
REPLICAS    AGE
nginx     Deployment/nginx   <unknown>/25%    1          5
1           32s
nginx     Deployment/nginx   46%/25%          1          5
1           71s
nginx     Deployment/nginx   46%/25%          1          5
2           92s
nginx     Deployment/nginx   92%/25%          1          5
4           2m2s
nginx     Deployment/nginx   66%/25%          1          5
5           2m32s
nginx     Deployment/nginx   57%/25%          1          5
5           2m41s
nginx     Deployment/nginx   27%/25%          1          5
5           3m11s
nginx     Deployment/nginx   23%/25%          1          5
5           3m41s
nginx     Deployment/nginx   0%/25%           1          5
4           4m23s
nginx     Deployment/nginx   0%/25%           1          5
2           5m53s
nginx     Deployment/nginx   0%/25%           1          5
1           6m30s
```

Likewise, we will see the replicas of the deployment changing when the
`HorizontalPodAutoscaler` actions the changes:

```
$ kubectl get deployment nginx -w
NAME      READY    UP-TO-DATE    AVAILABLE    AGE
nginx     1/1      1             1            18s
nginx     1/2      1             1            77s
nginx     2/2      2             2            79s
nginx     2/4      2             2            107s
nginx     3/4      4             3            108s
nginx     4/4      4             4            109s
nginx     4/5      4             4            2m17s
nginx     5/5      5             5            2m19s
nginx     4/4      4             4            4m23s
nginx     2/2      2             2            5m53s
nginx     1/1      1             1            6m30s
```

Apart from using the CPU and memory, you can use other parameters to scale your
workloads, such as network traffic. You can also use external metrics such as latency
and other factors that you can use to decide when to scale your traffic.

> **Tip**
> While you should use the `HorizontalPodAutoscaler` resource with
> CPU and memory, you should also consider scaling on external metrics such
> as response time and network latency. That will ensure better reliability as they
> directly impact customer experience and are therefore crucial to your business.

Till now, we have been dealing with stateless workloads. However, pragmatically speaking,
there is a sizeable number of stateful resources worldwide, and applications need to save
the state. Let's look at some considerations for managing the state.

Managing stateful applications

`Deployment` resources are beneficial for stateless workloads, as it does not need to
add any state considerations while updating `ReplicaSet` resources, but it cannot
work effectively with stateful workloads. To manage such workloads, you can use a
`StatefulSet` resource.

StatefulSet resource

StatefulSet is a resource that helps manage stateful applications. They are similar to Deployment resources, but unlike the Deployment resource, they also keep track of state and require volumes and `Service` resources in order to operate. `StatefulSet` resources maintain a sticky identity to each `Pod`. This means that the volume mounted on one `Pod` cannot be used by the other. In a `StatefulSet` resource, Kubernetes orders Pods by numbering them instead of generating a random hash. Pods within a `StatefulSet` resource are also rolled out in order and scaling also happens in order. If a particular `Pod` goes down and is recreated, the same volume is mounted to the `Pod`.

The following diagram illustrates the `StatefulSet` resource:

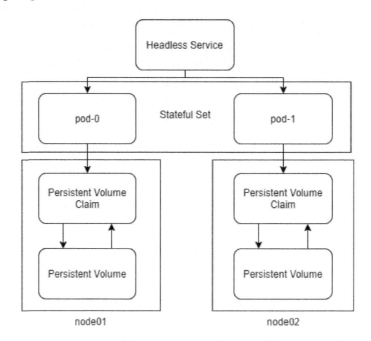

Figure 5.7 – StatefulSet

A `StatefulSet` resource has a stable and unique network identifier and therefore requires a **headless Service** resource to operate. Headless Services are `Service` resources that do not have a cluster IP. Instead, the Kubernetes DNS resolves the `Service` resource's FQDN directly to the Pods.

As a `StatefulSet` resource is supposed to persist data, it requires a persistent volume to operate. Therefore, let's look at how to manage volumes using Kubernetes.

Managing persistent volumes

Persistent volumes are Kubernetes resources that deal with storage. They can help you manage and mount hard disks, SSDs, filestores, and other block and network storage entities. You can provision persistent volumes manually or use dynamic provisioning within Kubernetes. When you use dynamic provisioning, Kubernetes will request the cloud provider via the cloud controller manager to provide the required storage. Let's look at both methods to understand how they work.

Static provisioning

Static provisioning is the traditional method of provisioning volumes. It requires someone (typically an administrator) to manually provision a disk and create the PersistentVolume resource using the disk information. The developer can then use the PersistentVolume resource within their StatefulSet resource, as in the following diagram:

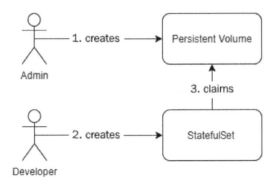

Figure 5.8 – Static provisioning

Let's now look at a static provisioning example.

To access the resources for this section, cd into the following:

```
$ cd ~/modern-devops/ch5/statefulsets/
```

So, we first need to create a disk within the cloud platform. Since we're using Google Cloud, let's proceed and use the gcloud commands to do so.

Use the following command to create a persistent zonal disk. Ensure that you use the same zone as your Kubernetes cluster. As we are using the us-central1-a zone for the Kubernetes cluster, we will use the same in the following command:

```
$ gcloud compute disks create nginx-manual --size 50GB \
--type pd-ssd --zone us-central1-a
```

```
Created [https://www.googleapis.com/compute/v1/
projects/<project_id>/zones/us-central1-a/disks/nginx-manual].
NAME          ZONE            SIZE_GB  TYPE     STATUS
nginx-manual  us-central1-a   50       pd-ssd   READY
```

As the disk is now ready, we can then create a PersistentVolume resource from it.

The manifest file, nginx-manual-pv.yaml, looks like the following:

```
apiVersion: v1
kind: PersistentVolume
metadata:
  name: nginx-manual-pv
  labels:
    usage: nginx-manual-disk
spec:
  capacity:
    storage: 50G
  accessModes:
    - ReadWriteOnce
  gcePersistentDisk:
    pdName: nginx-manual
    fsType: ext4
```

The spec section contains capacity, accessModes, and the kind of disk it needs to provision. You can specify one or more access modes to a persistent volume:

- ReadWriteOnce: Only one Pod can read and write to the disk at a time, and therefore you cannot mount such a volume to multiple Pods.

- ReadOnlyMany: Multiple Pods can read from the same volume at a time, but no Pod can write to the disk.

- ReadWriteMany: Multiple Pods can read and write to the same volume at once.

> **Tip**
> Not all kinds of storage support all access modes. You need to decide the type of volume during the initial requirement analysis and architectural assessment phase.

OK, let's now go and apply the manifest to provision the `PersistentVolume` resource using the following command:

```
$ kubectl apply -f nginx-manual-pv.yaml
```

Let's now check whether the persistent volume is available by using the following command:

```
$ kubectl get pv
NAME              CAPACITY    ACCESS MODES      RECLAIM POLICY
STATUS       CLAIM    STORAGECLASS     REASON    AGE
nginx-manual-pv   50G         RWO               Retain
Available                                                 8s
```

As the persistent volume is now available, we need to create the headless `Service` resource that will help maintain network identity in the `StatefulSet` resource. The manifest for the `nginx-manual-service.yaml` `Service` resource looks like the following:

```yaml
apiVersion: v1
kind: Service
metadata:
  name: nginx-manual
  labels:
    app: nginx-manual
spec:
  ports:
  - port: 80
    name: web
  clusterIP: None
  selector:
    app: nginx-manual
```

It is very similar to the regular `Service` resource, except that we have specified `clusterIP` as None.

Now let's go and apply the manifest using the following command:

```
$ kubectl apply -f nginx-manual-service.yaml
```

As the `Service` resource is created, we can create the `StatefulSet` resource that uses the created `PersistentVolume` and `Service` resources. The `StatefulSet` resource manifest, `nginx-manual-statefulset.yaml`, looks like the following:

```yaml
apiVersion: apps/v1
kind: StatefulSet
metadata:
  name: nginx-manual
spec:
  selector:
    matchLabels:
      app: nginx-manual
  serviceName: "nginx-manual"
  replicas: 1
  template:
    metadata:
      labels:
        app: nginx-manual
    spec:
      containers:
      - name: nginx
        image: nginx
        volumeMounts:
        - name: html
          mountPath: /usr/share/nginx/html
  volumeClaimTemplates:
  - metadata:
      name: html
    spec:
      accessModes: [ "ReadWriteOnce" ]
      resources:
        requests:
          storage: 40Gi
      selector:
        matchLabels:
          usage: nginx-manual-disk
```

The manifest contains various sections. While most are similar to the Deployment resource manifest, this requires a volume definition and a separate volumeClaimTemplates section. The volumeClaimTemplates section consists of the accessModes, resources, and selector sections. The selector section defines matchLabels, which help to select a particular PersistentVolume resource. In this case, it selects the PersistentVolume resource we defined previously. It also contains the serviceName attribute that defines the headless Service resource it will use.

Now, let's go ahead and apply the manifest using the following command:

```
$ kubectl apply -f nginx-manual-statetfulset.yaml
```

Now, let's inspect a few elements to see where we are. The StatefulSet resource creates a PersistentVolumeClaim resource to claim the PersistentVolume resource we created before.

Get the **PersistentVolumeClaim** using the following command:

```
$ kubectl get pvc
NAME                     STATUS    VOLUME             CAPACITY
ACCESS MODES   STORAGECLASS   AGE
html-nginx-manual-0      Bound     nginx-manual-pv    50G           RWO
4s
```

As we can see, StatefulSet resource has created a PersistentVolumeClaim resource called html-nginx-manual-0 that is bound to the nginx-manual-pv PersistentVolume resource. Therefore, manual provisioning has worked correctly.

If we query the PersistentVolume resource using the following command, we will see that the status is now showing as Bound:

```
$ kubectl get pv
NAME            CAPACITY    ACCESS MODES    RECLAIM POLICY
STATUS    CLAIM                             STORAGECLASS    REASON
nginx-manual-pv  50G         RWO             Retain
Bound     default/html-nginx-manual-0
```

Now, let's have a look at the Pods using the following command:

```
$ kubectl get pod
NAME             READY   STATUS    RESTARTS   AGE
nginx-manual-0   1/1     Running   0          14s
```

And as we see, `StatefulSet` resource has created a `Pod` and appended it with a serial number instead of a random hash. It wants to maintain ordering between the Pods and mount the same volumes to the same Pods that they mounted previously.

Now, let's open a shell into the `Pod` and create a file within the `/usr/share/nginx/html` directory using the following commands:

```
$ kubectl exec -it nginx-manual-0 -- /bin/bash
root@nginx-manual-0:/# cd /usr/share/nginx/html/
root@nginx-manual-0:/usr/share/nginx/html# echo 'Hello, world'
> index.html
root@nginx-manual-0:/usr/share/nginx/html# exit
```

Great! So, let's go ahead and delete the `Pod` and see whether we can get the file in the same location again using the following commands:

```
$ kubectl delete pod nginx-manual-0
$ kubectl get pod
NAME              READY    STATUS                RESTARTS    AGE
nginx-manual-0    1/1      Running               0           3s
$ kubectl exec -it nginx-manual-0 -- /bin/bash
root@nginx-manual-0:/# cd /usr/share/nginx/html/ && cat index.
html
Hello, world
root@nginx-manual-0:/usr/share/nginx/html# exit
```

And, as we can see, the file still exists, even after we deleted the `Pod`.

Static provisioning isn't one of the best ways of doing things, as you have to keep track of volumes and have to provision volumes manually. That involves a lot of manual activities and may be error-prone. Some organizations that want to keep a line between Dev and Ops can use this technique. Kubernetes allows this provision. However, for more DevOps-friendly organizations, there is a better way of doing it – *dynamic provisioning*.

Dynamic provisioning

Dynamic provisioning is when Kubernetes provides storage resources for you by interacting with the cloud provider. When we provisioned the disk manually, we interacted with the cloud APIs using the `gcloud` command line. What if your organization decides to move to some other cloud provider later? Well, that would break a lot of your existing scripts, and you have to rewrite the storage provisioning steps. Kubernetes is inherently portable and platform-independent. You can provision resources in the same way on any cloud platform.

But then different cloud providers have different storage offerings. How would Kubernetes know what kind of storage it needs to provision? Well, Kubernetes uses `StorageClass` resources for that. `StorageClasses` are Kubernetes resources that define the type of storage they need to provide when someone uses it.

The following diagram illustrates dynamic provisioning:

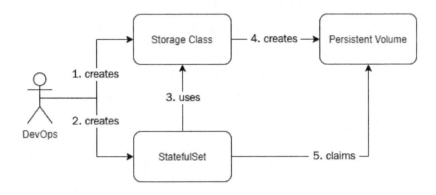

Figure 5.9 – Dynamic provisioning

Let's see an example storage class manifest, `fast-storage-class.yaml`, that provisions an SSD within Google Cloud Platform:

```
apiVersion: storage.k8s.io/v1
kind: StorageClass
metadata:
  name: fast
provisioner: kubernetes.io/gce-pd
parameters:
  type: pd-ssd
```

The `StorageClass` resource contains a provisioner and any parameters the provisioner requires. You may have noticed that I have kept the name `fast` instead of `gce-ssd` or something of that sort. The reason for that is because we want to keep the names as generic as possible.

> **Tip**
>
> Keep generic storage class names such as *fast*, *standard*, *block*, and *shared*, and avoid names specific to the cloud platform. Because storage class names are used in the persistent volume claims, and if you migrate to another cloud provider, you may end up changing a lot of manifests just to avoid confusion.

Let's go ahead and apply the manifest using the following command:

```
$ kubectl apply -f fast-storage-class.yaml
```

As the `StorageClass` resource is created, let's use it to provision an NGINX `StatefulSet` resource dynamically.

We need to create a `Service` resource manifest, `nginx-dynamic-service.yaml`, first:

```yaml
apiVersion: v1
kind: Service
metadata:
  name: nginx-dynamic
  labels:
    app: nginx-dynamic
spec:
  ports:
  - port: 80
    name: web
  clusterIP: None
  selector:
    app: nginx-dynamic
```

The manifest is very similar to the manual `Service` resource. Let's go ahead and apply it using the following command:

```
$ kubectl apply -f nginx-dynamic-service.yaml
```

Now, let's look at the StatefulSet resource manifest, nginx-dynamic-statefulset.yaml:

```yaml
apiVersion: apps/v1
kind: StatefulSet
metadata:
  name: nginx-dynamic
spec:
  selector:
    matchLabels:
      app: nginx-dynamic
  serviceName: "nginx-dynamic"
  replicas: 1
  template:
    metadata:
      labels:
        app: nginx-dynamic
    spec:
      containers:
      - name: nginx
        image: nginx
        volumeMounts:
        - name: html
          mountPath: /usr/share/nginx/html
  volumeClaimTemplates:
  - metadata:
      name: html
    spec:
      storageClassName: "fast"
      accessModes: [ "ReadWriteOnce" ]
      resources:
        requests:
          storage: 40Gi
```

The manifest is similar to the manual one, but this one contains the `storageClassName` attribute in the `volumeClaimTemplates` section, and lacks the `selector` section, as we are dynamically provisioning the storage. Use the following command to apply the manifest:

```
$ kubectl apply -f nginx-dynamic-statefulset.yaml
```

As the `StatefulSet` resource is created, let's go ahead and check the `PersistentVolumeClaim` and `PersistentVolume` resources using the following commands:

```
$ kubectl get pvc
NAME                       STATUS    VOLUME
CAPACITY    ACCESS MODES    STORAGECLASS
html-nginx-dynamic-0       Bound     pvc-d30a8462-f53d-4152-b16d-
6ba7a5967b78    40Gi        RWO             fast
$ kubectl get pv
NAME                                              CAPACITY
ACCESS MODES    RECLAIM POLICY    STATUS    CLAIM
STORAGECLASS    REASON
pvc-d30a8462-f53d-4152-b16d-6ba7a5967b78    40Gi         RWO
Delete             Bound      default/html-nginx-dynamic-0    fast
```

And we can see that the claim is bound to a persistent volume that is dynamically provisioned. Now, let's proceed and run the following command to do similar tests with this `StatefulSet` resource.

Let's create a file in the `nginx-dynamic-0` Pod using the following command:

```
$ kubectl exec -it nginx-dynamic-0 -- bash
root@nginx-dynamic-0:/# cd /usr/share/nginx/html/
root@nginx-dynamic-0:/usr/share/nginx/html# echo 'Hello,
dynamic world' > index.html
root@nginx-dynamic-0:/usr/share/nginx/html# exit
```

Now, delete the `Pod` and open a shell again to check whether the file exists by using the following commands:

```
$ kubectl delete pod nginx-dynamic-0
$ kubectl get pod nginx-dynamic-0
NAME               READY    STATUS     RESTARTS    AGE
nginx-dynamic-0    1/1      Running    0           13s
$ kubectl exec -it nginx-dynamic-0 -- bash
root@nginx-dynamic-0:/# cd /usr/share/nginx/html/
root@nginx-dynamic-0:/usr/share/nginx/html# cat index.html
Hello, dynamic world
```

```
root@nginx-dynamic-0:/usr/share/nginx/html# exit
```

And as we can see, the file exists in the volume even if the Pod was deleted. You would have observed that we have used the kubectl command multiple times throughout this chapter. When you perform activities throughout the day, it makes sense to use shortcuts and best practices wherever you can. Let's look at some of the best practices while using kubectl.

Kubernetes command-line best practices

For a seasoned Kubernetes developer and admin, kubectl is the command they run most of the time. The following steps will make your life simple and save you a ton of time and will also let you focus on more essential activities and set you apart from the rest.

Using alias

Most system administrators use aliases, and for an excellent reason. They save valuable time. Aliases in Linux are a different name for a command, and it is mostly used to shorten most frequently used commands; for example, ls -l becomes ll.

You can use the following aliases with kubectl to make your life easier.

k for kubectl

Yes, that's right. By using the following alias, you can use k instead of typing kubectl:

```
$ alias k='kubectl'
$ k get node
NAME                    STATUS     ROLES     AGE       VERSION
kind-control-plane      Ready      master    5m7s      v1.19.1
kind-worker             Ready      <none>    4m33s     v1.19.1
```

That will save a lot of your time and save yourself from a lot of hassle.

Using kubectl dry run

`kubectl --dry-run` helps you to generate YAML manifests from imperative commands and saves you a lot of typing time. You can write an imperative command to generate a resource and append that with a `--dry-run=client -o yaml` string to generate a YAML manifest from the imperative command. The command does not create the resource within the cluster, but instead just outputs the manifest. The following command will generate a `Pod` manifest using `dry-run`:

```
$ kubectl run nginx --image=nginx --dry-run=client -o yaml
apiVersion: v1
kind: Pod
metadata:
  creationTimestamp: null
  labels:
    run: nginx
  name: nginx
spec:
  containers:
  - image: nginx
    name: nginx
    resources: {}
  dnsPolicy: ClusterFirst
  restartPolicy: Always
status: {}
```

And you now have the skeleton YAML file that you can edit according to your liking.

Now imagine that you need to type this command multiple times during the day! At some point it becomes tiring. Why not shorten it by using the following alias?

```
$ alias kdr='kubectl --dry-run=client -o yaml'
```

You can then use the alias to generate other manifests.

To generate a `Deployment` resource manifest, use the following command:

```
$ kdr create deployment nginx --image=nginx
```

You can use the dry run to generate almost all resources from imperative commands. However, some resources do not have an imperative command, such as a `DaemonSet`. For such resources, you can generate the manifest for the closest resource and modify it. The `DaemonSet` manifest is very similar to the `Deployment` manifest, so you can generate a `Deployment` manifest and change it to match the `DameonSet` manifest.

Now, let's look at one of the most frequently used `kubectl` commands and their possible aliases.

kubectl apply and delete aliases

If you use manifests, you will use the `kubectl apply` and `kubectl delete` commands most of the time within your cluster, so it makes sense to use the following aliases:

```
$ alias kap='kubectl apply -f'
$ alias kad='kubectl delete -f'
```

You can then use them to apply or delete resources using the following commands:

```
$ kap nginx-deployment.yaml
$ kad nginx-deployment.yaml
```

While troubleshooting containers, most of us use `busybox`. Let's see how to optimize it.

Troubleshooting containers with busybox using an alias

We use the following commands to open a `busybox` session:

```
$ kubectl run busybox-test --image=busybox -it --rm \
--restart=Never -- <command>
```

Now, this can be tiring if you open several `busybox` sessions during the day. How about minimizing the overhead by using the following alias?

```
$ alias kbb='kubectl run busybox-test --image=busybox -it \
--rm --restart=Never --'
```

And then we can open a shell session to a new `busybox` Pod using the following command:

```
$ kbb sh
/ #
```

Now, that is much cleaner and easier. Likewise, you can also create aliases of other commands that you use frequently, for example:

```
$ alias kgp='kubectl get pods'
$ alias kgn='kubectl get nodes'
$ alias kgs='kubectl get svc'
$ alias kdb='kubectl describe'
$ alias kl='kubectl logs'
$ alias ke='kubectl exec -it'
```

And so on according to your needs. You may also be used to autocompletion within bash, where your commands autocomplete when you press Tab after typing a few words. kubectl also provides autocompletion of commands, but not by default. Let's now look at how to enable kubectl autocompletion within bash.

Using kubectl bash autocompletion

To enable kubectl bash autocompletion, use the following command:

```
$ echo "source <(kubectl completion bash)" >> ~/.bashrc
```

The command adds the kubectl completion bash command as a source to your .bashrc file. So, the next time you log in to your shell, you should be able to use kubectl autocomplete. That will save you a ton of time when typing commands.

Summary

We began this chapter by managing Pods with Deployment resources and ReplicaSet resources and discussed some of the critical Kubernetes deployment strategies. We then looked into Kubernetes service discovery and models and understood why we required a separate entity to expose containers to the internal or external world. We then looked at different Service resources and where to use them. We talked about Ingress resources and how to use them to create reverse proxies to our container workloads. We then delved into **Horizontal Pod Autoscaling** and used multiple metrics to scale our Pods automatically.

We looked at state considerations and learned about static and dynamic storage provisioning using PersistentVolumes, PersistentVolumeClaims, and StorageClass, and talked about some best practices surrounding them. We looked at StatefulSet resources as an essential resource that helps you schedule and manage stateful containers. Finally, we looked at some best practices, tips, and tricks surrounding the kubectl command line and how to use them effectively.

The topics covered in this and the previous chapter are just the core of Kubernetes. Kubernetes is a vast tool with enough functionality to write an entire book on it, so these chapters just give you a gist of what it is all about. Please feel free to read about the resources in detail in the Kubernetes official documentation at `https://kubernetes.io`.

In the next chapter, we will delve into the world of the cloud and Infrastructure as Code with Terraform.

Questions

1. A Kubernetes deployment deletes an old `ReplicaSet` resource when the image is updated – True/False?

2. What are the primary deployment strategies supported by Kubernetes?

   A. Recreate

   B. Rolling update

   C. Ramped slow rollout

   D. Best effort controlled rollout

3. What types of resources can you use to expose containers externally?

   A. `ClusterIP Service`

   B. `NodePort Service`

   C. `LoadBalancer Service`

   D. `Ingress`

4. It is a best practice to start with a ClusterIP service and change the service type later if needed – True/False?

5. `Deployment` resources are suitable for stateful workloads – True/False?

6. What kind of workloads can you run with ingresses?

   A. HTTP

   B. TCP

   C. FTP

   D. SMTP

7. What resources would you define for dynamic volume provisioning?

    A. `StorageClass`

    B. `PersistentVolumeClaim`

    C. `PersistentVolume`

    D. `StatefulSet`

8. To make your horizontal scaling more meaningful, what parameters should you use to scale your Pods?

    A. CPU

    B. Memory

    C. External metrics, such as response time

    D. Packets per second

9. What are the forms of routing within an `Ingress` resource?

    A. Simple

    B. Path-based

    C. Name-based

    D. Complex

Answers

1. False. An image deployment just scales the old `ReplicaSet` resource to `0`.

2. a, b

3. b, c, and d

4. True

5. False. Use StatefulSet resources instead.

6. a

7. a, b

8. a, b, c

9. b, c

Section 2: Delivering Containers

This section forms the book's core and explains various tools and techniques to implement modern DevOps for the cloud effectively. While the section heavily focuses on containers, we will also look at the modern DevOps approach using virtual machines and IaaS-based systems with infrastructure automation, configuration management, and immutable infrastructure. We will also learn about the cutting-edge CI/CD tools with a heavy focus on security.

This section comprises the following chapters:

6

Infrastructure as Code (IaC) with Terraform

Cloud computing is one of the primary factors of DevOps' enablement today. The initial apprehensions that there were about the cloud are a thing of the past. With an army of security and compliance experts manning cloud platforms 24x7, organizations are now trusting the *public cloud* like never before. Along with cloud computing, another buzzword is taking the industry by storm – **Infrastructure as Code (IaC)**. This chapter will focus on IaC with Terraform, and by the end of this chapter, you will understand the concept and have enough hands-on experience with Terraform to get you started in your journey.

In this chapter, we're going to cover the following main topics:

- Introduction to IaC
- Setting up Terraform and Azure providers
- Understanding Terraform workflows and creating your first resource using Terraform
- Terraform state and backends

- Terraform workspaces

- Terraform outputs, state, console, and graphs

Technical requirements

For this chapter, you can use any machine to run Terraform. Terraform supports a large number of platforms, including Windows, Linux, macOS, and others.

You will need an active Azure subscription to follow the exercises. Currently, Azure is offering a free trial for 30 days with $200 worth of free credits; you can sign up at `https://azure.microsoft.com/en-in/free`.

You will also need to clone the following GitHub repository for some of the exercises:

`https://github.com/PacktPublishing/Modern-DevOps-Practices`

Run the following command to clone the repository into your home directory, and `cd` into the `ch6` directory to access the required resources:

```
$ git clone https://github.com/PacktPublishing/Modern-DevOps-\
Practices.git modern-devops
$ cd modern-devops/ch6
```

So, let's get started!

Introduction to IaC

IaC is the concept of using code to define infrastructure. While most people can visualize infrastructure as tangible, virtual infrastructure is already commonplace and has existed for around two decades. Cloud providers provide a web-based console through which you can manage your infrastructure intuitively. But the process is not repeatable or recorded.

If you spin up a set of infrastructure components using the console in one environment and want to replicate it in another, it is a duplication of effort. To solve this problem, cloud platforms provide APIs to manipulate resources within the cloud and some command-line tools that can help trigger the APIs. You can then start writing scripts using commands to create the infrastructure and parameterize them to use the same scripts in another environment. Well, that kind of solves the problem, right?

Not really! Writing scripts is an imperative way of managing infrastructure. Though you can still call it IaC, its problem is that it does not effectively manage infrastructure changes. Let me give you a few examples:

- What would happen if you needed to modify something that was already in the script? If you change the script somewhere in the middle and rerun the entire thing, it may create havoc with your infrastructure. Imperative management of infrastructure is not idempotent. So, managing changes becomes a problem.

- What if someone changes the infrastructure managed by your script manually using the console? Will your script be able to detect it correctly? What if you want to change the same thing using a script? It will soon start to get messy.

- With the advent of hybrid cloud architecture, most organizations use multiple cloud platforms for their needs. When you are in such a situation, it soon becomes a problem to manage multiple clouds with imperative scripts. Different clouds have different ways of interacting with their APIs and various command-line tools to do so.

The solution to all these problems is a declarative IaC solution such as Terraform. HashiCorp's Terraform is the most popular IaC tool available in the market. It helps you automate and manage your infrastructure using code and can run on a variety of platforms. And as it is declarative, you just need to define what you need (the desired end state) instead of describing how to achieve it. It has the following features:

- It supports multiple cloud platforms via providers and exposes a single declarative **Hashicorp configuration language (HCL)**-based interface to interact with it. Therefore, it allows for managing various cloud platforms using a similar language and syntax. So, having a few Terraform experts within your team can take care of all your IaC needs.

- It tracks the state of the resources it manages using `state` files and supports local and remote backends to store and manage them. That helps in making the Terraform configuration idempotent. So, if someone makes changes manually to a Terraform-managed resource, Terraform can detect the difference in the next run and prompt corrective action to bring it to the defined configuration. The admin can then choose to absorb the change or resolve any conflicts before applying it.

- It enables GitOps in infrastructure management. With Terraform, you can have the infrastructure configuration alongside application code, making versioning, managing, and releasing infrastructure the same as managing code. You can also include code scanning and gating using Pull requests so that someone can review and approve the changes to higher environments before you apply them. A great power indeed!

Terraform has multiple offerings – open source, cloud, and enterprise. The open source offering is a simple **command-line interface (CLI)**-based tool that you can download on any supported operating system (OS) and use. The cloud and enterprise offerings are more of a wrapper over the open source. They provide a web-based GUI and other advanced features such as **Policy as Code** with **Sentinel**, **cost analysis**, **private modules**, **GitOps**, and **CI/CD pipelines**.

This chapter will look at the open source offering and its core functions.

Terraform open source is divided into two main parts – **Terraform Core** and **Terraform providers**, as seen in the following diagram:

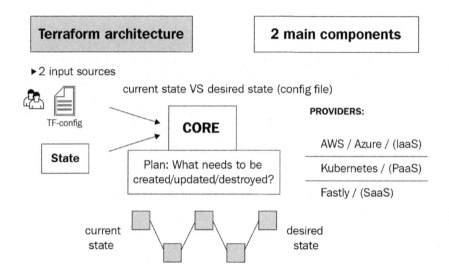

Figure 6.1 – Terraform architecture

Let's look at the functions of both components:

- **Terraform Core** is the CLI that we will use to interact with Terraform. It takes two main inputs – your Terraform configuration files and the existing state. It then takes the difference in configuration and applies it.

- **Terraform providers** are plugins that Terraform uses to interact with the cloud providers. The providers translate the Terraform configuration into the REST API calls of the cloud provider so that Terraform can manage the infrastructure associated with the cloud provider. For example, if you want Terraform to manage AWS infrastructure, you'll have to use the Terraform AWS provider.

Now let's see how we can install open source Terraform.

Installing Terraform

Installing Terraform is simple; go to `https://www.terraform.io/downloads.html` and follow the instructions for your platform. Most of it will require you to download a binary and move it to your system path.

Since we were using Ubuntu from the beginning, I will show the installation on Ubuntu.

Use the following commands to download Terraform, unzip and move the binary to the system path, and make the binary executable:

```
$ wget https://releases.hashicorp.com/terraform\
/0.14.3/terraform_0.14.3_linux_amd64.zip
$ unzip terraform_0.14.3_linux_amd64.zip
$ sudo mv terraform /usr/local/bin
$ sudo chmod +x /usr/local/bin/terraform
```

To check whether Terraform has installed successfully, run the following command:

```
$ terraform -version
Terraform v0.14.3
```

It shows that Terraform has been installed successfully. Terraform uses *Terraform providers* to interact with the cloud providers, so let's look at those in the next section.

Terraform providers

Terraform has a decentralized architecture. While the **Terraform CLI** contains Terraform's core functionality and provides all functionalities not related to any specific cloud provider, **Terraform providers** provide the interface between the Terraform CLI and the cloud providers themselves. This decentralized approach has allowed public cloud vendors to offer their Terraform providers so that their customers can use Terraform to manage infrastructure in their cloud. Such is Terraform's popularity that it has now become an essential requirement for every public cloud provider to offer a Terraform provider.

We will be interacting with Azure for this chapter's entirety; therefore, we will use the Azure Terraform provider for our activity.

To access the resources for this section, `cd` into the following:

```
$ cd ~/modern-devops/ch6/terraform-exercise/
```

Before we go ahead and configure the provider, we need to understand how Terraform needs to authenticate and authorize with the Azure APIs.

Authentication and authorization with Azure

The simplest way of providing authentication and authorization with Azure is to log in to your account using the Azure CLI. When you use the Azure provider within your Terraform file, it will automatically act as your account and do whatever it needs to. Now, this sounds dangerous. Admins generally have a lot of access, and having a tool that acts as an admin might not be a great idea. What if you want to plug Terraform into your CI/CD pipelines? Well, there is another way to do it – by using **Azure service principals**. Azure service principals allow you to access the required features without using a named user account. You can then apply the principle of least privilege on the service principal and provide only the necessary access.

Before configuring the service principal, let's first install the Azure CLI on our machine. To do so, run the following command:

```
$ curl -sL https://aka.ms/InstallAzureCLIDeb | sudo bash
```

The preceding command will download a `bash` script and will execute it using `bash`. The script will then automatically download and configure the Azure CLI. To confirm whether the Azure CLI is installed successfully, run the following command:

```
$ az --version
azure-cli                    2.17.1
```

And we see that the Azure CLI is correctly installed on the system. Now let's go ahead and configure the service principal.

To configure the Azure service principal, follow these steps.

Log in to Azure first using the following command and follow all the steps that the command prompts. You will have to browse to a specified URL and enter the given code. Once you've logged in, you will get a JSON response that will include some details, something like the following:

```
$ az login
To sign in, use a web browser to open the page https://
microsoft.com/devicelogin and enter the code XXXXXXXX to
authenticate.
[
  {
```

```
    "id": "00000000-0000-0000-0000-0000000000000",
    ...
  }
]
```

Make a note of the `id` attribute, which is the subscription `id`, and if you have more than
one subscription, you can use the following to set it to the correct one:

```
$ az account set --subscription="<SUBSCRIPTION_ID>"
```

Use the following command to create a service principal with the contributor role to allow
Terraform to manage the subscription's infrastructure.

> **Tip:**
> Follow the principle of least privilege while granting access to the service
> principal. Do not give privileges thinking that you might need them in the
> future. If any access is required in the future, you can grant it later.

We use contributor access for simplicity, but finer-grained access is possible and should be
used:

```
$ az ad sp create-for-rbac --role="Contributor"\
--scopes="/subscriptions/<SUBSCRIPTION_ID>"
Creating 'Contributor' role assignment under scope '/
subscriptions/<SUBSCRIPTION_ID>'
  Retrying role assignment creation: 1/36
The output includes credentials that you must protect. Be sure
that you do not include these credentials in your code or check
the credentials into your source control. For more information,
see https://aka.ms/azadsp-cli
{
  "appId": "00000000-0000-0000-0000-0000000000000",
  "displayName": "azure-cli-2021-01-07-05-59-24",
  "name": "http://azure-cli-2021-01-07-05-59-24",
  "password": "00000000000.xx-00000000000000000",
  "tenant": "00000000-0000-0000-0000-0000000000000"
}
```

We've successfully created the service principal. The response JSON consists of `appId`, `password`, and `tenant`. We will need these to configure Terraform to use the service principal. In the next section, let's define the Azure Terraform provider with the details.

Using the Azure Terraform provider

Before we define the Azure Terraform provider, let's understand what makes a Terraform root module. The Terraform root module is just a working directory within your filesystem containing one or more `.tf` files that help you define your configuration and are where you would typically run your Terraform commands.

Terraform scans all your `.tf` files, combines them, and processes them internally as one. Therefore, you can have one or more `.tf` files that you can split according to your needs. While there are no defined standards of naming `.tf` files, most conventions use `main.tf` as the main Terraform file where they define resources, a `vars.tf` file for defining variables, and `outputs.tf` for defining outputs.

For this discussion, let's create a `main.tf` file within your working directory and add a `provider` configuration like the following:

```
terraform {
  required_providers {
    azurerm = {
      source  = "azurerm"
      version = "=2.4.0"
    }
  }
}
provider "azurerm" {
  subscription_id = var.subscription_id
  client_id       = var.client_id
  client_secret   = var.client_secret
  tenant_id       = var.tenant_id
  features {}
}
```

The preceding file contains two blocks. The `terraform` block contains the `required_providers` block, which declares the `version` constraint for the `azurerm` provider. The `provider` block declares an `azurerm` provider, which requires four parameters.

> **Tip:**
> Always constrain the provider version as providers are released without notice, and if you don't include the version number, something that works on your machine might not work on someone else's machine or the CI/CD pipeline. Using a version constraint avoids breaking changes and keeps you in control.

You might have noticed that we have declared several variables within the preceding file instead of directly inputting the values. There are two main reasons for that – we want to make our template as generic as possible to promote reuse. So, suppose we want to apply a similar configuration in another subscription or use another service principal, we should be able to change it by changing the variable values. Secondly, we don't want to check `client_id` and `client_secret` into source control. It is a bad practice as we expose our service principal to users beyond those who need to know about it.

> **Tip:**
> Never check sensitive data into source control. Instead, use a `tfvars` file to manage sensitive information and keep it in a secret management system such as Hashicorp's Vault.

Okay, so as we've defined the provider resource and the attribute values are sourced from variables, the next step would be to declare variables. Let's have a look at that now.

Terraform variables

To declare variables, we will need to create a `vars.tf` file with the following data:

```
variable "subscription_id" {
  type        = string
  description = "The azure subscription id"
}
variable "client_id" {
  type        = string
  description = "The azure service principal appId"
}
variable "client_secret" {
  type        = string
  description = "The azure service principal password"
  sensitive   = true
}
```

```
variable "tenant_id" {
  type        = string
  description = "The azure tenant id"
}
```

So, we've defined four variables here using variable blocks. Variable blocks typically have a type and a description. The `type` attribute defines the datatype of the variable we are declaring and defaults to the `string` datatype. It can be a primitive datatype such as `string`, `number`, or `bool`, or a complex data structure such as `list`, `set`, `map`, `object`, or `tuple`. We will look at types in detail when we use them later in the exercises. The `description` attribute provides more information regarding the variable so that users can refer to it for better understanding.

> **Tip:**
> Always set the `description` attribute right from the beginning as it is user-friendly and promotes the reuse of your template.

The `client_secret` variable also contains a third attribute called `sensitive`, which is a Boolean attribute set to `true`. When the `sensitive` attribute is set to `true`, the Terraform CLI does not display it in the screen's output. It is highly recommended to use this attribute for sensitive variables such as passwords and secrets.

> **Tip:**
> Always declare a sensitive variable as `sensitive`. This is because if you are using Terraform within your CI/CD pipelines, unprivileged users might get access to sensitive information by looking at the build output.

Apart from the other three, an attribute called `default` will help you specify default values for variables. The default values help you provide the best possible value for a variable, which your users have the option of overriding if they need to.

> **Tip:**
> Always use default values where possible as they allow you to provide soft guidance about your enterprise standard to users and save a ton of their time.

The next step would be to provide values for the variables. Let's have a look at that.

Providing variable values

There are a few ways to provide variable values within Terraform:

- **Via the console using** `-var` **flags** – You can use multiple `-var` flags with the `variable_name=variable_value` string to supply the values.

- **Via a variable definitions file (the** `.tfvars` **file)** – You can use a file containing the list of variables and their values ending with an extension of `.tfvars` (if you prefer HCL) or `.tfvars.json` (if you prefer `json`) via the command line with the `-var-file` flag.

- **Via default variable definitions files** – If you don't want to supply the variable definition file via the command line, you can create a file with the name `terraform.tfvars` or end it with an extension of `.auto.tfvars` within the Terraform workspace. Terraform will automatically scan these files and take the values from there.

- **Environment variables** – If you don't want to use a file or pass the information via the command line, you can use environment variables to supply it. You need to create environment variables with the `TF_VAR_<var-name>` structure, containing the variable value.

- **Default** – When you run a Terraform plan without providing values to variables in any other way, the Terraform CLI will prompt for the values, and you have to enter them manually.

If multiple methods are used to provide the same variable's value, the first method in the preceding list has the highest precedence for a specific variable. It overrides anything that is defined in the methods listed later.

We will use the `terraform.tfvars` file for this activity and provide the values for the variables.

Add the following data into the `terraform.tfvars` file:

```
subscription_id="<SUBSCRIPTION_ID>"
client_id="<SERVICE_PRINCIPAL_APP_ID>"
client_secret="<SERVICE_PRINCIPAL_SECRET>"
tenant_id="<TENANT_ID>"
```

If you are checking the Terraform configuration into source control, add the file to the ignore list to avoid accidentally checking it in.

If you using `git`, adding the following to the `.gitignore` file will suffice:

```
*.tfvars
.terraform*
```

Now, let's go ahead and look at the Terraform workflow to progress further.

Terraform workflow

The Terraform workflow typically consists of the following:

- `init` – Initializes the Terraform workspace and backend (more on them later) and downloads all required providers. You can run the `init` command multiple times during your build as it does not make changes to your workspace or state.

- `plan` – Runs a speculative plan on the requested resources. This command typically connects with the cloud provider, then checks whether the objects managed by Terraform exist within the cloud provider and whether they have the same configuration as defined in the Terraform template. It then shows the delta in the planned output that an admin can review and change the configuration if they are not satisfied. If they are satisfied, they can apply the plan to commit the changes to the cloud platform. The `plan` command does not make any changes to the current infrastructure.

- `apply` – This applies the delta configuration to the cloud platform. When you use `apply` by itself, it runs `plan` first and asks for confirmation. If you supply a plan to it, it applies the plan directly. You can also use `apply` without running `plan` by using the `-auto-approve` flag.

- `destroy` – The `destroy` command is used to destroy the entire infrastructure that is managed by Terraform. It is, therefore, not a very popular command and is rarely used in a production environment. That does not mean that the `destroy` command is not helpful. Suppose you are spinning up a development infrastructure for temporary purposes and don't need it later. In that case, it takes a few minutes to destroy everything that you created by using this command.

To access the resources for this section, `cd` into the following:

```
$ cd ~/modern-devops/ch6/terraform-exercise/
```

Now let's look at each one of these in detail with hands-on exercises.

terraform init

So, to initialize a Terraform workspace, run the following command:

```
$ terraform init
Initializing the backend...
Initializing provider plugins...
- Finding hashicorp/azurerm versions matching "2.4.0"...
- Installing hashicorp/azurerm v2.4.0...
- Installed hashicorp/azurerm v2.4.0 (signed by HashiCorp)
Terraform has been successfully initialized!
You may now begin working with Terraform. Try running
"terraform plan" to see any changes that are required for your
Infrastructure. All Terraform commands should now work.

If you ever set or change modules or backend configuration
for Terraform, rerun this command to reinitialize your working
directory. If you forget, other commands will detect it and
remind you to do so if necessary.
```

As the Terraform workspace has initialized, we can create an Azure resource group to start working with the cloud.

Creating the first resource – Azure resource group

To create a resource group, we need to use the `azurerm_resource_group` resource within the `main.tf` file. Add the following to your `main.tf` file to create the resource group:

```
resource "azurerm_resource_group" "rg" {
  name     = var.rg_name
  location = var.rg_location
}
```

As we've used two variables, we've got to declare those, so add the following to the `vars.tf` file:

```
variable "rg_name" {
  type        = string
  description = "The resource group name"
}
```

```
variable "rg_location" {
  type        = string
  description = "The resource group location"
}
```

And then, we need to add the resource group name and location to the `terraform.tfvars` file. Therefore, add the following to the `terraform.tfvars` file:

```
rg_name=terraform-exercise
rg_location="West Europe"
```

So, now we're ready to run a plan, but before we do so let's use `terraform fmt` to format our files into the canonical standard.

terraform fmt

The `terraform fmt` command formats the `.tf` files into a canonical standard. Use the following command to format your files:

```
$ terraform fmt
terraform.tfvars
vars.tf
```

The command lists the files that it formatted. The next step is to validate your configuration.

terraform validate

The `terraform validate` command validates the current configuration and checks whether there are any syntax errors. To validate your configuration, run the following:

```
$ terraform validate
Success! The configuration is valid.
```

The success output denotes that our configuration is valid. If there were any errors, it would have highlighted them in the validated output.

> **Tip:**
> Always run `fmt` and `validate` before every Terraform plan. It saves you a ton of planning time and helps you keep your configuration in good shape.

As the configuration is valid, we are ready to run a plan.

terraform plan

To run a Terraform plan, use the following command:

```
$ terraform plan
An execution plan has been generated and is shown below.
Resource actions are indicated with the following symbols:
  + create
Terraform will perform the following actions:
  # azurerm_resource_group.rg will be created
  + resource "azurerm_resource_group" "rg" {
      + id       = (known after apply)
      + location = "westeurope"
      + name     = "terraform-exercise"
    }
Plan: 1 to add, 0 to change, 0 to destroy.
-----------------------------------------------------------------
Note: You didn't specify an "-out" parameter to save this plan,
so Terraform can't guarantee that exactly these actions will be
performed if "terraform apply" is subsequently run.
```

Right, so the `plan` output tells us that if we run `terraform apply` immediately, it will create a single `terraform_exercise` resource group. It also gives a note that since we did not save this plan, it is not guaranteed that the subsequent `apply` will result in the same action. Meanwhile, things might have changed; therefore, Terraform will rerun `plan` and prompt us for `yes` when applying. Thus, if you don't want surprises, you should save the plan to a file.

> Tip:
>
> Always save `terraform plan` output to a file and use the file to apply the changes. This is to avoid any last-minute surprises with things that might have changed in the background and `apply` not doing what it intended to do, especially when you get your plan reviewed as a part of your process.

So, let's go ahead and save the plan to a file first using the following command:

```
$ terraform plan -out rg_terraform_exercise.tfplan
```

And this time, the plan is saved to a file called `rg_terraform_exercise.tfplan`. We can use this file to apply the changes subsequently.

terraform apply

To apply the changes using the plan file, run the following command:

```
$ terraform apply "rg_terraform_exercise.tfplan"
azurerm_resource_group.rg: Creating...
azurerm_resource_group.rg: Creation complete after 1s [id=/
subscriptions/<SUBSCRIPTION_ID>/resourceGroups/terraform-
exercise]

Apply complete! Resources: 1 added, 0 changed, 0 destroyed.

The state of your infrastructure has been saved to the path
below. This state is required to modify and destroy your
infrastructure, so keep it safe. To inspect the complete state
use the `terraform show` command.

State path: terraform.tfstate
```

And that's it! Terraform has applied the configuration. Let's use the Azure CLI to verify whether the resource group is created.

Run the following command to list all resource groups within your subscription:

```
$ az group list
[
  {
    "id": "/subscriptions/<SUBSCRIPTION_ID>/resourceGroups/
terraform-exercise",
    "location": "westeurope",
    "name": "terraform-exercise",
    ...
  },
  . . .
]
```

And we see that our resource group is created and within the list.

There might be instances when `apply` was partially successful. In that case, Terraform will automatically taint resources that it believes weren't created successfully. Such resources will be recreated automatically in the next run. If you want to taint a resource for recreation manually, you can use the `terraform taint` command:

```
$ terraform taint <resource>
```

Let's suppose we want to destroy the resource group as we no longer need it. We can use `terraform destroy` for that.

terraform destroy

To destroy the resource group, we can run a speculative plan first. It is always a best practice to run a speculative plan, to confirm that what we need to destroy is within the output to have no surprises later. Terraform, like Linux, does not have an undo button.

To run a speculative destroy plan, use the following command:

```
$ terraform plan -destroy
An execution plan has been generated and is shown below.
Resource actions are indicated with the following symbols:
  - destroy
Terraform will perform the following actions:
  # azurerm_resource_group.rg will be destroyed
  - resource "azurerm_resource_group" "rg" {
      - id        = "/subscriptions/<SUBSCRIPTION_ID>/
resourceGroups/terraform-exercise" -> null
      - location = "westeurope" -> null
      - name      = "terraform-exercise" -> null
    }
Plan: 0 to add, 0 to change, 1 to destroy.
------------------------------------------------------------
Note: You didn't specify an "-out" parameter to save this plan,
so Terraform can't guarantee that exactly these actions will be
performed if "terraform apply" is subsequently run.
```

And as we see, as the resource group was the only resource managed by Terraform, it has listed that as the resource that will be destroyed. There are two ways of destroying the resource, either by using `terraform destroy` on its own or saving the speculative plan using the `out` parameter and running `terraform apply` on the destroy plan.

Let's use the first method for now.

Run the following command to destroy all resources managed by Terraform:

```
$ terraform destroy
An execution plan has been generated and is shown below.
Resource actions are indicated with the following symbols:
  - destroy


Terraform will perform the following actions:

  # azurerm_resource_group.rg will be destroyed
  ...
Plan: 0 to add, 0 to change, 1 to destroy.

Do you really want to destroy all resources?
  Terraform will destroy all your managed infrastructure, as
shown above. There is no undo. Only 'yes' will be accepted to
confirm.

  Enter a value:
```

Now, this time Terraform reruns `plan` and prompts for a value. It will only accept `yes` as confirmation. So, you can review the output and type `yes` and hit *Enter* to confirm:

```
  Enter a value: yes
azurerm_resource_group.rg: Destroying... [id=/
subscriptions/<SUBSCRIPTION_ID>/resourceGroups/terraform-
exercise]
azurerm_resource_group.rg: Still destroying... [id=/
subscriptions/<SUBSCRIPTION_ID>/resourceGroups/terraform-
exercise, 10s elapsed]


azurerm_resource_group.rg: Destruction complete after 19s
```

And it has now destroyed the resource group.

But how does Terraform know what it had created before and what it needs to destroy? Well, it uses a state file for that. Let's have a look.

terraform state

Terraform uses a state file to track what it has deployed and what resources it is managing. The state file is essential as it contains a record of all the infrastructure Terraform is maintaining, and if you lose it, Terraform will lose track of what it has done so far and start treating resources as if they are new and need to be created again. Therefore, you should protect your state as you would protect code.

Terraform stores state in backends. By default, Terraform stores the state file as a file called `terraform.tfstate` within the `workspace` directory, which is called the local backend. However, that is not one of the best ways of managing the state. There are several reasons why you should not store state in a local system:

- Multiple admins cannot work on the same infrastructure if the state file is stored within someone's local directory.
- Local workstations are not backed up, and therefore even if you have a single admin doing the job, the risk of losing the state file is high.

You might argue that we can resolve these problems by checking the state file into source control with the `.tf` files. Well, don't do that! The state files are plaintext, and if your infrastructure configuration contains sensitive information such as passwords, anyone can see it. Therefore, you need to store a state file securely. Also, storing state files in source control does not provide state locking, resulting in conflicts if multiple people are simultaneously modifying the state file.

> **Tip:**
> Never store state files in source control. Use a `.gitignore` file entry to bypass the `terraform.tfstate` file.

The best place to store your Terraform state is on remote cloud storage. Terraform provides a remote backend to store state remotely. There are multiple types of remote backends you can use. At the time of writing this book, you have the following options – Artifactory, Azure store, Consul, `cos`, `etcd`, `etcdv3`, `gcs`, `http`, Kubernetes, Manta, `oss`, `pg`, S3, Swift, Terraform Cloud, and Terraform Enterprise.

> **Tip:**
> While choosing the `state` storage solution, you should prefer storage with
> state locking in place. That will allow multiple people to manipulate the
> resources without stepping on each other's shoes and causing conflict, as once a
> state file is locked, others cannot acquire it until the lock is released.

As we're using Azure, we can use Azure Storage to store our state. The advantages are
three-fold:

- Your state file is centralized. You can have multiple admins working together and
  managing the same infrastructure.

- The store is encrypted at rest.

- You get automatic backup and redundancy, and high availability.

To access the resources for this section, `cd` into the following:

```
$ cd ~/modern-devops/ch6/terraform-exercise/
```

Let's now use the `azurerm` backend and use the Azure Storage to persist our Terraform
state.

Using the Azure Storage backend

As we will end up in a chicken-or-egg situation if we use Terraform to build a backend to
store its state, we will have to configure this bit without using Terraform.

Therefore, let's use the `az` command to configure the storage account in a different
resource group that Terraform will not manage.

Creating Azure Storage resources

Let's start by defining a few variables:

```
$ RESOURCE_GROUP=tfstate
$ STORAGE_ACCOUNT_NAME=tfstate$RANDOM
$ CONTAINER_NAME=tfstate
```

Create a resource group first using the following command:

```
$ az group create --name $RESOURCE_GROUP --location westeurope
```

Now, let's go ahead and create a storage account within the resource group using the following command:

```
$ az storage account create --resource-group $RESOURCE_GROUP \
--name $STORAGE_ACCOUNT_NAME --sku Standard_LRS \
--encryption-services BLOB
```

The next step is to fetch the account key using the following command:

```
$ ACCOUNT_KEY=$(az storage account keys list \
--resource-group tfstate --account-name $STORAGE_ACCOUNT_NAME \
--query '[0].value' -o tsv)
```

Now, we can go ahead and create a Blob Storage container using the following command:

```
$ az storage container create --name $CONTAINER_NAME \
--account-name $STORAGE_ACCOUNT_NAME --account-key $ACCOUNT_KEY
```

And if we receive a `created` response, the storage account is created and ready for use.

Now, we can go and define the backend configuration file in Terraform.

Creating a backend configuration in Terraform

Before we create the backend, we will need the STORAGE_ACCOUNT_NAME value. To get this, run the following command:

```
$ echo $STORAGE_ACCOUNT_NAME
tfstate15153
```

To create the backend configuration in Terraform, create a file called `backend.tf` within the workspace:

```
terraform {
  backend "azurerm" {
    resource_group_name   = "tfstate"
    storage_account_name  = "tfstate15153"
    container_name        = "tfstate"
    key                   = "example.tfstate"
  }
}
```

In the backend configuration, we've defined the backend `resource_group_name` where the Blob Storage instance exists, `storage_account_name`, `container_name`, and `key`. The `key` attribute specifies the filename that we will use to define the state of this configuration. There might be multiple projects that you are managing using Terraform, and all of them will need separate state files. Therefore, the `key` attribute defines the state file's name that we will use for our project. That allows multiple Terraform projects to use the same Azure Blob Storage to store the state.

> **Tip:**
> Always use the name of the project as the name of the key. For example, if your project name is `foo`, name the key `foo.tfstate`. That will prevent potential conflicts with others and also allow you to locate your state file quickly.

To initialize the Terraform workspace with the new backend configuration, run the following command:

```
$ terraform init
Initializing the backend...
Backend configuration changed!
Terraform has detected that the configuration specified for
the backend has changed. Terraform will now check for existing
state in the backends.
Successfully configured the backend "azurerm"! Terraform will
automatically use this backend unless the backend configuration
changes.
...
```

And when we initialize that, Terraform detects that the backend has changed and checks whether anything is available in the existing backend. If it finds something, it asks whether we want to migrate the current state to the new backend. If it does not, then it automatically switches to the new backend, as we see here.

Now, let's go ahead and use the `terraform plan` command to run a plan:

```
$ terraform plan
Acquiring state lock. This may take a few moments...
Terraform will perform the following actions:
  # azurerm_resource_group.rg will be created
  + resource "azurerm_resource_group" "rg" {
    ...
```

```
    }
Plan: 1 to add, 0 to change, 0 to destroy.
----------------------------------------------------------------
Releasing state lock. This may take a few moments...
```

So as we see, `terraform plan` tells us that it will create a new resource group called `terraform-exercise`. Let's apply the configuration, and this time with an `auto-approve` flag so that the plan does not run again, and Terraform immediately applies the changes using the following command:

```
$ terraform apply -auto-approve
Acquiring state lock. This may take a few moments...
azurerm_resource_group.rg: Creating...
azurerm_resource_group.rg: Creation complete after 2s [id=/
subscriptions/<SUBSCRIPTION_ID>/resourceGroups/terraform-
exercise]

Apply complete! Resources: 1 added, 0 changed, 0 destroyed.
Releasing state lock. This may take a few moments...
```

And we have now the resource created successfully.

Now, let's go to Azure Blob Storage and see whether we have a `tfstate` file there:

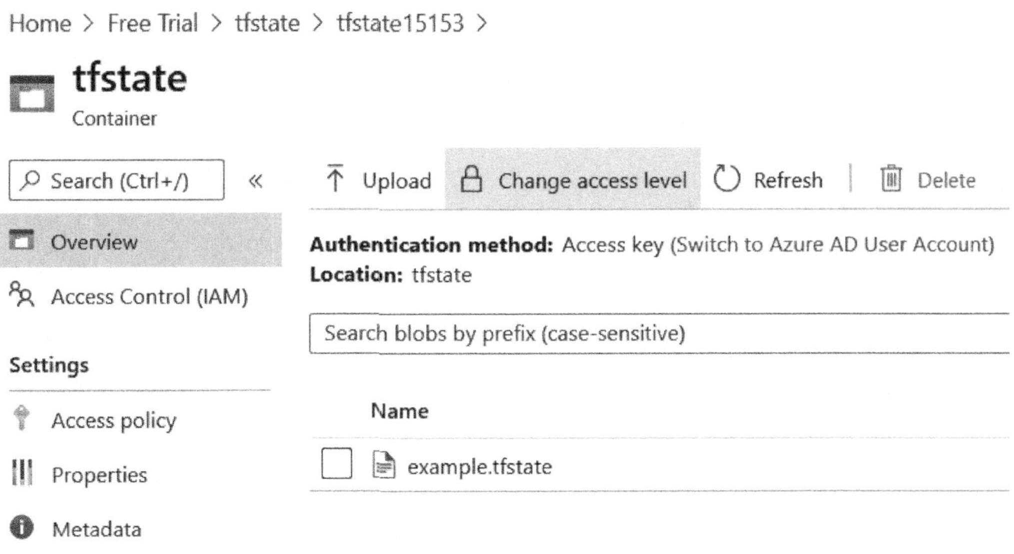

Figure 6.2 – Terraform state

And as we see, we have a file called `example.tfstate` within the blob container. That is how remote storage works, and now anyone who has access to the Blob Storage instance can use the Terraform configuration and make changes.

So far, we've been managing resources using the default workspace, but what if there are multiple environments that you need to control using the same configuration? Well, Terraform offers workspaces for those scenarios.

Terraform workspaces

Software development requires multiple environments. You develop software within your workspace, deploy it into the development environment, unit test it, and then promote the tested code to a test environment. Your QA team will test the code extensively in the test environment, and once all test cases pass, you can promote your code to production.

Well, that means you need to maintain a similar infrastructure in all environments. With an IaC tool such as Terraform, infrastructure is represented as code, and we have to manage our code to fit multiple environments. But Terraform is not just code, it also contains state files, and we have to maintain state files for every environment.

Let's suppose you need to create three resource groups, `terraform-exercise-dev`, `terraform-exercise-test`, and `terraform-exercise-prod`. Each resource group will contain a similar set of infrastructure with similar properties. For example, let's say each resource group includes an Ubuntu **virtual machine** (**VM**).

A simple method to approach the problem is by creating a structure like the following:

```
├── dev
│   ├── backend.tf
│   ├── main.tf
│   ├── terraform.tfvars
│   └── vars.tf
├── prod
│   ├── backend.tf
│   ├── main.tf
│   ├── terraform.tfvars
│   └── vars.tf
└── test
    ├── backend.tf
    ├── main.tf
    ├── terraform.tfvars
    └── vars.tf
```

Can you see the duplication? The same files are occurring multiple times, and all of them contain the same configuration. The only thing that might change is the `terraform.tfvars` file for each environment.

So, this does not sound like a great way to approach this problem, and that's why Terraform provides workspaces for it.

Terraform workspaces are nothing but independent state files. So, you have a single configuration and multiple state files for each environment. Sounds simple, right? Let's have a look.

Another way to represent the same configuration by using Terraform workspaces is the following:

```
├── backend.tf
├── main.tf
├── terraform.tfvars
└── vars.tf
```

Now, this looks simple. We just contain a single set of files. Let's have a look at each of them to understand better.

To access the resources for this section, `cd` into the following:

```
$ cd ~/modern-devops/ch6/terraform-workspaces/
```

The `main.tf` file contains a `resource_group` resource with a name that includes an environment suffix, along with other resources that we need to create within the resource group such as vnet, subnet, and virtual machine, something like the following:

```
...
resource "azurerm_resource_group" "main" {
  name     = "${var.rg_prefix}-${var.env}"
  location = var.rg_location
}
...
```

We have declared the env variable in the `vars.tf` file as follows:

```
...
variable "env" {
  type        = string
  description = "env: dev, test, or prod"
}
...
```

So, the template is now ready to take configuration for any environment, and we will have a separate resource group for each environment.

Now let's initialize the Terraform workspace by using the following command:

```
$ terraform init
```

Now, once Terraform has initialized, let's create a dev workspace by using the following command:

```
$ terraform workspace new dev
Created and switched to workspace "dev"!
You're now on a new, empty workspace. Workspaces isolate heir
state, so if you run "terraform plan" Terraform will not see
any existing state for this configuration.
```

So, as we're in a new empty workspace called dev, let's run a plan. We need to pass the value for the env variable while running the plan as we haven't declared it in the tfvars file.

Use the following command to run a plan on the dev environment:

```
$ terraform plan -var env=dev -out dev.tfplan
Acquiring state lock. This may take a few moments...
An execution plan has been generated and is shown below.
Resource actions are indicated with the following symbols:
  + create

Terraform will perform the following actions:

  # azurerm_network_interface.main will be created
  + resource "azurerm_network_interface" "main" {
      ...
    }

  # azurerm_resource_group.main will be created
  + resource "azurerm_resource_group" "main" {
      + id       = (known after apply)
      + location = "westeurope"
      + name     = "terraform-ws-dev"
    }

  # azurerm_subnet.internal will be created
  + resource "azurerm_subnet" "internal" {
      ...
```

```
      }

  # azurerm_virtual_machine.main will be created
  + resource "azurerm_virtual_machine" "main" {
      ...
  }

  # azurerm_virtual_network.main will be created
  + resource "azurerm_virtual_network" "main" {
      ...
      }
Plan: 5 to add, 0 to change, 0 to destroy.
------------------------------------------------------------------
This plan was saved to: dev.tfplan
To perform exactly these actions, run the following command to
apply: terraform apply "dev.tfplan"
Releasing state lock. This may take a few moments...
```

Now, let's go ahead and apply the plan using the following command:

```
$ terraform apply "dev.tfplan"
Acquiring state lock. This may take a few moments...
azurerm_resource_group.main: Creating...
...
azurerm_virtual_network.main: Creating...
...
azurerm_subnet.internal: Creating...
...
azurerm_network_interface.main: Creating...
...
azurerm_virtual_machine.main: Creating...
...
Apply complete! Resources: 5 added, 0 changed, 0 destroyed.
Releasing state lock. This may take a few moments...
```

As the dev plan has been applied and the resources are created in the dev resource group, let's create a workspace for testing:

```
$ terraform workspace new test
```

As the new workspace is created, let's run a plan on the test workspace with `env=test` using the following command and save it to the `test.tfplan` file:

```
$ terraform plan -var env=test -out test.tfplan
...
# azurerm_resource_group.main will be created
 + resource "azurerm_resource_group" "main" {
     + id       = (known after apply)
     + location = "westeurope"
     + name     = "terraform-ws-test"
   }
...
```

As we can see, the resources will be created in the `terraform-ws-test` resource group. So, let's go ahead and apply the plan using the following command:

```
$ terraform apply test.tfplan
```

And the `test` plan has been applied as well. Now let's go ahead and inspect the created resources.

Inspecting resources

Let's use the `az` command to list the resource groups. As we know, our resource groups have a resource group prefix of `terraform-ws`. Therefore, use the following command to list all resource groups containing the prefix:

```
$ az group list|grep name|grep terraform-ws
    "name": "terraform-ws-dev",
    "name": "terraform-ws-test",
```

As we can see, we have two resource groups, `terraform-ws-dev` and `terraform-ws-test`. So, two resource groups have been created successfully.

You can also verify this in the Azure portal:

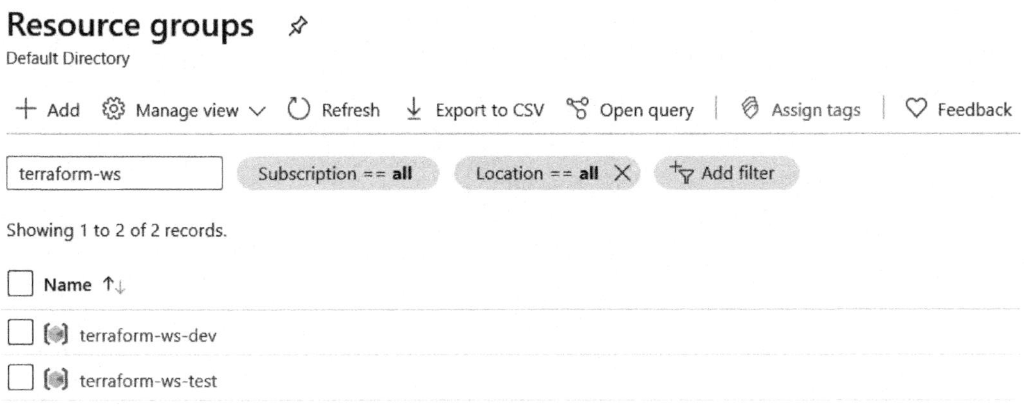

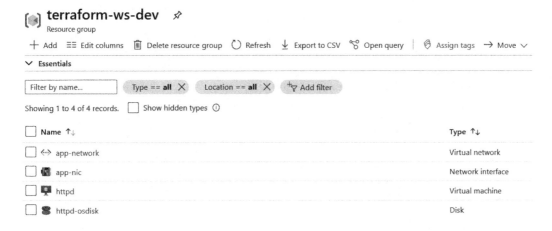

Figure 6.3 – Resource groups

Now, let's go ahead and inspect the resources on the `terraform-ws-dev` resource group using the Azure portal by clicking on `terraform-ws-dev`:

Figure 6.4 – Terraform dev resource group

As we see, we have a virtual network, a network interface, an OS disk, and a Virtual Machine within the resource group. We should expect similar resources with the same names in the `terraform-ws-test` resource group. Let's go ahead and have a look:

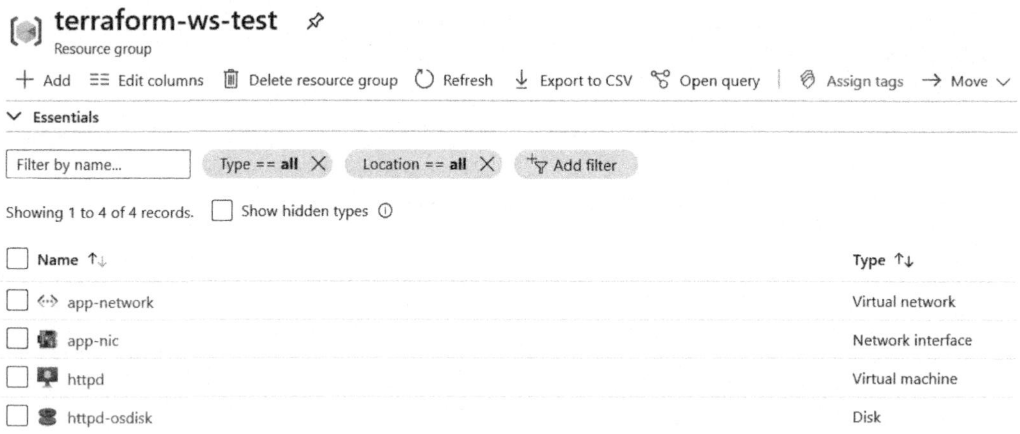

Figure 6.5 – Terraform test resource group

And as we can see, we have similar resources in the `terraform-ws-test` resource groups as well.

We did all of this using a single configuration, but there should be two state files for each workspace since they are two sets of resources. Let's have a look.

Inspecting state files

If we had used the local backend for the state files, we would have got the following structure:

```
|-- terraform.tfstate.d
|   |-- dev
|   |    `-- terraform.tfstate
|   `-- test
|        `-- terraform.tfstate
```

So, Terraform creates a directory called `terrafom.tfstate.d`, and within that, it creates directories for each workspace. Within the directories, it stores the state file for each workspace as `terraform.tfstate`.

But since we are using a remote backend and using Azure Blob Storage for it, let's inspect the files within it using the Azure console:

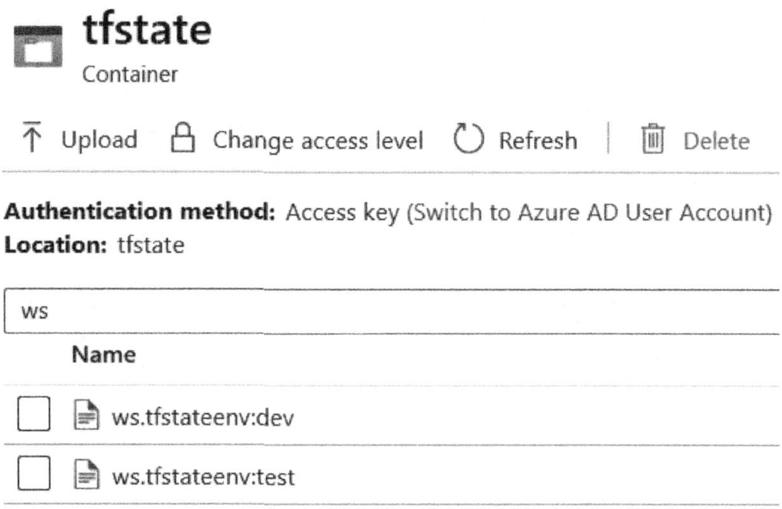

tfstate
Container

↑ Upload   🔒 Change access level   ○ Refresh | 🗑 Delete

Authentication method: Access key (Switch to Azure AD User Account)
Location: tfstate

ws

	Name
☐ 📄	ws.tfstateenv:dev
☐ 📄	ws.tfstateenv:test

Figure 6.6 – Terraform workspaces state

And as we see, there are two state files, one for each environment. Therefore, the state files are suffixed with an env:dev or env:test string. That is how workspaces are managed in Azure Blob Storage. The remote backend's structure for maintaining state files depends on the provider plugins, and therefore there might be different ways of managing multiple states for various backends. However, the Terraform CLI will interpret workspaces the same way irrespective of the backends, so nothing changes for the end user from a CLI perspective.

Cleaning up

Now let's go ahead and clean up both resource groups to avoid unnecessary charges.

As we're already within the test workspace, let's run the following command to destroy resources within the test workspace:

```
$ terraform destroy -auto-approve -var env=test
```

Now, let's switch to the dev workspace using the following command:

```
$ terraform workspace select dev
Switched to workspace "dev".
```

As we're within the `dev` workspace, use the following command to destroy all resources within the `dev` workspace:

```
$ terraform destroy -auto-approve -var env=dev
```

And in a while, we should see that both resource groups are gone. Now, let's look at some of the advanced concepts of Terraform in the next section.

Terraform output, state, console, and graphs

While we understand that Terraform uses state files to manage resources, let's look at some advanced commands that will help us appreciate and make more sense of the Terraform state concept.

To access the resources for this section, `cd` into the following:

```
$ cd ~/modern-devops/ch6/terraform-workspaces/
```

Now, let's go ahead and look at our first command – `terraform output`.

terraform output

So far, we've looked at variables, but we haven't yet discussed outputs. Terraform outputs are return values of a Terraform configuration that allow users to export configuration to users or any modules that might use the current module. We won't be creating modules in this book, however, to learn more about it, refer the official documentation at `https://learn.hashicorp.com/tutorials/terraform/module`.

For now, let's go with the last example and add an output variable that exports the private IP of the network interface attached to the Virtual Machine in the `outputs.tf` file:

```
output "vm_ip_addr" {
  value = azurerm_network_interface.main.private_ip_address
}
```

Now, let's go ahead and apply the configuration:

```
$ terraform apply -auto-approve -var env=dev
...
Outputs:
vm_ip_addr = "10.0.2.4"
```

After Terraform has applied the configuration, it shows the outputs at the end of the console result. You can run the following to inspect the output anytime later:

```
$ terraform output
vm_ip_addr = "10.0.2.4"
```

Outputs are stored in the state file like everything else, so let's look at how we can manage Terraform state using the CLI.

Managing Terraform state

Terraform stores the configuration it manages in state files, and therefore it provides a command for advanced state management. The `terraform state` commands help you manage the state of the current configuration. While the state file is plaintext and you can manually modify it, using the `terraform state` command is the recommended approach for managing it.

But before we get into details, we need to understand why we would want to do that. Things might not always go according to plan, and therefore the state file may have corrupt data. You also might want to see specific attributes of a particular resource after you've applied it. There might be a need to investigate the state file for the root cause analysis of a specific infrastructure provisioning problem. Let's have a look at the most common use cases.

Viewing the current state

To view the current state, we can simply run the following command:

```
$ terraform show
```

That will output all resources that Terraform has created and is currently managing, including outputs. Of course, this can be overwhelming for some, and we may want to view the list of resources managed by Terraform.

Listing resources in the current state

To list the resources in the Terraform state file, run the following command:

```
$ terraform state list
azurerm_network_interface.main
azurerm_resource_group.main
azurerm_subnet.internal
azurerm_virtual_machine.main
azurerm_virtual_network.main
```

And as we see, there are five resources managed by Terraform. You might want to remove a resource from the Terraform state. It might be possible that someone has removed a resource manually as it is no longer required, but it isn't removed from the Terraform configuration.

Removing a resource from the state

To remove a state manually from the Terraform state file, run the following command:

```
$ terraform state rm azurerm_virtual_machine.main
Acquiring state lock. This may take a few moments...
Removed azurerm_virtual_machine.main
Successfully removed 1 resource instance(s).
Releasing state lock. This may take a few moments...
```

Bear in mind that this has merely removed the resource from the state file and has not touched the actual resource sitting on Azure. There might be instances where someone spun up a virtual machine manually within Azure, and we now want Terraform to manage it. This kind of situation happens mostly in brownfield projects. We have to declare the same configuration within Terraform and then import existing resources in the Terraform state. To do so, we can use the terraform import command.

Importing existing resources into Terraform state

To import existing resources into Terraform state, you can use the terraform import command. The terraform import command is structured as follows:

```
terraform import <resource> <resource_id>
```

For example, to reimport the `httpd` virtual machine into the state, run the following command:

```
$ terraform import -var env=dev azurerm_virtual_machine.\
main "/subscriptions/<SUBSCRIPTION_ID>/resourceGroups\
/terraform-ws-dev/providers/Microsoft.Compute/\
virtualMachines/httpd"
azurerm_virtual_machine.main: Importing from ID "/
subscriptions/<SUBSCRIPTION_ID>/resourceGroups/terraform-ws-
dev/providers/Microsoft.Compute/virtualMachines/httpd"...
azurerm_virtual_machine.main: Import prepared!
  Prepared azurerm_virtual_machine for import
azurerm_virtual_machine.main: Refreshing state... [id=/
subscriptions/<SUBSCRIPTION_ID>/resourceGroups/terraform-ws-
dev/providers/Microsoft.Compute/virtualMachines/httpd]
Import successful!
The resources that were imported are shown above. These
resources are now in your Terraform state and will henceforth
be managed by Terraform.
Releasing state lock. This may take a few moments...
```

To check whether the resource is imported to the state, we can list the resources again using the following command:

```
$ terraform state list
azurerm_network_interface.main
azurerm_resource_group.main
azurerm_subnet.internal
azurerm_virtual_machine.main
azurerm_virtual_network.main
```

And as we see, we have the virtual machine within the state file. If we want to dig down further into the resources, we can use `terraform console`.

terraform console

The `terraform console` command provides an interactive console that we can use to investigate state files, build paths dynamically, and evaluate expressions even before using them in resources. It is a potent tool that is used by most advanced Terraform users. For example, let's launch the console and look through the configuration of the virtual machine resource we just imported.

Use the following commands to launch the console and get the resource group of the virtual machine and the `id` value:

```
$ terraform console
Acquiring state lock. This may take a few moments...
> azurerm_virtual_machine.main.resource_group_name
"terraform-ws-dev"
> azurerm_virtual_machine.main.id
"/subscriptions/<SUBSCRIPTION_ID>/resourceGroups/terraform-ws-
dev/providers/Microsoft.Compute/virtualMachines/httpd"
> exit
Releasing state lock. This may take a few moments...
```

And as we can see, the virtual machine is in the correct resource group, and we're satisfied that the import was correct.

Terraform dependencies and graph

Terraform uses a dependency model so that it can manage in what order resources are created and destroyed. There are two kinds of dependencies – *implicit* and *explicit*. We've been using implicit dependencies until now, where the virtual machine depended upon the network interface, and the network interface depended upon the subnet. The subnet depended upon the virtual network, and all of these resources depended on the resource group. These dependencies naturally occur when we use the output of one resource as the input of another.

However, sometimes we might want to define an explicit dependency on a resource, especially when there is no way to define an implicit dependency on them. You can use the `depends_on` attribute for that kind of operation.

> Tip:
> Avoid explicit dependencies unless they are needed, as Terraform uses parallelism to manage resources. If there are explicit dependencies that are not required, it will slow down Terraform runs because it can process multiple parallel resources.

To visualize the dependencies between resources, we can export a graph from the state file and convert that into a PNG file using a tool such as **Graphviz**.

Run the following command to export the dependency graph:

```
$ terraform graph > vm.dot
```

We can then process the graphfile using the Graphviz tool. To install the tool on Ubuntu, run the following command:

```
$ sudo apt install graphviz -y
```

Now run the following command to convert the graphfile to a PNG file:

```
$ cat vm.dot | dot -T png -o vm.png
```

The graph is available on https://github.com/PacktPublishing/Modern-DevOps-Practices/blob/main/ch6/terraform-graph.png. Now, let's go ahead and see how we can clean up our resources.

Cleaning up resources

Removing resources that are managed by Terraform is easy. Use the following command to clean up the resources:

```
$ terraform destroy -var env=dev -auto-approve
```

It will clear resources from the resource group and delete the resource group after that.

While using terraform destroy can be an easy way to get rid of resources you don't need, it is best if you stick to this only in the dev environment and never use it in production. Instead, you can manage by removing resources that you don't need from the configuration itself.

Summary

In this chapter, we've discussed Terraform's core and understood some of the most common commands and functionalities from a hands-on perspective. We started with understanding IaC, introduced Terraform as an IaC tool, installed Terraform, understood Terraform providers, and used the Azure Terraform provider to manage infrastructure in Azure.

We then looked at Terraform variables and multiple ways of supplying values to the variables. We discussed the core Terraform workflow, where we talked about several commands that you would use to manage infrastructure using Terraform. We then looked at Terraform state as an essential component that helps Terraform keep track of the infrastructure it is managing.

We looked at local and remote state storage and used Azure Blob Storage as the remote state backend. We then discussed Terraform workspaces and how they enable us to use the same Terraform configuration to build multiple environments with hands-on exercises.

We then looked at some advanced operations with Terraform state using outputs, states, and the console. We finally looked at how Terraform manages dependencies and viewed a dependency graph using the `graph` command.

In the next chapter, we will delve into configuration management using Ansible.

Questions

1. Why should we constrain the provider version?

2. You should always use the `fmt` and `validate` functions before a Terraform plan – True/False?

3. What does the Terraform `plan` command do? (Multiple answers are possible.)

    A. Refreshes the current state with the existing infrastructure state

    B. Gets the delta between the current configuration and the expected configuration

    C. Applies the configuration to the cloud

    D. Destroys the configuration in the cloud

4. What does the `terraform apply` command do? (Multiple answers are possible.)

    A. Refreshes the current state with the existing infrastructure

    B. Gets the delta between the current configuration and the expected configuration

    C. Applies the configuration to the cloud

    D. Destroys the configuration in the cloud

5. Why should you never store state files in source control? (Multiple answers are possible.)

    A. State files are plaintext, and therefore you expose sensitive information to unprivileged users.

B. Source control does not support state locking, and therefore they might result in potential conflicts between users.

C. Multiple admins cannot work on the same configuration.

6. Which of the following are valid Terraform remote backends? (Multiple answers are possible.)

   A. S3

   B. Azure Blob Storage

   C. Artifactory

   D. Git

   E. HTTP

   F. Terraform Enterprise

7. Which command will mark a resource for recreation in the next `apply`?

8. Where are state files stored in the local backend if you use workspaces?

9. What command should we use to remove a Terraform resource from the state?

10. What command should we use to import an existing cloud resource within the state?

Answers

1. Because Terraform providers are released separately to the Terraform CLI, different versions might break the existing configuration

2. True

3. A, B

4. A, B, C

5. A, B

6. A, B, C, E, F

7. The taint command

8. `terraform.tfstate.d`

9. `terraform state rm <resource>`

10. `terraform import <resource> <id>`

7

Configuration Management with Ansible

In the last chapter, we looked at **Infrastructure as Code (IaC)** with Terraform, with its core concepts, IaC workflow, state, and debugging techniques. We will now delve into configuration management and **Configuration as Code (CaC)** with Ansible. Ansible is a configuration management tool that helps you to define configuration as idempotent chunks of code.

In this chapter, we're going to cover the following main topics:

- Introduction to config management
- Setting up Ansible
- Introduction to Ansible playbooks
- Ansible playbooks in action
- Designing for reusability

Technical requirements

For this chapter, you will need an active Azure subscription to follow the exercises. Currently, Azure is offering a free trial for 30 days with $200 worth of free credits, and you can sign up at `https://azure.microsoft.com/en-in/free`.

You will also need to clone the following GitHub repository for some of the exercises:

`https://github.com/PacktPublishing/Modern-DevOps-Practices`

Run the following command to clone the repository into your home directory, and `cd` into the `ch7` directory to access the required resources:

```
$ git clone https://github.com/PacktPublishing/Modern-DevOps-\
Practices.git modern-devops
$ cd modern-devops/ch7
```

You also need to install Terraform in your system. Refer to *Chapter 6, Infrastructure as Code (IaC) with Terraform*, for more details on how to install and set up Terraform.

Introduction to config management

Let's look at the traditional way of hosting and managing applications. We first create a virtual machine from physical infrastructure and then log in manually to virtual machines. We can then choose to either run a set of scripts or do the setup manually. At least that's what we are doing till now, even in this book.

There are a number of problems with this approach. Let's look at some of them:

- If we set up the server manually, the process is not repeatable. For example, if we need to build another server with a similar configuration, we will have to repeat the entire process.

- Even if we use scripts, the scripts themselves are not idempotent. This means they cannot identify the delta configuration and apply them only if it is needed.

- Typical production environments consist of a huge number of servers, and therefore setting everything up manually is a labor-intensive task and adds to the toil. Software engineers should focus on novel ways of automating the processes that cause toil.

- While you can store scripts within source control, they are *imperative*. We always encourage a *declarative* way of managing things.

Modern configuration management tools such as Ansible solve all these problems by providing the following:

- They manage configuration through a set of declarative code pieces.

- You can store the code in version control.

- You can apply the code to multiple servers from a single control node.

- As they are idempotent, they only apply the delta configuration.

- It is a repeatable process, and you can use variables and templates to apply the same configuration to multiple environments.

- They provide deployment orchestration and therefore are mostly used within CI/CD pipelines.

Although there are many tools available in the market that provide configuration management, such as **Ansible**, **Puppet**, **Chef**, and **Saltstack**, Ansible is the most popular and straightforward tool used for configuration management. It is more efficient, and because of its simplicity, it is less time-consuming than others.

It is an open source configuration management tool built using Python and currently owned by **RedHat**. It provides the following features:

- It helps you to automate routine tasks such as OS upgrades and patches, creating backups, while also creating all OS-level configurations such as users, groups, permissions, and others.

- The configuration is written using simple YAML syntax.

- It uses **Secure Shell** (**SSH**) to communicate with managed nodes and sends commands via it.

- The commands are executed sequentially within each node in an idempotent manner.

- It connects to the nodes parallelly to save time.

Ansible has a simple architecture. It has a control node that takes care of managing multiple managed nodes. All you need is a control node server to install Ansible and the nodes to manage using the control node (also known as managed nodes). The managed nodes should allow an SSH connection from the Ansible control node, something like the following diagram:

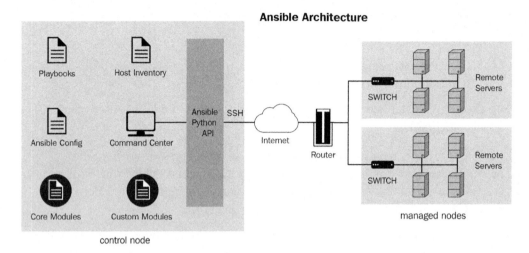

Figure 7.1 – Ansible Architecture

Now let's go ahead and see how we can install and set up the required configuration using Ansible. Let's look at how to install Ansible in the next section.

Setting up Ansible

We need to set up and install Ansible in the control node, but before we do that, we will have to spin three servers to start the activity – an Ansible control node and two managed nodes.

Setting up inventory

The idea is to set up a two-tier architecture with **Apache** and **MySQL**. So let's use Terraform to spin up the three servers.

Let's first cd into the directory where the Terraform templates are located, and then edit the terraform.tfvars file to fill in the required details. (Please refer to *Chapter 6, Infrastructure as Code (IaC) with Terraform*, for more details about how to get the attributes):

```
$ cd ~/modern-devops/ch7/setup-ansible-terraform
$ vim terraform.tfvars
```

Then, use the following commands to spin up the servers using Terraform:

```
$ terraform init
$ terraform plan -out ansible.tfplan
$ terraform apply ansible.tfplan
```

Once we have the `terraform apply` command completed successfully, we will see three servers – `ansible-control-node`, `web`, and `db`, and the associated resources created within the `ansible-exercise` resource group.

The `terraform apply` output also provides the public IP addresses of the Ansible control node and the `web` virtual machine. You should see the public IP address we got in the output.

> **Note**
>
> It might take a while for Azure to report the output, and if you did not get the IP addresses during `apply`, you could subsequently run `terraform output` to get the details.

So, let's use an `ssh` client to log in to `ansible-control-node` using the IP address we got in the last step. We will use the username and password we configured in the `terraform.tfvars` file:

```
$ ssh ssh_admin@104.46.61.213
```

Now, as we've logged in to the `control` node, let's go and install Ansible in it.

Installing Ansible in the control node

Now, as we're within the Ansible control node, we need to set it up. Ansible requires a Linux/UNIX machine (preferably), and you should have Python **2.x** or **3.x** installed.

As the Ansible control node uses Ubuntu, Ansible provides a PPA repository that we can configure to download and install Ansible using `apt` commands.

Use the following commands to install Ansible on the server:

```
$ sudo apt update
$ sudo apt install software-properties-common -y
$ sudo apt-add-repository --yes --update ppa:ansible/ansible
$ sudo apt install ansible -y
```

To check whether Ansible has been installed successfully, run the following command:

```
$ ansible --version
ansible 2.9.16
```

And, as we see, `ansible 2.9.16` is successfully installed on your control node. Now let's move on and look at whether we can communicate with our managed nodes (also known as inventory servers).

Connecting the Ansible control node with inventory servers

We'll create an Ansible user called `ansible` and set up passwordless `ssh` to connect to the inventory servers from the Ansible control node.

Run the following commands within your control node to create an `ansible` user, add the user to the sudoers list, and generate an `ssh` key pair for passwordless authentication:

```
$ sudo su - root
$ useradd -m ansible
$ echo 'ansible ALL=(ALL) NOPASSWD:ALL' >> /etc/sudoers
$ sudo su - ansible
$ ssh-keygen -t rsa -N "" -f ~/.ssh/id_rsa
```

Once the key is generated, print the public key using the following command to configure them to the web and db servers:

```
$ cat ~/.ssh/id_rsa.pub
```

Now, exit `ansible` and the root shell sessions and, using the shell session of the user we defined in the Terraform template, `ssh` into the web server:

```
$ ssh web
```

Enter the password, and you should land on the web server. Repeat the same steps that we did for the control node using the following commands:

```
$ sudo su - root
$ useradd -m ansible
$ echo 'ansible ALL=(ALL) NOPASSWD:ALL' >> /etc/sudoers
$ sudo su - ansible
$ ssh-keygen -t rsa -N "" -f ~/.ssh/id_rsa
```

Additionally, we will also have to add the public key of our control node to the `authorized_keys` file of the `ansible` user. That will allow passwordless connectivity from the control node to the `web` server using the `ansible` user. Use the following command to do so:

```
$ vim ~/.ssh/authorized_keys
```

Add the contents of the `id_rsa.pub` file that we had printed when we were in the control node to the file and then save and exit.

The next step would be to assign proper permissions to the `authorized_keys` file using the following command:

```
$ sudo chmod 600 /home/ansible/.ssh/authorized_keys
```

And once we are done, we will exit from the prompts until we reach the control node.

Once you are in the control node server, switch the user to `ansible` and try doing an `ssh` to the `web` server using the following commands:

```
$ sudo su - ansible
$ ssh web
```

And if you land on the `web` server, passwordless authentication is working correctly.

Repeat the same steps to set up the `db` server as well.

Ansible uses an inventory file to manage nodes, and therefore the next step is to set up an inventory file.

Setting up an inventory file

An inventory file within Ansible is a file that allows you to group your managed nodes according to roles. For example, you can define roles such as `webserver` and `dbserver` and group related servers together. You can use IP addresses, hostnames, or aliases for that.

> **Tip**
> Always use aliases as they provide some room for IP address and hostname changes.

You can run Ansible commands on hosts or a group of hosts using the role tagged to them. There is no limit to servers that can have a particular role. If your server uses a non-standard SSH port, you can use that port within the inventory file.

The default location of the Ansible inventory file is /etc/ansible/hosts. If you look at the /etc/ansible directory ownership, it is owned by the root user. We want to use the ansible user that we created for security purposes. Therefore, we have to change the /etc/ansible directory ownership and its subdirectories and files to ansible. Use the following command to do so:

```
$ sudo chown -R ansible:ansible /etc/ansible
```

We can then switch user to ansible and clone the Git repository that contains the required files into the control server using the following commands:

```
$ sudo su - ansible
$ git clone https://github.com/PacktPublishing/Modern-DevOps-\
Practices.git modern-devops
$ cd ~/modern-devops/ch7/ansible-exercise
```

In our scenario, we have a web server called web, and a dbserver called db. Therefore, if you check the hosts file called hosts within the repository, you will see the following:

```
[webservers]
web ansible_host=web
[dbservers]
db ansible_host=db
[all:vars]
ansible_python_interpreter=/usr/bin/python3
```

The [all:vars] section has a provision for variables that will apply to all groups. Here, we're explicitly defining ansible_python_interpreter to python3 so that Ansible uses python3 instead of python2. As we're using Ubuntu, python3 comes installed as default, and python2 is deprecated.

We also see that instead of using web directly, we've specified an ansible_host section. That defines web as an alias that is pointing to a host with the hostname web. You can also use the IP address instead of the hostname if required.

> **Tip**
>
> Always group the inventory according to the function performed. That helps us to apply a similar configuration to a large number of machines with a similar role.

As we want to keep the configuration with code, we would wish to stay within the Git repository itself. So, we need to tell Ansible that the inventory file is located in a non-standard location. To do so, we will create an Ansible configuration file.

Setting up the Ansible configuration file

The Ansible configuration file defines global properties that are specific to our setup. The following are the ways in which you can specify the Ansible configuration file, and the first method overrides the next. The settings are not merged, so keep that in mind:

- By setting an environment variable, `ANSIBLE_CONFIG`, pointing to the Ansible configuration file
- By creating an `ansible.cfg` file in the current directory
- By creating an `ansible.cfg` file in the home directory of the current user
- By creating an `ansible.cfg` file in the `/etc/ansible` directory.

> **Tip**
>
> If you manage multiple applications, with each application in its Git repositories, having a local `ansible.cfg` file in every repository will help keep the applications decentralized. It will also enable GitOps and make Git the single source of truth.

So, if you check the `ansible.cfg` file in the current directory, you will see the following:

```
[defaults]
inventory = ./hosts
host_key_checking = False
```

Now, to check whether our `inventory` file is correct, let's list our inventory by using the following command:

```
$ ansible-inventory --list -y
all:
  children:
```

```
      dbservers:
        hosts:
          db:
            ansible_host: db
            ansible_python_interpreter: /usr/bin/python3
      ungrouped: {}
      webservers:
        hosts:
          web:
            ansible_host: web
            ansible_python_interpreter: /usr/bin/python3
```

And we see that there are two groups, dbservers containing db, and webservers containing web, each using python3 as the ansible_python_interpreter.

If we want to see all the hosts, you can use the following command:

```
$ ansible --list-hosts all
  hosts (2):
    web
    db
```

If we want to list all hosts that have the webservers role, use the following command:

```
$ ansible --list-hosts webservers
  hosts (1):
    web
```

Now, let's check whether Ansible can connect to these servers by using the following command:

```
$ ansible all -m ping
web | SUCCESS => {
    "changed": false,
    "ping": "pong"
}
db | SUCCESS => {
    "changed": false,
    "ping": "pong"
}
```

And as we can observe, we get a successful response for both servers. So, we're all set up, and we can start defining the infrastructure. Ansible offers tasks and modules to provide configuration management. Let's look at these in the next section.

Ansible tasks and modules

Ansible tasks form the basic building block of running Ansible commands. Ansible tasks are structured in the following format:

```
$ ansible <options> <inventory>
```

Ansible modules are a reusable unit of code that does a particular thing very well, such as running a shell command, and creating and managing users. You can use Ansible modules with Ansible tasks to manage the configuration within the managed nodes. For example, the following command will run the uname command on each server we are managing:

```
$ ansible -m shell -a "uname" all
db | CHANGED | rc=0 >>
Linux
web | CHANGED | rc=0 >>
Linux
```

So we get a reply from the db server and the web server, each providing a return code, 0, and an output, Linux. If you look at the command, you will see that we have provided the following flags:

- -m: The name of the module (shell module here)

- -a: The parameters to the module (uname in this case)

The command finally ends with where we want to run this task. Since we've specified all, it runs the task on all servers. We can pick and choose to run this on a single server, a set of servers, a role, or multiple roles, or use a wildcard to select the combination we want.

The tasks have three possible statuses – SUCCESS, CHANGED, and FAILURE. The SUCCESS status denotes that the task was successful, and Ansible took no action. The CHANGED status denotes that Ansible had to change the existing configuration to apply the expected configuration, and FAILURE denotes an error while executing the task.

Ansible modules are reusable scripts that we can use to define configuration within servers. Each module targets a particular aspect of configuration management. Modules are used in both Ansible tasks and playbooks. There are a large number of modules available for consumption, and they are available at `https://docs.ansible.com/ansible/2.9/modules/modules_by_category.html`. You can pick and choose modules according to your requirement and use cases.

> **Tip**
>
> As Ansible is idempotent, always use modules specific to your task and avoid using command and shell modules. For example, use the `apt` module to install a package instead of using the command module to run `apt install <package> -y`. If your playbook starts to look like code, then you're doing something fundamentally wrong.

Now, tasks on their own do not make sense when we have a series of steps that we need to follow while setting up a server. Therefore, Ansible provides *playbooks* for this activity. Let's have a look in the next section.

Introduction to Ansible playbooks

Ansible playbooks are a collection of Ansible tasks to produce the desired configuration within target managed nodes. They have the following features:

- They help in managing configuration within multiple remote servers using declarative steps.
- They use a sequential list of idempotent steps and steps that match the expected configuration are not applied again.
- The tasks within the playbook can be synchronous and asynchronous.
- They enable GitOps by allowing the steps to be stored using a simple YAML file to keep in source control, providing **configuration management as code (CaC)**.

Ansible playbooks consist of multiple plays, and each play is mapped to a group of hosts using a role and consists of a series of tasks required to achieve them, something like the following diagram:

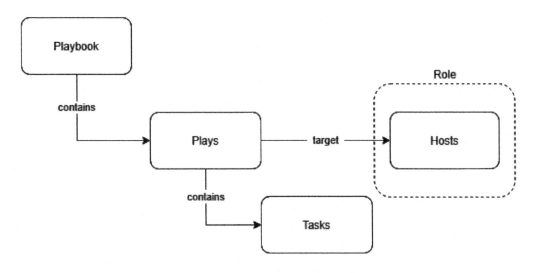

Figure 7.2 – Playbooks

The following is an example of a simple playbook that pings all servers.

Create a file called `ping.yaml` with the following content:

```
---
 - hosts: all
   tasks:
     - name: Ping all servers
       action: ping
```

The YAML file contains a list of plays, as evident by the list directive. Each play consists of a `hosts` attribute that defines the role where we want to apply the play. The `tasks` section consist of a list of tasks, each with a `name` and `action` attributes. In the preceding example, we have a single play with a single task that pings all servers.

Checking playbook syntax

It is a best practice to check the playbook syntax before applying it to your inventory. To check your playbook's syntax, run the following command:

```
$ ansible-playbook ping.yaml --syntax-check
playbook: ping.yaml
```

As we get the response with the playbook name, this means that the syntax is correct. Now let's go ahead and apply the playbook.

Applying the first playbook

To apply the playbook, run the following command:

```
$ ansible-playbook ping.yaml
PLAY [all] ***********************************************
TASK [Gathering Facts] ***********************************
ok: [db]
ok: [web]
TASK [Ping all servers] **********************************
ok: [web]
ok: [db]
PLAY RECAP ***********************************************
db  : ok=2     changed=0     unreachable=0     failed=0
skipped=0     rescued=0     ignored=0
web : ok=2     changed=0     unreachable=0     failed=0
skipped=0     rescued=0     ignored=0
```

There are three elements of play execution:

- **Gathering facts**: This is where Ansible checks for all hosts that are part of the role, logs into each instance, and gathers information from each host that it uses while executing the tasks from the plays.

- **Run tasks**: Then it runs the tasks of each play, as defined in the playbook.

- **Play recap**: Ansible then provides a recap of the tasks it executed and the hosts it ran that on. This includes a list of all successful and failure responses.

As we've looked into an elementary example on playbooks, we need to understand how to use Ansible playbooks effectively. Let's have a look at Ansible playbooks in action with a better example in the next section.

Ansible playbooks in action

Let's suppose you are creating an Apache server that serves a custom website. It also connects with a MySQL backend. In short, we are setting up a **Linux, Apache, MySQL, and PHP (LAMP)** stack using Ansible.

The following directory contains all resources for the exercises in this section:

```
$ cd ~/modern-devops/ch7/lamp-stack
```

We have created the following custom index.php page that tests the connection to the MySQL database and displays whether it can connect or not:

```
...
<?php
mysqli_connect('db', 'testuser', 'Password@1') or die('Could
not connect the database : Username or password incorrect');
echo 'Database Connected successfully';
?>
...
```

We create several Ansible playbooks according to the logical steps we follow with configuration management.

It is an excellent practice to update the packages and repositories at the start of every configuration. Therefore, we need to start our playbook with this step.

Updating packages and repositories

As we're using Ubuntu in this case, we can use the apt module to update the packages. We need to update packages and repositories to ensure that the latest package index is available with all our apt repositories. It will avoid any untoward issues while installing packages. The following playbook, apt-update.yaml, performs the update:

```
---
- hosts: webservers:dbservers
  become: true
  tasks:
    - name: Update apt packages
      apt: update_cache=yes cache_valid_time=3600
```

The YAML file begins with a list of plays, and contains a single play in this case. The hosts attribute defines a colon-separated list of roles/hosts inventory to apply to the playbook. In this case, we've specified that as webservers and dbservers. The become attribute specifies whether we want to execute the play as a root user. So, as we've set become to true, Ansible will perform all play tasks with sudo privileges. The play contains a single task – Update apt packages. The task uses the apt module and consists of update_cache=yes. It will run an apt update on all nodes with the webservers and dbservers roles. The next step is to install packages and services.

Installing application packages and services

To install the packages on Ubuntu, we will use the apt module, and we will use the service module to start and enable the service.

Let's start by installing Apache on the web servers by using the following install-webserver.yaml playbook:

```
---
- hosts: webservers
  become: true
  tasks:
    - name: Install packages
      apt:
        name:
        - apache2
        - php
        - libapache2-mod-php
        - php-mysql
        update_cache: yes
        cache_valid_time: 3600
        state: present
    - name: Start and Enable Apache service
      service: name=apache2 state=started enabled=yes
```

As this configuration is for `webservers`, we've specified that within the `hosts` attribute. The `tasks` section defines two tasks – `Install packages` and `Start and Enable Apache Service`. The `Install packages` task uses the apt module to install `apache2`, `php`, `libapache2-mod-php`, and `php-mysql`. The `Start and Enable Apache service` task will start and enable the `apache2` service.

Similarly, we will install and set up the MySQL service using the following `install-dbserver.yaml` playbook:

```
- hosts: dbservers
  become: true
  tasks:
  - name: Install packages
    apt:
      name:
      - python-pymysql
      - mysql-server
      update_cache: yes
      cache_valid_time: 3600
      state: present
  - name: Start and enable MySQL service
    service:
      name: mysql
      state: started
      enabled: true
```

This playbook will run two tasks – `Install packages` and the `Start and enable MySQL service`. The `Install packages` task will install the `python-mysql` and `mysql-server` packages using the apt module. The `start and enable MySQL service` task will start and enable the MySQL service.

Configuring applications

The next step in the chain is to configure the applications. There are two playbooks for this. The first will configure Apache on `webservers`, and the second will configure MySQL on `dbservers`.

The following `setup-webservers.yaml` playbook will configure `webservers`:

```yaml
---
- hosts: webservers
  become: true
  tasks:
  - name: Delete index.html file
    file:
      path: /var/www/html/index.html
      state: absent
  - name: Upload application file
    copy:
      src: index.php
      dest: /var/www/html
      mode: 0755
    notify:
      - Restart Apache
  handlers:
  - name: Restart Apache
    service: name=apache2 state=restarted
```

This playbook runs on all nodes with the `webservers` role, and there are three tasks in this playbook. The `Delete index.html file` task uses the `file` module to delete the `/var/www/html/index.html` file from the web server. That is because we are using `index.php` as the index page and not `index.html`. The `Upload application file` task then uses the `copy` module to copy the `index.php` file from the Ansible control node to the web server on the `/var/www/html` destination, with a mode of `0755`. The `Upload application file` task also has a `notify` action that will call the `Restart Apache` handler if this task has a status of CHANGED. There is a `handlers` section within the playbook that defines handlers that listen to notify events. In this scenario, if there is a change in the `Upload application file` task, then the `Restart Apache` handler will be triggered and will restart the apache2 service.

We will use the following `setup-dbservers.yaml` playbook to configure MySQL on `dbservers`:

```yaml
---
- hosts: dbservers
  become: true
  vars:
    mysql_root_password: "Password@1"
  tasks:
  - name: Set the root password
```

```
    copy:
      src: client.my.cnf
      dest: "/root/.my.cnf"
      mode: 0600
    notify:
      - Restart MySQL
  - name: Create a test user
    mysql_user:
      name: testuser
      password: "Password@1"
      login_user: root
      login_password: "{{ mysql_root_password }}"
      state: present
      priv: '*.*:ALL,GRANT'
      host: '%'
  - name: Remove all anonymous user accounts
    mysql_user:
      name: ''
      host_all: yes
      state: absent
      login_user: root
      login_password: "{{ mysql_root_password }}"
    notify:
    - Restart MySQL
  - name: Remove the MySQL test database
    mysql_db:
      name: test
      state: absent
      login_user: root
      login_password: "{{ mysql_root_password }}"
    notify:
    - Restart MySQL
  - name: Change bind address
    lineinfile:
      path:  /etc/mysql/mysql.conf.d/mysqld.cnf
      regexp: ^bind-address
      line: 'bind-address            = 0.0.0.0'
    notify:
    - Restart MySQL
handlers:
- name: Restart MySQL
  service: name=mysql state=restarted
```

This playbook is a bit more complicated, but let's break it down into parts to facilitate our understanding:

There is a `vars` section in this playbook, and that defines a `mysql_root_password` variable. We need this password while executing MySQL tasks. The first task is to set up the root password. The best way to set that up is by defining a `/root/.my.cnf` file within MySQL that contains the root credentials. We are copying the following `client.my.cnf` file to `/root/.my.cnf` using the `copy` module:

```
[client]
user=root
password=Password@1
```

Then the `Create a test user` task uses the `mysql_user` module to create a user called `testuser`. You can see that it requires values for the `login_user` and `login_password` attributes, and we are supplying `root` and `{{ mysql_root_password }}`, respectively. It then goes ahead and removes all anonymous users and also removes the test database. It then changes the bind address to `0.0.0.0` using the `lineinfile` module. The `lineinfile` module is a powerful module that helps in manipulating files by first grepping a file using a regex and then replacing those lines with the line attribute's value. All of these tasks notify the `Restart MySQL` handler that restarts the MySQL database service.

Combining the playbooks

As we've written multiple playbooks, we need to execute them in order. We cannot configure the services before installing packages and services, and there is no point in running an `apt` update after installing the packages. Therefore, we can create a playbook of playbooks.

To do so, we've created a YAML file – `playbook.yaml`, that has the following content:

```
---
 - import_playbook: apt-update.yaml
 - import_playbook: install-webserver.yaml
 - import_playbook: install-dbserver.yaml
 - import_playbook: setup-webservers.yaml
 - import_playbook: setup-dbservers.yaml
```

This YAML contains a list of plays, and every play contains an `import_playbook` statement. The plays are executed in order as specified in the file. Now let's go ahead and execute the playbook.

Executing the playbooks

Executing the playbook is simple. We will use the `ansible-playbook` command followed by the playbook YAML file. As we've combined playbooks in a `playbook.yaml` file, the following command will run the playbook:

```
$ ansible-playbook playbook.yaml
...
PLAY RECAP ************************************************
db: ok=0    changed=11    unreachable=0    failed=0    skipped=0
rescued=0    ignored=0
web: ok=0    changed=8    unreachable=0    failed=0
skipped=0    rescued=0    ignored=0
```

As we can see, the configuration is applied on both `webservers` and `dbservers`, and so let's `curl` the web server to see what we get:

```
$ curl web
<html>
<head>
<title>PHP to MQSQL</title>
</head>
<body>Database Connected successfully</body>
</html>
```

As we can see, the database is connected successfully! That proves that the setup was successful.

There are several reasons why the way we approached the problem is not the best way of doing it. First of all, there are several sections within the playbook where we've hardcoded things. While we have used variables in a few playbooks, we've also assigned values to variables within it. That does not make the playbooks a candidate for reuse. The best way to design software is to keep reusability in mind. Therefore, there are many ways in which we can redesign the playbooks to foster reusability.

Designing for reusability

Ansible provides variables for turning Ansible playbooks into reusable templates. You can substitute variables in the right places using **Jinja2** markup, which we've already used in the last playbook. Let's now look at Ansible variables, their types, and how to use them.

Ansible variables

Ansible variables, like any other variables, are used to manage differences between managed nodes. You can use a similar playbook for multiple servers, but sometimes there are some differences in configuration. Ansible variables help you template your playbooks so that you can reuse them for a variety of similar systems. There are multiple places where you can define your variables:

- Within the Ansible playbook within the `vars` section
- In your inventory
- In reusable files or roles
- Passing variables through the command line
- Registering variables by assigning the return values of a task

Ansible variable names can include letters, numbers, and underscores. You cannot have a Python keyword as a variable as Ansible uses Python in the background. Also, a variable name cannot begin with a number but can start with an underscore.

You can define variables using a simple key-value pair within the YAML files and by following the standard YAML syntax.

Variables can broadly be of three types – *simple variables*, *list variables*, and *dictionary variables*.

Simple variables

Simple variables are variables that just hold a single value. They can have string, integer, double, or Boolean values. To refer to simple Ansible variables within the playbook, you need to use them within Jinja expressions, such as `{{ var_name }}`. You should always quote Jinja expressions as the YAML files will fail to parse without that.

The following is an example of a simple variable declaration:

```
mysql_root_password: bar
```

And this is how you should reference it:

```
- name: Remove the MySQL test database
  mysql_db:
    name: test
    state: absent
    login_user: root
    login_password: "{{ mysql_root_password }}"
```

Now let's look at list variables.

List variables

List variables hold a list of values that you can reference by using an index. You can also use list variables within loops. To define a list variable, you can use the standard YAML syntax for a list, for example:

```
region:
    - europe-west1
    - europe-west2
    - europe-west3
```

To access the variable, we can use the index format, for example, as follows:

```
region: " {{ region[0] }} "
```

Ansible also supports more complex dictionary variables. Let's have a look.

Dictionary variables

Dictionary variables hold a complex combination of key-value pairs, and it is the same as a Python dictionary. You can define dictionary variables using the standard YAML syntax, for example:

```
foo:
  bar: one
  baz: two
```

There are two ways in which to refer to these variables' values. For example, in dot notation, we can write the following:

```
bar: {{ foo.bar }}
```

And in bracket notation, we can depict the same thing using the following command:

```
bar: {{ foo[bar] }}
```

We can use either dot or bracket notation, the same way as in Python.

> **Tip**
> While both dot and bracket notations signify the same thing, using bracket notification is a better option. With dot notation, some keys can collide with the methods and attributes of Python dictionaries.

Now let's look at ways of sourcing variable values.

Sourcing variable values

While you can manually define variables and provide their values, sometimes we need dynamically generated values; for example, if we need to know the server's hostname where Ansible is executing the playbook or want to use a specific value returned from a task within a variable. Ansible provides a list of variables and system metadata during the gathering facts phase for the former requirement. That helps to determine what variables are available and how we can use them. Let's understand how we can gather that information.

Finding metadata using Ansible facts

Ansible facts are metadata information associated with the managed nodes. Ansible gets the facts during the gathering facts stage, and we can use the facts variable directly within the playbook. To determine the facts, we can use the `setup` module as an Ansible task. For example, you can run the following command to get the Ansible facts for all nodes with the `webservers` role:

```
$ ansible -m setup webservers
web | SUCCESS => {
    "ansible_facts": {
        "ansible_all_ipv4_addresses": [
            "10.0.2.5"
        ],
        ...
        "ansible_hostname": "web",
```

So, as we can see, we get `ansible_facts` with multiple variables associated with the inventory item. As we just have a single server here, we get details of the web server. Within the piece, we have an `ansible_hostname` attribute called web. We can use that `ansible_hostname` attribute within our playbook if we need to.

Sometimes, we want to source a task's output to a particular variable to use the variable in any subsequent tasks of the playbook. Let's look at how we can do that.

Registering variables

Say, for example, a task within your playbook needs a value from the result of a preceding task. Well, we can use the register attribute for that.

The following directory contains all the resources for exercises in this section:

```
$ cd ~/modern-devops/ch7/vars-exercise
```

Let's look at the following example `register.yaml` file:

```
- hosts: webservers
  tasks:
    - name: Get free space
      command: df -h
      register: free_space
      ignore_errors: true
    - name: Print the free space from the previous task
      debug:
          msg: "{{ free_space }}"
```

The playbook contains two tasks. The first task uses the `command` module to execute a command, `df -h`, and registers the result in the `free_space` variable. The subsequent task uses the previous task's output using the `debug` module to print `free_space` as a message to the console.

Now, as we've looked into variables, let's look at some other aspects that will help us to improve the last playbook.

Jinja2 templates

Ansible allows for templating files using dynamic Jinja2 templates. You can use the Python syntax within the file, starting with { { and ending with } }. That will allow you to substitute variables during runtime and run complex computations on variables. To understand this further, let's modify the `index.php` file to supply the MySQL `username` and `password` dynamically during execution:

```
<html>
<head>
<title>PHP to MQSQL</title>
</head>
<body>
<?php
mysqli_connect('db', '{{ mysql_user }}', '{{ mysql_password
}}') or die('Could not connect the database : Username or
password incorrect');
echo 'Database Connected successfully';
?>
</body>
```

```
</html>
```

As we can see, instead of hardcoding the username and password, we can use templates to substitute the variable values during runtime. That will make the file more reusable and will fit multiple environments. Ansible provides another important aspect of coding reusability within your playbooks – Ansible roles. Let's have a look at this in the next section.

Ansible roles

Well, the last playbook looks a bit cluttered. You have a lot of files within them, and none of them are reusable. The code we've written can only set up the configuration in a particular way. This may work fine for smaller teams where you have limited configurations to manage, but it is not as simple as it looks for most enterprises.

Ansible roles help to standardize an Ansible setup and promote reusability. With roles, you can automatically load var files, handlers, tasks, and other Ansible artifacts by using a standard directory structure relative to your playbooks. The directory structure is as follows:

```
<playbook>.yaml
roles/
    <role>/
        tasks/
        handlers/
        library/
        files/
        templates/
        vars/
        defaults/
        meta/
```

The `roles` directory contains multiple subdirectories for each role. Each role directory contains multiple standard directories:

- `tasks`: This directory contains a list of tasks' `yaml` files. It should contain a file called `main.yaml` (or `main.yml` or `main`), containing the entire list of tasks or importing tasks from other files within the directory.

- `handlers`: This directory contains a list of handlers associated with the role within a file called `main.yaml`.

- `library`: This directory contains Python modules that can be used with the role.

- `files`: This directory contains all files that we require for our configuration.

- `templates`: This directory contains the Jinja2 templates that the role deploys.

- `vars`: This directory contains a `main.yaml` file with a list of variables associated with the role.

- `defaults`: This directory contains a `main.yaml` file containing the default variables associated with the role that can be easily overridden by any other variable that includes inventory variables.

- `meta`: This directory contains the metadata and dependencies associated with the role within a `main.yaml` file.

Some best practices revolve around managing your Ansible configuration through the folder structure. Let's look at some of these next.

> **Tip**
> While choosing between the `vars` and `defaults` directories, the thumb rule is to put variables that will not change within the `vars` directory. Put the variables that are likely to change within the `defaults` directory.

So, we'll go and use the `defaults` directory as much as we can. There are some best practices regarding roles as well that we should follow. Let's look at some of them.

> **Tip**
> Think about the full life cycle of a specific service while designing roles rather than building the entire stack, in other words, instead of using `lamp` as a role, use `apache` and `mysql` roles instead.

We will create three roles for our use – `common`, `apache`, and `mysql`.

> **Tip**
> Use specific roles, such as `apache` or `mysql`, instead of using `webserver` or `dbserver`. Typical enterprises have a mix and match of multiple web server and database technologies. Therefore, giving a generic name to a role will confuse things.

The following directory contains all the resources for the exercises in this section:

```
$ cd ~/modern-devops/ch7/lamp-stack-roles
```

The following is the directory structure we will follow for our scenario:

```
├── ansible.cfg
├── custom-playbook.yaml
├── hosts
├── output.log
├── playbook.yaml
```

There are two roles that we'll create – apache and mysql. Let's look at the directory structure of the apache role first:

```
└── roles
    ├── apache
    │   ├── defaults
    │   │   └── main.yaml
    │   ├── handlers
    │   │   └── main.yaml
    │   ├── tasks
    │   │   ├── install-apache.yaml
    │   │   ├── main.yaml
    │   │   └── setup-apache.yaml
    │   └── templates
    │       └── index.php.j2
```

There is also a common role that will apply to all scenarios. The following directory structure defines that:

```
    ├── common
    │   └── tasks
    │       └── main.yaml
```

Finally, let's define the mysql role through the following directory structure:

```
    └── mysql
        ├── defaults
        │   └── main.yaml
        ├── files
        ├── handlers
        │   └── main.yaml
        ├── tasks
        │   ├── install-mysql.yaml
        │   ├── main.yaml
        │   └── setup-mysql.yaml
        └── templates
```

```
└── client.my.cnf.j2
```

The apache directory consists of the following:

- We've used the same index.php file we created in the last exercise, converted it to a Jinja2 template called index.php.j2, and copied it to roles/apache/templates.

- The handlers directory contains a main.yaml file that contains the Restart Apache handler.

- The tasks directory contains an install-apache.yaml file that includes all tasks required to install Apache. The setup-apache.yaml file consists of a list of tasks that will set up Apache similar to how we did in the previous exercise. The main.yaml file contains tasks from both files, using include directives such as the following:

```
---
- include: install-apache.yaml
- include: setup-apache.yaml
```

- The defaults directory contains the main.yaml file, which consists of the mysql_username and mysql_password variables and their default values.

> **Tip**
> Use the least amount of variables as possible and try to default them. Use sane defaults for variables in such a way that minimal custom configuration is needed.

The mysql directory consists of the following:

- We've modified client.my.cnf and converted that to a j2 file. The j2 file is a Jinja2 template file that we will use in the role through the template module in the Set the root password task. The file exists within the templates directory:

```
[client]
user=root
password={{ mysql_root_password }}
```

As we can see, we're providing the password through a Jinja2 expression. When we run the mysql role through the playbook, the value of mysql_root_password will be substituted in the password section.

- The `handlers` directory contains the `Restart MySQL` handler.

- The `tasks` directory consists of three files. The `install-mysql.yaml` file contains tasks that install `mysql`, and the `setup-mysql.yaml` file contains tasks that set up `mysql`. The `main.yaml` file combines both these files using `include` task directives, as follows:

```
---
- include: install-mysql.yaml
- include: setup-mysql.yaml
```

- The `defaults` directory contains a `main.yaml` file with a list of variables we will use within the role. In this case, it just contains the value of `mysql_root_password`.

The `common` directory contains a single directory called `tasks` that includes a `main.yaml` file with a single task to run an `apt update`.

The main directory contains the `ansible.cfg`, `hosts`, and `playbook.yaml` files. While the `hosts` and `ansible.cfg` files are the same as the last exercise, the `playbook.yaml` file looks like the following:

```
---
- hosts: webservers
  become: true
  roles:
     - common
     - apache
- hosts: dbservers
  become: true
  roles:
     - common
     - mysql
```

The playbook is now a concise one with a lot of reusable elements. It consists of two plays. The first play will run on all web servers with the root user and apply the `common` and `apache` roles to them. The second play will run on all nodes with the `dbservers` role with the root user and use the `common` and `mysql` roles.

> **Tip**
>
> Always keep roles loosely coupled. In the preceding example, the `apache` role has no dependency on `mysql` and vice versa. This will allow us to reuse configuration with ease.

Now, let's go ahead and execute the playbook:

```
$ ansible-playbook playbook.yaml
PLAY [webservers]
...
PLAY [dbservers]
...
PLAY RECAP
db  : ok=10     changed=0      unreachable=0      failed=0
skipped=0       rescued=0      ignored=0
web : ok=7      changed=0      unreachable=0      failed=0
skipped=0       rescued=0      ignored=0
```

And as we can see, there are no changes to the configuration. We've applied the same configuration but in a better way. If we want to share our configuration with people within the team, we can share the `roles` directory, and they can simply apply the role within their playbook.

There may be instances where we want to use a different value for the variable we've defined in the `roles` section. You can override variables within the playbook by supplying the variable values while defining roles, something like the following:

```
---
- hosts: webservers
  become: true
  roles:
    - common
    - role: apache
      vars:
        mysql_user: "foo"
        mysql_password: "bar@123"
- hosts: dbservers
  become: true
  roles:
    - common
    - role: mysql
      vars:
```

```
      mysql_user: "foo"
      mysql_password: "bar@123"
```

When we apply the playbook using the following command, we'll see that the user now changes to `foo` and that the password changes to `bar` in both the Apache and MySQL configurations:

```
$ ansible-playbook custom-playbook.yaml
...
PLAY RECAP
db  : ok=9    changed=1    unreachable=0    failed=0
skipped=0    rescued=0    ignored=0
web : ok=7    changed=2    unreachable=0    failed=0
skipped=0    rescued=0    ignored=0
```

So if we `curl` the web host, we will get the same response as before:

```
...
<body>Database Connected successfully</body>
...
```

Our setup is working correctly with roles. We've set up the Ansible playbook by following all the best practices and using reusable roles and templates. That is the way to go forward in designing powerful Ansible playbooks.

Summary

In this chapter, we've discussed Ansible and its core functionalities from a hands-on perspective. We began by understanding Configuration as Code, looked at Ansible and Ansible architecture, installed Ansible, understood Ansible modules, tasks, and playbooks, and then applied our first Ansible configuration. We then looked at fostering reusability with Ansible variables, Jinja2 templates, and roles, and then reorganized our configuration with reusability in mind. We also looked at several best practices along the way.

In the next chapter, we will combine Terraform with Ansible to spin up something useful and look at HashiCorp's Packer to create immutable infrastructure.

Questions

1. It is a best practice to avoid using command and shell modules as much as possible. (True/False)

2. Aliases help in keeping your inventory generic. (True/False)

3. What does the `ansible-playbook` command do? (Choose one)

    a. It runs an ad hoc task on the inventory.

    b. It runs a series of tasks on the inventory.

    c. It applies the plays and tasks configured with the playbook.

    d. It destroys the configuration from managed nodes.

4. Which of the following techniques help in building reusability within your Ansible configuration? (Multiple answers are possible)

    a. Use variables.

    b. Use Jinja2 templates.

    c. Use roles.

    d. Use tasks.

5. While naming roles, what should we consider? (Multiple answers are possible)

    a. Name roles as precisely as possible.

    b. While thinking of roles, think of the service instead of the full stack.

    c. Use generic names for roles.

6. In which directory should you define variables within roles if the variable's value is likely to change? (Choose one)

    a. defaults

    b. vars

7. Handlers are triggered when the output of the task associated with the handler is …? (Choose one)

    a. SUCCESS

    b. CHANGED

    c. FAILED

8. Does a SUCCESS status denote that the task did not detect any changed configuration? (True/False)

9. What are the best practices for inventory management? (Multiple answers are possible)

    a. Use a separate inventory for each environment.

    b. Group the inventory by functions.

c. Use aliases.

d. Keep the inventory file in a central location.

Answers

1. True

2. True

3. c

4. a, b, c

5. a, b

6. a

7. b

8. True

9. a, b, and c

8
IaC and Config Management in Action

In the previous chapter, we looked at configuration management with Ansible and the technology's core concepts. We also discussed Terraform and IaC in *Chapter 6, Infrastructure as Code (IaC) with Terraform*. Now let's apply the principles of both technologies to a practical situation. Let's boot up a scalable **Linux Apache MySQL and PHP (LAMP)** stack on Azure with Terraform, Ansible, and another tool Packer that we'll discuss in this chapter.

In this chapter, we're going to cover the following main topics:

- Immutable infrastructure with Hashicorp's Packer
- Creating the Apache and MySQL playbook
- Building the Apache and MySQL images using Packer and Ansible provisioners
- Creating the required infrastructure with Terraform

Technical requirements

For this chapter, you will need an active Azure subscription for following the exercises. Currently, Azure is offering a free trial for 30 days with $200 worth of free credits; sign up at `https://azure.microsoft.com/en-in/free`.

You will also need to clone the following GitHub repository for some of the exercises:

`https://github.com/PacktPublishing/Modern-DevOps-Practices`

Run the following command to clone the repository into your home directory, and `cd` into the `ch8` directory to access the required resources:

```
$ git clone https://github.com/PacktPublishing/Modern-DevOps-\
Practices.git modern-devops
$ cd modern-devops/ch8
```

You also need to install **Terraform** and **Ansible** in your system. Refer to *Chapter 6, Infrastructure as Code (IaC) with Terraform*, and *Chapter 7, Configuration Management with Ansible*, for more details on installing and setting up Terraform.

Immutable infrastructure with Hashicorp's Packer

The traditional method of setting up applications via Terraform and Ansible would be to use Terraform to spin up the infrastructure and then use Ansible on top to apply the relevant configuration to the infrastructure. That is what we did in the last chapter. While that is a viable approach and many enterprises use it, there is a better way to do it with modern DevOps approaches and **immutable infrastructure**.

Immutable infrastructure is a ground-breaking concept that has resulted because of the problems of **mutable infrastructure**. In a mutable infrastructure approach, we generally update servers in place. So, when we install **Apache** in a **Virtual Machine (VM)** using Ansible and then customize it further, we follow a mutable approach. We may want to update the servers from time to time, patch them, update our Apache to a newer version from time to time, and update our application code from time to time.

The issue with this approach is that while we can manage it well with Ansible (or related tools such as **Puppet**, **Chef**, and **Saltstack**), the problem always remains that we are making live changes in a production environment that might go wrong for various reasons. Worse, it updates something to a version we did not anticipate or test in the first place. We also might end up in a partial upgrade state that might be difficult to roll back.

With the scalable infrastructure that the cloud provides, you can have a dynamic horizontal scaling model where Virtual Machines scale with traffic. Therefore, you can have the best possible utilization of your infrastructure – the best bang for your buck! The problem with the traditional approach is that even if we use Ansible to apply the configuration to new machines, it is slower to get ready. Therefore, the scaling is not optimal, especially for bursty traffic.

Immutable infrastructure helps you manage these problems by taking the same approach we took for containers – baking configuration directly into the OS image using modern DevOps tools and practices. Immutable infrastructure helps you deploy tested configuration to production by replacing the existing VM and without doing any updates in place. It is faster to start and easy to roll back. You can also version infrastructure changes with this approach.

Hashicorp has an excellent suite of DevOps products related to infrastructure and configuration management. Hashicorp provides **Packer** to help you create immutable infrastructure by baking configurations directly in your Virtual Machine image, rather than the slow process of creating a Virtual Machine with a generic OS image and then customizing it later.

Packer uses a staging Virtual Machine to customize the image. The following is the process that Packer follows while building the custom image:

1. You start with a `packer.json` file to define the base image you want to start from and where you want to build the image. You also define the provisioner for building the custom image, such as Ansible, and specify what playbooks to use.

2. When you run a Packer build, Packer uses the details in the `packer.json` file to create a **build VM** from the **base image**, run the **provisioner** on it to customize it, turn off the build VM, take a snapshot, and save that as a **disk image**. It finally saves the image in an image repository.

3. You can then build the Virtual Machine from the custom image using Terraform or other tools.

The following figure explains the process in detail:

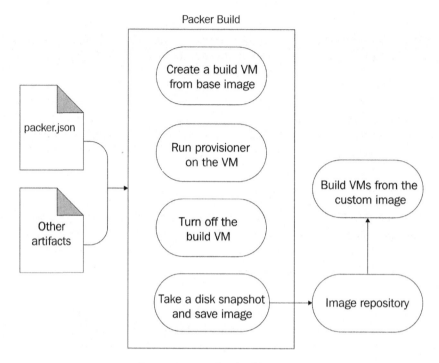

Figure 8.1 – Packer build process

The result of this is that your application is quick to start up and scales very well. For any changes you have within your configuration, you create a new OS image with Packer and Ansible and then use Terraform to apply the changes to your resources. Terraform will then spin down the old Virtual Machines and spin up new ones with the new configuration. If you can relate it with the container deployment workflow, you can make real sense of it. We've used the container workflow within the Virtual Machine world! But is immutable infrastructure for everyone? Let's understand where it fits best.

When to use immutable infrastructure

Deciding to switch to immutable infrastructure is difficult, especially when your Ops team treats servers as pets. Most people get paranoid about the idea of deleting an existing server and creating a new one for every update. Well, you need to do a lot of convincing when you first come up with the idea of doing it. And it does not mean that you will have to do immutable infrastructure to do proper DevOps. It all depends on your use case.

Let's look at some of the pros and cons of each approach to understand them better.

Pros of mutable infrastructure

Let's begin with the pros of mutable infrastructure:

- If adequately managed, mutable infrastructure is faster to upgrade and make changes to. It makes security patches quicker.

- It is simpler to manage, as we don't have to worry about building the entire Virtual Machine image and redeploying it for every update.

Cons of mutable infrastructure

Next, let's see the cons of mutable infrastructure:

- It eventually results in configuration drift. When people start making changes manually in the server and do not use a config management tool, it becomes difficult to know what's in the server after a particular point. Then you will have to start relying on snapshots.

- Versioning is not possible with mutable infrastructure, and rolling back changes is a troublesome process.

- There is a possibility of partial updates because of technical issues such as a patchy network, unresponsive apt repositories, and so on.

- There is a risk because changes are applied directly to the production environment. There is also a chance that you will end up in an unanticipated state that is difficult to troubleshoot.

- Because of configuration drift, it is impossible to say that the current configuration is the same as being tracked in version control. Therefore, building a new server from scratch may require manual intervention and comprehensive testing.

Similarly, now let's look at the pros and cons of immutable infrastructure.

Pros of immutable infrastructure

The pros of immutable infrastructure are as follows:

- It eliminates configuration drift as the infrastructure cannot change once deployed, and any changes should come via the CI/CD process.

- It is DevOps-friendly as every build and deployment process inherently follows modern DevOps practices.

- It makes discrete versioning possible as every image generated out of an image build can be versioned and kept within an image repository. That makes rollouts and rollbacks much more straightforward and promotes modern DevOps practices such as **Canary** and **Blue-Green** deployments with A/B testing.

- As the image is pre-built and tested, we always get a predictable state out of immutable infrastructure. We, therefore, reduce a lot of risk from production implementations.

- It helps horizontal scaling on the cloud because you can now create servers from pre-built images that make new Virtual Machines faster to start up and get ready.

Cons of immutable infrastructure

The cons of immutable infrastructure are as follows:

- The process of building and deploying immutable infrastructure is a bit complex, and it is slow to add updates and manage urgent hotfixes.

- There are storage and network overheads in generating and managing Virtual Machine images.

So, as we've looked at the pros and cons of both approaches, it ultimately depends on how you currently do infrastructure management and your end goal. Immutable infrastructure has a huge benefit, and therefore, it is something that every modern DevOps engineer should understand and implement if possible. However, there are technical and process constraints that prevent people from doing it – while some are related to the technology stack, most are simply processes and red tape.

We all know that DevOps is not all about tools, but it is a cultural change that should originate from the very top. If it is not possible to use immutable infrastructure for some reason, you always have the option of using a **config management** tool such as Ansible on top of live servers. That makes things manageable to a certain extent.

Now, moving on to Packer, let's look at how to install it.

Installing Packer

Installing Packer is very simple. Just download the required Packer binary and move it to your system path. The following commands show how to install Packer on Linux:

```
$ wget https://releases.hashicorp.com/packer\
/1.6.6/packer_1.6.6_linux_amd64.zip
$ unzip packer_1.6.6_linux_amd64.zip
$ sudo mv packer /usr/bin
```

```
$ sudo chmod +x /usr/bin/packer
```

To verify the installation, run the following command:

```
$ packer version
Packer v1.6.6
```

And as we see, Packer is installed successfully. We can go ahead with the next activity in our goal – creating playbooks.

Creating the Apache and MySQL playbooks

As our goal is to spin up a scalable LAMP stack in this chapter, we need to start by defining Ansible playbooks that would run on the build Virtual Machine. We've already created some roles for Apache and MySQL in *Chapter 7, Configuration Management with Ansible*. We will use the same roles within this setup as well.

Therefore, we will have the following directory structure within the ch8 directory:

```
.
├── dbserver-playbook.yaml
├── dbserver-packer.json
├── roles
│   ├── apache
│   ├── common
│   └── mysql
├── webserver-playbook.json
└── webserver-packer.yaml
```

We have two playbooks here – webserver-playbook.yaml and dbserver-playbook.yaml. Let's look at each one to understand how we write our playbooks for Ansible.

The webserver-playbook.yaml looks like the following:

```
---
- hosts: default
  become: true
  roles:
    - common
    - apache
```

The `dbserver-playbook.yaml` looks like the following:

```
---
- hosts: default
  become: true
  roles:
    - common
    - mysql
```

As we see, both playbooks have the `hosts` mentioned as default. That is because we will not define the inventory for this playbook. Instead, Packer will use the build Virtual Machine to build the image and dynamically generate the inventory.

> **Note**
>
> Packer will also ignore any `remote_user` attributes within the task and use the user present in the Ansible provisioner's JSON config.
>
> You cannot use **Jinja2** `{{ function }}` macro syntax within the Packer JSON to pass it as is to your Ansible provisioner. That is because Packer also uses Jinja2 templating to pass variables. You can, though, use Jinja2 templates within your playbooks without any changes.

As we've already tested this configuration in the previous chapter, all we need now is to define Packer configuration, so let's go ahead and do that in the next section.

Building the Apache and MySQL images using Packer and Ansible provisioners

We will now use Packer to create the Apache and MySQL images. Before defining the Packer configuration, we have a few prerequisites to allow Packer to build custom images.

Prerequisites

We would need to create a service principal for Packer to interact with Azure and build the image.

First, log in using the Azure CLI to your Azure account using the following command:

```
$ az login
```

Now, set the subscription to the subscription id we got in response to `az login` using the following command:

```
$ az account set --subscription="<SUBSCRIPTION_ID>"
```

Then create the service principal with contributor access using the following command:

```
$ az ad sp create-for-rbac --role="Contributor" \
--scopes="/subscriptions/<SUBSCRIPTION_ID>"
Creating 'Contributor' role assignment under scope '/
subscriptions/<SUBSCRIPTION_ID>'
  Retrying role assignment creation: 1/36
The output includes credentials that you must protect. Be sure
that you do not include these credentials in your code or check
the credentials into your source control. For more information,
see https://aka.ms/azadsp-cli
{
  "appId": "00000000-0000-0000-0000-0000000000000",
  "displayName": "azure-cli-2021-01-07-05-59-24",
  "name": "http://azure-cli-2021-01-07-05-59-24",
  "password": "xxxxxxxxxxxxxxxxxxxxxxxxxxxxxxxx",
  "tenant": "00000000-0000-0000-0000-0000000000000"
}
```

We've successfully created the service principal. The response JSON consists of an `appId`, `password`, and `tenant` that we will use in the subsequent sections.

> **Note**
> You can also reuse the service principal we created in *Chapter 6, Infrastructure as Code (IaC) Using Terraform* instead.

Now let's go ahead and set a few environment variables with the details we gathered using the following commands:

```
$ export CLIENT_ID=<VALUE_OF_APP_ID>
$ export CLIENT_SECRET=<VALUE_OF_PASSWORD>
$ export TENANT_ID=<VALUE_OF_TENANT>
$ export SUBSCRIPTION_ID=<SUBSCRIPTION_ID>
```

We will use these environment variables in our Packer build. We also need a resource group for storing the built images.

To create the resource group, run the following command:

```
$ az group create -n packer-rg -l westeurope
```

Now let's go ahead and define the Packer configuration.

Defining the Packer configuration

Packer allows us to define configuration in JSON as well as HCL files. As JSON is a widely used syntax in Packer's case and HCL is still in beta when writing this book, let's create two JSON files for the Packer configuration – one for the webserver and the other for the dbserver.

The webserver-packer.json file looks like the following:

```json
{
  "variables": {
    "client_id": "{{env `CLIENT_ID`}}",
    "client_secret": "{{env `CLIENT_SECRET`}}",
    "tenant_id": "{{env `TENANT_ID`}}",
    "subscription_id": "{{env `SUBSCRIPTION_ID`}}"
  },
  "builders": [{
    "type": "azure-arm",
    "client_id": "{{user `client_id`}}",
    "client_secret": "{{user `client_secret`}}",
    "tenant_id": "{{user `tenant_id`}}",
    "subscription_id": "{{user `subscription_id`}}",
    "managed_image_resource_group_name": "packer-rg",
    "managed_image_name": "apache-webserver",
    "os_type": "Linux",
    "image_publisher": "Canonical",
    "image_offer": "UbuntuServer",
    "image_sku": "16.04-LTS",
    "azure_tags": {},
    "location": "West Europe",
    "vm_size": "Standard_DS2_v2"
  }],
  "provisioners": [{
      "type": "ansible",
```

```
        "playbook_file": "./webserver-playbook.yaml"
    }]
}
```

The JSON file consists of three sections – `variables`, `builders`, and `provisioners`.

The `variables` section defines a list of user variables that we can use within the `builders` and `provisioners` section of the Packer configuration. We've defined four variables – `client_id`, `client_secret`, `tenant_id`, and `subscription_id` and are sourcing the values of these variables from the environment variables we described in the previous section. That is because we don't want to commit the values of these attributes in source control.

> **Tip**
> Always source sensitive data from external variables, such as environment variables, or a secret manager such as Hashicorp's Vault. You should never commit sensitive information with code.

The `builders` section consists of an array of builders. Every builder has a mandatory `type` attribute that defines the builder's type for the Packer build. Different types of builders have different attributes that help us connect and authenticate with the cloud provider that the builder is associated with. Other attributes define the build Virtual Machine's specification and the base image that the build Virtual Machine will use. It also describes the properties of the custom image we're trying to create. Since we're using Azure in this case, it contains the type as `azure-arm` and consists of `client_id`, `client_secret`, `tenant_id`, and `subscription_id`, which helps Packer authenticate with the Azure API server. As you see, these attributes' values are sourced from the user variables we defined in the *variables* section.

> **Tip**
> The managed image name can also contain a version. That will help you build a new image for every new version you want to deploy.

The `provisioners` section defines how we're going to customize our Virtual Machine. There are a lot of provisioners that Packer provides. Luckily, Packer provides the Ansible provisioner out of the box. Therefore, we've specified the type as `ansible`. The Ansible provisioner requires the path to the playbook file, and therefore in the preceding case, we've provided `webserver-playbook.yaml`.

Tip

You can specify multiple builders in the `builders` section, each with the same or different types. Similarly, we can have numerous provisioners with the `provisioners` section. Each will be executed in parallel. So, if you want to build the same configuration for multiple cloud providers, you can specify multiple builders for each cloud provider.

Now let's go ahead and build the image using the following command:

```
$ packer build webserver-packer.json
==> azure-arm: Running builder ...
==> azure-arm: Getting tokens using client secret
==> azure-arm: Getting tokens using client secret
    azure-arm: Creating Azure Resource Manager (ARM) client
```

Packer first creates a temporary resource group to spin up a staging Virtual Machine:

```
==> azure-arm: Creating resource group ...
==> azure-arm:    -> ResourceGroupName : 'pkr-Resource-Group-
1si4o8mas1'
==> azure-arm:    -> Location          : 'West Europe'
```

Packer then validates and deploys the deployment template and gets the IP address of the staging Virtual Machine:

```
==> azure-arm: Validating deployment template ...
==> azure-arm: Deploying deployment template ...
==> azure-arm: Getting the VM's IP address ...
==> azure-arm:    -> IP Address        : '52.166.65.8'
```

Then Packer uses SSH to connect with the staging Virtual Machine and provisions it with Ansible:

```
==> azure-arm: Waiting for SSH to become available...
==> azure-arm: Connected to SSH!
==> azure-arm: Provisioning with Ansible...
    azure-arm: Setting up proxy adapter for Ansible....
```

```
==> azure-arm: Executing Ansible: ansible-playbook -e
packer_build_name="azure-arm" -e packer_builder_type=azure-
arm --ssh-extra-args '-o IdentitiesOnly=yes' -e ansible_ssh_
private_key_file=/tmp/ansible-key696541413 -i /tmp/packer-
provisioner-ansible576226560 /home/gaurava/modern-devops/ch8/
webserver-playbook.yaml
    azure-arm: PLAY [default] ********************************
    azure-arm: TASK [Gathering Facts] ************************
    azure-arm: ok: [default]
    azure-arm: TASK [common : Update apt packages] ***********
    azure-arm: ok: [default]
    azure-arm: TASK [apache : Install packages] **************
    azure-arm: changed: [default]
    azure-arm: TASK [apache : Start and Enable Apache service]
    azure-arm: ok: [default]
    azure-arm: TASK [apache : Delete index.html file] *********
    azure-arm: changed: [default]
    azure-arm: TASK [apache : Upload application file] ********
    azure-arm: changed: [default]
    azure-arm: RUNNING HANDLER [apache : Restart Apache] ******
    azure-arm: changed: [default]
    azure-arm: PLAY RECAP ************************************
    azure-arm: default: ok=7    changed=4    unreachable=0
failed=0    skipped=0    rescued=0    ignored=0
```

Once the Ansible run is complete, Packer gets the disk details, captures the image, and creates the machine image in the resource group we specified in the Packer configuration:

```
==> azure-arm: Querying the machine's properties ...
==> azure-arm:  -> Managed OS Disk   : '/
subscriptions/<SUBSCRIPTION_ID>/resourceGroups/pkr-Resource-
Group-1si4o8mas1/providers/Microsoft.Compute/disks/
pkros1si4o8mas1'
==> azure-arm: Querying the machine's additional disks
properties ...
==> azure-arm: Powering off machine ...
==> azure-arm: Capturing image ...
==> azure-arm:  -> Image ResourceGroupName: 'packer-rg'
==> azure-arm:  -> Image Name             : 'apache-webserver'
==> azure-arm:  -> Image Location         : 'West Europe'
```

Finally, it removes the deployment object and the temporary resource group it created:

```
==> azure-arm: Removing the created Deployment object:
'pkrdplsi4o8mas1'
==> azure-arm: Cleanup requested, deleting resource group ...
==> azure-arm: Resource group has been deleted.
```

It then provides the list of artifacts it has generated:

```
==> Builds finished. The artifacts of successful builds are:
--> azure-arm: Azure.ResourceManagement.VMImage:
OSType: Linux
ManagedImageResourceGroupName: packer-rg
ManagedImageName: apache-webserver
ManagedImageId: /subscriptions/<SUBSCRIPTION_ID>/
resourceGroups/packer-rg/providers/Microsoft.Compute/images/
apache-webserver
ManagedImageLocation: West Europe
```

If we look at the `packer-rg` resource group, we will find that there is a Virtual Machine image within it:

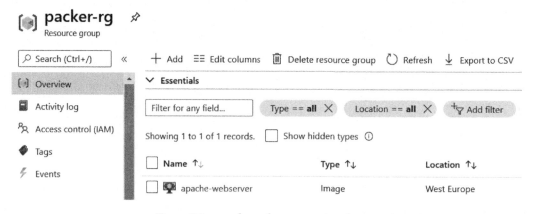

Figure 8.2 – apache-webserver custom image

We've successfully built a custom image with Packer! Now, let's go ahead and do the same with the database configuration as well.

First, let's create a `dbserver-packer.json` file that looks like the following:

```json
{
  "variables": {
    "client_id": "{{env `CLIENT_ID`}}",
    "client_secret": "{{env `CLIENT_SECRET`}}",
    "tenant_id": "{{env `TENANT_ID`}}",
    "subscription_id": "{{env `SUBSCRIPTION_ID`}}"
  },
  "builders": [{
    "type": "azure-arm",
    "client_id": "{{user `client_id`}}",
    "client_secret": "{{user `client_secret`}}",
    "tenant_id": "{{user `tenant_id`}}",
    "subscription_id": "{{user `subscription_id`}}",
    "managed_image_resource_group_name": "packer-rg",
    "managed_image_name": "mysql-dbserver",
    "os_type": "Linux",
    "image_publisher": "Canonical",
    "image_offer": "UbuntuServer",
    "image_sku": "16.04-LTS",
    "azure_tags": {},
    "location": "West Europe",
    "vm_size": "Standard_DS2_v2"
  }],
  "provisioners": [{
      "type": "ansible",
      "playbook_file": "./dbserver-playbook.yaml"
  }]
}
```

The configuration is similar to `webserver-packer.json`, but instead of using `webserver-playbook.yaml`, we will be using `dbserver-playbook.yaml`.

Now, let's go ahead and apply the configuration using the following command:

```
$ packer build dbserver-packer.json
==> Builds finished. The artifacts of successful builds are:
--> azure-arm: Azure.ResourceManagement.VMImage:
OSType: Linux
ManagedImageResourceGroupName: packer-rg
ManagedImageName: mysql-dbserver
ManagedImageId: /subscriptions/<SUBSCRIPTION_ID>/
resourceGroups/packer-rg/providers/Microsoft.Compute/images/
mysql-dbserver
ManagedImageLocation: West Europe
```

This will build the Virtual Machine using similar steps and save the image within the `packer-rg` resource group.

Now let's look into the resource group and check if `mysql-dbserver` is present:

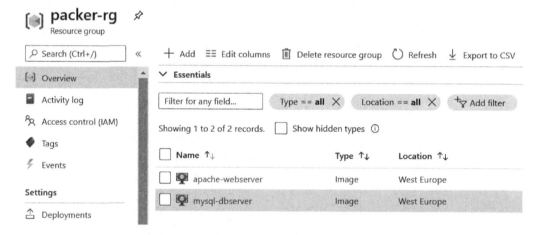

Figure 8.3 – MySQL database server custom image

As shown in *Figure 8.3*, we can see both images present in the resource group.

> **Tip**
>
> It isn't possible to rerun Packer with the same managed image name once the image is created in the resource group. That is because we don't want to override an existing image accidentally. While you can override it by using the `-force` flag with `packer build`, you should include a version within the image name to allow multiple versions of the image to exist in the resource group. For example, instead of using `apache-webserver`, you can use `apache-webserver-0.0.1`.

Now it's time to use these images and create our infrastructure with them.

Creating the required infrastructure with Terraform

As our goal was to build a scalable LAMP stack, we will define a **VM scale set** using the `apache-webserver` image we created and a single Virtual Machine with the `mysql-dbserver` image. A VM scale set is an autoscaling group of Virtual Machines that will scale out and scale back horizontally based on traffic, similar to how we did with containers on Kubernetes.

We will create the following resources:

- A new resource group called `lamp-rg`
- A virtual network with a resource group called `lampvnet`
- A subnet within `lampvnet` called `lampsub`
- Within the subnet, we create a NIC for the database called `db-nic` that contains the following:

  - A network security group called `db-nsg`

  - A Virtual Machine called `db` that uses the custom `mysql-dbserver` image
- We then create a VM scale set that includes the following:

  - A network profile called `webnp`

  - A backend address pool

  - A load balancer called `web-lb`

  - A public IP address attached to `web-lb`

  - An HTTP probe that checks the health of port `80`

The following figure explains the topology graphically:

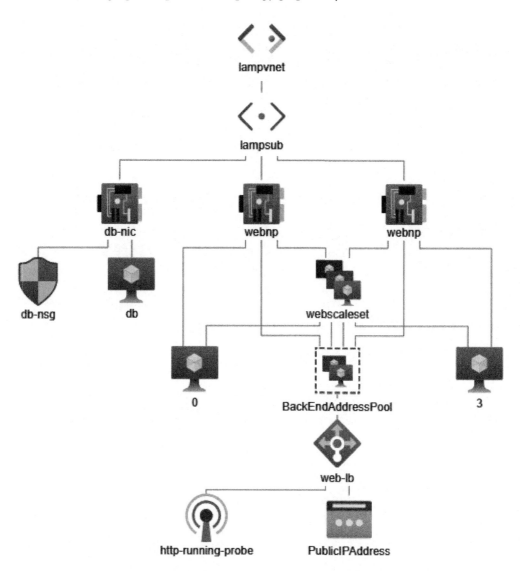

Figure 8.4 – Scalable LAMP stack topology diagram

We use the following Terraform template, `main.tf`, to define the configuration.

We first define the Terraform providers:

```
terraform {
  required_providers {
    azurerm = {
      source  = "azurerm"
    }
  }
}
provider "azurerm" {
  subscription_id = var.subscription_id
  client_id       = var.client_id
  client_secret   = var.client_secret
  tenant_id       = var.tenant_id
  features {}
}
```

We then define the custom image data sources so that we can use them within our configuration:

```
data "azurerm_image" "websig" {
  name                = "apache-webserver"
  resource_group_name = "packer-rg"
}
data "azurerm_image" "dbsig" {
  name                = "mysql-dbserver"
  resource_group_name = "packer-rg"
}
```

We then define the resource group, vnet, and the subnet:

```
resource "azurerm_resource_group" "main" {
  name     = var.rg_name
  location = var.location
}
resource "azurerm_virtual_network" "main" {
  name                = "lampvnet"
  address_space       = ["10.0.0.0/16"]
  location            = var.location
  resource_group_name = azurerm_resource_group.main.name
}
resource "azurerm_subnet" "main" {
```

```
  name                  = "lampsub"
  resource_group_name   = azurerm_resource_group.main.name
  virtual_network_name  = azurerm_virtual_network.main.name
  address_prefixes      = ["10.0.2.0/24"]
}
```

As the Apache web servers will remain behind a network load balancer, we will define the load balancer and the public IP address that we will attach to it:

```
resource "azurerm_public_ip" "main" {
  name                  = "webip"
  location              = var.location
  resource_group_name   = azurerm_resource_group.main.name
  allocation_method     = "Static"
  domain_name_label     = azurerm_resource_group.main.name
}
resource "azurerm_lb" "main" {
  name                  = "web-lb"
  location              = var.location
  resource_group_name   = azurerm_resource_group.main.name
  frontend_ip_configuration {
    name                = "PublicIPAddress"
    public_ip_address_id = azurerm_public_ip.main.id
  }
  tags = {}
}
```

We will then define a backend address pool to the load balancer so that we can use this within the Apache VM scale set:

```
resource "azurerm_lb_backend_address_pool" "bpepool" {
  resource_group_name = azurerm_resource_group.main.name
  loadbalancer_id     = azurerm_lb.main.id
  name                = "BackEndAddressPool"
}
```

We will define an HTTP probe on port 80 for a health check and attach it to the load balancer:

```
resource "azurerm_lb_probe" "main" {
  resource_group_name = azurerm_resource_group.main.name
  loadbalancer_id     = azurerm_lb.main.id
  name                = "http-running-probe"
  port                = 80
}
```

We need a NAT rule to map the load balancer ports to the backend pool port, and therefore we will define a load balancer rule that will map port 80 on the load balancer with port 80 of the backend pool Virtual Machines We will also attach the http health check probe in this config:

```
resource "azurerm_lb_rule" "lbnatrule" {
  resource_group_name            = azurerm_resource_group.main.name
  loadbalancer_id                = azurerm_lb.main.id
  name                           = "http"
  protocol                       = "Tcp"
  frontend_port                  = 80
  backend_port                   = 80
  backend_address_pool_id        = azurerm_lb_backend_address_
pool.bpepool.id
  frontend_ip_configuration_name = "PublicIPAddress"
  probe_id                       = azurerm_lb_probe.main.id
}
```

Now, we will define the Virtual Machine scale set with the resource group using the custom image and the load balancer we defined before:

```
resource "azurerm_virtual_machine_scale_set" "main" {
  name                = "webscaleset"
  location            = var.location
  resource_group_name = azurerm_resource_group.main.name
  upgrade_policy_mode = "Manual"
  sku {
    name     = "Standard_DS1_v2"
    tier     = "Standard"
    capacity = 2
  }
  storage_profile_image_reference {
```

```
      id=data.azurerm_image.websig.id
  }
```

We then go ahead and define the OS disk and the data disk:

```
storage_profile_os_disk {
  name                = ""
  caching             = "ReadWrite"
  create_option       = "FromImage"
  managed_disk_type   = "Standard_LRS"
}
storage_profile_data_disk {
  lun           = 0
  caching       = "ReadWrite"
  create_option = "Empty"
  disk_size_gb  = 10
}
```

The OS profile defines how we log in to the Virtual Machine:

```
os_profile {
  computer_name_prefix = "web"
  admin_username       = var.admin_username
  admin_password       = var.admin_password
}
os_profile_linux_config {
  disable_password_authentication = false
}
```

We then define a network profile that will associate the scale set with the load balancer we defined before:

```
network_profile {
  name    = "webnp"
  primary = true
  ip_configuration {
    name                                   = "IPConfiguration"
    subnet_id                              = azurerm_subnet.main.id
    load_balancer_backend_address_pool_ids = [azurerm_lb_
backend_address_pool.bpepool.id]
    primary = true
  }
}
tags = {}
```

```
}
```

Now moving on to the database configuration, we will start by defining a network security group for the database servers to allow port 22 and 3306 from internal servers within the virtual network:

```
resource "azurerm_network_security_group" "db_nsg" {
    name                = "db-nsg"
    location            = var.location
    resource_group_name = azurerm_resource_group.main.name
    security_rule {
        name                       = "SSH"
        priority                   = 1001
        direction                  = "Inbound"
        access                     = "Allow"
        protocol                   = "Tcp"
        source_port_range          = "*"
        destination_port_range     = "22"
        source_address_prefix      = "*"
        destination_address_prefix = "*"
    }
    security_rule {
        name                       = "SQL"
        priority                   = 1002
        direction                  = "Inbound"
        access                     = "Allow"
        protocol                   = "Tcp"
        source_port_range          = "*"
        destination_port_range     = "3306"
        source_address_prefix      = "*"
        destination_address_prefix = "*"
    }
    tags = {}
}
```

We then define an NIC to provide an internal IP to the Virtual Machine:

```
resource "azurerm_network_interface" "db" {
  name                = "db-nic"
  location            = var.location
  resource_group_name = azurerm_resource_group.main.name
  ip_configuration {
    name                          = "db-ipconfiguration"
```

```
    subnet_id                        = azurerm_subnet.main.id
    private_ip_address_allocation = "Dynamic"
  }
}
```

We will then associate the network security group to the network interface:

```
resource "azurerm_network_interface_security_group_association"
"db" {
    network_interface_id     = azurerm_network_interface.db.id
    network_security_group_id = azurerm_network_security_group.
db_nsg.id
}
```

Finally, we'll define the database Virtual Machine using the custom image:

```
resource "azurerm_virtual_machine" "db" {
  name                  = "db"
  location              = var.location
  resource_group_name   = azurerm_resource_group.main.name
  network_interface_ids = [azurerm_network_interface.db.id]
  vm_size               = var.vm_size
  delete_os_disk_on_termination = true
  storage_image_reference {
    id    = data.azurerm_image.dbsig.id
  }
  storage_os_disk {
    name              = "db-osdisk"
    caching           = "ReadWrite"
    create_option     = "FromImage"
    managed_disk_type = "Standard_LRS"
  }
  os_profile {
    computer_name  = "db"
    admin_username = var.admin_username
    admin_password = var.admin_password
  }
  os_profile_linux_config {
    disable_password_authentication = false
  }
  tags = {}
}
```

Now, as we've defined everything we needed, fill the `terraform.tfvars` file with the required information, and go ahead and initialize our Terraform workspace by using the following command:

```
$ terraform init
```

As Terraform has initialized successfully, use the following command to apply the Terraform configuration:

```
$ terraform apply
Apply complete! Resources: 13 added, 0 changed, 0 destroyed.
Outputs:
web_ip_addr = "40.115.61.69"
```

As Terraform has applied the configuration and provided the load balancer IP address as an output, let's use that to navigate to the web server:

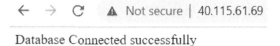

Database Connected successfully

Figure 8.5 – LAMP stack working correctly

And as we get the `Database Connected successfully` message, we see that the configuration is successful! We've successfully created a scalable LAMP stack by using Packer, Ansible, and Terraform. It combines Infrastructure as Code, Configuration as Code, immutable infrastructure, and modern DevOps practices to create a seamless environment without any manual intervention.

Summary

In this chapter, we have covered immutable infrastructure and how to use Packer to create immutable infrastructure. We then used Packer with the Ansible provisioner to build custom images for Apache and MySQL. We used the custom images to create a scalable LAMP stack using Terraform. The chapter introduced you to the era of modern DevOps, where everything is automated. We follow the same principles for building and deploying all kinds of infrastructure, be it containers or Virtual Machines. In the next chapter, we will move to the world of **Container as a Service** (**CaaS**) and serverless computing for containers.

Questions

1. Immutable infrastructure helps avoid configuration drift. (True/False)

2. It is a best practice to source sensitive data from external variables such as environment variables or a secret management tool such as Hashicorp's Vault. (True/False)

3. What modifications do we need to make to our existing playbooks to allow Packer to use them? (Choose one.)

    A. Remove any existing `ansible.cfg` files from the current working directory.

    B. Remove any host files from the current working directory.

    C. Update the `hosts` attribute to default within the playbook.

    D. None of the above.

4. Which of the following are limitations of using the Ansible provisioner with Packer? (Choose all that apply.)

    A. You cannot pass Jinja2 macros as is to your Ansible playbooks.

    B. You cannot define `remote_user` within your Ansible playbooks.

    C. You cannot use Jinja2 templates within your Ansible playbooks.

    D. You cannot use roles and variables within your Ansible playbooks.

5. While naming managed images, what should we consider? (Choose all that apply.)

    A. Name images as specifically as possible.

    B. Use the version as part of the image.

    C. Don't use the version as part of the image name. Instead, always use the `-force` flag within the Packer build.

6. When using multiple provisioners, how are configurations applied to the build Virtual Machine?

    A. One after the other based on occurrence in the JSON file

    B. Parallelly

7. We can use a single Packer JSON file to build images with the same configuration in multiple cloud environments. (True/False)

8. What features does a Virtual Machine scale set provide? (Choose all that apply.)

   A. It helps you horizontally scale Virtual Machine instances with traffic.

   B. It helps you auto-heal faulty Virtual Machines.

   C. It helps you do canary deployments.

   D. None of the above.

Answers

1. True
2. True
3. C
4. A, B
5. A, B
6. B
7. True
8. A,B,C

9

Containers as a Service (CaaS) and Serverless Computing for Containers

In the last three chapters, we have covered immutable infrastructure, configuration as code, and infrastructure as code and how to use Packer, Ansible, and Terraform to create one. These chapters introduced you to the era of modern DevOps, where everything is automated. We follow the same principles for building and deploying all kinds of infrastructure, be it containers or virtual machines.

Now, let's get back to the container world and look at other ways of automating and managing container deployments – **Containers as a Service (CaaS)** and **Serverless computing for containers**. CaaS provides container-based virtualization that abstracts away all management behind the scenes and helps you manage your containers, without worrying about the underlying infrastructure and orchestration. For simple deployments and less complex applications, CaaS can be a savior. Serverless computing is a broad term that encompasses applications that can be run without us having to worry about the infrastructure behind the scenes. It has an additional benefit that you can focus purely on the application. We will discuss CaaS technologies such as **AWS ECS with Fargate** in detail and briefly discuss other cloud-based CaaS offerings such as **Azure Kubernetes Services**, **Google Kubernetes Engine**, and **Google Cloud Run**. We will then delve into the popular open source serverless CaaS solution known as **Knative**.

In this chapter, we're going to cover the following main topics:

- The need for serverless offerings
- Amazon ECS with EC2 and Fargate
- Other CaaS services
- Open source CaaS with Knative

Technical requirements

You will need an active AWS subscription for this chapter's exercises. Currently, AWS is offering a free tier for some products. You can sign up at `https://aws.amazon.com/ free`. This chapter uses some paid services, but we will try to minimize how many we use as much as possible during the exercises.

You will also need to clone the following GitHub repository for some of the exercises:

`https://github.com/PacktPublishing/Modern-DevOps-Practices`.

Run the following command to clone the repository into your home directory. Then, `cd` into the `ch9` directory to access the required resources:

```
$ git clone https://github.com/PacktPublishing/Modern-DevOps-\
Practices.git modern-devops
$ cd modern-devops/ch9
```

As the repository contains files with placeholders, you will have to replace the `<your_dockerhub_user>` string with the your actual Docker Hub user. Use the following commands to substitute the placeholders.

```
$ find ./ -type f -exec sed -i -e 's/\
<your_dockerhub_user>/<your actual docker hub user>/g' {} \;
```

So, let's get started!

The need for serverless offerings

So far, we've been spinning up and down compute instances such as virtual machines. Somehow, we were aware of and optimized the number of resources, machines, and all the infrastructure surrounding the applications we'd built. Still, you want your team to focus on what they do best – code development. Unless your organization wants to invest heavily in an expensive infrastructure team to do a lot of heavy lifting behind the scenes, you'd be better off concentrating on writing and building quality applications, rather than focusing on where and how to run them and how to optimize them.

Serverless offerings come as a reprieve for this problem. Instead of concentrating on how to host your infrastructure to run your applications, you can declare what you want to run, and the serverless offering manages it for you. This has come as a boon for small enterprises that do not have the budget to invest heavily in infrastructure and want to get started quickly, without wasting too much time standing up and maintaining infrastructure to run the applications.

Serverless offerings also offer automatic placement and scaling for your container and application workloads. You can spin from 0 to 100 instances in some cases in a matter of minutes, if not seconds. The best part is that you pay for what you use in some services rather than what you allocate.

This chapter will concentrate on a very popular AWS container management offering called **Elastic Container Service** (**ECS**), along with the AWS container serverless offering **AWS Fargate**. We will then briefly look at offerings from other cloud platforms and, finally, the open source standard for container-based serverless, known as Knative.

Now, let's go ahead and look at Amazon ECS.

Amazon ECS with EC2 and Fargate

Amazon **Elastic Container Service** (**ECS**) is a container orchestration platform that AWS offers. It is simple to use and manage, uses Docker behind the scenes, and can deploy your workloads to **Amazon EC2**, a virtual machine-based solution, or Amazon Fargate, a serverless solution.

It is a highly scalable solution that helps you host your containers in minutes. It makes it easy to host, run, stop, and start your containers. Similar to how Kubernetes offers **pods**, ECS offers **tasks**, which help you run your container workloads. A task can contain one or more containers, grouped according to a logical relationship. You can also group one or more tasks into **services**. Services are similar to Kubernetes controllers, which manage tasks and can ensure that the required number of replicas of your tasks are running in the right places at a time. ECS uses simple API calls to provide many functionalities, such as creating, updating, reading, and deleting tasks and services.

ECS also allows you to place your containers according to multiple placement strategies while keeping high availability and resource optimization in mind. You can tweak the placement algorithm according to your priority – cost, availability, or a mix of both. So, you can use ECS to run one-time batch workloads or long-running microservices, all using a simple to use API interface.

ECS architecture

ECS is a cloud-based regional service. When you spin up an ECS cluster, the instances span across multiple availability zones, where you can schedule your tasks and services using simple manifests. These ECS manifests are very similar to the `docker-compose` YAML manifests, where we specify what tasks to run and what tasks make a service.

You can run ECS within an existing **virtual private cloud** (**VPC**). The VPC consists of multiple **Availability Zones** (**AZ**). We have the option to schedule tasks in either AWS EC2 or AWS Fargate.

Your ECS cluster can have one or more EC2 instances attached to it. You also have the option to attach an existing EC2 instance to a cluster by installing the ECS node agent within your EC2 instance. The agent sends information about your containers' state and the tasks to the ECS scheduler. It then interacts with the container runtime to schedule containers within the node. They are similar to `kubelet` in the Kubernetes ecosystem. If you run your containers within EC2 instances, you pay for the number of EC2 instances you allocate to the cluster.

If you plan to use Fargate, the infrastructure is wholly abstracted from you, and you just have to specify the amount of CPU and memory your container is set to consume. You pay for the amount of CPU and memory that your container consumes rather than the resources you allocate to the machines.

> **Tip**
>
> Although you only pay for the resources you consume in Fargate, it turns out to be more expensive than running your tasks on EC2, especially when you're running daemon services such as a web server. The rule of thumb is to run daemon tasks within EC2 and batch tasks with Fargate. That will give you the best cost optimization.

When we schedule a task, AWS spins up the container on a managed EC2 or Fargate server by pulling the required container image from a **Container Registry**. Every task has an elastic network interface attached to it. Multiple tasks are grouped as a service, and the service ensures that all the required tasks run at once.

AWS ECS uses a task scheduler to schedule containers on your cluster. It places your containers in your cluster's right node based on placement logic, availability, and cost requirements. The scheduler also ensures that the desired number of tasks are running on the right node at a given time.

The following diagram explains the ECS cluster architecture beautifully:

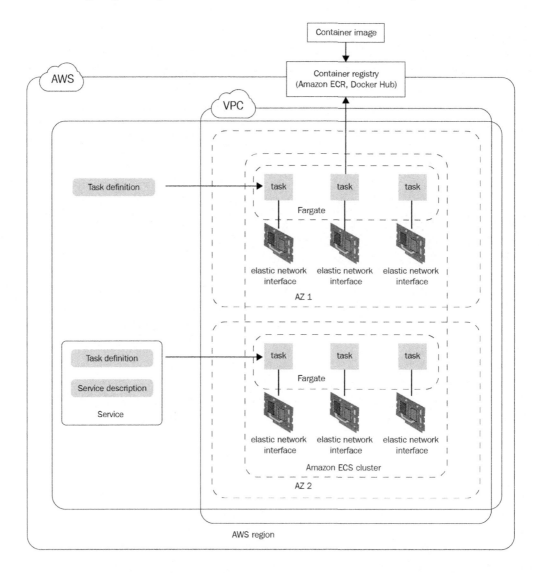

Figure 9.1 – ECS architecture

Amazon provides the ECS CLI for interacting with the ECS cluster. It is a simple command-line tool that you can use to administer an ECS cluster and create and manage tasks and services on the ECS cluster.

Now, let's go ahead and install the ECS CLI.

Installing the AWS and ECS CLIs

The AWS CLI is available as a `deb` package within the public `apt` repositories. To install it, run the following commands:

```
$ sudo apt update
$ sudo apt install awscli -y
$ aws --version
aws-cli/1.18.69 Python/3.5.2 Linux/4.4.0-1121-aws
botocore/1.16.19
```

Installing the ECS CLI in the Linux ecosystem is simple. We just need to download the binary and move to the system path using the following command:

```
$ sudo curl -Lo /usr/local/bin/ecs-cli https://\
amazon-ecs-cli.s3.amazonaws.com/ecs-cli-linux-amd64-latest
$ sudo chmod +x /usr/local/bin/ecs-cli
```

Run the following command to check if `ecs-cli` has been installed correctly:

```
$ ecs-cli --version
ecs-cli version 1.21.0 (bb0b8f0)
```

As we can see, `ecs-cli` has been successfully installed on our system.

The next step is to allow `ecs-cli` to connect with your AWS API. You need to export a few environment variables for this. Run the following commands to do so:

```
$ export AWS_SECRET_ACCESS_KEY=...
$ export AWS_ACCESS_KEY_ID=...
$ export AWS_DEFAULT_REGION=...
```

Once we've set the environment variables, `ecs-cli` will use them to authenticate with the AWS API. In the next section, we'll spin up an ECS cluster using the ECS CLI.

Spinning up an ECS cluster

We can use the ECS CLI commands to spin up an ECS cluster. You can run your containers in EC2 and Fargate, so first, we will create a cluster that runs EC2 instances. Then, we will add Fargate tasks within the cluster.

To connect with your EC2 instances, you need to generate a key pair within AWS. To do so, run the following command:

```
$ aws ec2 create-key-pair --key-name ecs-keypair
```

The output of this command will provide the key pair in a JSON file. Extract the JSON file's key material and save that in a separate file called `ecs-keypair.pem`. Remember to replace the \n characters with a new line when you save the file.

Once we've generated the key pair, we can use the following command to create an ECS cluster using the ECS CLI:

```
$ ecs-cli up --keypair ecs-keypair --instance-type \
t2.micro --size 2 --cluster cluster-1 --capability-iam
INFO[0003] Using recommended Amazon Linux 2 AMI with ECS Agent
1.50.1 and Docker version 19.03.13-ce
INFO[0004] Created cluster
cluster=cluster-1 region=us-east-1
INFO[0006] Waiting for your cluster resources to be created...
INFO[0006] Cloudformation stack status
stackStatus=CREATE_IN_PROGRESS
VPC created: vpc-06aaea0bc4a8c7459
Security Group created: sg-097206175813aa7e7
Subnet created: subnet-088b52c91a6f40fd7
Subnet created: subnet-032cd63290da67271
Cluster creation succeeded.
```

When we issue this command, in the background, AWS spins up a stack of resources using **CloudFormation**. CloudFormation is AWS's **Infrastructure as Code (IaC)** solution, similar to Terraform, but it caters only to AWS. The Cloud Formation template consists of several resources such as a VPC, a security group, a subnet within the VPC, a route table, a route, a subnet route table association, an internet gateway, an **Identity Access Management (IAM)** role, an instance profile, a launch configuration, an Auto Scaling group, a VPC gateway attachment, and the cluster itself. The Auto Scaling group contains two EC2 instances that are running and serving the cluster. Keep a copy of the output as we would need the details later on during the course of the exercises.

Now that our cluster is running fine, we will go ahead and spin up our first task.

Creating task definitions

ECS tasks are similar to Kubernetes pods. They are the basic building blocks of ECS and are comprised of one or more related containers. Task definitions are the blueprints for ECS tasks and define what the ECS task should look like. They are very similar to `docker-compose` files and written in YAML format. ECS also uses all versions of `docker-compose` to allow us to define tasks. They help you define the containers and their image, their resource requirements, where they should run (EC2 or Fargate), their volume and port mappings, and other networking requirements.

> **Tip**
> Using the `docker-compose` manifest to spin up tasks and services is a great idea as it will help you align your configuration with an open standard.

A task is a finite process and only runs once. Even if it's a daemon process such as a web server, the task still runs once as it waits for the daemon process to end (which runs indefinitely in theory). The task's life cycle follows the *Pending -> Running -> Stopped* states. So, when you schedule your task, the task enters the *Pending* state, attempting to pull the image from the container registry. Then, it tries to start the container. Once the container has started, it enters the *Running* state. When the container has completed executing or errored out, it ends up in the *Stopped* state. If there are startup errors with a container, it directly transitions from the *Pending* state to the *Stopped* state.

Now, let's go ahead and deploy an `nginx` web server task within the ECS cluster we just created.

To access the resources for this section, `cd` into the following directory:

```
$ cd ~/modern-devops/ch9/ECS/tasks/EC2/
```

We'll use `docker-compose` task definitions here. So, let's start by defining the following `docker-compose.yml` file:

```
version: '3'
services:
  web:
    image: nginx
    ports:
      - "80:80"
    logging:
      driver: awslogs
      options:
        awslogs-group: /aws/webserver
```

```
        awslogs-region: us-east-1
        awslogs-stream-prefix: ecs
```

The YAML file defines a container `web` with an `nginx` image with host port `80` mapped to container port `80`. It uses the `awslogs` logging driver, which streams logs into **AWS CloudWatch**. It will stream the logs to the `/aws/webserver` log group in the `us-east-1` region with the `ecs` stream prefix.

The task definition also includes the resource definition; that is, the amount of resources we want to reserve for our task. Therefore, we will have to define the following `ecs-params.yaml` file:

```
version: 1
task_definition:
  services:
    web:
      cpu_shares: 100
      mem_limit: 524288000
```

This YAML file defines `cpu_shares` in millicores and `mem_limit` in bytes for the container we're planning to fire. Now, let's look at how we can schedule this task as an EC2 task.

Scheduling EC2 tasks on ECS

Let's use `ecs-cli` to apply the configuration and schedule our task using the following command:

```
$ ecs-cli compose up --create-log-groups \
--cluster cluster-1 --launch-type EC2
```

Now that the task has been scheduled and the container is running, let's list all the tasks to get the container's details and find out where it is running. To do so, run the following command:

```
$ ecs-cli ps --cluster cluster-1
Name                                                     State     Ports
TaskDefinition  Health
cluster-1/738c4ad7d89944a085142b8e18f0c171/web   RUNNING
3.82.112.105:80->80/tcp  ch9:1              UNKNOWN
```

As we can see, the web container is running on `cluster-1` on `3.82.112.105:80`. Now, use the following command to `curl` this endpoint to see what we get:

```
$ curl 3.82.112.105:80
<html>
<head>
<title>Welcome to nginx!</title>
...
</html>
```

Here, we get the default NGINX home page! We've successfully scheduled a container on ECS using the EC2 launch type. You might want to duplicate this task for more traffic. This is known as horizontal scaling. We'll see how in the next section.

Scaling tasks

We can easily scale tasks using `ecs-cli`. Use the following command to scale the tasks to two:

```
$ ecs-cli compose scale 2 --cluster cluster-1 --launch-type EC2
```

Now, use the following command to check if two containers are running on the cluster:

```
$ ecs-cli ps --cluster cluster-1
Name                                                       State      Ports
TaskDefinition  Health
cluster-1/738c4ad7d89944a085142b8e18f0c171/web  RUNNING
3.82.112.105:80->80/tcp    ch9:1                UNKNOWN
cluster-1/b545856ff79a407d9c813ee3c86f8e47/web  RUNNING
3.237.240.116:80->80/tcp   ch9:1                UNKNOWN
```

As we can see, two containers are running on the cluster. Now, let's query CloudWatch to get the logs of the containers.

Querying container logs from CloudWatch

CloudWatch is AWS's monitoring and log analytics tool. It helps us monitor our infrastructure and applications running on AWS. To query logs from Cloudwatch, we must list the log streams using the following command:

```
$ aws logs describe-log-streams --log-group-name \
/aws/webserver --log-stream-name-prefix ecs|grep logStreamName
```

```
"logStreamName": "ecs/web/738c4ad7d89944a085142b8e18f0c171",
"logStreamName": "ecs/web/b545856ff79a407d9c813ee3c86f8e47",
```

As we can see, there are two log streams for this – one for each task. `logStreamName` follows the convention `<log_stream_prefix>/<task_name>/<task_id>`. So, to get the logs for `cluster-1/738c4ad7d89944a085142b8e18f0c171/web`, run the following command:

```
$ aws logs get-log-events --log-group-name /aws/webserver \
    --log-stream ecs/web/738c4ad7d89944a085142b8e18f0c171
```

Here, you will see a stream of logs in JSON format in the response. Now, let's look at how we can stop running tasks.

Stopping tasks

`ecs-cli` uses the friendly `docker-compose` syntax for everything. Use the following command to stop the tasks in the cluster:

```
$ ecs-cli compose down --cluster cluster-1
```

Let's list the containers to see if the tasks have stopped by using the following command:

```
$ ecs-cli ps --cluster cluster-1
Name                                                        State
Ports                           TaskDefinition   Health
cluster-1/738c4ad7d89944a085142b8e18f0c171/web   STOPPED
ExitCode: 0   3.82.112.105:80->80/tcp   ch9:1              UNKNOWN
cluster-1/b545856ff79a407d9c813ee3c86f8e47/web   STOPPED
ExitCode: 0   3.237.240.116:80->80/tcp   ch9:1             UNKNOWN
```

As we can see, both containers have stopped.

Running tasks on EC2 is not a serverless way of doing things. You still have to provision and manage the EC2 instances, and although ECS takes care of managing workloads on the cluster, you still have to pay for the number of resources you've provisioned in the form of EC2 instances. AWS offers Fargate as a serverless solution where you pay per resource consumption. Let's look at how we can create the same task as a Fargate task.

Scheduling Fargate tasks on ECS

Scheduling tasks on Fargate is very similar to EC2. Here, we just need to specify `launch-type` as Fargate.

To schedule the same task on Fargate, run the following command:

```
$ ecs-cli compose up --create-log-groups \
--cluster cluster-1 --launch-type FARGATE
FATA[0001] ClientException: Fargate only supports network mode
'awsvpc'.
```

Oops! We have a problem! Well, it's complaining about the network type. For a Fargate task, we need to supply the network type as awsvpc instead of the default bridge network. The awsvpc network is an overlay network that implements the **container network interface (CNI)**. To understand more about Docker networking, please refer to *Chapter 1, The Move to Containers*. For now, let's go ahead and configure the awsvpc network type. But before that, the Fargate task requires a few configurations.

To access the resources for this section, cd into the following directory:

```
$ cd ~/modern-devops/ch9/ECS/tasks/FARGATE/
```

First of all, we'll have to assume a task execution role for the ECS agent to authenticate with the AWS API and interact with Fargate.

To do so, create the following task-execution-assume-role.json file:

```
{
    "Version": "2012-10-17",
    "Statement": [
      {
        "Sid": "",
        "Effect": "Allow",
        "Principal": {
          "Service": "ecs-tasks.amazonaws.com"
        },
        "Action": "sts:AssumeRole"
      }
    ]
}
```

Then, use the following command to assume the task execution role:

```
$ aws iam --region us-east-1 create-role --role-name \
ecsTaskExecutionRole --assume-role-policy-document \
file://task-execution-assume-role.json
```

ECS provides a default Role Policy called `AmazonECSTaskExecutionRolePolicy`, which contains various permissions that help you interact with Cloudwatch and Elastic Container Registry. The following `json` outlines the permission the policy has:

```json
{
    "Version": "2012-10-17",
    "Statement": [
        {
            "Effect": "Allow",
            "Action": [
                "ecr:GetAuthorizationToken",
                "ecr:BatchCheckLayerAvailability",
                "ecr:GetDownloadUrlForLayer",
                "ecr:BatchGetImage",
                "logs:CreateLogStream",
                "logs:PutLogEvents"
            ],
            "Resource": "*"
        }
    ]
}
```

We have to assign this Role Policy to the `ecsTaskExecution` role we assumed previously by using the following command:

```
$ aws iam attach-role-policy --policy-arn \
arn:aws:iam::aws:policy/service-role\
/AmazonECSTaskExecutionRolePolicy \
--role-name ecsTaskExecutionRole
```

Once we've assigned the policy to the `ecsTaskExecution` role, we need to source the ID of both subnets and the security group of the ECS cluster when we created it. You can find those details in the command-line output from when we created the cluster. We will use these details in the following `ecs-params.yml` file:

```yaml
version: 1
task_definition:
  task_execution_role: ecsTaskExecutionRole
  ecs_network_mode: awsvpc
  task_size:
    mem_limit: 0.5GB
    cpu_limit: 256
run_params:
```

```
network_configuration:
  awsvpc_configuration:
    subnets:
      - "subnet-088b52c91a6f40fd7"
      - "subnet-032cd63290da67271"
    security_groups:
      - "sg-097206175813aa7e7"
    assign_public_ip: ENABLED
```

The ecs-params.yml file consists of a task_execution_role, which we created, and ecs_network_mode set to awsvpc, as required by Fargate. We've defined task_size so that it has 0.5GB of memory and 256 millicores of CPU. So, since Fargate is a serverless solution, we only pay for the CPU cores and memory we consume. The run_params section consists of network_configuration, which contains awsvpc_configuration. Here, we specify both subnets that were created when we created the ECS cluster. We must also specify security_groups, which we created with the ECS cluster.

> **Note**
>
> Use the subnets and security group of your ECS cluster instead of copying the ones in this example.

Now that we're ready to fire the task on Fargate, let's run the following command:

```
$ ecs-cli compose up --create-log-groups \
--cluster cluster-1 --launch-type FARGATE
```

Now, let's check if the task is running successfully by using the following command:

```
$ ecs-cli ps --cluster cluster-1
Name                                                    State

Ports                      TaskDefinition  Health
cluster-1/93972076615d49c589b80aa7d58834cf/web  RUNNING

3.91.62.193:80->80/tcp  FARGATE:1         UNKNOWN
```

As we can see, the task is running on `3.91.62.193:80` as a Fargate task. Let's `curl` this URL to see if we get a response by using the following command:

```
$ curl 3.91.62.193:80
<html>
<head>
<title>Welcome to nginx!</title>
...
</body>
</html>
```

As we can see, we get the default NGINX home page.

Now, let's go ahead and delete the task we created by using the following command:

```
$ ecs-cli compose down --cluster cluster-1
```

As we already know, tasks have a set life cycle, and once they stop, they stop. You cannot start the same task again. Therefore, if we want to ensure that a certain number of tasks are always running, we must create a service. We'll create a service in the next section.

Scheduling services on ECS

ECS services are similar to Kubernetes **ReplicaSets**. They ensure that a certain number of tasks are always running at a particular time. To schedule a service, we can use the `ecs-cli` command line.

> **Tip**
>
> Always uses services for applications that run as daemons, such as web servers. For batch jobs, always use tasks; as we don't want to recreate the job once it's ended.

To run the `nginx` web server as a service, we can use the following command:

```
$ ecs-cli compose service up --create-log-groups \
  --cluster cluster-1 --launch-type FARGATE
INFO[0001] Using ECS task definition
TaskDefinition="FARGATE:1"
WARN[0002] Failed to create log group /aws/webserver in
us-east-1: The specified log group already exists
INFO[0002] Auto-enabling ECS Managed Tags
```

```
INFO[0008] (service FARGATE) has started 1 tasks: (task
eb5ff0b96af549dda69136adaac57a59).  timestamp="2021-02-18
14:57:15 +0000 UTC"
INFO[0034] Service status
desiredCount=1 runningCount=1 serviceName=FARGATE
INFO[0034] ECS Service has reached a stable state
desiredCount=1 runningCount=1 serviceName=FARGATE
INFO[0034] Created an ECS service
service=FARGATE taskDefinition="FARGATE:1"
```

By looking at the logs, we can see that the service is trying to ensure that the tasks' desired count matches the tasks' running count. If for some reason, your task is deleted, ECS will replace it with a new one.

Let's list the tasks and see what we get by using the following command:

```
$ ecs-cli ps --cluster cluster-1
Name                                        State

Ports                    TaskDefinition  Health
cluster-1/eb5ff0b96af549dda69136adaac57a59/web  RUNNING

3.88.145.147:80->80/tcp  FARGATE:1       UNKNOWN
```

As we can see, the service has created a new task that is running on 3.88.145.147:80. Let's try to access this URL using the following command:

```
$ curl 3.88.145.147
<!DOCTYPE html>
<html>
<head>
<title>Welcome to nginx!</title>
...
</html>
```

We still get the default NGINX home page in the response. Now, let's try to browse the logs of the task.

Browsing container logs using the ECS CLI

Apart from using AWS Cloudwatch, you can also use the friendly ECS CLI to do this, irrespective of where your logs are stored. This helps us see everything from a single pane of glass.

Run the following command to do so:

```
$ ecs-cli logs --task-id eb5ff0b96af549dda69136adaac57a59 \
--cluster cluster-1
/docker-entrypoint.sh: /docker-entrypoint.d/ is not empty, will
attempt to perform configuration
/docker-entrypoint.sh: Looking for shell scripts in /docker-
entrypoint.d/
/docker-entrypoint.sh: Launching /docker-entrypoint.d/10-
listen-on-ipv6-by-default.sh
10-listen-on-ipv6-by-default.sh: info: Getting the checksum of
/etc/nginx/conf.d/default.conf
10-listen-on-ipv6-by-default.sh: info: Enabled listen on IPv6
in /etc/nginx/conf.d/default.conf
/docker-entrypoint.sh: Launching /docker-entrypoint.d/20-
envsubst-on-templates.sh
/docker-entrypoint.sh: Launching /docker-entrypoint.d/30-tune-
worker-processes.sh
/docker-entrypoint.sh: Configuration complete; ready for start
up
65.1.110.35 - - [18/Feb/2021:15:01:12 +0000] "GET / HTTP/1.1"
200 612 "-" "curl/7.47.0" "-"
```

As we can see, we can browse the logs for the particular task this service is running. Now, let's go ahead and delete the service.

Deleting an ECS service

To delete the service, run the following command:

```
$ ecs-cli compose service down --cluster cluster-1
INFO[0001] Deleted ECS service
service=FARGATE
INFO[0001] Service status
desiredCount=0 runningCount=1 serviceName=FARGATE
INFO[0006] Service status
desiredCount=0 runningCount=0 serviceName=FARGATE
INFO[0006] (service FARGATE) has stopped 1 running tasks:
(task eb5ff0b96af549dda69136adaac57a59).  timestamp="2021-02-18
15:06:21 +0000 UTC"
INFO[0006] ECS Service has reached a stable state
```

```
desiredCount=0 runningCount=0 serviceName=FARGATE
```

As we can see, the service has been deleted.

As we can see, even if we create multiple instances of tasks, they run on different IP addresses and can be accessed separately. However, in reality, tasks need to be load balanced, and we would need to provide a single endpoint. Let's look at a solution we can use to manage this.

Load balancing containers running on ECS

Load balancing is an essential functionality of multi-instance applications. They help us serve the application on a single endpoint. Therefore, you can have multiple instances of your applications running at a time, and the end user doesn't need to worry about what instance they're calling. AWS provides two main types of load balancing solutions – **layer 4** load balancing with the Network Load Balancer and **layer 7** load balancing with the Application Load Balancer.

> **Tip**
>
> While both load balancers have their use cases, using a layer 7 load balancer provides a significant advantage for HTTP-based applications. It offers advanced traffic management such as path-based and host-based routing.

So, let's go ahead a create an Application Load Balancer to frontend our tasks using the following command:

```
$ aws elbv2 create-load-balancer --name ecs-alb \
--subnets <SUBNET-1> <SUBNET-2> \
--security-groups <SECURITY_GROUP_ID> \
--region us-east-1
```

The output of the preceding command contains values for LoadBalancerARN and DNSName. We will need to use them in the subsequent steps, so keep a copy of the output safe.

The next step will be to create a target group. The target group defines the group of tasks and the port they will be listening to, and the load balancer will forward traffic to it. Use the following command to define a target group:

```
$ aws elbv2 create-target-group --name target-group \
--protocol HTTP --port 80 --target-type ip \
--vpc-id <VPC_ID> --region us-east-1
```

You will get the target group ARN in the response. Keep it safe as we will need it in the next step.

Next, we will need a listener running on the load balancer. This should forward traffic from the load balancer to the target group. Use the following command to do so:

```
$ aws elbv2 create-listener --load-balancer-arn \
<LOAD_BALANCER_ARN> --protocol HTTP --port 80 \
--default-actions Type=forward,TargetGroupArn=\
<TARGET_GROUP_ARN> --region us-east-1
```

You will get the listener ARN in response to this command. Please keep that handy as we will need it in the next step.

Now that we've defined the load balancer, we need to run `ecs-cli compose service up` to deploy our service. We will also provide the target group as a parameter to associate our service with the load balancer.

To access the resources for this section, `cd` into the following directory:

```
$ cd ~/modern-devops/ch9/ECS/loadbalancing/
```

Run the following command to do so:

```
$ ecs-cli compose service up --create-log-groups \
--cluster cluster-1 --launch-type FARGATE \
--target-group-arn <TARGET_GROUP_ARN> \
--container-name web --container-port 80
```

Now that the service is running and we have our task running on Fargate, we can scale our service to three desired tasks. To do so, run the following command:

```
$ ecs-cli compose service scale 3 --cluster cluster-1
```

Since our service has scaled to three tasks, let's go ahead and hit the load balancer DNS endpoint we captured in the first step. This should provide us with the default NGINX response. Run the following command to do so:

```
$ curl ecs-alb-1660189891.us-east-1.elb.amazonaws.com
<html>
<head>
<title>Welcome to nginx!</title>
...
</html>
```

As we can see, we get a default NGINX response from the load balancer. This shows that load balancing is working well!

ECS provides a host of other features, such as horizontal autoscaling, customizable task placement algorithms, and others, but they are beyond the scope of this book. Please read the ECS documentation to learn more about other aspects of the tool. Now, let's look at some of the other popular **Container as a Service (CaaS)** products available on the market.

Other CaaS products

Amazon ECS provides a versatile way of managing your container workloads. It works great when you have a smaller, simpler architecture and don't want to add the additional overhead of using a complex container orchestration engine such as Kubernetes.

> Tip
>
> If you run exclusively on AWS and you don't have a need for a future multi-cloud or hybrid-cloud strategy, ECS is an excellent tool choice. Fargate makes it easier to deploy your containers and run them without worrying about the infrastructure behind the scenes.

ECS is tightly coupled with AWS and its architecture. To solve this problem, we can use managed services within AWS, such as the **Elastic Kubernetes Service (EKS)**. It offers the Kubernetes API to schedule your workloads. This makes managing containers even more versatile as you can spin up a Kubernetes cluster with ease and use a standard, open source solution that you can install and run anywhere you like. This does not tie you to a particular vendor. However, EKS is slightly more expensive than ECS and adds a *$0.10* per hour cluster management charge. That is nothing in comparison to the benefits you get out of it.

If you aren't running on AWS, there are options from other providers too. The next of the big three cloud providers is Azure, which offers the **Azure Kubernetes Service** (**AKS**), a managed Kubernetes solution that can help you get started in minutes. AKS provides a fully managed solution with event-driven Elastic provisioning for worker nodes as and when required. It also integrates quite nicely with Azure DevOps, which gives you a faster end-to-end development experience. The best part of this is that you don't have to pay a cluster management charge (at the time of writing this book).

Google Kubernetes Engine (**GKE**) is one of the most robust Kubernetes platforms available. Since the Kubernetes project came from Google and they are the largest contributor to this project in the open source community, GKE is generally quicker to roll out newer versions and are the first to release security patches into the solution. Also, it is one of the most feature-rich and customizable solutions and offers several plugins as a cluster configuration. Therefore, you can choose what you need to install on bootstrap and harden your cluster even further. All these come at a cost, though, as GKE charges a *$0.10* cluster management charge per hour, just like Amazon.

If you don't want to use Kubernetes because your architecture is not complicated and there are only a few containers to manage, you can use Google Cloud Run. Google Cloud Run is a serverless CaaS solution built on the open source Knative project. It helps you run your containers without any vendor lock-in. Since it is serverless, you pay for the number of containers you use and their resource utilization. It is a fully scalable solution and very well-integrated with Google Cloud's DevOps and monitoring solutions such as Cloud Code, Cloud Build, Cloud Monitoring, and Cloud Logging. The best part is that it is comparable to AWS Fargate, and it abstracts all infrastructure behind the scenes. So, it's kind of a minimal Ops or NoOps solution.

Now that we've talked about Knative as an open source CaaS solution, let's discuss it in more detail.

Open source CaaS with Knative

As we've seen, there are several vendor-specific CaaS services available on the market. Still, the problem with most of them is that they are tied up to a single cloud provider. Our container deployment specification then becomes vendor-specific and results in vendor lock-in. As modern DevOps engineers, we also have to ensure that the solution we propose best fits the architecture's needs, and avoiding vendor lock-in is one of the most important ones.

However, Kubernetes in itself is not serverless. You have to have infrastructure defined, and daemon services should have at least a single instance running at a particular time. This makes managing microservices applications a pain and resource-intensive.

But wait! We said that microservices help optimize infrastructure consumption. Yes, that's correct, they do, but they do so within the container space. Imagine that you have a shared cluster of VMs where parts of the application scale with traffic, and each part of the application has its peaks and troughs. By doing this, you will save a lot of infrastructure by performing this simple multi-tenancy.

However, it also means that you will have to have at least one instance of each microservice running every time – even if there is zero traffic! Well, that's not the best utilization we have. How about creating instances when you get the first hit and not having any when you don't have traffic? This would save a lot of resources, especially when things are silent. You can have hundreds of microservices making up the application that would not have any instances during an idle period, and if you'd combined it with a managed service that runs Kubernetes and then autoscales your virtual machine instances with traffic, you can have minimal instances during the silent period.

There have been attempts within the open source and cloud-native space to develop an open source, vendor-agnostic, serverless framework for containers. We have **Knative** for this, which the **Cloud Native Computing Foundation** (**CNCF**) has recently adopted.

> **Tip**
> If you are running on Google Cloud, the Cloud Run service uses Knative behind the scenes. Therefore, you can use Cloud Run instead to take advantage of a fully managed serverless offering.

To understand how Knative works, let's look at the Knative architecture.

Knative architecture

The Knative project combines elements of multiple existing CNCF projects such as Kubernetes, **Istio**, **Prometheus**, and **Grafana** and eventing engines such as **Kafka** and **Google Pub/Sub**. Knative runs as a Kubernetes operator using Kubernetes **Custom Resource Definitions (CRDs)**, which helps operators administer Knative using the kubectl command line. For developers, Knative provides its API, which the kn command-line utility can use. The users are provided access through Istio, which, with its traffic management features, is a crucial component of Knative. The following diagram describes this graphically:

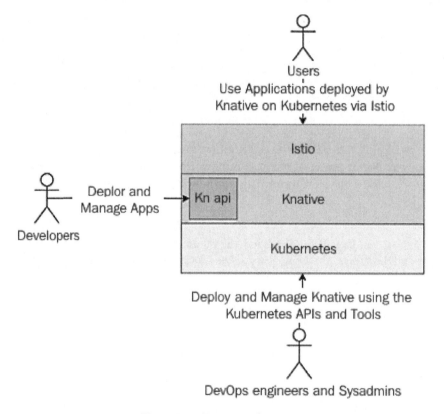

Figure 9.2 – Knative architecture

Knative consists of two main modules – *serving* and *eventing*. While the **serving** module helps us maintain stateless applications using HTTP/S endpoints, the **eventing** module integrates with eventing engines such as Kafka and Google Pub/Sub. As we've discussed mostly HTTP/S traffic so far, we will scope our discussion to Knative serving for this book.

Knative maintains *serving* pods, which help route traffic within workload pods and therefore act as proxies by using the Istio Ingress Gateway component. It provides a virtual endpoint for your service and listens to it. When it discovers a hit on the endpoint, it creates the required Kubernetes components to serve that traffic. Therefore, Knative has the functionality to scale from zero workload pods as it will spin up a pod when it receives traffic for it. The following diagram shows how:

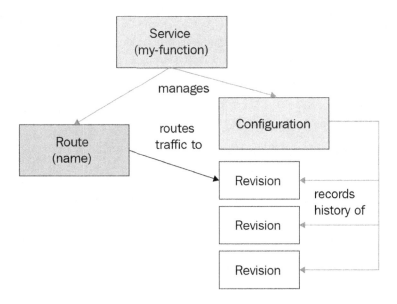

Figure 9.3 – Knative serving architecture

Knative endpoints are made up of three basic parts – `<app-name>`, `<namespace>`, and `<custom-domain>`. While `name` and `namespace` are similar to Kubernetes services, `custom-domain` is defined by us. It can either be a legitimate domain for your organization or something internal, such as `example.com`, or a Magic DNS solution, such as sslip.io, which we will use in our hands-on exercises. If you are using your organization domain, you will have to create your DNS configuration so that the domain resolves to the Istio Ingress Gateway IP addresses.

Now, let's go ahead and install Knative.

For the exercises, we will use **Google Kubernetes Engine** (**GKE**). Since GKE is a highly robust Kubernetes cluster, it is a great choice for integrating with Knative. As we mentioned previously, Google Cloud provides a free trial of $300 for 90 days. You can sign up at `https://cloud.google.com/free`, if you've not done so already.

Spinning up Google Kubernetes Engine

Once you've signed up and are on your console, you can open the Google Cloud Shell CLI to run the following commands.

You need to enable the Kubernetes Engine API first using the following command:

```
$ gcloud services enable container.googleapis.com
```

Knative requires **Kubernetes 1.17** or newer. As GKE provides **1.18** by default, at the time of writing this book, we will use the default settings as much as possible. To create a single-node autoscaling GKE cluster that scales from 1 node to 5 nodes, run the following command:

```
$ gcloud container clusters create cluster-1 \
--num-nodes 2 --enable-autoscaling \
--min-nodes 1 --max-nodes 5 --zone us-central1-a
```

And that's it! The cluster is up and running.

You will also need to clone the following GitHub repository for some of the exercises: `https://github.com/PacktPublishing/Modern-DevOps-Practices`.

Run the following command to clone the repository into your home directory. Then, `cd` into the `ch9` directory to access the required resources:

```
$ git clone https://github.com/PacktPublishing/Modern-DevOps-\
Practices.git modern-devops
```

Now that the cluster is up and running, let's go ahead and install Knative.

Installing Knative

We will start by installing the **Custom Resource Definitions** (**CRDs**) that define Knative resources as Kubernetes API resources.

To access the resources for this section, `cd` into the following directory:

```
$ cd ~/modern-devops/ch9/knative/
```

Run the following command to install the CRDs:

```
$ kubectl apply -f https://github.com/knative/serving/\
releases/download/v0.23.1/serving-crds.yaml
```

As we can see, Kubernetes has installed some CRDs. Next, we must install the core components of Knative serving. Use the following command to do so:

```
$ kubectl apply -f https://github.com/knative/serving\
/releases/download/v0.23.1/serving-core.yaml
```

Now that the core serving components have been installed, the next step is installing Istio within the Kubernetes cluster. To do so, run the following commands:

```
$ curl -L https://istio.io/downloadIstio | ISTIO_\
VERSION=1.7.0 sh - && cd istio-1.7.0 && export \
PATH=$PWD/bin:$PATH
$ istioctl install --set profile=demo
$ kubectl label namespace knative-serving \
istio-injection=enabled
```

Now that Istio has been installed, we will wait for the Istio Ingress Gateway to be assigned an external IP address. Run the following command to check this until you get an external IP in the response:

```
$ kubectl -n istio-system get service istio-ingressgateway
NAME                        TYPE              CLUSTER-IP
EXTERNAL-IP       PORT(S)
AGE
istio-ingressgateway    LoadBalancer      10.15.240.239
35.226.198.46    15021:30829/TCP,80:30199/TCP,443:32099/
TCP,31400:32240/TCP,15443:32592/TCP    117s
```

As we can see, we've been assigned an external IP – 35.226.198.46. We will use this IP for the rest of this exercise.

Now, we will install the Knative Istio controller by using the following command:

```
$ kubectl apply -f https://github.com/knative/\
net-istio/releases/download/v0.23.1/release.yaml
```

Now that the controller has been installed, we must configure the DNS so that Knative can provide us with custom endpoints. To do so, we can use the Magic DNS known as `sslip.io`, which Knative offers to use for experimentation. The Magic DNS resolves any endpoint to the IP address present in the subdomain. For example, `35.226.198.46.sslip.io` resolves to `35.226.198.46`.

> **Note**
>
> Do not use Magic DNS in production. It is an experimental DNS service and should only be used for evaluating Knative.

Run the following command to configure the DNS:

```
$ kubectl apply -f https://github.com/knative/serving/releases\
/download/v0.23.1/serving-default-domain.yaml
```

As you can see, it provides a batch job that gets fired whenever there is a DNS request.

Now, let's install the HPA add-on to help us autoscale pods on the cluster with traffic automatically. To do so, run the following command:

```
$ kubectl apply -f https://github.com/knative/serving/releases\
/download/v0.23.1/serving-hpa.yaml
```

That completes our Knative installation.

Now, we need to install and configure the kn command-line utility. Use the following commands to do so:

```
$ sudo curl -Lo /usr/local/bin/kn \
https://storage.googleapis.com/knativenightly\
/client/latest/kn-linux-amd64
$ sudo chmod +x /usr/local/bin/kn
```

In the next section, we'll deploy our first application on Knative.

Deploying a Python Flask app on Knative

To understand Knative, let's try to build and deploy a **Flask** application that outputs the current timestamp in the response. Let's start by building the app.

Building the Python Flask app

To build such an app, we will have to create a few files.

The app.py file looks like this:

```python
import os
import datetime
from flask import Flask
app = Flask(__name__)
@app.route('/')
def current_time():
  ct = datetime.datetime.now()
  return 'The current time is : {}!\n'.format(ct)
if __name__ == "__main__":
  app.run(debug=True,host='0.0.0.0')
```

We will need a Dockerfile to build this app, so use the following Dockerfile for this:

```dockerfile
FROM python:3.7-slim
ENV PYTHONUNBUFFERED True
ENV APP_HOME /app
WORKDIR $APP_HOME
COPY . ./
RUN pip install Flask gunicorn
CMD exec gunicorn --bind :$PORT --workers 1 --threads 8
--timeout 0 app:app
```

Now, let's go ahead and build the Docker container using the following command:

```
$ docker build -t <your_dockerhub_user>/py-time .
```

Now that the image is ready, let's push it to Docker Hub by using the following command:

```
$ docker push <your_dockerhub_user>/py-time
```

Now that we've successfully pushed the image, we can run this on Knative.

Deploying the Python Flask app on Knative

To deploy the app, we can either use the kn command line or create a manifest file.

Let's start by using the `kn` command line. Use the following command to deploy the application:

```
$ kn service create py-time --image \
<your_dockerhub_user>/py-time
Creating service 'py-time' in namespace 'default':
 14.230s Configuration "py-time" is waiting for a Revision to
become ready.
 14.345s Ingress has not yet been reconciled.
 14.503s Waiting for load balancer to be ready
 14.754s Ready to serve.
Service 'py-time' created to latest revision 'py-time-gglyx-1'
is available at URL:
http://py-time.default.35.226.198.46.sslip.io
```

As we can see, Knative has deployed the app and provided a custom endpoint. Let's `curl` the endpoint to see what we get:

```
$ curl http://py-time.default.35.226.198.46.sslip.io
The current time is : 2021-02-22 08:24:09.159317!
```

We get the current time in the response. As we already know, Knative should detect if there is traffic coming into the pod and delete it. Let's watch the pods for some time and see what happens:

```
$ kubectl get pod -w
NAME                                               READY   STATUS
RESTARTS    AGE
py-time-gglyx-1-deployment-78bdb7c5d-95d61    2/2     Running
0          5s
py-time-gglyx-1-deployment-78bdb7c5d-95d61    2/2
Terminating          0               65s
```

As we can see, just after 1 minute of inactivity, Knative starts terminating the pod. Now, that's what we mean by scaling from zero.

To delete the service permanently, we can use the following command:

```
$ kn service delete py-time
```

We've just looked at the imperative way of deploying and managing the application. But what if we want to declare the configuration, as we did previously? We can create a custom resource definition manifest with the `Service` resource provided by `apiVersion`, known as `serving.knative.dev/v1`.

We will create the following manifest file, called `py-time-deploy.yaml`, for this:

```
apiVersion: serving.knative.dev/v1
kind: Service
metadata:
  name: py-time
spec:
  template:
    spec:
      containers:
        - image: <your_dockerhub_user>/py-time
```

Now that we've created this file, we will use the `kubectl` command line to apply it. It makes deployment consistent with Kubernetes.

> **Note**
>
> Though it is a service resource, don't confuse this with the typical Kubernetes service resource. It is a custom resource provided by `apiVersion` `serving.knative.dev/v1`. That is why `apiVersion` is very important.

Let's go ahead and run the following command to do so:

```
$ kubectl apply -f py-time-deploy.yaml
service.serving.knative.dev/py-time created
```

With that, the service has been created. To get the endpoint of the service, we will have to query the `ksvc` resource using `kubectl`. Run the following command to do so:

```
$ kubectl get ksvc py-time
NAME         URL
LATESTCREATED    LATESTREADY        READY    REASON
py-time    http://py-time.default.35.226.198.46.sslip.io
py-time-00001    py-time-00001    True
```

The URL is the custom endpoint we have to target. Let's `curl` the custom endpoint using the following command:

```
$ curl http://py-time.default.35.226.198.46.sslip.io
The current time is : 2021-02-22 08:39:06.051857!
```

We get the same response this time as well! So, if you want to keep using `kubectl` for managing Knative, you can easily do so.

Knative helps scale applications based on the amount of load it receives – automatic horizontal scaling. Let's run load testing on our application to see that in action.

Load testing your app on Knative

We will use the `hey` utility to perform load testing. Since your application has already been deployed, run the following command to do the load test:

```
hey -z 30s -c 500 http://py-time.default.35.226.198.46.sslip.io
```

Once the command has executed, run the following code to get the currently running instances of the `py-time` pods:

```
$ kubectl get pod
NAME                                        READY STATUS  RESTARTS   AGE
py-time-00001-deployment-5c59c467b-52vjv    2/2   Running    0       44s
py-time-00001-deployment-5c59c467b-bhhvm    2/2   Running    0       44s
py-time-00001-deployment-5c59c467b-h6qr5    2/2   Running    0       42s
py-time-00001-deployment-5c59c467b-h92jp    2/2   Running    0       40s
py-time-00001-deployment-5c59c467b-p27gl    2/2   Running    0       88s
py-time-00001-deployment-5c59c467b-tdwrh    2/2   Running    0       38s
py-time-00001-deployment-5c59c467b-zsgcg    2/2   Running    0       42s
```

As we can see, Knative has created seven instances of the `py-time` pod. This is horizontal autoscaling in action.

Now, let's look at the cluster nodes by running the following command:

```
$ kubectl get nodes
NAME                                    STATUS    AGE
gke-cluster-2-default-pool-353b3ed4-js71    Ready   3m17s
gke-cluster-2-default-pool-353b3ed4-mx83    Ready   106m
gke-cluster-2-default-pool-353b3ed4-vf7q    Ready   106m
```

As we can see, GKE has created another node in the node pool because of the extra burst of traffic it received. This is phenomenal as we have the Kubernetes API to do what we want. We have automatically horizontally autoscaled our pods. We have also automatically horizontally autoscaled our cluster worker nodes. This means that we have a fully automated solution for running containers, without having to worry about the management nuances! That is open source serverless in action for you!

Summary

This chapter covered CaaS and serverless CaaS services. These help us manage container applications with ease, without worrying about the underlying infrastructure and managing them. We used Amazon's ECS as an example and deep dived into it with an example. Then, we briefly discussed other solutions that are available on the market. Finally, we looked at Knative, an open source serverless solution for containers that runs on top of Kubernetes and uses many other open source CNCF projects.

In the next chapter, we will delve into continuous integration in the container world.

Questions

1.   ECS allows us to deploy to which of the following? (Multiple answers are possible)

     A. EC2

     B. AWS Lambda

     C. Fargate

     D. AWS Lightsail

2.   ECS uses Kubernetes in the background – True/False?

3.   We should always use services in ECS instead of tasks for batch jobs – True/False?

4.   We should always use Fargate for batch jobs as it runs for a short period, and we only pay for the resources that are consumed during that time – True/False?

5.   Which of the following are CaaS services that implement the Kubernetes API? (Multiple answers are possible)

     A. GKE

     B. AKS

     C. EKS

     D. ECS

6. Google Cloud Run is a serverless offering that uses Knative behind the scenes – True/False?

7. Which one of the following is offered as a Knative module? (Multiple answers are possible)

   A. Serving

   B. Eventing

   C. Computing

   D. Containers

Answers

1. a, c

2. False

3. False

4. True

5. a, b, c

6. True

7. a, b

10
Continuous Integration

In the last chapters, we've looked at individual tools that will help us to implement several aspects of modern DevOps. Now, it's time to look at how we can bring all of the tools and concepts we've learned together and use them to create a continuous integration pipeline. We will look at some of the popular open source and SaaS-based tools that can get us started quickly with **Continuous Integration (CI)**. We will begin with **GitHub Actions**, **Jenkins with Kaniko**, and some cloud-specific SaaS tools, such as **AWS Code Commit** and **Code Build**. Finally, we will cover some best practices related to build performance.

In this chapter, we're going to cover the following main topics:

- The importance of automation
- Building a CI pipeline with GitHub Actions
- Scalable Jenkins on Kubernetes with Kaniko
- Automating a build with triggers
- CI with AWS Code Commit and Code Build
- Build performance best practices

Technical requirements

For this chapter, you will need to clone the following GitHub repository for some of the exercises:

`https://github.com/PacktPublishing/Modern-DevOps-Practices`

Run the following command to clone the repository into your home directory, and `cd` into the `ch10` directory to access the required resources:

```
$ git clone https://github.com/PacktPublishing/Modern-DevOps-\
Practices.git modern-devops
$ cd modern-devops/ch10
```

So, let's get started!

The importance of automation

Software development and delivery have moved away from traditional project-based teams to product-based teams. So, gone are the days when you would get a new project and form a new team to deliver it. It would take years to deliver it with a diligent army of enterprise and solution architects, business analysts, software developers, QA analysts, and the operations team working at different phases of the software development life cycle. The manner in which technology is changing is so rapid that what is relevant today might not be relevant in a year's time. Therefore, the traditional project-based waterfall model would not work at the current time.

The project management function is quickly diluting, and software development teams are transitioning to Agile teams that deliver in Sprints iteratively. Therefore, if there is a new requirement, we don't wait for the entire thing to be signed off before we start to do design, development, QA, and so on. Instead, we break software down into workable features and deliver them in smaller chunks to get value and feedback from customers quickly. That means rapid software development with less risk of failure.

Well, the teams are agile, and they develop software faster, but there are a lot of things in the **Software Development Lifecycle (SDLC)** process that are conducted manually, such as the fact that the code is built after all development has been done for that cycle, and what would happen if you then find bugs? Or your builds do not run? How do we trace what caused that problem in the first place?

What if you know the cause of a broken build as soon as you check the code into source control? What if you can understand that particular software fails some tests when deploying it to the test environment? Well, that's **CI** for you in a nutshell.

CI is a process through which developers check-in code frequently to a source code repository, perhaps several times a day. Automated tooling behind the scenes can detect these commits and then build, run some tests, and tell you upfront whether the commit has caused any issues. This means that your developers, testers, product owners, operations team, everyone comes to know what has caused the issue, and the developer can fix the problem quickly. That creates a feedback loop in software development. We always had a manual feedback loop within software development, but that loop was slow. So either you wait for a long time before doing your next task, or you carry on doing the wrong thing until you realize that it is too late to undo all of that. That adds to the rework effort of everything you have done hitherto.

As we all know, the cost of fixing a bug earlier in the SDLC cycle is way cheaper than fixing it later on. Therefore, CI aims to provide continuous feedback on the code quality early in the SDLC. That saves your developers and the organization a lot of time and money on fixing bugs they detect when most of your code is tested and ready to go to production. Therefore, CI helps software development teams to develop better software faster.

Agile is a way of working and is silent on the tools, techniques, and automation required to achieve it. DevOps is an extension of the Agile mindset and helps you to implement it effectively. DevOps focuses heavily on automation and looks at avoiding manual work wherever possible. It also looks at software delivery automation and seeks to amplify or replace traditional tools and frameworks. With the advent of modern DevOps, there are specific tools, techniques, and best practices that simplify the life of a developer, QA, and operator. Modern public cloud platforms and DevOps provide teams with ready-to-use dynamic infrastructure that helps businesses reduce the time to market and build scalable, elastic, high-performant infrastructure to keep enterprises live with minimal downtime.

To implement CI, we will need a CI tool. Let's look at some of the popular tools and the options you have in the next section.

Building a CI pipeline with GitHub Actions

GitHub Actions is a SaaS-based tool that comes with GitHub. So, when you create your GitHub repository, you get access to this service out of the box. Therefore, for people who are new to CI/CD and want to get started quickly, GitHub Actions is one of the best tools.

Now, let's try to create a CI pipeline for a **Python Flask** app running on a **Docker** container, and run some tests. If the tests pass, the build will pass, otherwise, it fails.

To access the resources for this section, cd into the following:

```
$ cd ~/modern-devops/ch10/flask-app
```

The app.py file consists of the following:

```
from flask import Flask
from flask import make_response

app = Flask(__name__)

@app.route('/')
def index():
  return "Hello World!"

@app.route('/<page>')
def default(page):
  response = make_response('The page %s does not exist.' %
page, 404)
  return response
if __name__ == '__main__':
  app.run(debug=True)
```

It is a Python Flask application that returns Hello World! in the response when we hit the home page, /, and for any other page, it returns The page <page> does not exist.

We will also write a test for this in the following app.test.py file:

```
import unittest
from app import app

class AppTestCase(unittest.TestCase):
  def test_index(self):
    tester = app.test_client(self)
    response = tester.get('/', content_type='html/text')
```

```
      self.assertEqual(response.status_code, 200)
      self.assertEqual(response.data, b'Hello World!')

  def test_default(self):
    tester = app.test_client(self)
    response = tester.get('xyz', content_type='html/text')
    self.assertEqual(response.status_code, 404)
    self.assertTrue(b'does not exist' in response.data)

if __name__ == '__main__':
  unittest.main()
```

It defines two tests in the test case. The first test checks whether the Flask application returns `Hello World!` and `HTTP 200` in the response if we hit the home page. The second test checks whether the application returns `does not exist` in the response with a `404` HTTP code when we hit the `/xyz` page in the application.

Now, as we're all aware that Docker is inherently CI-compliant, we can run the tests using the `Dockerfile` itself. We create the following `Dockerfile`:

```
FROM python:3.7-alpine
ENV FLASK_APP=app.py
ENV FLASK_RUN_HOST=0.0.0.0
RUN apk add --no-cache gcc musl-dev linux-headers
COPY requirements.txt requirements.txt
RUN pip install -r requirements.txt
EXPOSE 5000
COPY . .
RUN python3 app.test.py
CMD ["flask", "run"]
```

The Dockerfile starts with the `python:3.7-alpine` base image and then installs the requirements and copies the code into the working directory. It runs the `app.test.py` unit test to check whether the code would work if we deploy it. Finally, the `CMD` command defines a `flask run` command that would run when we fire the container.

Let's build the `Dockerfile` and see what we get:

```
$ docker build -t flask-app .
Sending build context to Docker daemon  5.632kB
Step 1/10 : FROM python:3.7-alpine
 ---> 72e4ef8abf8e
...
Step 9/10 : RUN python3 app.test.py
 ---> Running in a1a83e215d28
-------------------------------------------------------------
Ran 2 tests in 0.008s
OK
Removing intermediate container a1a83e215d28
 ---> 39ba88d774ef
Step 10/10 : CMD ["flask", "run"]
 ---> Running in e96171503e6c
Removing intermediate container e96171503e6c
 ---> 2d9f3462767f
Successfully built 2d9f3462767f
Successfully tagged flask-app:latest
```

As we can see, it built the container, and it also executed a test on it and responded with `Ran 2 tests in 0.008s` and an `OK` message. Therefore, we were able to use `Dockerfile` to do the build and test this app.

Let's now look at GitHub Actions and how we can automate this step.

Creating a GitHub repository

Before we use GitHub Actions, we would need to create a GitHub repository. To do so, go to `https://github.com/new` and create a new repository. Give an appropriate name to it. For this exercise, I am going to use `flask-app-gh-actions`.

Once you've created it, clone the repository by using the following command:

```
$ git clone https://github.com/<GitHub_Username>\
/flask-app-gh-actions.git
```

Then, change the directory into the repository directory and copy the app.py, app.test.py, requirements.txt, and Dockerfile files into the repository directory using the following commands:

```
$ cd flask-app-gh-actions
$ cp ~/modern-devops/ch10/flask-app/* .
```

Now, we need to create a GitHub Actions workflow file. Let's look at that in the next section.

Creating a GitHub Actions workflow

The GitHub Actions workflow is a simple YAML file that contains the build steps. We need to create the workflow in the .github/workflows directory within the repository. Let's do that using the following command:

```
$ mkdir -p .github/workflows
```

We will use the following GitHub Actions workflow file, build.yaml, for this exercise:

```
name: Build and Test App
on:
  push:
    branches: [ master ]
  pull_request:
    branches: [ master ]
jobs:
  build:
    runs-on: ubuntu-latest
    steps:
    - uses: actions/checkout@v2
    - name: Login to Docker Hub
      id: login
      run: docker login -u ${{ secrets.DOCKER_USER  }} -p ${{
secrets.DOCKER_PASSWORD }}
    - name: Build the Docker image
      id: build
      run: docker build . --file Dockerfile --tag ${{ secrets.
DOCKER_USER  }}/flask-app-gh-actions
    - name: Push the Docker image
```

```
        id: push
        run: docker push ${{ secrets.DOCKER_USER  }}/flask-app-
gh-actions
```

The file comprises the following:

- name: The name of the workflow – Build and Test App in this case.

- on: Describes when this workflow will run. In this case, it will run if a push or pull request is sent on the master branch.

- jobs: A GitHub Actions workflow contains one or more jobs that run in parallel by default. This attribute contains all jobs.

- jobs.build: This is a job that does the container build.

- jobs.build.runs-on: This describes where the build job will run. We've specified ubuntu-latest here. This means that this job will run on an Ubuntu VM.

- jobs.build.steps: This consists of the steps that run sequentially within the job. The build job consists of four build steps: checkout, which will check out the code from your repository; login, which will log in to DockerHub; build, which will run a Docker build on your code; and push, which will push your Docker image to DockerHub.

- jobs.build.steps.uses: It is the first step and describes an action that you will run as a part of your job. Actions are reusable pieces of code that you can execute in your pipeline. In this case, it runs the checkout action. That checks out the code from the current branch where the action is triggered.

> **Tip**
> Always use a version with your actions. That will prevent your build from breaking if a later version is not compatible with your pipeline.

- jobs.build.steps.name: This is the name of your build step.

- jobs.build.steps.id: This is a unique identifier of your build step.

- jobs.build.steps.run: This is the command it executes as part of the build step.

The workflow also contains variables within ${{ }}. We can define multiple variables within the workflow and use them in the subsequent steps. In this case, we've used two variables – ${{ secrets.DOCKER_USER }} and ${{ secrets.DOCKER_PASSWORD }}. These variables are sourced from GitHub secrets.

> **Tip**
> It is a best practice to use GitHub secrets for storing sensitive information. Never check these details into the repository.

You will have to define two secrets within your repository by going to the following URL: https://github.com/<your_user>/flask-app-gh-actions/settings/secrets/actions.

Define two secrets within the repository:

```
DOCKER_USER=<Your DockerHub username>
DOCKER_PASSWORD=<Your DockerHub password>
```

Now, let's move this build.yml file to the workflows directory by using the following command:

```
$ mv build.yml .github/workflows/
```

And now, we're ready to push this code to GitHub. Run the following commands to commit and push the changes to your GitHub repository:

```
$ git add --all
$ git commit -m 'Initial commit'
$ git push
```

Now, go to the **workflows** tab of your GitHub repository by visiting `https://github.com/<your_user>/flask-app-gh-actions/actions`, and you should see something like the following screenshot:

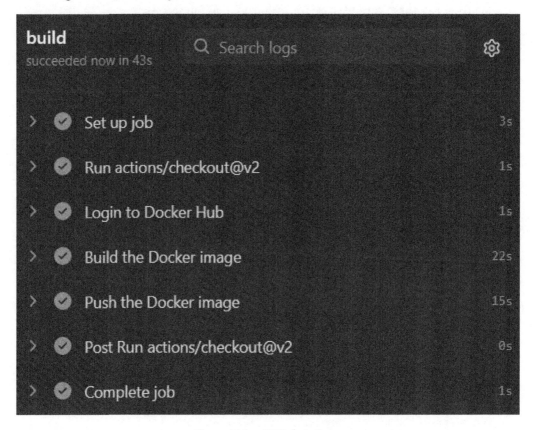

Figure 10.1 – GitHub Actions

As we can see, GitHub has run a build using our workflow file, and it has built the code and pushed the image to DockerHub. You can visit your DockerHub account, and you should see your image pushed to your account:

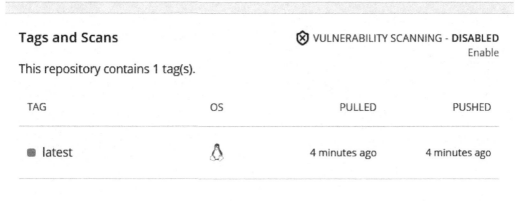

Figure 10.2 – DockerHub image

Now, let's try to break our code somehow. Let's suppose that someone from your team changed the `app.py` code, and instead of returning `Hello World!`, it started returning `Hello, World!`. Let's see what would happen in that scenario.

Make the following changes to the `index` function in the `app.py` file:

```
...
def index():
  return "Hello, World!"
...
```

Now, commit and push the code to GitHub using the following commands:

```
$ git add --all
$ git commit -m 'Updated Hello World'
$ git push
```

Now, go to GitHub Actions and find the latest build. You will see that the build will error out and give the following output:

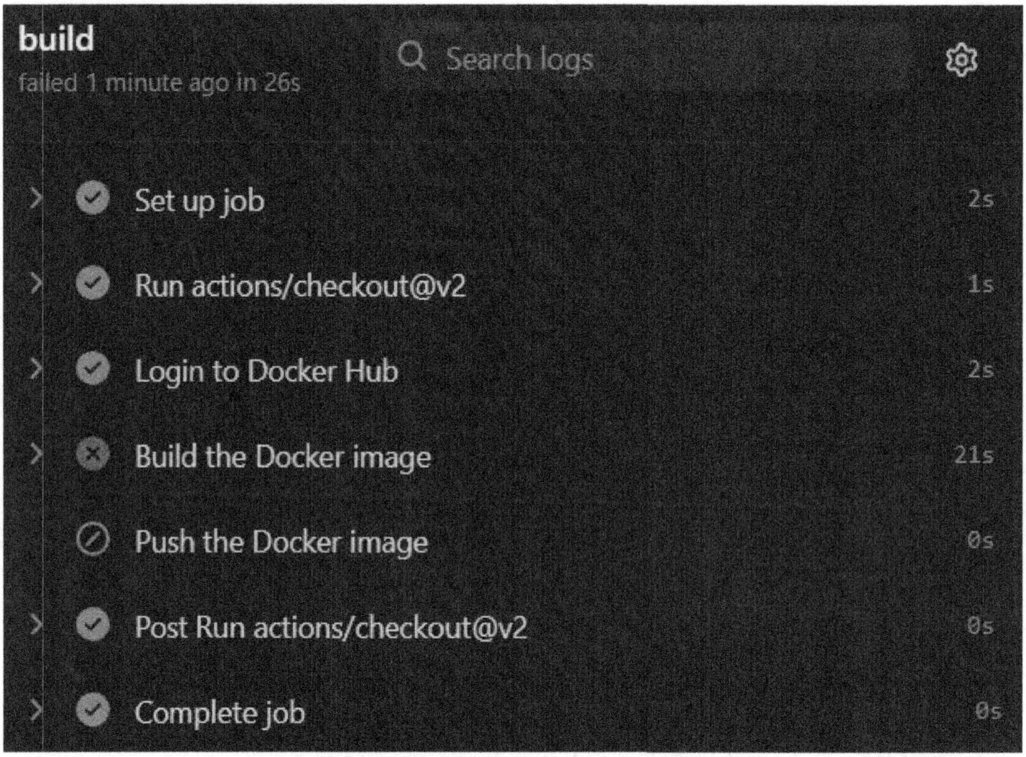

Figure 10.3 – GitHub Actions – Build failure

The *Build the Docker image* step has failed. If you click on the step and scroll down to see what happened with it, you will find that the app.test.py execution failed. That is because of a test case failure with AssertionError: b'Hello, World!' != b'Hello World!'. This means that as Hello, World! didn't match the expected Hello World! output, the test case failed, as shown in the following screenshot:

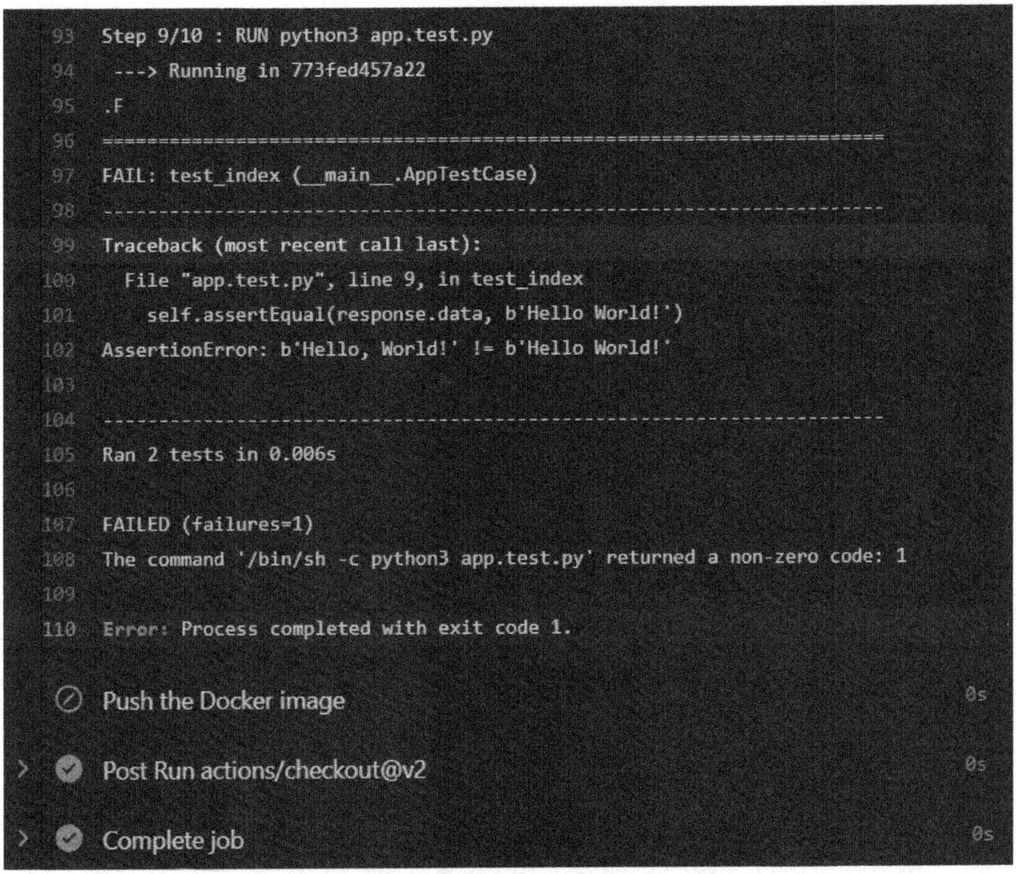

```
93   Step 9/10 : RUN python3 app.test.py
94    ---> Running in 773fed457a22
95   .F
96   =================================================================
97   FAIL: test_index (__main__.AppTestCase)
98   -----------------------------------------------------------------
99   Traceback (most recent call last):
100    File "app.test.py", line 9, in test_index
101      self.assertEqual(response.data, b'Hello World!')
102   AssertionError: b'Hello, World!' != b'Hello World!'
103
104   -----------------------------------------------------------------
105   Ran 2 tests in 0.006s
106
107   FAILED (failures=1)
108   The command '/bin/sh -c python3 app.test.py' returned a non-zero code: 1
109
110   Error: Process completed with exit code 1.

   ⊘  Push the Docker image                                            0s

>  ✅  Post Run actions/checkout@v2                                     0s

>  ✅  Complete job                                                     0s
```

Figure 10.4 – GitHub Actions – Test failure

We've uncovered the error as soon as someone pushed the buggy code to the Git repository. Are you able to see the benefits of CI already?

Now, let's go and fix the code, and commit the code back again.

Modify the index function of app.py to the following:

```
...
def index():
  return "Hello World!"
...
```

And then `commit` and `push` the code to GitHub using the following commands:

```
$ git add --all
$ git commit -m 'Updated Hello World'
$ git push
```

And this time, the build will be successful:

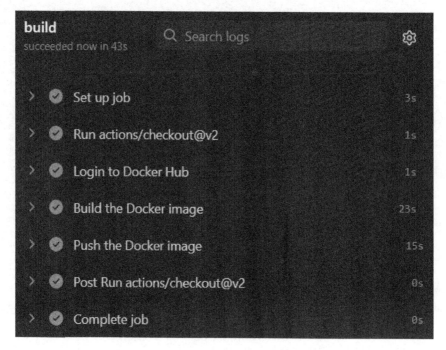

Figure 10.5 – GitHub Actions – Build success

Not everyone uses GitHub, and therefore, the SaaS offering might not be an option for them. Therefore, let's look at the most popular open source CI tool, **Jenkins**, in the next section.

Scalable Jenkins on Kubernetes with Kaniko

Jenkins is the most popular CI tool available in the market. It is open source, simple to install, and runs with ease. It is a Java-based tool with a plugin-based architecture designed to support several integrations, such as with a source code management tool such as *Git*, *SVN*, and *Mercurial*, or with popular artifact repositories such as *Nexus* and *Artifactory*. It also integrates well with well-known build tools such as *Ant*, *Maven*, and *Gradle*, aside from the standard shell scripting and windows batch file executions.

Jenkins follows a master-agent model. Though technically, you can run all your builds on the master machine itself, it makes sense to offload your CI builds to other machines in your network so as to have a distributed architecture. That does not overload your master machine. You can use it simply to store the build configurations and other management data and manage the entire CI Build cluster, something along the lines of the following diagram:

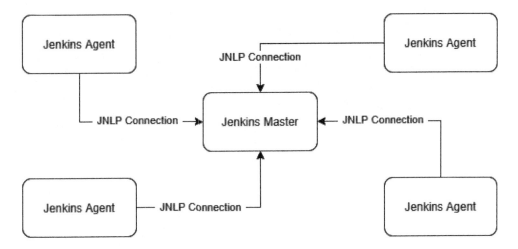

Figure 10.6 – Scalable Jenkins

In the diagram, multiple static Jenkins agents connect to a Jenkins Master. Now, this architecture works well, but it isn't scalable enough. Modern DevOps emphasizes resource utilization, and therefore, we want to roll out an agent machine only when we want to build. Therefore, a better way to do it is to automate your builds to roll out an agent machine when you require a build. Well, this might be overkill in the case of rolling out new virtual machines as it takes some minutes to provision a new machine even when using a prebuilt image with Packer. A better alternative is to use a container.

Jenkins integrates quite well with Kubernetes and therefore allows you to run your build on a Kubernetes cluster. That way, whenever you trigger a build on Jenkins, Jenkins instructs Kubernetes to create a new agent container that will then connect with the master machine and run the build within itself. That is build on-demand at its best. The following diagram shows the process in detail:

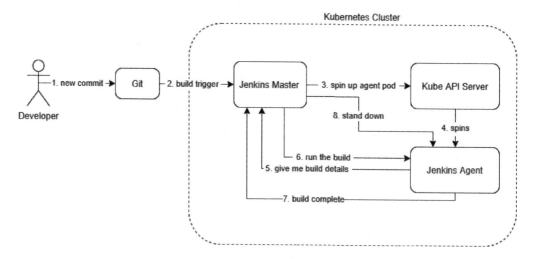

Figure 10.7 – Scalable Jenkins CI workflow

That sounds great, and we can go ahead and run this build, but there are issues with this approach. We need to understand that the Jenkins Master and Agents are running as containers, and they aren't full-fledged virtual machines. Therefore, if we want to run a Docker build within the container, you will have to run the container in privileged mode. That isn't a security best practice, and your admin should already have disabled that. That is because running a container in privileged mode exposes your host filesystem to the container. A hacker who can access your container will have full access to do whatever in your system.

To solve that problem, you can use a container build tool such as **Kaniko**. Kaniko is a build tool provided by Google that helps you build your containers without access to the Docker daemon, and you do not even need Docker installed in your container. That is a great way to run your builds within a **Kubernetes cluster** and create a scalable continuous integration environment. It is effortless to use, not hacky, and provides a secure way of building your containers, as we will see in the subsequent sections.

For this section, we will use the **Google Kubernetes Engine (GKE)**. As mentioned before, Google Cloud provides a free trial of $300 for 90 days. You can sign up at https://cloud.google.com/free if you have not already done so.

Spinning up Google Kubernetes Engine

Once you've signed up and are in your console, you can open the Google Cloud Shell CLI to run the commands.

You need to enable the Kubernetes Engine API first using the following command:

```
$ gcloud services enable container.googleapis.com
```

To create a two-node autoscaling GKE cluster that scales from one to five nodes, run the following command:

```
$ gcloud container clusters create cluster-1 \
--num-nodes 2 --enable-autoscaling \
--min-nodes 1 --max-nodes 5 --zone us-central1-a
```

And that's it! The cluster is up and running.

You will also need to clone the following GitHub repository for some of the exercises: `https://github.com/PacktPublishing/Modern-DevOps-Practices`.

Run the following command to clone the repository into your home directory and cd into the ch10 directory to access the required resources:

```
$ git clone https://github.com/PacktPublishing/Modern-DevOps-\
Practices.git modern-devops
$ cd modern-devops/ch10/jenkins/jenkins-master
```

As the repository contains files with placeholders, you will have to replace the <your_ dockerhub_user> string with the your actual Docker Hub user. Use the following commands to substitute the placeholders.

```
$ find ./ -type f -exec sed -i -e 's/\
<your_dockerhub_user>/<your actual docker hub user>/g' {} \;
```

As the cluster is now up and running, let's go ahead and install Jenkins in the next section.

Installing Jenkins

As we're running on a Kubernetes cluster, all we need is the latest official Jenkins image from DockerHub, and we will customize the image according to our requirements.

The following Dockerfile will help us to create the image with the required plugins:

```
FROM jenkins/jenkins
RUN /usr/local/bin/install-plugins.sh ssh-slaves email-ext
```

```
mailer slack htmlpublisher greenballs simple-theme-plugin
kubernetes git github
```

The Dockerfile starts from the Jenkins base image and installs the required plugins.

> **Tip**
> You can customize further and install more plugins to the master image based
> on your requirements.

Let's build the image from the Dockerfile using the following command:

```
$ docker build -t <your_dockerhub_user>/jenkins-master-kaniko .
```

Now, as we've built the image, use the following command to push it to DockerHub:

```
$ docker push <your_dockerhub_user>/jenkins-master-kaniko
```

We also have to build the Jenkins agent image to run our builds. Remember that Jenkins agents need to have all the supporting tools you need in order to run your builds. You will find the resources for the agents in the following directory:

```
$ cd ~/modern-devops/ch10/jenkins/jenkins-agent
```

We will use the following Dockerfile to do that:

```
FROM gcr.io/kaniko-project/executor:v0.11.0 as kaniko
FROM jenkins/jnlp-slave
COPY --from=kaniko /kaniko /kaniko
WORKDIR /kaniko
USER root
```

This Dockerfile uses a multi-stage build to take the kaniko base image and copy the kaniko binary from the kaniko base image to the jnlp base image. Let's go ahead and build and push the container using the following commands:

```
$ docker build -t <your_dockerhub_user>/jenkins-jnlp-kaniko .
$ docker push <your_dockerhub_user>/jenkins-jnlp-kaniko
```

To deploy Jenkins on our Kubernetes cluster, we will first create a `jenkins` service account. A Kubernetes service account resource helps Pods to authenticate with the Kube API Server. We will give the service account permission to interact with the Kube API server as a `cluster-admin` using a cluster role binding. A Kubernetes `ClusterRoleBinding` resource helps provide permissions to a service account to perform certain actions in the Kubernetes cluster. The `jenkins-sa-crb.yaml` manifest describes that. To access these resources, run the following command:

```
$ cd ~/modern-devops/ch10/jenkins/jenkins-master
```

To apply the manifest, run the following command:

```
$ kubectl apply -f jenkins-sa-crb.yaml
```

The next step involves creating a `PersistentVolumeClaim` resource to store Jenkins data to ensure that the Jenkins data persists beyond the Pod's life cycle and will exist even when we delete the Pod.

To apply the manifest, run the following command:

```
$ kubectl apply -f jenkins-pvc.yaml
```

We will then create a Kubernetes `Secret` called `regcred` to help the Jenkins Pod authenticate with the Docker registry. Use the following command to do so:

```
$ kubectl create secret docker-registry regcred \
  --dockerserver=https://index.docker.io/v1/ \
  --docker-username=<username> --docker-password=<password>
```

Now, we'll define a `Deployment` resource, `jenkins-deployment.yaml`, that will run the Jenkins container. The Pod uses the `jenkins` service account and defines a `PersistentVolume` resource called `jenkins-pv-storage` using the `PersistentVolumeClaim` resource called `jenkins-pv-claim` that we defined. We define the Jenkins container that uses the Jenkins master image we created. It exposes the HTTP port `8080` for the *Web UI*, and port `50000` for *JNLP*, which the agents would use to interact with the Jenkins master. We will also mount the `jenkins-pv-storage` volume to `/var/jenkins_home` to persist the Jenkins data beyond the Pod's life cycle. We specify `regcred` as the `imagePullSecret` attribute in the Pod image. We also use an `initContainer` to assign the ownership to `jenkins` for `/var/jenkins_home`.

Apply the manifest by using the following command:

```
$ kubectl apply -f jenkins-deployment.yaml
```

As we've created the deployment, we can expose the deployment on a `LoadBalancer` service using the `jenkins-svc.yaml` manifest. This service exposes ports `8080` and `50000` on a Load Balancer. Use the following command to apply the manifest:

```
$ kubectl apply -f jenkins-svc.yaml
```

Let's get the service to find the external IP to use that to access Jenkins:

```
$ kubectl get svc jenkins-service
NAME                     TYPE              CLUSTER-IP        EXTERNAL-IP
PORT(S)                                    AGE
jenkins-service      LoadBalancer    10.3.246.64      LOAD_BALANCER_
EXTERNAL_IP      8080:30251/TCP,50000:30302/TCP      2m12s
```

Now, to access the service, hit `http://<LOAD_BALANCER_EXTERNAL_IP>:8080` in your browser window:

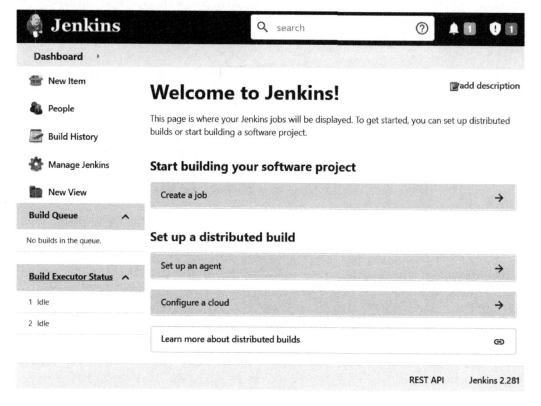

Figure 10.8 – Jenkins home page

The first step with Jenkins set up is to enable global security. Currently, your cluster is open to the world, and anyone can do anything with it.

To enable **Global Security**, go to `http://LOAD_BALANCER_EXTERNAL_IP:8080/configureSecurity/`.

Set the following options to get started:

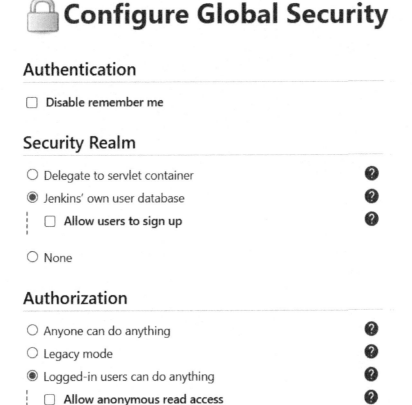

Figure 10.9 – Configure Global Security

Jenkins will prompt you to create an admin account after this step. Use the form to create an admin account to your liking. Next, we will go ahead and connect with the Kubernetes cluster.

Connecting Jenkins with the cluster

To connect Jenkins with the cluster, go to `http://LOAD_BALANCER_EXTERNAL_IP:8080/configureClouds/`.

Click on the **Add a new cloud** button and select **Kubernetes**, as shown in the following screenshot:

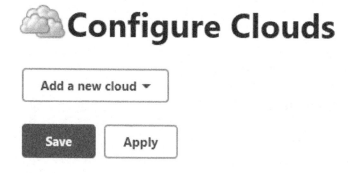

Figure 10.10 – Configure Clouds

After you've selected **Kubernetes**, you should get the following screen. Click on the **Kubernetes Cloud details...** button:

Figure 10.11 – Selecting Kubernetes Cloud

After that, we need a few details from `kubectl`. Run the following command to get the control-plane IP address:

```
$ kubectl cluster-info | grep "control plane"
Kubernetes control plane is running at https://35.224.6.58
```

Add the preceding URL to the **Kubernetes URL** field and click on **Test Connection**. You should get a **Connected to Kubernetes v1.18.12-gke.1210** response:

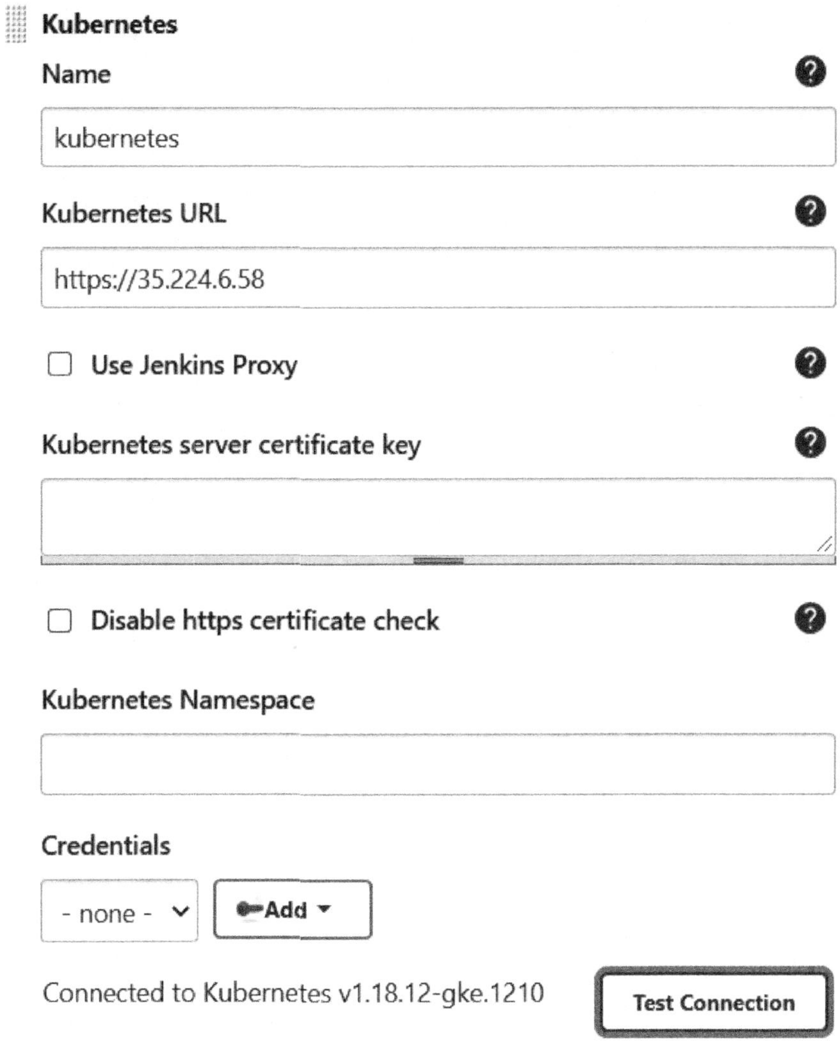

Figure 10.12 – Kubernetes connection

As the connection test is successful, we will start filling up the rest of the form. In **Jenkins URL**, add `http://jenkins-service:8080`, and in **Jenkins tunnel**, add `jenkins-service:50000`. Click on **Pod Labels** and add a pod label with `key=jenkins` and `value=agent`, as in the following screenshot. Leave the rest as their defaults:

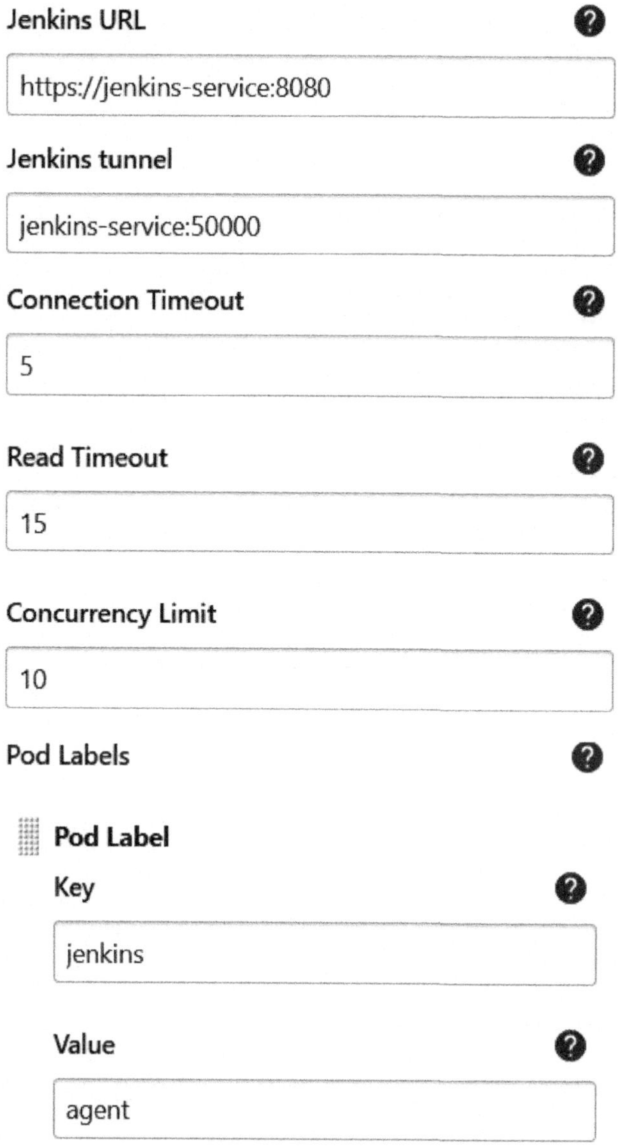

Jenkins URL   ❓

```
https://jenkins-service:8080
```

Jenkins tunnel   ❓

```
jenkins-service:50000
```

Connection Timeout   ❓

```
5
```

Read Timeout   ❓

```
15
```

Concurrency Limit   ❓

```
10
```

Pod Labels   ❓

Pod Label

Key   ❓

```
jenkins
```

Value   ❓

```
agent
```

Figure 10.13 – Kubernetes service level configuration

Now, we'll add a pod template. To do so, click on **Pod Templates | Add Pod Template**. Add the following details to the **Pod template** field:

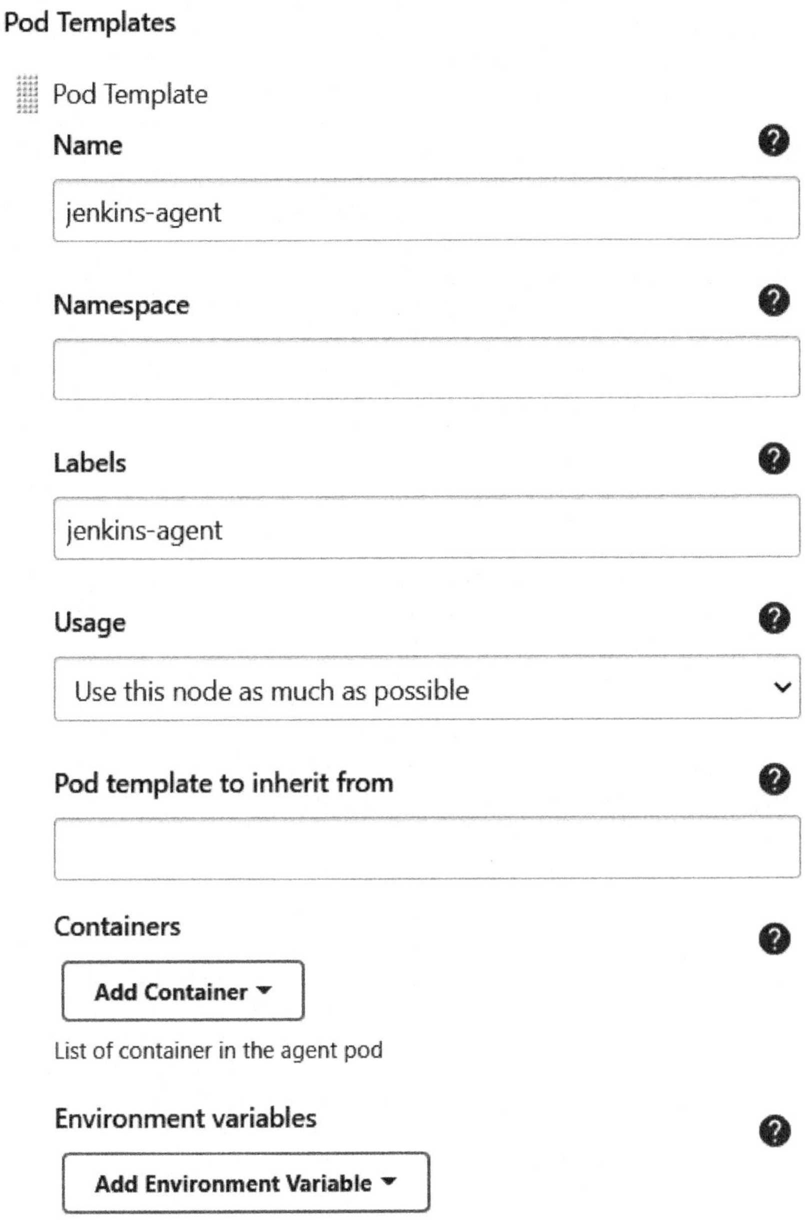

Pod Templates

Pod Template

Name   ?

    jenkins-agent

Namespace   ?

Labels   ?

    jenkins-agent

Usage   ?

    Use this node as much as possible   ⌄

Pod template to inherit from   ?

Containers   ?

    Add Container ▼

List of container in the agent pod

Environment variables   ?

    Add Environment Variable ▼

Figure 10.14 – Kubernetes pod configuration

Now, we'll add the container details. Click on the **Add Container** button. Within that, specify the name as `jnlp` and in the **Docker image** field, add the *Docker agent image* you built in the previous step:

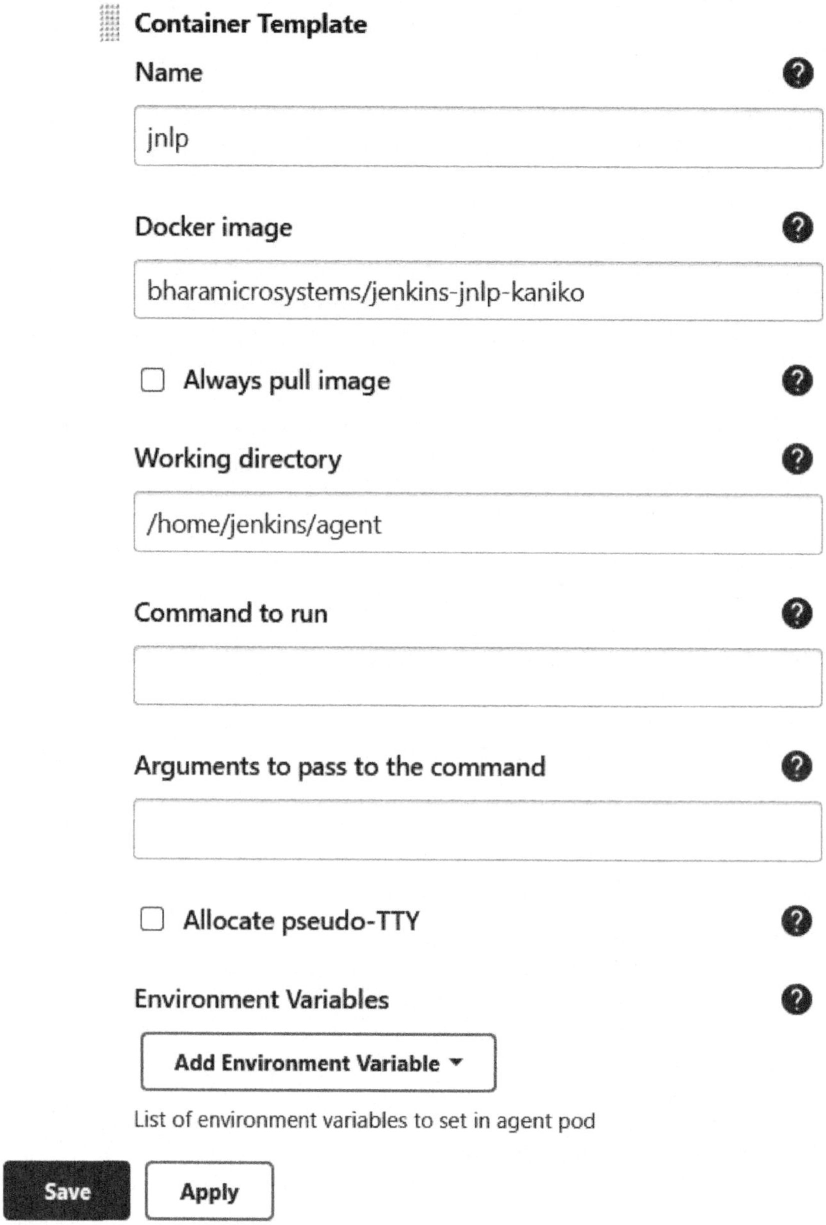

Container Template

Name   ❓

> jnlp

Docker image   ❓

> bharamicrosystems/jenkins-jnlp-kaniko

☐   Always pull image   ❓

Working directory   ❓

> /home/jenkins/agent

Command to run   ❓

Arguments to pass to the command   ❓

☐   Allocate pseudo-TTY   ❓

Environment Variables   ❓

Add Environment Variable ▼

List of environment variables to set in agent pod

Save   Apply

Figure 10.15 – Kubernetes container configuration

We will then need to mount the `regcred` secret to the file `kaniko/.docker` as a volume. As `regcred` contains the Docker registry credentials, Kaniko will use this to connect with your container registry. Click on **Volumes** and add the following secret volume to the Pod:

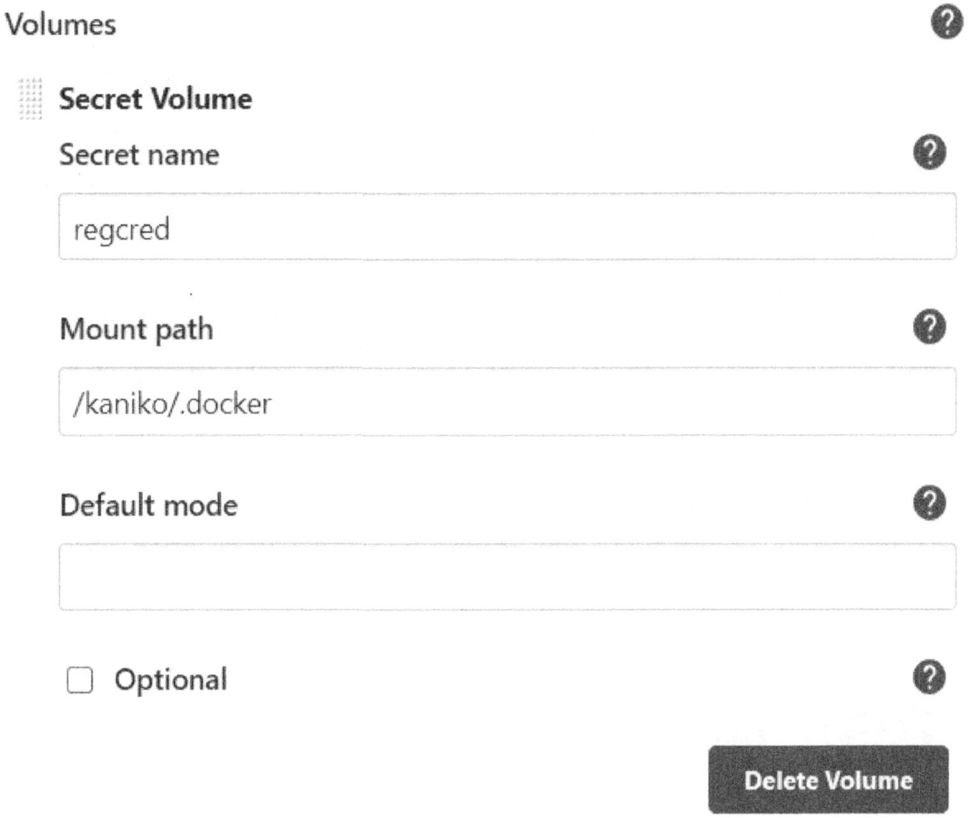

Volumes

Secret Volume

Secret name

```
regcred
```

Mount path

```
/kaniko/.docker
```

Default mode

```
```

☐ Optional

Delete Volume

Figure 10.16 – Kubernetes volume configuration

We will also have to provide an image pull secret to authenticate with the Container Registry to pull the `jnlp` image. Add `regcred` as the image pull secret. As we want to run this Pod using the `jenkins` service account, add that to the **Service Account** section as shown:

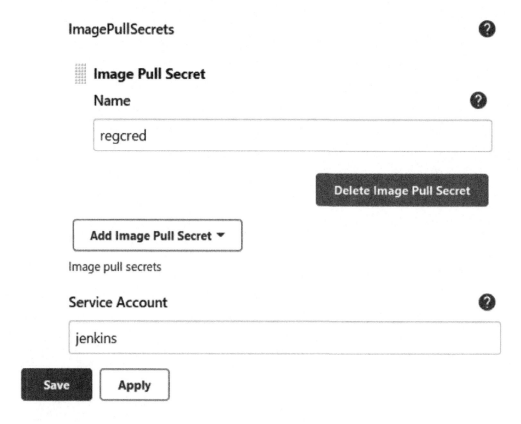

Figure 10.17 – Kubernetes service account configuration

We already have two executors in the master node. We'll have to set executors on the master node to zero as we don't want to run any builds on the Jenkins master. To do so, go to `http://LOAD_BALANCER_ EXTERNAL_IP:8080/computer/(master)/ configure` and set the number of executors to `0`. We're now ready to fire up our first job on Jenkins.

Running our first Jenkins job

Before we create our first job, we'll have to prepare our repository to run the job. So, just create a repository on GitHub and run the following commands:

```
$ cd ~/modern-devops/ch10
$ git clone [REPO_URL]
$ cp -a flask-app/* [REPO_NAME]
$ cp jenkins/jenkins-agent/build.sh [REPO_NAME]
```

Then cd into your local repository, and commit and push your changes to GitHub. Once done, we're ready to create a job in Jenkins.

To create a new job in Jenkins, go to the **Jenkins** home page | **New Item** | **Freestyle Job**. Provide a job name (preferably the same as the Git repository name) and then click **Next**.

Click on **Source Code Management**, select **Git**, and add your Git repository URL, as in the following example. Specify the branch from where you want to build:

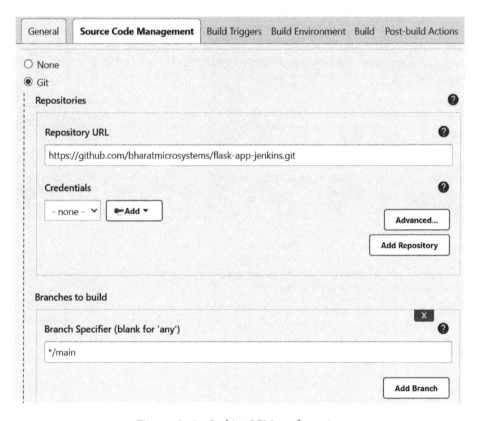

Figure 10.18 – Jenkins SCM configuration

Go to the **Build Triggers** tab, select **Poll SCM**, and add the following details:

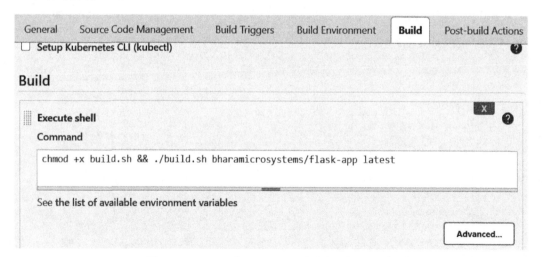

Figure 10.19 – Jenkins build triggers configuration

Then, click on **Build | Add Build Step | Execute shell**. The **Execute shell** build step executes a sequence of shell commands on the Linux CLI. In this example, we're running the `build.sh` script with the `<your_dockerhub_user>/<image>` arguments and the image tag. Change the details according to your requirements. Once you've finished, click on **Save**:

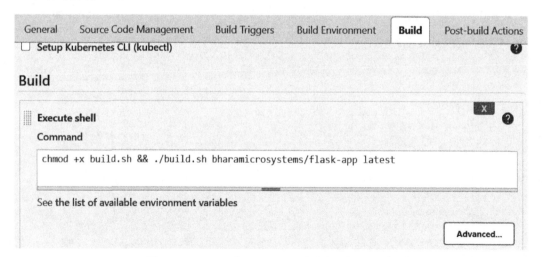

Figure 10.20 – Jenkins Execute shell configuration

Now we're ready to build this job. To do so, you can either go to your job configuration and click on **Build**, or you can push a change to GitHub. You should see something like the following:

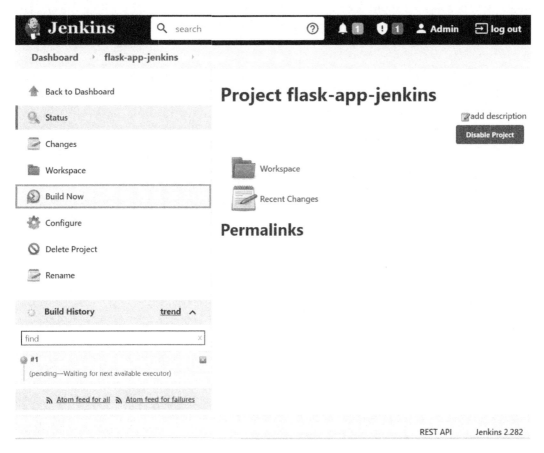

Figure 10.21 – Jenkins job page

We'll wait for Jenkins to spin up an agent pod in Kubernetes, where it will run this job, and soon the job should start building. Once it starts building, click on **Build | Console Output**. If everything is OK, you'll see that the build is successful and that Jenkins has built the `flask-app` application and executed a unit test on it before pushing the Docker image to the registry. Verify that the image is in the repository:

```
Collecting Werkzeug>=0.15
  Downloading Werkzeug-1.0.1-py2.py3-none-any.whl (298 kB)
Collecting click>=5.1
  Downloading click-7.1.2-py2.py3-none-any.whl (82 kB)
Collecting MarkupSafe>=0.23
  Downloading MarkupSafe-1.1.1.tar.gz (19 kB)
Building wheels for collected packages: MarkupSafe
  Building wheel for MarkupSafe (setup.py): started
  Building wheel for MarkupSafe (setup.py): finished with status 'done'
  Created wheel for MarkupSafe: filename=MarkupSafe-1.1.1-cp37-cp37m-linux_x86_64.whl size=17026
sha256=ed65c6a2b98932cf4c3f02c3359d80d24f71a17debb91eb52832331c4419cdee
  Stored in directory: /root/.cache/pip/wheels/b9/d9/ae/63bf9056b0a22b13ade9f6b9e08187c1bb71c47ef21a8c9924
Successfully built MarkupSafe
Installing collected packages: MarkupSafe, Werkzeug, Jinja2, itsdangerous, click, flask
Successfully installed Jinja2-2.11.3 MarkupSafe-1.1.1 Werkzeug-1.0.1 click-7.1.2 flask-1.1.2 itsdangerous-1.1.0
[36mINFO[0m[0028] Taking snapshot of full filesystem...
[36mINFO[0m[0033] EXPOSE 5000
[36mINFO[0m[0033] cmd: EXPOSE
[36mINFO[0m[0033] Adding exposed port: 5000/tcp
[36mINFO[0m[0033] Using files from context: [/home/jenkins/agent/workspace/flask-app-jenkins]
[36mINFO[0m[0033] COPY . .
[36mINFO[0m[0033] Taking snapshot of files...
[36mINFO[0m[0033] RUN python3 app.test.py
[36mINFO[0m[0033] cmd: /bin/sh
[36mINFO[0m[0033] args: [-c python3 app.test.py]
..
----------------------------------------------------------------------
Ran 2 tests in 0.009s

OK
[36mINFO[0m[0033] Taking snapshot of full filesystem...
[36mINFO[0m[0037] CMD ["flask", "run"]
Finished: SUCCESS
```

Figure 10.22 – Jenkins console output

And we're able to run a Docker build by using a scalable Jenkins server. As we can see, we've set up polling on the SCM settings to look for changes every minute and build the job if we detect any. But this is resource-intensive and does not help in the long run. Just imagine that you have hundreds of jobs interacting with multiple GitHub repositories, and the Jenkins master is polling them every minute. A better approach would be that if GitHub can trigger a post-commit webhook on Jenkins, Jenkins can build the job whenever there are changes in the repository. Let's look at that scenario in the next section.

Automating a build with triggers

The best way to allow your CI build to trigger when you make changes to your code is to use a post-commit webhook. We've already looked at such an example in the GitHub Actions workflow. Let's try to automate the build with triggers in the case of Jenkins. We'll have to make some changes on both the Jenkins side and the GitHub side to do so. Let's deal with Jenkins first, and then we'll make changes to GitHub.

Go to **Job configuration** | **Build Triggers** and make the following changes:

General
Source Code Management
Build Triggers
Build Environment
Build
Post-build Actions
Trigger builds remotely (e.g., from scripts)
Build after other projects are built
Build periodically
GitHub hook trigger for GITScm polling
Poll SCM

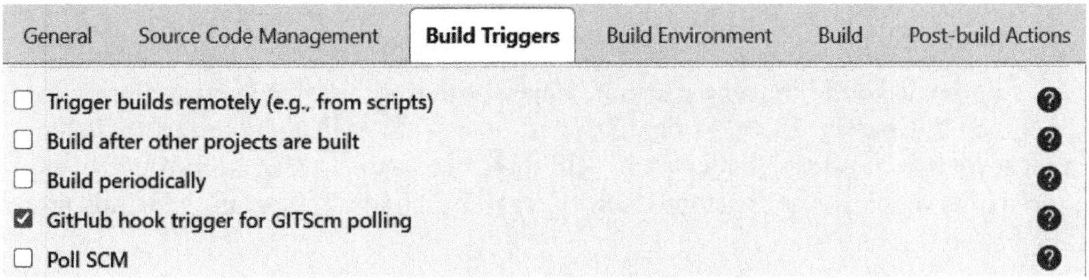

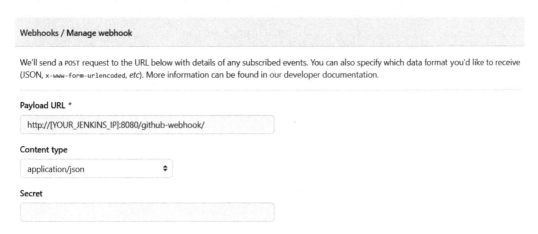

Figure 10.23 – Jenkins GitHub hook trigger

Save the configuration by clicking on **Save**. Now, go to your GitHub repository, click on **Settings** | **Webhooks** | **Add Webhook**, add the following details, and then click on **Add Webhook**:

Webhooks / Manage webhook
We'll send a POST request to the URL below with details of any subscribed events. You can also specify which data format you'd like to receive (JSON, x-www-form-urlencoded, etc). More information can be found in our developer documentation.
Payload URL *
http://[YOUR_JENKINS_IP]:8080/github-webhook/
Content type
application/json
Secret

Figure 10.24 – GitHub webhook

, push a change to the repository and you should see that the job on Jenkins will start building:

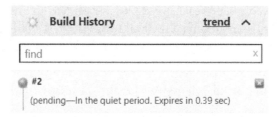

Figure 10.25 – Jenkins GitHub webhook trigger

This is automated build triggers in action. Jenkins is one of the most popular open source CI tools on the market. The most significant advantage of it is that you can pretty much run it anywhere. However, it does come with some management overhead. You may have noticed how simple it was to get started with GitHub Actions, but Jenkins is slightly more complicated.

Several other SaaS platforms offer Continous Integration and Continuous Delivery as a service. For instance, if you are running on AWS, you'd get their inbuilt CI with **AWS Code Commit** and **Code Build**. Let's have a look at this.

CI with AWS Code Commit and Code Build

AWS Code Commit is a Git repository, while Code Build, on the other hand, is a CI tool. Both are SaaS products offered by AWS. If you exclusively run on AWS and don't have a future multi-cloud roadmap, using these products can quickly get you started with your CI.

For this section, you will need an active AWS subscription to follow the exercises. Currently, AWS is offering a free tier on some products. You can sign up at https://aws.amazon.com/free. This chapter uses some paid services, but we will minimize the amount as much as possible.

Once you've created your account, install the AWS CLI: https://docs.aws.amazon.com/cli/latest/userguide/install-cliv1.html.

To access the resources for this section, run the following command:

```
cd ~/modern-devops/ch10/codebuild
```

Then, configure the following environment variables to get started:

```
$ export AWS_ACCESS_KEY_ID=[YOUR_AWS_ACCESS_KEY_ID]
$ export AWS_SECRET_ACCESS_KEY=[YOUR_AWS_SECRET_ACCESS_KEY]
```

```
$ export AWS_DEFAULT_REGION=[YOUR_AWS_DEFAULT_REGION]
```

Now, let's go ahead and create an AWS Code Commit repository.

Creating an AWS Code Commit repository

To create an AWS Code Commit repository called `flask-app`, run the following command:

```
$ aws codecommit create-repository --repository-name flask-app
...
      "cloneUrlHttp": "https://git-codecommit.us-east-1.
amazonaws.com/v1/repos/flask-app",
         "cloneUrlSsh": "ssh://git-codecommit.us-east-1.
amazonaws.com/v1/repos/flask-app",
...
```

In the response, we'll get `cloneUrlHttp` and `cloneUrlSsh`. We can use either of these options to clone our repository. But before we clone, we'll have to set up credentials for the Git command line to access our repository. Assuming that your IAM user already has permissions to clone a repository, we can configure the following credential helper to authenticate with AWS Code Commit:

```
$ git config --global credential.helper '!aws \
codecommit credential-helper $@'
$ git config --global credential.UseHttpPath true
```

Now let's clone by using the `https` URL for this example:

```
$ cd ~
$ git clone https://git-codecommit\
.us-east-1.amazonaws.com/v1/repos/flask-app
Cloning into 'flask-app'...
warning: You appear to have cloned an empty repository.
Checking connectivity... done.
```

And we've cloned the blank repository from AWS Code Commit. Now, let's copy the contents of `flask-app` and push this to this repository using the following commands:

```
$ cp -a modern-devops/ch10/flask-app/* flask-app/
$ cd flask-app
$ git add -all
$ git commit -m 'Initial commit'
$ git push
```

So, we now have our code in the AWS Code Commit repository. Let's now look at AWS Code Build.

Creating an AWS Code Build job

First, we will have to create an AWS Code Build project. The Code Build project will contain configurations to build the code from the AWS Code Commit repository. The Code Build project needs to assume a particular role to act on behalf of an IAM user to connect with the respective services, such as Code Commit. The role and policy files are already present in the shared Git repository. Run the following command to create the Code Build service role:

```
$ aws iam create-role --role-name CodeBuildServiceRole \
  --assume-role-policy-document file://create-role.json
```

The output contains the role's ARN. Keep that handy, as we will need that in the Code Build project configuration file.

We will also have to assign a policy to the CodeBuildServiceRole role to have the required permissions to interact with the required AWS services. To assign the policy to the role, run the following command:

```
$ aws iam put-role-policy --role-name CodeBuildServiceRole \
  --policy-name CodeBuildServiceRolePolicy \
  --policy-document file://put-role-policy.json
```

We'll create an AWS Code Build project file that we will use to create the Code Build project. To create the file, replace the placeholder values in the code-build-project.json file and then run the following command:

```
$ aws codebuild create-project \
  --cli-input-json file://codebuild-project.json
```

Once the project is created, we will need a buildspec file. The buildspec file is a YAML file that specifies the steps of the build. In this case, create the following buildspec.yaml file within the flask-app directory:

```
version: 0.2
phases:
  pre_build:
    commands:
      - echo Logging in to Docker Hub
      - docker login --username $DOCKER_USER --password
$DOCKER_PASSWORD
```

```
build:
  commands:
    - docker build -t $IMAGE_REPO_NAME:$IMAGE_TAG .
post_build:
  commands:
    - docker push $IMAGE_REPO_NAME:$IMAGE_TAG
```

You can then commit and push the code to the Code Commit repository.

From the AWS console, go to **Code Build | flask-app** and then click on **Start Build**. You can go and check the build logs. You will find that AWS Code Build has built the Docker container and pushed the image to DockerHub, as shown in the following screenshot:

```
⊘ Succeeded                                                    Start time: 1 minute ago

125  Step 9/10 : RUN python3 app.test.py
126   ---> Running in 8d1d4ba68db0
127  ..
128  ----------------------------------------------------------------------
129  Ran 2 tests in 0.005s
130
131  OK
132  Removing intermediate container 8d1d4ba68db0
133   ---> b40419bc02e2
134  Step 10/10 : CMD ["flask", "run"]
135   ---> Running in fcd19fa41266
136  Removing intermediate container fcd19fa41266
137   ---> 546f49191db4
138  Successfully built 546f49191db4
139  Successfully tagged bharamicrosystems/flask-app:latest
140
141  [Container] 2021/03/07 16:01:46 Phase complete: BUILD State: SUCCEEDED
142  [Container] 2021/03/07 16:01:46 Phase context status code:  Message:
143  [Container] 2021/03/07 16:01:46 Entering phase POST_BUILD
144  [Container] 2021/03/07 16:01:46 Running command docker push bharamicrosystems/flask-app
145  The push refers to repository [docker.io/bharamicrosystems/flask-app]
146  ac2cfe9ff0f1: Preparing
147  76429a61e3d3: Preparing
```

Figure 10.26 – AWS Cloud Build console output

At the moment, there is no direct way for triggering Code Build on every push to Code Commit. There are workarounds available, such as writing a Lambda function that can listen to Code Commit events and trigger Code Build as a result, or you can use the AWS Code Pipeline service to do so. Covering these is beyond the scope of this book.

CI follows the same principle regardless of the tooling you choose to implement. It is more of a process and a cultural change within your organization. Let's now look at some of the best practices regarding CI.

Build performance best practices

CI is an ongoing process, and therefore, you will have a lot of parallel builds running within your environment at a given time. In such a situation, let's look at how we can optimize them using a number of best practices.

Aim for faster builds

The faster you can complete your build, the quicker you will get feedback and run your next iteration. A slow build slows down your development team. Take steps to ensure that builds are faster. For example, in Docker's case, it makes sense to use smaller base images as it will download the code from the image registry every time it does a build. Using a single base image for most of your builds will also speed up your build time. Using tests will help, but make sure that they aren't long-running. We want to avoid a CI build that runs for hours. Therefore, it would be good to offload long-running tests into another job or use a pipeline. Run activities in parallel if possible.

Always use post-commit triggers

Post-commit triggers help your team significantly. They will not have to log in to the CI server and trigger the build manually. That completely decouples your development team from CI management.

Configure build reporting

You don't want your development team to log in to the CI tool and check how the build is running. Instead, all they want to know is the result of the build and the build logs. Therefore, you can configure build reporting at the end so that you can send your build status via email or, even better, using a Slack channel.

Customize the build server size

Not all builds work the same in similar kinds of build machines. You may want to choose machines based on what suits your build environment best. If your builds tend to consume more CPU than memory, it will make sense to choose such machines to run your builds instead of the standard ones.

Ensure that your builds only contain what you need

Builds move across networks. You download base images, build your application image, and push that to the container registry. Bloated images not only take a lot of network bandwidth and time to transmit, but also make your build vulnerable to security issues. Therefore, it is always best practice to only include what you require in the build and avoid bloat. You can use Docker's multi-stage builds for these kinds of situations.

These are some of the best practices on a high level, and they are not exhaustive, but they are good enough to start optimizing your CI environment.

Summary

This chapter has covered CI, and you have understood the need for CI and the basic CI workflow for a container application. We then looked at GitHub Actions to build an effective Continous Integration pipeline. We then looked at the Jenkins open source offering and deployed a scalable Jenkins on Kubernetes with Kaniko, setting up a Jenkins master-agent model. We then understood how to use hooks for automating builds, both in the GitHub Actions-based workflow and the Jenkins-based workflow. We then delved into AWS's CI stack using AWS Code Commit and Code Build. Finally, we learned about build performance best practices and dos and don'ts.

By now, you should be familiar with CI and its nuances, along with the various tooling you can use to implement it.

In the next chapter, we will delve into Continuous Deployment/Delivery in the container world.

Questions

1. Which of the following are CI tools? (Multiple answers are possible)

   a. Jenkins

   b. GitHub Actions

   c. Kubernetes

   d. AWS Cloudbuild

2. It is a best practice to configure post-commit triggers – True/False?

3. Jenkins is a SaaS-based CI tool – True/False?

4. Kaniko requires Docker to build your containers – True/False?

5. Jenkins agents are required for which of the following reasons? (Multiple answers are possible)

    a. They make builds more scalable.

    b. They help offload the management function from the Jenkins master.

    c. They allow for parallel builds.

    d. They keep the Jenkins master less busy.

6. AWS Cloudbuild does not have an out-of-the-box build trigger solution – True/False?

7. Which of the following is required for a scalable Jenkins server as described in the example? (Multiple answers are possible)

    a. Kubernetes cluster

    b. Jenkins master node

    c. Jenkins agent node

    d. Credentials to interact with the container registry.

Answers

1. a, b, d
2. True
3. False
4. False
5. a, c, d
6. True
7. a, b, d

11

Continuous Deployment/ Delivery with Spinnaker

In the last chapter, we looked at one of the key aspects of modern DevOps – Continuous Integration. Continuous Integration is the first thing most organizations implement when they embrace DevOps, but things don't end with Continuous Integration. Continuous Integration ends with a tested build being available in an artifact repository. In this chapter, we'll implement the next part of the DevOps toolchain – **Continuous Deployment/Delivery**.

In this chapter, we're going to cover the following main topics:

- Importance of Continuous Deployment and automation

- Continuous deployment models and tools

- Introduction to Spinnaker

- Setting up Spinnaker

- Deploying a sample application using a Spinnaker pipeline

Technical requirements

For this chapter, we will spin up a cloud-based Kubernetes cluster, Google Kubernetes Engine, for the exercises. Currently, Google Cloud Platform provides a free $300 trial for 90 days, so you can go ahead and sign up for one at `https://console.cloud.google.com/`.

You will also need to clone the following GitHub repository for some of the exercises: `https://github.com/PacktPublishing/Modern-DevOps-Practices`.

Run the following command to clone the repository into your home directory, and `cd` into the `ch11` directory to access the required resources:

```
$ git clone https://github.com/PacktPublishing/Modern-DevOps-\
Practices.git modern-devops
$ cd modern-devops/ch11
```

As the repository contains files with placeholders, you will have to replace the "<your_dockerhub_user>" string with the your actual Docker Hub user. Use the following commands to substitute the placeholders.

```
$ find ./ -type f -exec sed -i -e 's/\
<your_dockerhub_user>/\
<your_actual_docker_hub_user>/g' {} \;
```

So, let's get started!

Importance of Continuous Deployment and automation

Continuous delivery/deployments form the Ops part of your DevOps toolchain. So, while your developers are continuously building and pushing your code and your **Continuous Integration** (**CI**) pipeline is building, testing, and publishing the builds to your artifact repository, the Ops team will deploy the build to the test and staging environments. The QA team are the gatekeepers who will ensure that the code meets a certain quality, and only then does the Ops team deploy the code to production.

Now, for organizations that have implemented only the CI part, the rest of the activities are manual. For example, operators will pull the artifacts and run commands to do the deployments manually. Therefore, your deployment's velocity will depend on the availability of your Ops team to do it. As the deployments are manual, the process is error-prone, and human beings tend to make mistakes in repeatable jobs.

One of the essential principles of modern DevOps is to avoid **Toil**. Toil is nothing but repeatable jobs that developers and operators do day in and day out, and all of that toil can be removed by automation. That will help your team to focus on the more important things at hand.

With **Continuous Delivery** in place, standard tooling can deploy code to higher environments based on certain gate conditions. Continuous Delivery pipelines will trigger as soon as a tested build arrives at the artifact repository. The pipeline then decides, based on a set configuration, where and how to deploy the code. It also establishes whether any manual checks are required, such as raising a change ticket and checking whether it's approved.

While Continuous Deployment and delivery are often confused with being the same thing, there is a slight difference between them. Continuous delivery enables your team to deliver tested code in your environment based on a human trigger. So, while you don't have to do anything more than just press a button to do a deployment to production, it would still be initiated by someone at a convenient time (a maintenance window). Continuous deployments go a step further where they integrate with the CI process and will start the deployment process as soon as a new tested build is available for it to consume. There is no need for any manual intervention, and Continuous Deployment will only stop in case of a failed test.

The monitoring tool forms the next part of the DevOps toolchain. The operations team can learn from managing their production environment and provide developers with feedback regarding what they need to do better. That feedback ends up in the development backlog, and they can deliver it as features in future releases. That completes the cycle, and now you have your team churning out a technology product continuously.

There are several models and tools available to implement Continuous Deployment/ delivery. Let's have a look at some of them in the next section.

Continuous deployment models and tools

A typical CI/CD workflow looks like the following:

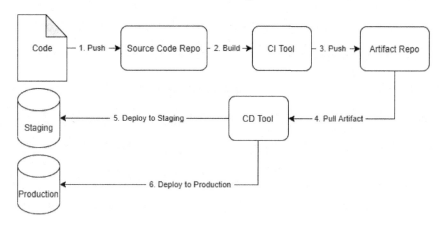

Figure 11.1 – CI/CD workflow

1. Your developers write code and push it to a code repository (typically a Git repository).

2. Your CI tool builds the code, runs a series of tests, and pushes the tested build to an artifact repository. Your Continuous Deployment tool then picks up the artifact and deploys it to your test and staging environments. Based on whether you want to do Continuous Deployment or delivery, it automatically deploys the artifact to the production environment.

Well, what do you then choose for a delivery tool? Let's look at the example we covered in *Chapter 10, Continuous Integration.* We picked up a **Flask** app and used a CI tool such as GitHub Actions/Jenkins/AWS Code build that uses **Docker** to create a container out of it and push it to our Docker Hub container registry. Well, we could have used the same tool for also doing the deployment to our environment.

For example, if we wanted to deploy to Kubernetes, it would have been a simple YAML update and apply. That we could easily do with any of those tools, but we chose not to do it. Why? The answer is simple – CI tools are meant for CI, and if you want to use them for anything else, you'll get stuck at a certain point. That does not mean that you cannot use the tools for doing Continuous Deployment. It will only suit a minimal amount of use cases, based on the deployment model you follow.

Several deployment models exist based on your application, technology stack, customers, risk appetite, and cost consciousness. Let's look at some of the popular deployment models used within the industry.

Simple deployment model

The **simple deployment model** is one of the most straightforward of all. You deploy the required version of your application after removing the old one. It completely replaces the previous version, and rolling back is generally redeploying the older version after removing the deployed one:

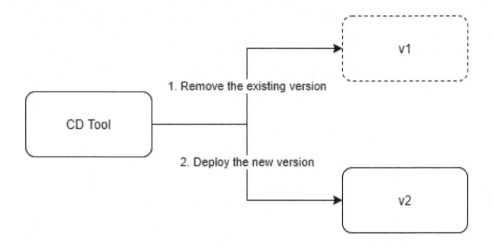

Figure 11.2 – Simple deployment model

As it is a simple way of deploying things, you can manage this by using a CI tool such as **Jenkins**, **GitHub actions**, or **AWS Cloud Build**. However, the simple deployment model is not the most desired way of doing deployments because of some inherent risks. This kind of change is disruptive and typically needs downtime. That means your service would remain unavailable to your customers for the upgrade period. It might be OK for organizations that do not have users 24x7, but disruptions eat into their **Service Level Objectives (SLOs)** and **Agreements (SLAs)** for global organizations. Even if there isn't one, they hamper customer experience and the organization's reputation as a result.

Therefore, to manage such kinds of situations, we have some complex deployment models.

Complex deployment models

Complex Deployment Models, unlike simple deployment models, try to minimize disruptions and downtimes within the application and make rolling out releases more seamless to the extent that most users don't even notice when the upgrade is being conducted. There are two main kinds of complex deployments that are prevalent in the industry.

Blue/Green deployments

Blue/Green deployments (also known as **Red/Black deployments**) roll out the new version (Green) in addition to the existing version (Blue). You can then do sanity checks and other activities with the latest version to ensure that everything is good to go. Then, you can switch traffic from the old version to the new version and monitor for any issues. If you encounter problems, you switch back traffic to the old version, otherwise you keep the latest version running and remove the old version:

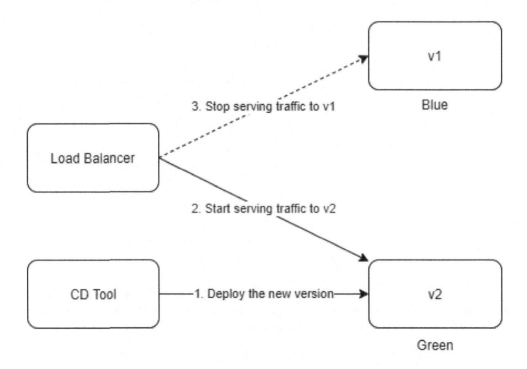

Figure 11.3 – Blue/Green deployments

You can take Blue/Green deployments to the next level by using canary deployments.

Canary deployment and A/B testing

Canary Deployments are similar to Blue/Green deployments, but are generally utilized for risky upgrades. So, like Blue/Green deployments, we deploy the new version alongside the existing one. Instead of switching all traffic to the latest version at once, we will only switch traffic to a small subset of users. As we do that, we can understand from our logs and user behaviors whether the switchover is causing any issues. That is called A/B testing. When we do A/B testing, we can target a specific group of users based on location, language, age group, or users who have opted for testing Beta versions of a product. That will help organizations gather feedback without disrupting general users and make changes to the product once they're satisfied with what they are rolling out. You can make the release generally available by switching over the total traffic to the new version and getting rid of the old version:

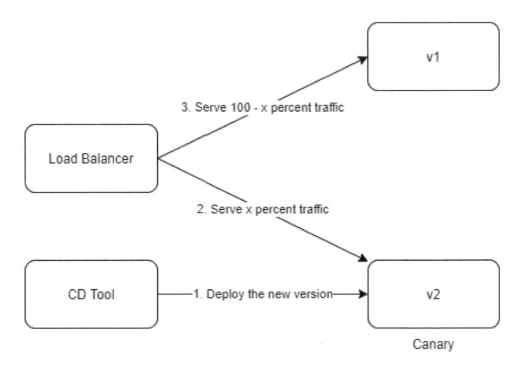

Figure 11.4 – Canary deployments

While complex deployments cause the least disruption to users, they are generally complex to manage using traditional CI tools such as Jenkins. Therefore, we need to get the tooling right on it. Several Continuous Deployment tools are available in the market, including **Spinnaker**, **Argo CD**, **Circle CI**, and **AWS Code Deploy**. For this chapter, we will focus on Spinnaker.

Introduction to Spinnaker

Spinnaker is an open source, multi-cloud continuous delivery tool developed by **Netflix** and **Google** and which was then open sourced to the **Cloud Native Computing Foundation** (CNCF). This tool can help you deploy your applications across multiple clouds and Kubernetes clusters and manage them using a single control plane. That provides organizations with immense power in managing their deployments across several estates, geographical locations, and cloud accounts.

The tool is potent and flexible with its pipelines. Currently, it supports many target cloud platforms, including **AWS EC2, EKS, Kubernetes, Google Compute Engine, Google Kubernetes Engine, Google App Engine, Microsoft Azure, Openstack, Oracle Cloud Infrastructure**, and **Cloud Foundry**. They also have plans to integrate it with on-premises data centers.

It helps you run robust deployment pipelines that can run system and integration tests, manage your infrastructure using a concept called server groups, and monitor deployment rollouts. The pipelines can be triggered in many ways, such as **Git events, Jenkins, Docker, CRON**, other Spinnaker pipelines, and **Artifacts** in a container registry.

They also support immutable infrastructure in the cloud using immutable images with **Packer**, resulting in faster rollouts, easier rollback, and avoiding configuration drifts that occur with traditional configuration management. They offer blue/green and canary deployment strategies by default.

Spinnaker offers Integration with **Chaos Monkey** for your tests, which helps you test your system resiliency by terminating instances on purpose. Chaos Monkey simulates an environment of Chaos within your environment with services by causing random outages within processes and services, so as to test the resilience of your application. While it is an interesting bit to learn, it forms a part of the QA function and so is not within the scope of this book.

Spinnaker also offers a manual judgment task within its pipelines. So, if you're implementing a continuous delivery pipeline, it becomes easier to do so.

> Tip
> Using the manual judgment task, you can pause the deployment to production until someone manually approves the deployment.

Spinnaker is inherently a microservices application. Several components of it interact with each other to provide a complete experience.

The following diagram depicts each component:

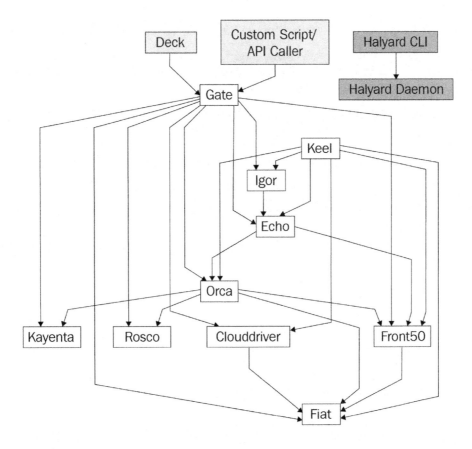

Figure 11.5 – Spinnaker architecture

Spinnaker is made up of the following microservices:

- **Deck**: A simple browser-based UI that takes care of the user interactions.

- **Gate**: The API Gateway that frontends all **Spinnaker** components and listens to calls from the **Spinnaker UI** and **API Callers**.

- **Orca**: This is the orchestration engine that takes care of all ad hoc operations and pipelines.

- **Clouddriver**: This indexes/caches deployed resources and makes calls to cloud providers.

- **Front50**: This is the persistent store and stores the application, pipeline, project, and notification metadata.

- **Rosco**: This helps in baking custom VM images by providing a wrapper over **Packer**.

- **Igor**: This is used to trigger **Jenkins** and **Travis** pipeline jobs from Spinnaker.

- **Echo**: This is Spinnaker's **Eventing** engine. It allows for all communications between multiple systems, such as sending notifications to Slack or receiving webhooks from systems such as Jenkins.

- **Fait**: This is the authorization service and provides RBAC.

- **Kayenta**: This provides automatic canary analysis for deployments.

- **Keel**: This provides managed delivery.

- **halyard**: This is Spinnaker's configuration tool. We will use this to configure Spinnaker.

So, without further ado, let's spin up Spinnaker.

Setting up Spinnaker

Setting up Spinnaker is relatively complex, but once you have set it up, it becomes effortless to manage your deployments. Spinnaker is also a little heavy on resources. We will create the following in our deployment:

- A **VM for running halyard**. The VM should have at least 12 GB of memory. Since we're using GCP, the nearest machine I can find is `e2-standard-4`.

- A **Google Kubernetes Engine cluster** that has at least four cores and 16 GB of RAM in the cluster. Therefore, we'll spin up a three-node cluster with `e2-standard-2` machines.

- A **Google Cloud Storage Bucket** to store Spinnaker configurations. This entails cheaper storage, and we don't want to store metadata on disks.

> Tip
> While there are other ways of deploying Spinnaker (notably **Helm**), using **halyard** has its advantages as it helps you to configure Spinnaker easily and has tremendous community support.

Let's start by spinning up the Google Kubernetes Engine. Remember that you'll be using your local system for setting everything up and not the cloud shell in this exercise. Therefore, you first have to install the Google SDK within your machine. Use the instructions from `https://cloud.google.com/sdk/docs/install` and install the SDK within your system.

Spinning up Google Kubernetes Engine

Once you've installed the Google Cloud SDK, open up the command-line interface on your system. Windows users can use `cmd`, and Linux and Mac users can use the Terminal.

Run the following command to log in to your account from the CLI:

```
$ gcloud auth login
```

A browser window will pop up where you can log in using your Google Cloud account and allow access to your CLI to act on your behalf. Once you've done that, you will get back to the prompt.

You then need to enable the **Kubernetes Engine API**, **Google IAM API**, and **Google Cloud Resource Manager API** using the following commands:

```
$ gcloud services enable container.googleapis.com
$ gcloud services enable iam.googleapis.com
$ gcloud services enable cloudresourcemanager.googleapis.com
```

To create a three-node GKE cluster with `e2-standard-2` machines, run the following command:

```
$ gcloud container clusters create cluster-1 \
--zone us-central1-a -m e2-standard-2
```

It will take a few minutes for your cluster to get ready, and you should see that it will soon start running.

Next, let's go and set up some service accounts and add IAM policies to them.

Setting up service accounts and permissions

We'll first create a service account for the halyard host VM and provide the required permissions. That is the VM that we'll install halyard on and administer our Spinnaker deployment from here:

```
$ PROJECT_ID=<project_id>
$ gcloud iam service-accounts create halyard-service-account \
--project=${PROJECT_ID} --display-name halyard-service-account
$ gcloud projects add-iam-policy-binding ${PROJECT_ID} \
--role roles/iam.serviceAccountKeyAdmin \
--member serviceAccount:halyard-service-account@\
${PROJECT_ID}.iam.gserviceaccount.com
$ gcloud projects add-iam-policy-binding ${PROJECT_ID} \
--role roles/container.admin \
--member serviceAccount:halyard-service-account@\
${PROJECT_ID}.iam.gserviceaccount.com
```

The service account is created.

> **Tip**
> While we've assigned the `container.admin` role to `halyard-service-account`, it is best to only give the permissions required to do the deployments.

Next, we'll create a service account for **Google Cloud Storage** and assign the relevant permissions to it using the following commands:

```
$ gcloud iam service-accounts create gcs-service-account \
--project=${PROJECT_ID} --display-name gcs-service-account
$ gcloud projects add-iam-policy-binding ${PROJECT_ID} \
--role roles/storage.admin \
--member serviceAccount:gcs-serviceaccount@\
${PROJECT_ID}.iam.gserviceaccount.com
$ gcloud projects add-iam-policy-binding ${PROJECT_ID} \
--member serviceAccount:gcs-serviceaccount@\
${PROJECT_ID}.iam.gserviceaccount.com \
--role roles/browser
```

As we've set up the service accounts correctly, let's go ahead and create a halyard host VM.

Creating a halyard host VM

To create a halyard host VM, use the following command:

```
$ gcloud compute instances create halyard \
--project=${PROJECT_ID} --zone=us-central1-f \
--scopes=cloud-platform --service-account=halyard\
-service-account@${PROJECT_ID}.iam.gserviceaccount.com \
--image-project=ubuntu-os-cloud --image-\
family=ubuntu-1604-lts --machine-type=e2-standard-4
```

Next, we'll SSH into the halyard host VM and run the next set of commands from there. We'll port forward from your workstation to this VM and from the VM to Spinnaker running on Kubernetes. So that is why you cannot use a cloud shell for this exercise.

Make sure that the SSH port 22 and the ports 8084 and 9000 are open on your firewall. Run the following command if they're not open already:

```
$ gcloud compute instances \
--project=${PROJECT_ID} add-tags halyard --tags=halyard
$ gcloud compute firewall-rules create allow-halyard-access \
--target-tags halyard --source-ranges 0.0.0.0/0 \
--action=allow --direction=ingress \
--rules tcp:22,tcp:8084,tcp:9000 --priority 50
```

Let's ssh into the halyard VM using the following command:

```
$ gcloud compute ssh halyard \
--project=${PROJECT_ID} --zone=uscentral1-f \
--ssh-flag="-L 9000:localhost:9000" \
--ssh-flag="-L 8084:localhost:8084"
```

Depending upon your system's platform, it will either fire a puTTy window or ssh into the halyard VM using your terminal.

> **Tip**
> If you're using a Windows workstation, it is good to install puTTy as it provides a better experience than other tools.

Now, let's go ahead and install halyard.

Installing halyard

Before installing halyard, we need to have `kubectl` installed within the system as halyard will use that to interact with our **Kubernetes cluster**. To do so, run the following command:

```
$ curl -LO \
https://storage.googleapis.com/kubernetes-release/release/\
$(curl -s https://storage.googleapis.com/\
kubernetesrelease/release/stable.txt)/bin/linux/amd64/kubectl
$ chmod +x kubectl
$ sudo mv kubectl /usr/local/bin/kubectl
```

Run the following command to check whether `kubectl` has been installed successfully:

```
$ kubectl version --client
Client Version: version.Info{Major:"1",
Minor:"20", GitVersion:"v1.20.5",
GitCommit:"6b1d87acf3c8253c123756b9e61dac642678305f",
GitTreeState:"clean", BuildDate:"2021-03-18T01:10:43Z",
GoVersion:"go1.15.8", Compiler:"gc", Platform:"linux/amd64"}
```

Next, we've got to install Java within the system. Halyard supports **Java 11**, so run the following command to install it.

```
$ sudo add-apt-repository ppa:openjdk-r/ppa
$ sudo apt update
$ sudo apt install openjdk-11-jdk
```

Now, let's go ahead and install halyard using the following commands:

```
$ curl -O https://raw.githubusercontent.com/spinnaker\
/halyard/master/install/debian/InstallHalyard.sh
$ sudo bash InstallHalyard.sh
```

When you run the install script, halyard will prompt you for a non-root user to run halyard as. Use the current user you're logged on as, or create a separate user for halyard and use that.

Once you've done that, it takes a while for halyard daemon to start running. You may have to wait for a minute for that. It will then prompt you whether you want to enable bash autocompletion. Press *y* and *Enter*.

> **Tip**
> If your halyard daemon does not run for some reason, troubleshoot the problem using the logs at `/var/log/spinnaker`.

Next, we'll manually take the configuration from the `bashrc` file to enable autocompletion in the current session. To do so, run the following command:

```
$ . ~/.bashrc
```

And that's it! halyard is successfully installed. Now, let's use halyard to deploy Spinnaker for us.

Setting up the required credentials

Now, we need to set up credentials for accessing the GKE cluster and the cloud storage. Although we've created the service accounts already, we need to get the credentials for them in this VM.

First, get the Kubernetes credentials by running the following command:

```
$ gcloud container clusters get-credentials cluster-1 \
    --zone=us-central1-a
```

The next step is to get the GCS credentials. For that, we'll generate a **JSON** credentials file for the GCS service account and store it in a particular directory. Run the following commands to do so:

```
$ mkdir -p ~/.gcp/gcp.json
$ gcloud iam service-accounts keys create ~/.gcp/gcp.json \
--iam-account gcs-service-account@\
${PROJECT_ID}.iam.gserviceaccount.com
```

Now, as we have the right credentials in place, the next step involves setting up the Spinnaker configuration.

Setting up the Spinnaker configuration

First, we'll have to tell halyard what version of Spinnaker to use. We'll just go ahead and use the latest version. Use the following command to do so:

```
$ hal config version edit --version $(hal version latest -q)
```

The next step is to configure where we want to persist Spinnaker data. Spinnaker supports multiple data stores. We'll use GCS as it's a cheap cloud storage option and costs us much less than storing it in a persistent disk. To do so, run the following command:

```
$ hal config storage gcs edit \
--project $(gcloud config get-value project) \
--json-path ~/.gcp/gcp.json
$ hal config storage edit --type gcs
```

As we're using **Docker Hub** for our exercises, we will enable the container registry for Docker Hub. Docker Hub does not provide an index to list all repositories. We don't want to track all of it. We'll have to specify the repositories we'll be checking for changes. In this case, we'll use two repositories, <your_dockerhub_user>/flask-app and <your_dockerhub_user>/flask-app-gh-actions. To do so, run the following commands:

```
$ hal config provider docker-registry enable
$ hal config provider docker-registry account add \
my-docker-registry --address index.docker.io \
--repositories <your_dockerhub_user>\
/flask-app-gh-actions <your_dockerhub_user>/flask-app
```

The next thing we need to tell halyard is that we want to deploy to a Kubernetes environment. To do so, we will have to set up the Kubernetes provider. Use the following commands to do so:

```
$ hal config provider kubernetes enable
$ hal config provider kubernetes account add my-k8s-account \
--docker-registries my-docker-registry \
--context $(kubectlconfig current-context)
```

Now, as we've finished configuring Spinnaker, we can go ahead and deploy it.

Deploying Spinnaker

To deploy Spinnaker, we'll have to tell halyard where we want to deploy Spinnaker. As we'll deploy it within the Kubernetes cluster that we've created, run the following command to set it:

```
$ hal config deploy edit --account-name my-k8s-account \
--type distributed
```

We're now ready to deploy Spinnaker. To do so, run the following command:

```
$ hal deploy apply
```

It will deploy several resources, and when the deployment completes, you'll get a prompt to run `hal deploy connect`. Let's do so to connect with Spinnaker.

```
$ hal deploy connect
```

Now, it will start doing a port-forward from ports `8084` and `9000`.

> **Tip**
> While port forwarding is a secure way of connecting to Spinnaker, it is not very practical for many users as you don't want to provide all of them with halyard access. In such a situation, you can expose the spin-gate deployment via a `LoadBalancer` or `Ingress` resource.

Open your favorite browser from your workstation, go to `localhost:9000`, and you should see the following.

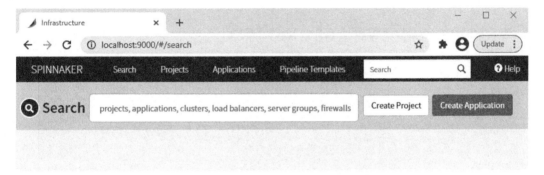

Figure 11.6 – Spinnaker home page

Congratulations! Spinnaker is running successfully on your system!

Now let's go ahead and run a Continuous Deployment pipeline using Spinnaker.

Deploying a sample application using a Spinnaker pipeline

The Continuous Deployment pipeline will start after delivering a change to the Docker Hub registry through the CI process.

But as we're going to do continuous delivery, we require a manual check that will ensure that someone approves it prior to deployment.

In this case, we'll deploy the code directly to the `staging` namespace as soon as a new version of the container is available in the Docker Hub registry. We will then add a **Manual Check** to ensure that we do our tests and only approve the production deployment once we're satisfied. Once we've approved the manual deployment, Spinnaker will deploy the code to the `production` namespace.

The application is a simple Flask application that will respond with the current version it's running. It will also contain unit tests to ensure that we don't break anything. They are all part of the CI process, so we will not cover the tooling aspects. They are already covered in *Chapter 10*, *Continuous Integration*. In this chapter, we will focus on the Continuous Deployment part. So, let's start by creating a deployment manifest for the application.

Creating a deployment manifest

We will create a single `manifest.yaml` file that will contain three resources – a `Namespace`, a `Deployment`, and a `Service`.

The namespace part looks like the following:

```
apiVersion: v1
kind: Namespace
metadata:
  name: '${namespace}'
```

The deployment part deploys three replicas of the Flask application and appears as follows:

```
apiVersion: apps/v1
kind: Deployment
metadata:
  labels:
    app: flask-app
```

```
  name: flask-app
  namespace: '${namespace}'
spec:
  replicas: 3
  selector:
    matchLabels:
      app: flask-app
  template:
    metadata:
      labels:
        app: flask-app
    spec:
      containers:
        - image: '<your_dockerhub_user>/flask-
app:${trigger[''tag'']}'
          name: flask-app
          ports:
            - containerPort: 5000
```

We then expose the deployment using a Load Balancer service on port 80. The service manifest looks like the following:

```
apiVersion: v1
kind: Service
metadata:
  name: flask-app
  namespace: '${namespace}'
spec:
  ports:
    - port: 80
      protocol: TCP
      targetPort: 5000
  selector:
    app: flask-app
  type: LoadBalancer
```

Create a GitHub repository of your choice, clone it, copy the `manifest.yaml` file from the `ch11` directory, and `commit` and `push` it to your repository. Use the following as an example:

```
$ git clone https://github.com/<YOUR_REPO>/flask-app.git
$ cd flask-app
$ cp -a ~/modern-devops/ch11/manifest.yaml .
$ git add --all
$ git commit -m 'Initial commit'
$ git push
```

Now, as we're going to use the GitHub repository as our source for deploying the manifest, we have to add the GitHub repository as a Spinnaker artifact. To do so, we'll have to make some changes to the halyard configuration.

First, go to `https://github.com/settings/tokens` to generate an access token. Add the `repository` scope to the token and keep the token handy.

Then, run the following commands:

```
$ echo [YOUR_TOKEN] > token
$ hal config artifact github enable
$ hal config artifact github account add \
[YOUR_GITHUB_USER_ID] --token-file token
$ hal deploy apply
```

Now, we're ready to create the Spinnaker application.

Creating a Spinnaker application

A Spinnaker application denotes the application that it is managing. It will contain all settings related to the **Application** and **Deployment pipelines**, **Clusters**, and **Server Groups**.

A server group within Spinnaker is the deployable software unit, such as a **Docker container image** or a **VM image**. It also contains its settings, such as the number of instances, autoscaling policies, and other associated metadata. You can also associate a server group with a load balancer and a firewall.

A cluster within Spinnaker is a logical grouping of server groups. Please don't confuse it with the Kubernetes cluster where the server groups are deployed.

Now, let's move on and create a **Spinnaker application** using the **Spinnaker UI**.

Go to `http://localhost:9000/#/applications` and click on the **Create Application** button. You will be prompted with a form. Supply a name, email, in the **Repo Type** field, select **GitHub**, and then specify the GitHub project and **Repo Name**. Keep everything else as their default settings and then click on the **Create** button:

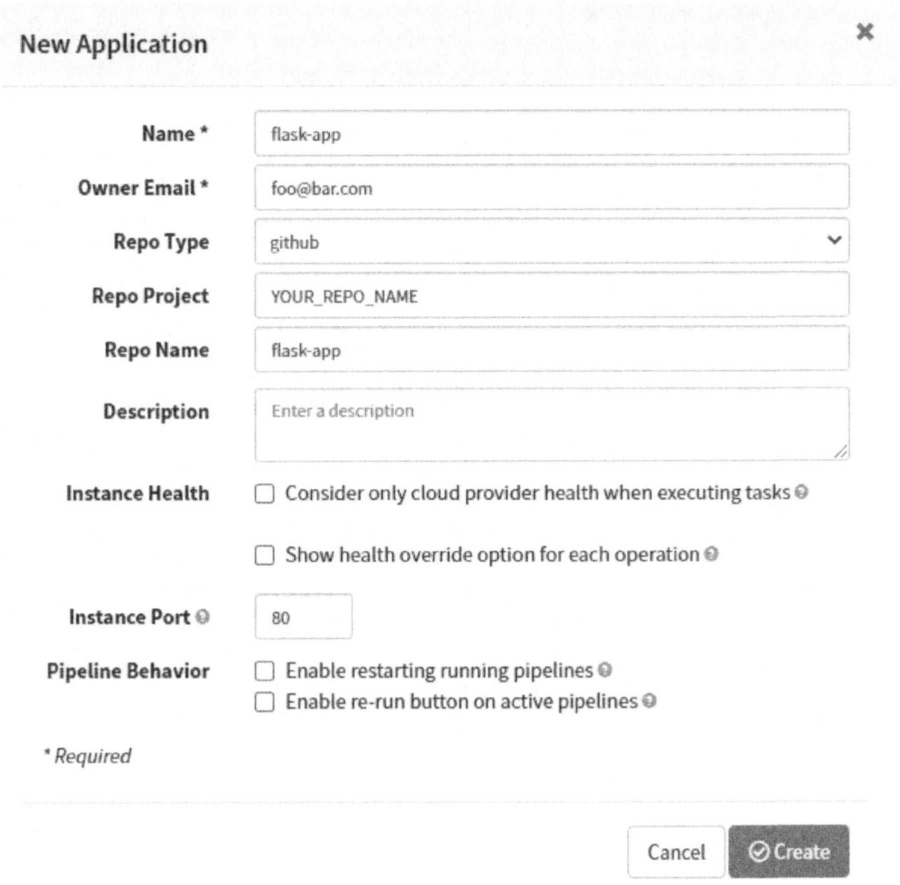

New Application   ✖

Name *	flask-app
Owner Email *	foo@bar.com
Repo Type	github ⌄
Repo Project	YOUR_REPO_NAME
Repo Name	flask-app
Description	Enter a description
Instance Health	☐ Consider only cloud provider health when executing tasks ❷
	☐ Show health override option for each operation ❷
Instance Port ❷	80
Pipeline Behavior	☐ Enable restarting running pipelines ❷
	☐ Enable re-run button on active pipelines ❷

*Required

Cancel   ⊘ Create

Figure 11.7 – New application

Now, let's go ahead and create the pipeline within the application.

Creating a Spinnaker pipeline

To create a Spinnaker pipeline, click on the **Pipelines** button on the left pane and you will see a **Configure a new pipeline** link on the main page – click on that. You'll be prompted by a form, supply a pipeline name of your choice, and click on **Create**:

Figure 11.8 – Create New Pipeline

You can then configure the pipeline as per your requirements. Let's understand what we need in the first place. We want the following:

- The pipeline should be triggered when there is an image pushed to `<your_dockerhub_user>/flask-app`.

- It should then deploy to the `staging` namespace.

- We will then need a manual gate that will wait for someone to confirm before the next step.

- On confirmation, we want to deploy the code to the `production` namespace.

So, let's start by creating a **Trigger** first. In the **Automated Triggers** section, click on the **Add Trigger** button. Then, select the type as **Docker Registry**. As we've preconfigured the Flask app when we did the halyard configuration, you will see that pre-populated within the **Registry Name**, **Organization**, and **Image** dropdowns. Select the `flask-app` image:

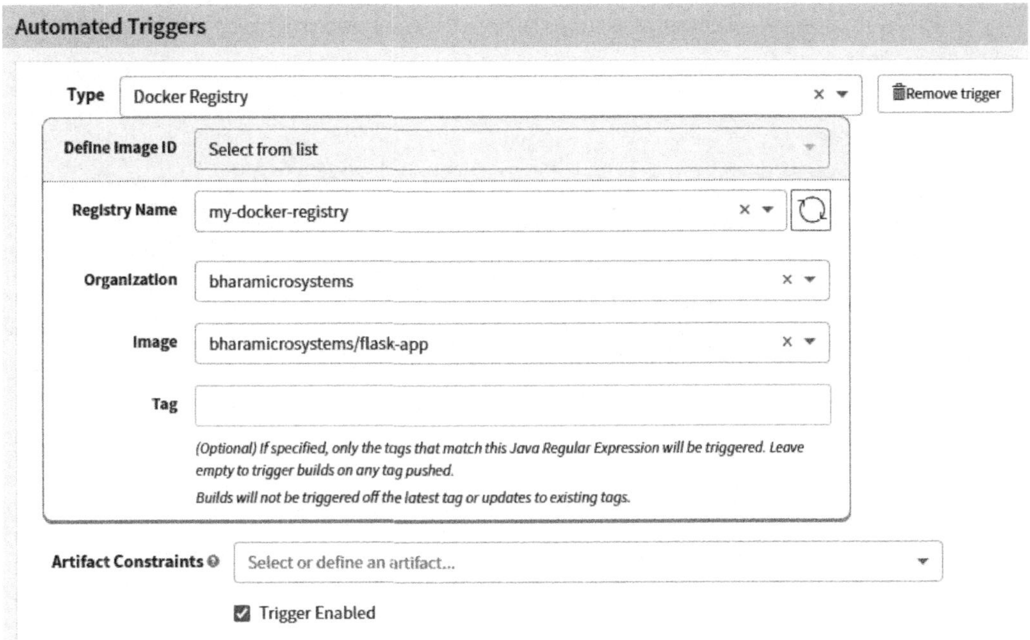

Figure 11.9 – Automated Triggers

Now, we can start adding stages to the pipeline. The first task will be to set the
`namespace` variable to `staging`. Remember that we've added the `namespace`
placeholder within our `manifest.yaml` file. We need to specify the variable value
within the pipeline. To add the variable, click on **Add Stage**. Select **Evaluate Variable**
as the type, insert `Set Staging Namespace` in the **Stage Name** field, and keep the
Depends On field blank. Then, create a variable with the name `namespace` and the
value `staging`:

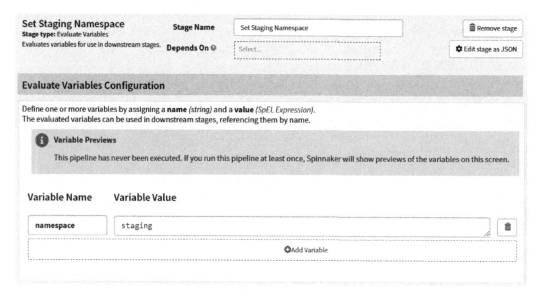

Figure 11.10 – Set Staging Namespace

Now, as we've set the namespace correctly, we can go ahead and deploy the application to the staging environment. Click on the **Add Stage** button in the **Configuration** section. Set **Deploy (Manifest)** as the type and the stage name as `Deploy to Staging`:

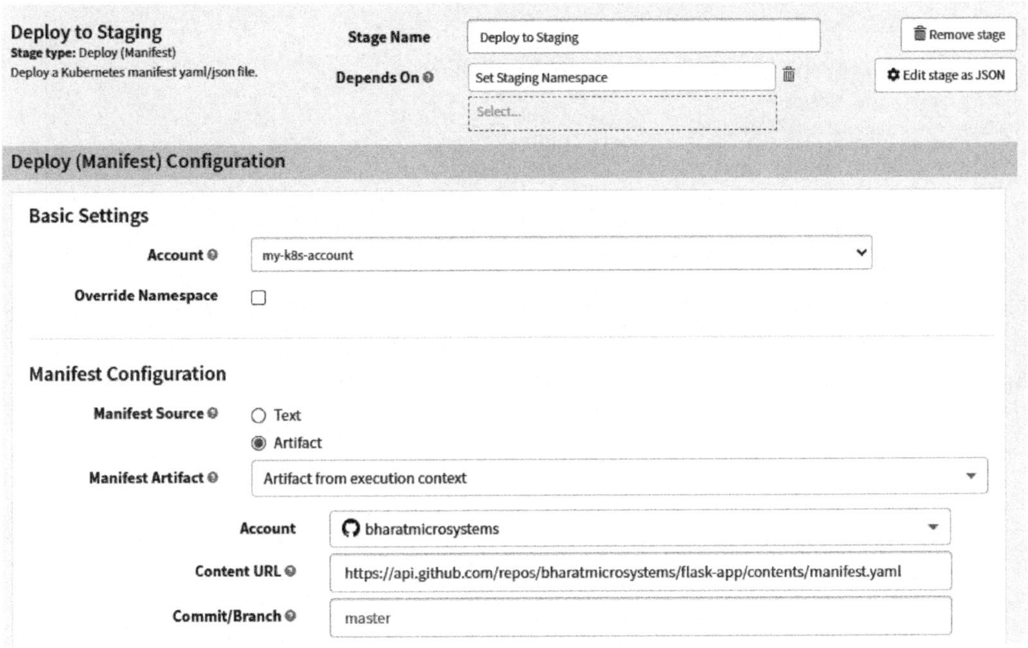

Figure 11.11 – Deploy to Staging

In the **Basic Settings** section of **Deploy (Manifest) Configuration**, select `my-k8s-account` in the **Account** field (it should come pre-populated as we've set that in the halyard configuration). Next, in the **Manifest Configuration** section, select **Artifact** for **Manifest Source**. Within **Manifest Artifact**, click on **Define new Artifact**. That will give you some other fields you need to fill. Remember that we need to get the manifest from our GitHub repository.

So, select the GitHub account that you've defined in the halyard configuration. The content URL should be the URL of your manifest file in the form `https://api.github.com/repos/<ACCOUNT_NAME>/flask-app/contents/manifest.yaml`. Keep the rest as their default settings.

The next stage is **Manual Judgment**. It is at this point that we'll decide whether we want to go ahead with the production deployment. To add **Manual Judgment**, click on **Add stage** and then select **Type** as **Manual Judgment**. Leave everything as their default settings in this instance:

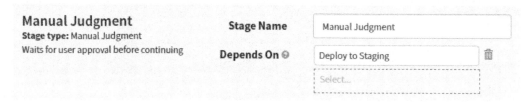

Figure 11.12 – Manual Judgment

Next, we'll move on to setting the `production` namespace. Similar to how we did for the staging environment, click on **Add Stage.** Select **Evaluate Variable** for **Type** and insert `Set Production Namespace` in the **Stage Name** field. Then, create a variable with the name `namespace` and the value `production`:

Figure 11.13 – Set Production Namespace

Finally, we want to deploy the manifest to production. Therefore, we need to add another stage called **Deploy to Production**. Click on the **Add Stage** button in the **Configuration** section. Set **Deploy (Manifest)** as the type and `Deploy to Production` as the stage name:

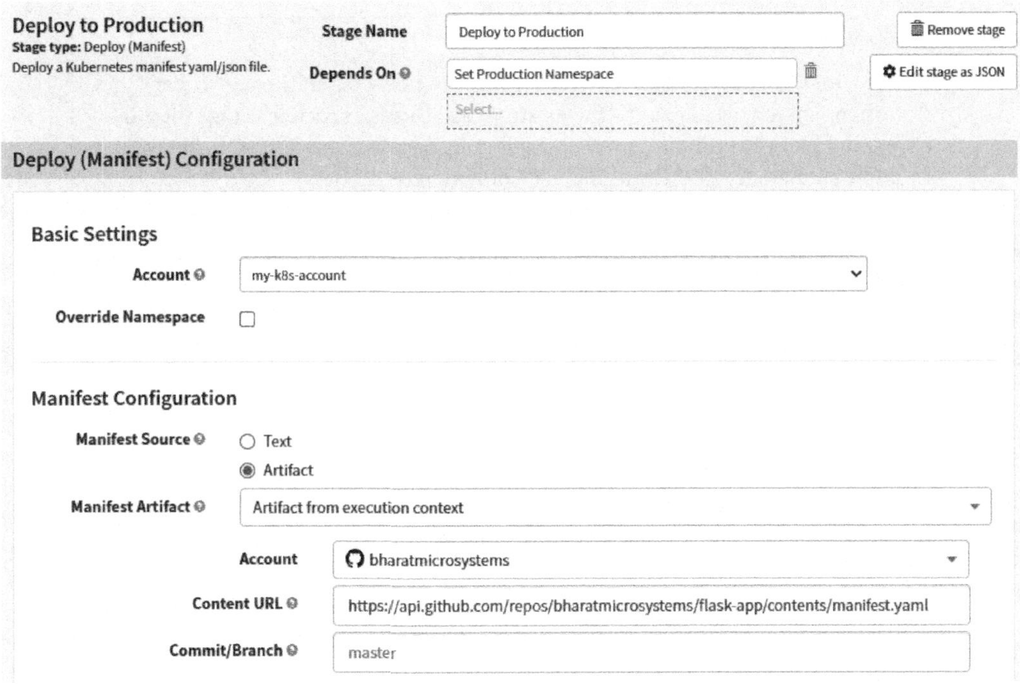

Figure 11.14 – Deploy to Production

In the **Basic Settings** section of **Deploy (Manifest) Configuration**, select `my-k8s-account` as the account (it should come pre-populated as we've set that in the halyard configuration). Next, in the **Manifest Configuration** section, select **Artifact** for **Manifest Source**. Within **Manifest Artifact**, click on **Define new Artifact**. That will provide you with some other fields that you need to fill. Remember that we need to get the manifest from our GitHub repository.

So, select the GitHub account that you've defined in the halyard configuration. The content URL should be the URL of your manifest file in the form `https://api.github.com/repos/<ACCOUNT_NAME>/flask-app/contents/manifest.yaml`. Keep the rest as their default settings.

And that's it. We're now ready to fire the pipeline.

Testing the pipeline

Now that the pipeline is ready, we can go ahead and test it. As we've created a trigger, we would expect that the pipeline should trigger when there is an image with a new tag pushed to the container registry. In this case, we'll use Docker Hub.

> **Note**
>
> The pipeline will auto-trigger only when there is a new tag in the registry and not when you make changes to the existing tag. This is expected as tags should be immutable. You can use semantic versioning to make sure that you can push multiple changes to your Continuous Deployment pipeline.

Now, let's go ahead and deploy version 1 of the Flask app. Let's change the directory to `~/modern-devops/ch11/flask-app-v1` using the following command:

```
$ cd ~/modern-devops/ch11/flask-app-v1
```

Now, let's run a Docker build. We could have used a CI pipeline for it, but for this chapter, let's go ahead and run it manually using the following command:

```
$ docker build -t <your_dockerhub_user>/flask-app:1 .
Successfully tagged <your_dockerhub_user>/flask-app:1
```

Now, as the container image is built and ready, let's push it to Docker Hub using the following command:

```
$ docker push <your_dockerhub_user>/flask-app:1
```

Now, if you look at your pipeline, you'll see that within a minute, Spinnaker will have detected a new tag in the Docker Hub registry and initiated a build. It will go through the **Set Staging Namespace** and **Deploy to Staging** stages, and the application gets deployed to the staging namespace of the Kubernetes cluster:

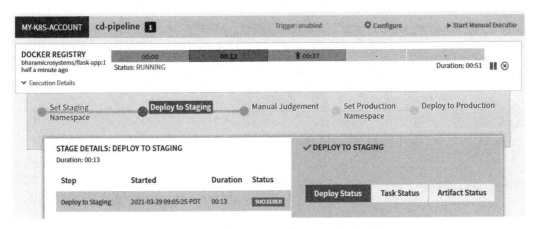

Figure 11.15 – Deployment pipeline – Deploy to Staging

To test the application, we can run the following to get the Load Balancer service endpoint we need to trigger in order to test the deployment. To get the service details, run the following command:

```
$ kubectl get service -n staging
#NAME           TYPE            CLUSTER-IP      EXTERNAL-IP
PORT(S)         AGE
flask-app       LoadBalancer    10.3.240.215    35.192.42.56
80:30484/TCP    5m9s
```

Now, as we've got the Load Balancer external IP address, we can use `curl` to hit the endpoint. Use the following command to do so:

```
$ curl 35.192.42.56
This is version 1
```

And as expected, we get the required output. The Spinnaker pipeline is awaiting manual input so that it can trigger a deployment to production. Click on the **Manual Judgment** stage and approve the deployment to production. Once you do that, the pipeline will transition to the **Set Production Namespace** stage and finally to **Deploy to Production**:

Figure 11.16 – Deployment pipeline – Deploy to Production

Now, as the application is deployed to production, let's run a test to prove that the deployment was successful. To do that, get the service details in the `production` namespace, extract the external IP of the Load Balancer service, and hit the endpoint using `curl` using the following commands:

```
$ kubectl get service -n production
NAME          TYPE          CLUSTER-IP     EXTERNAL-IP
PORT(S)       AGE
flask-app     LoadBalancer  10.3.246.185   35.232.135.252
80:32196/TCP  7m35s
$ curl 35.232.135.252
This is version 1
```

And as we see, the deployment worked well, and we see the same response from the production service.

Now, let's assume that a change was needed to the code, and we want to deploy the next version to production via staging. To do so, we'll have to go through the same process. The version 2 code is present in `~/modern-devops/ch11/flask-app-v2`. Change the directory to this by means of the following command:

```
$ cd ~/modern-devops/ch11/flask-app-v2
```

Now, run the following commands to `build` and `push` the v2 container image to Docker Hub:

```
$ docker build -t <your_dockerhub_user>/flask-app:2 .
Successfully tagged <your_dockerhub_user>/flask-app:2
$ docker push <your_dockerhub_user>/flask-app:2
```

Now, as we've pushed a new tag to the Docker Hub registry, it should also trigger a pipeline:

Figure 11.17 – Deployment pipeline – Deploy to Staging

Now, as it has deployed `flask-app:2` to the `staging` namespace, let's run a quick test as we did in version 2 using the following commands:

```
$ kubectl get service -n staging
#NAME          TYPE          CLUSTER-IP      EXTERNAL-IP
PORT(S)        AGE
flask-app    LoadBalancer   10.3.240.215    35.192.42.56
80:30484/TCP   5m9s
$ curl 35.192.42.56
This is version 2
```

As we can see, version 2 is running fine within the staging namespace, so let's move on and approve the deployment to production. Click on the **Manual Judgment** stage and approve the deployment:

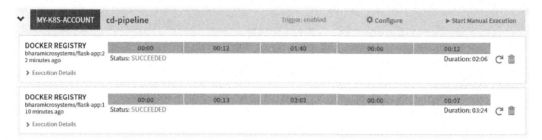

Figure 11.18 – Deployment pipeline – Deploy to Production

Once the pipeline finishes successfully, we can go ahead and test the deployment to production. Run the following commands to do so:

```
$ kubectl get service -n production
NAME           TYPE          CLUSTER-IP      EXTERNAL-IP
PORT(S)        AGE
flask-app      LoadBalancer  10.3.246.185    35.232.135.252
80:32196/TCP    7m35s
$ curl 35.232.135.252
This is version 2
```

And that's it! We get the expected response in this case as well. The Spinnaker-based Continuous Deployment pipeline is working perfectly.

Summary

This chapter has covered Continuous Deployment and delivery and we have understood the need for Continuous Deployment and the basic Continuous Deployment workflow for a container application. We then talked about several modern deployment strategies and how CI tools cannot take those responsibilities. We then looked at the Spinnaker as our Continuous Deployment tool, installed it, and deployed a Flask application using Spinnaker.

In the next chapter, we will explore another vital aspect of modern DevOps – securing the deployment pipeline.

Questions

1. Which of the following are **Continuous Deployment** tools? (Multiple answers are possible)

   a. Spinnaker

   b. GitHub

   c. Argo Continuous Deployment

   d. AWS Code Deploy

2. Continuous Delivery requires human input for deployment to production – True/False?

3. Spinnaker supports Blue/Green deployments out of the box – True/False?

4. The best way to configure Spinnaker is by using halyard – True/False?

5. What would you use to initiate Spinnaker deployment? (Multiple answers are possible)

   a. Trigger the pipeline manually.

   b. Use an auto-trigger such as Git hooks or new tags in the container registry.

   c. Use CI to trigger Spinnaker pipelines.

   d. Spinnaker pipelines don't react to external stimuli.

6. A Spinnaker server group is a group of servers on which Spinnaker deploys – True/False?

7. What are the ways of providing a Kubernetes deployment manifest to Spinnaker? (Multiple answers are possible)

   a. By adding an external artifact such as GitHub or GCS.

   b. By supplying the manifest manually.

   c. Spinnaker discovers artifacts automatically.

   d. Spinnaker doesn't need a manifest to manage Kubernetes resources.

Answers

1. a, c, and d

2. True

3. True

4. True

5. a, b, and c

6. False

7. a and b

12

Securing the Deployment Pipeline

In the previous chapters, we've looked at **continuous integration (CI)** and **continuous deployment/delivery (CD)**. Both concepts, and the tooling surrounding them, help us deliver better software faster. However, one of the most critical aspects of technology is security. Though security was not considered in DevOps' initial days, with the advent of **DevSecOps**, modern DevOps now places a great emphasis on security. In this chapter, we'll try to understand concepts surrounding container applications' security and how we can apply them within the realms of CI and CD.

In this chapter, we're going to cover the following main topics:

- Securing CI/CD pipelines
- Managing secrets
- Container vulnerability scanning
- Binary authorization
- Security of modern DevOps pipelines

Technical requirements

For this chapter, we will spin up a cloud-based Kubernetes cluster, **Google Kubernetes Engine (GKE)**, for the exercises. Currently, **Google Cloud Platform (GCP)** provides a free **US dollars (USD)** $300 trial for 90 days, so you can go ahead and sign up for one at `https://console.cloud.google.com/`.

You will also need to clone the following GitHub repository for some of the exercises:

`https://github.com/PacktPublishing/Modern-DevOps-Practices`

You can use the Cloud Shell offering available on GCP to follow this chapter. Go to Cloud Shell and start a new session. Run the following commands to clone the repository into your home directory, and cd into the `ch12` directory to access the required resources:

```
$ git clone https://github.com/PacktPublishing/Modern-DevOps-\
Practices.git modern-devops
$ cd modern-devops/ch12
```

As the repository contains files with placeholders, you will have to replace the <your_dockerhub_user> string with the your actual Docker Hub user. Use the following commands to substitute the placeholders.

```
$ find ./ -type f -exec sed -i -e 's/\
<your_dockerhub_user>/<your actual docker hub user>/g' {} \;
```

We will use GKE for this chapter, so let's create a Kubernetes cluster for ourselves. You need to enable some APIs first, using the following command:

```
$ gcloud services enable container.googleapis.com \
containerregistry.googleapis.com \
binaryauthorization.googleapis.com container.googleapis.com \
cloudkms.googleapis.com
```

To create a three-node GKE cluster, run the following command:

```
$ gcloud container clusters create cluster-1 \
--zone us-central1-a --enable-binauthz
```

It will take a few minutes for your cluster to get ready, and you should see that it will soon start running. Now, let's look at how to secure CI/CD pipelines in the next section.

Securing CI/CD pipelines

Security has always been the top priority for most organizations, and it also forms a significant part of a mature organization's investment. However, security comes with its own costs. Most organizations have cybersecurity teams that audit their code regularly and give feedback. However, that process is generally slow and happens when most of the code is already developed and difficult to modify.

Therefore, embedding security at the early stages of development is an important goal for modern DevOps. Embedding security with DevOps has led to the concept of DevSecOps, where developers, cybersecurity experts, and operations teams work together toward a common goal of creating better and more secure software faster.

There are many ways of embedding security within the software supply chain. Some of these might include static code analysis, security testing, and applying organization-specific security policies within the process, but the idea of security is not to slow down development. Instead of using human input, we can always use tools that can significantly improve the security posture of the software we develop.

Software always requires access to sensitive information such as user data, credentials, **Open Authorization (OAuth)** tokens, passwords, and other information known as secrets. Developing and managing software while keeping all these aspects secure has always been a concern. The CI/CD pipelines themselves might deal with them as they build and deliver working software by combining code and other dependencies from various sources that may include sensitive information. Keeping these bits secure is of utmost importance, and therefore the need arises to use modern DevOps tools and techniques to embed security within the CI/CD pipelines themselves.

CI/CD pipelines are one of the essential features of modern DevOps, and they orchestrate all processes and combine all tools to deliver better software faster, but how would you secure them? You may want to ask the following questions:

- How do I store and manage secrets securely?
- How do I scan a container image for vulnerabilities?
- How do I ensure that only approved images are deployed in our cluster?

Throughout the course of this chapter, we will try to answer these using best practices and tooling. For reference, look at the following workflow diagram:

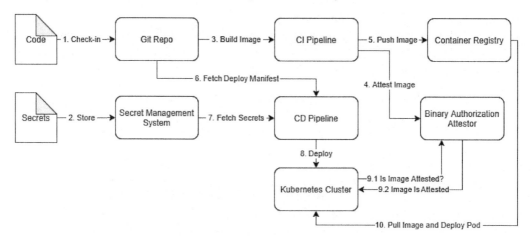

Figure 12.1 – Secure CI/CD workflow

We will try to cover all aspects of implementing this workflow in the subsequent sections, so let's look at managing secrets in the next section.

Managing secrets

Most application code requires access to sensitive information. These are called **secrets** in the DevOps world. A secret is any data that helps someone prove their identity, authenticate, and authorize privileged accounts, applications, and services. Some of the potential candidates that constitute secrets are listed here:

- Passwords
- API tokens, GitHub tokens, and any other application key
- **Secure Shell (SSH)** keys
- **Transport Layer Security (TLS)**, **Secure Sockets Layer (SSL)**, and **Pretty Good Privacy (PGP)** private keys
- One-time passwords

A good example could be a container running within Kubernetes that requires access to an API key to authenticate with a third-party API or username and password to authenticate with a backend database. Developers need to understand where and how to store secrets so that they are not exposed inadvertently to people who are not supposed to view them.

When we run a CI/CD pipeline, it becomes imperative to understand how we place those secrets, as in CI/CD pipelines we build everything from the source. *"Do not store secrets with code"* is a prominent piece of advice that we've all heard.

> **Tip**
>
> Never store hardcoded secrets within CI/CD pipelines or store secrets in a source code repository such as Git.

How can we manage to access secrets without including them in our code if we want to run a fully automated CI/CD pipeline? Well, that's something we need to figure out.

> **Tip**
>
> When using containers, the thing to avoid is baking the secrets within an image. While this is a prominent piece of advice, many developers do this inadvertently, which leads to a lot of security holes. It is very insecure, and you should avoid doing it at all costs.

The way you can overcome this problem is by using some form of **secrets management solution**. A secrets management solution or a **key management solution** helps store and manage your secrets and secure them with encryption at rest and in transit. There are key management tools within cloud providers, such as **Cloud Key Management Service (KMS)** in GCP and **Amazon Web Services (AWS)**, or you can use a third-party tool such as **HashiCorp Vault** if you want to go cloud-agnostic. All these solutions provide APIs to create and query secrets at runtime, and they secure the API via **HyperText Transfer Protocol Secure (HTTPS)** to allow encryption in transit. That way, you don't need to store your secrets with code or bake it within an image.

In this discussion, we'll use the Cloud KMS solution offered by GCP to store secrets, and we will access them while running the CI/CD pipeline. Cloud KMS is Google Cloud's secrets management system that helps you store and manage secrets in a central place. It is incredibly secure and uses **hardware security modules (HSMs)** to provide additional hardening of your secrets.

We will not use a specific CI/CD pipeline as such in this chapter, but I will provide pointers on how to access secrets so that you can integrate the solution with any CI/CD tool of your choice. So, let's first look at a sample application that will be using our secret.

Sample application

We'll use a Python Flask application for this exercise. This is a simple API that returns `The secret is <secret value>` and obtains a secret value from an environment variable called `SECRET`. We will not be storing the secret in the source code. The code is available in `~/modern-devops/ch12/kms/flask-app`.

Now, let's go ahead and build the application using Docker and push the image to Docker Hub. That is what you'll typically do in your CI solution. Use the following commands to do so:

```
$ docker login -u <your_dockerhub_user>
$ docker build -t <your_dockerhub_user>/flask-app-secret:1 .
$ docker push <your_dockerhub_user>/flask-app-secret:1
```

And as we've pushed the image to our Docker registry, we can start creating a secret manifest.

Creating a Secret manifest

To inject the secret using the environment variable, we will have to create a **Kubernetes Secret** resource. To do so, let's create the following manifest and save it as a file called `secret.yaml`. You can also use the existing `secret.yaml` file present in `~/modern-devops/ch12/kms`:

```
apiVersion: v1
data:
  SECRET: Zm9vYmFy
kind: Secret
metadata:
  name: flask-app-secret
```

The manifest consists of a secret called `flask-app-secret` that contains a secret with a `SECRET` key and a `Zm9vYmFy` value. The value is just a Base64-encoded version of `foobar`. That is the secret that we expect to see in the Flask API response.

> **Tip**
> A Kubernetes secret stores secrets as Base64-encoded strings. Therefore, they are not encrypted and are as bad as plaintext as far as the security posture is concerned. Never store Kubernetes secret manifests in your Git repository.

Now, as we have a `secret.yaml` file created, we can store the secret in Cloud KMS. To do so, let's set up a **Cloud KMS** secret first.

Creating a Cloud KMS secret

To create a Cloud KMS secret, you need the **Secret Manager Admin** role (`role/secretmanager.admin`) granted to your user or the service account you're using to manage the secrets.

We also need the **Cloud KMS API** enabled before we go ahead. To do so, run the following command:

```
$ gcloud services enable secretmanager.googleapis.com
```

We will create a secret called `flask-app-secret` with the `secret.yaml` file we created. To do so, we'll have to first create a secret in Cloud KMS. Run the following command for that:

```
$ gcloud secrets create flask-app-secret \
--replication-policy="automatic"
```

We can now store our file as a new version of our secret. Cloud KMS uses versioning on secrets, and therefore any new secret we create on the **secret identifier (ID)** (`flask-app-secret`) is versioned and stored within Cloud KMS. You can refer to a specific version by either its version number or by the `latest` keyword if you want to access the latest version of a secret.

Let's go ahead and create our first version of the secret using the `secret.yaml` file by running the following command:

```
$ gcloud secrets versions add flask-app-secret \
--data-file=secret.yaml
```

And as we see, we have the first version (version 1) of our secret created. You will typically do that during development, and it should remain outside of the CI/CD process. Thus instead of checking the secret manifest in to your source code repository, you can store it in Cloud KMS. Now, let's go ahead and create a `manifest.yaml` file that deploys our application and mounts the secret to the application's Pod.

Accessing the secret and deploying the application

You would run these steps during the CD process. Remember that you've already created a secret and stored it in Cloud KMS. You've also pushed the rest of your code and a Dockerfile into your source code repository, used the CI process to build a container out of it, and pushed it to the container registry. The manifest.yaml file is present in ~/modern-devops/ch12/kms. The manifest consists of a **Load Balancer Service** and a **Deployment** resource. If you look at the containers section within the Deployment resource, you will find the following:

```
...
    spec:
      containers:
        - image: '<your_dockerhub_user>/flask-app-secret:1'
          name: flask-app
          ports:
            - containerPort: 5000
          env:
            - name: SECRET
              valueFrom:
                secretKeyRef:
                  name: flask-app-secret
                  key: SECRET
```

The env section of the manifest creates an environment variable called SECRET that it mounts from the flask-app-secret secret that we created before from the value of it's SECRET key. Now, let's go ahead and apply the secret and the manifest.

As we've stored the secret.yaml file within Cloud KMS, we need to retrieve that and apply it. To do so, run the following command:

```
$ gcloud secrets versions access latest \
--secret=flask-app-secret | kubectl apply -f -
secret/flask-app-secret created
```

We're doing two things in this command—first, we run gcloud secrets versions access latest --secret=flask-app-secret to access the contents of the secret, and we pipe it directly to kubectl apply -f -. It does not store the secret either in the logs or in your shell history. We've directly retrieved the data from KMS and used it directly on Kubernetes. Things are secure at this point.

> **Tip**
> Never fetch secrets as local files within the CI/CD server. They tend to appear in the logs or the CD workspace that others can view. Be cautious about this, especially when you have a large team to work with.

Now, let's go ahead and deploy our application using the following command:

```
$ kubectl apply -f manifest.yaml
```

Now, let's wait for a minute and check your pod's status to ensure everything looks good. Run the following command to do so:

```
$ kubectl get pod
NAME                         READY   STATUS    RESTARTS   AGE
flask-app-55fbbfc946-jmnpc   1/1     Running   0          83s
flask-app-55fbbfc946-n9kkv   1/1     Running   0          83s
flask-app-55fbbfc946-nntqn   1/1     Running   0          83s
```

And as we see, all three pods are running and ready. Let's query the service and retrieve the external IP address to hit the request using the following command:

```
$ kubectl get svc flask-app
NAME         TYPE           CLUSTER-IP    EXTERNAL-IP
PORT(S)           AGE
flask-app    LoadBalancer   10.3.247.21   34.123.117.254
80:30711/TCP      2m41s
```

And as we see, we've got the external IP address of the service. Now, let's use the `curl` command to hit the endpoint, as follows, and see if we get the secret in the response:

```
$ curl 34.123.117.254/
The secret is foobar
```

And we get the secret as `foobar`, which is what we expected. That is proper secret management, as we did not store the secret in the source code repository (Git). We did not view or log the secret while applying it, which means that there is no trace of this secret anywhere in the logs, and only the application or people who have access to the namespace where this application is running can access it. Now, let's go ahead and look at another vital aspect of ensuring security within your deployment pipelines—vulnerability scanning.

Container vulnerability scanning

Perfect software is costly to write and maintain, and every time someone makes changes to running software, the chances of breaking something are high. Apart from other bugs, changes also add a lot of software vulnerabilities. You cannot avoid these as software developers. Cybersecurity experts and cybercriminals are at constant war with each other, and they evolve with time. Every day, a new set of vulnerabilities is found and reported.

In containers, vulnerabilities can exist on multiple fronts and may be completely unrelated to what you're responsible for. Well, developers write code, and excellent ones do it securely. Still, you never know whether a base image may also contain many vulnerabilities that your developers might completely overlook. In modern DevOps, vulnerabilities are expected, and the idea is to mitigate them as much as possible. We should reduce vulnerabilities, but doing so in a manual way is time-consuming, leading to toil.

Several tools are available on the market that provide container vulnerability scanning. Some of them are open source tools such as **Anchore**, **Clair**, **Dagda**, **OpenSCAP**, *Sysdig's Falco*, or **software-as-a-service** (**SaaS**) services available with **Google Container Registry** (**GCR**), **Amazon Elastic Container Registry** (**ECR**), and **Azure Defender**. For this chapter, we'll discuss **Anchore Grype**.

Anchore Grype (`https://github.com/anchore/grype`) is a container vulnerability scanner that scans your images for known vulnerabilities and reports on their severity. Based on that, you can take appropriate action to prevent vulnerabilities by either including a different base image or modifying the layers to remove vulnerable components.

Anchore Grype is a simple **command-line interface** (**CLI**)-based tool that you can install as a binary and run anywhere—within your local system or your CI pipelines. You can also configure it to fail your pipeline if the vulnerability level increases above a particular threshold, thereby embedding security within your automation—all of this happening without troubling your development or security team.

Now, let's go ahead and install Anchore Grype and see it in action.

Installing Anchore Grype

Anchore Grype offers an installation script within their GitHub repository that you can download and run, and it should set it up for you. To install it within a Linux environment, run the following command:

```
$ curl -sSfL https://raw.githubusercontent.com\
/anchore/grype/main/install.sh
$ sudo sh -s -- -b /usr/local/bin
```

To verify whether Anchore Grype is installed, run the following command:

```
$ grype version
```

You should then see the version information. As Grype is now installed, let's go ahead and run a vulnerability scan on our application.

We'll use the same application in this scenario, but we'll try different base images to see how container vulnerability scanning works.

Scanning images

So, let's start with building a flask-app image with the python:3.7-slim base image. The code for this exercise is in the ~/modern-devops/ch12/grype/flask-app-slim directory.

To build the image, run the following command:

```
$ docker build -t flask-app-secret:slim .
```

Once we've built the image, use the following command to run a container vulnerability scan:

```
$ grype flask-app-secret:slim
   Vulnerability DB          [updated]
   Loaded image
   Parsed image
   Cataloged image           [102 packages]
   Scanned image             [101 vulnerabilities]
NAME          INSTALLED    FIXED-IN   VULNERABILITY    SEVERITY
apt           1.8.2.2                 CVE-2011-3374    Negligible
bash          5.0-4                   CVE-2019-18276   Negligible
coreutils     8.30-3                  CVE-2016-2781    Low
coreutils     8.30-3                  CVE-2017-18018   Negligible
gcc-8-base    8.3.0-6                 CVE-2018-12886   Medium
...
```

You'll then get a summary, along with a list of vulnerabilities with severities—Negligible, Low, Medium, High, Critical, and Unknown. This package contains 101 vulnerabilities, and that's relatively high considering it's an app that returns a simple message. Well, as you might have guessed by now, it's because of the base image.

Let's see if we can reduce it by changing the base image to `python:3.7`. Change the directory to `~/modern-devops/ch12/grype/flask-app-latest` and run the following command to build the container:

```
$ docker build -t flask-app-secret:latest .
```

To run a vulnerability scan, use the following command:

```
$ grype flask-app-secret:latest
  Vulnerability DB            [no update available]
  Loaded image
  Parsed image
  Cataloged image             [442 packages]
  Scanned image               [1634 vulnerabilities]
...
```

And this one is even worse. We now have 1,634 vulnerabilities. It does not seem to go in the right direction, but what might have caused this? Let's list the image and see if we can find out more by using the following command:

```
$ docker images | grep flask-app-secret
flask-app-secret    latest    e46edc0dcce6    8 minutes ago
886MB
flask-app-secret    slim      7c00944120f0    24 minutes ago
122MB
```

And as we see, the size of the latest image is 886 MB! That's almost six times more than the slim version, which is 122 MB only. There's more bloatware within the latest image, and therefore we need to do the reverse: get a smaller image that can still do our job. Well, let's try the `alpine` image that we've already used before.

To run a vulnerability scan on the app with the `python:3.7-alpine` base image, change the directory to `~/modern-devops/ch12/grype/flask-app-alpine` and run the following command to build the container:

```
$ docker build -t flask-app-secret:alpine .
```

Now, let's run a vulnerability scan on this image using the following command:

```
$ grype flask-app-secret:alpine
  Vulnerability DB            [no update available]
```

```
   Loaded image
   Parsed image
   Cataloged image              [57 packages]
   Scanned image                [0 vulnerabilities]
No vulnerabilities found
```

Wow! It looks great! There are no vulnerabilities found in this. It shows that the `alpine` image is very secure and does not contain any known vulnerabilities.

> **Tip**
>
> Always use the `alpine` base image if possible. One way to do it is by starting with an `alpine` image initially and seeing if it fits your use case and runs your application without any issues. You can move to the slim or full-blown version if that does not suit your app.

Now, just out of curiosity, let's look at the size of the `alpine` image. Let's execute the following command to see this information:

```
$ docker images | grep flask-app-secret | grep alpine
flask-app-secret    alpine          499786ff8b21    44 seconds ago
52.4MB
```

And as we see, it's less than half of the slim image.

We can also set a threshold within Grype to fail when any vulnerabilities are equal to or worse than it. For example, if we don't want to allow any `High` or `Critical` vulnerabilities in the container, we can use the following command:

```
$ grype -f high <container-image>
```

Let's try it out on the slim image using the following command:

```
$ grype -f high flask-app-secret:slim
...
discovered vulnerabilities at or above the severity threshold
```

And it fails this time! This feature can help you integrate Grype into your CI pipelines. These will discover vulnerabilities and not allow any builds to end up in your container registry if they don't have a standard security posture. Now, while images are built and deployed using your CI/CD toolchain, there is nothing in between that can prevent someone from deploying an image in your Kubernetes cluster. You might be scanning all your images for vulnerabilities and mitigating them, but somewhere, someone might bypass all controls and deploy containers directly to your cluster. Now, how would you prevent such a situation? Well, the answer to that question is: through binary authorization. Let's look at this in the next section.

Binary authorization

Binary authorization is a deploy-time security mechanism that ensures that only trusted binary files are deployed within your environments. In the context of containers and Kubernetes, binary authorization uses signature validation and ensures that only container images signed by a trusted authority are deployed within your Kubernetes cluster.

Using binary authorization provides you with tighter control over what is deployed in your cluster. It ensures that only tested containers and those approved and verified by a particular authority (such as security tooling or personnel) are present in your cluster.

Binary authorization works by enforcing rules within your cluster via an admission controller. This means that you can create rulesets only to allow images signed by an attestation authority to be deployed in your cluster. Your **quality assurance (QA)** team can be a good attestor in a practical scenario. You can also embed the attestation within your CI/CD pipelines. The attestation means your images have been tested and scanned for vulnerabilities, and have crossed a minimum standard so that they are ready to be deployed to the cluster.

GCP provides binary authorization embedded within GKE, based on the open source project Kritis (`https://github.com/grafeas/kritis`). It uses a **public key infrastructure (PKI)** to attest and verify images—so, your images are signed by an attestor authority using the private key, and Kubernetes verifies the images by using the public key. In the hands-on exercise, we will set up binary authorization and a PKI using Cloud KMS. We will then create a default attestor, configure GKE to deny all images that the attestor didn't sign, attempt to deploy an unattested image, and finally attest and deploy it. So, let's get started by setting up some default variables.

Setting up binary authorization

We'll start by setting up some default variables that we will use in the exercise. Feel free to modify them according to your requirements. Run the following commands to do so:

```
$ PROJECT_ID=$(gcloud config list \
--format 'value(core.project)')
$ ATTESTOR_NAME=default-attestor
$ NOTE_ID=default-attestor-note
$ KMS_KEY_LOCATION=us-central1
$ KMS_KEYRING_NAME=${ATTESTOR_NAME}_keyring
$ KMS_KEY_NAME=${ATTESTOR_NAME}_key
$ KMS_KEY_VERSION=1
$ KMS_KEY_PURPOSE=asymmetric-signing
$ KMS_KEY_ALGORITHM=ec-sign-p256-sha256
$ KMS_PROTECTION_LEVEL=software
```

To create an attestor, we first need to create an **attestor note**. We will use this attestor note when we create an attestor. Run the following command to do so:

```
$ cat > /tmp/note_payload.json << EOM
{
  "name": "projects/${PROJECT_ID}/notes/${NOTE_ID}",
  "attestation": {
    "hint": {
      "human_readable_name": "Attestor Note"
    }
  }
}
EOM
$ curl -X POST -H "Content-Type: application/json" \
-H "Authorization: Bearer $(gcloud auth print-access-token)" \
--data-binary @/tmp/note_payload.json \
"https://containeranalysis.googleapis.com/v1\
/projects/${PROJECT_ID}/notes/?noteId=${NOTE_ID}"
```

Now, as the attestor note has been created, let's create an attestor using the attestor note by running the following command:

```
$ gcloud container binauthz attestors create ${ATTESTOR_NAME} \
--attestation-authority-note=${NOTE_ID} \
--attestationauthority-note-project=${PROJECT_ID}
```

OK—the next step is to set up a PKI. For that, we'll use Cloud KMS. We will create a Cloud KMS keyring and, within the keyring, we'll create a key. Use the following commands to do so:

```
$ gcloud kms keyrings create ${KMS_KEYRING_NAME} \
--location ${KMS_KEY_LOCATION}
$ gcloud kms keys create ${KMS_KEY_NAME} \
--location ${KMS_KEY_LOCATION} --keyring ${KMS_KEYRING_NAME} \
--purpose ${KMS_KEY_PURPOSE} \
--default-algorithm ${KMS_KEY_ALGORITHM} \
--protection-level ${KMS_PROTECTION_LEVEL}
```

Now, as we've created a key, we need to add the public key to the attestor. Use the following command to do that:

```
$ gcloud container binauthz attestors public-keys add \
--attestor="${ATTESTOR_NAME}" \
--keyversion-project="${PROJECT_ID}" \
--keyversion-location="${KMS_KEY_LOCATION}" \
--keyversion-keyring="$KMS_KEYRING_NAME}" \
--keyversion-key="${KMS_KEY_NAME}" \
--keyversion="${KMS_KEY_VERSION}"
```

And we've set up binary authorization and an attestor with GKE. Now, the next step is to create a default binary authorization policy.

Creating a default binary authorization policy

A default binary authorization policy defines how a cluster should behave when we want to deploy a container in it. In this situation, we do not want to deploy anything, apart from attested images. We create the following YAML file that has a few attributes. The globalPolicyEvaluationMode attribute is enabled because we do not want to enforce the policy on system images that Google manages. The defaultAdmissionRule section requires attestation using the attestor we created. Use the following commands to create and assign a policy to your cluster:

```
$ cat > /tmp/policy.yaml << EOM
    globalPolicyEvaluationMode: ENABLE
    defaultAdmissionRule:
      evaluationMode: REQUIRE_ATTESTATION
      enforcementMode: ENFORCED_BLOCK_AND_AUDIT_LOG
      requireAttestationsBy:
        - projects/${PROJECT_ID}/attestors/${ATTESTOR_NAME}
    name: projects/${PROJECT_ID}/policy
EOM
$ gcloud container binauthz policy import /tmp/policy.yaml
```

Wait for 2 minutes for the policy to be propagated in your cluster. After that, let's try to deploy a pod to your cluster that uses a `docker.io/<your_dockerhub_user>/flask-app-secret:1` image, using the following command:

```
$ kubectl run flask-app-secret \
--image docker.io/<your_dockerhub_user>/flask-app-secret:1 \
--port 5000
Error from server (VIOLATES_POLICY): admission webhook
"imagepolicywebhook.image-policy.k8s.io" denied the request:
Image docker.io/<your_dockerhub_user>/flask-app-secret:1 denied
by binary authorization default admission rule. Image docker.
io/<your_dockerhub_user>/flask-app-secret:1 denied by attestor
projects/<project_id>/attestors/default-attestor: Expected
digest with sha256 scheme, but got tag or malformed digest
```

Now, this one failed! That's what we expected, but it looks as though there's something else if you look at the reason. The failure has occurred because we specified a tag instead of a `sha256` digest. That's because when we use binary authorization, we need to deploy images with their `sha256` digest instead of the tag. Why? Because anyone can tag a different image than what was attested and push it to the container registry, but a digest is a hash created out of a Docker image. Therefore, as long as the image contents do not change, the digest remains the same, so no one can cheat through binary authorization control. Therefore, let's try to deploy the image again, but this time with a digest.

Now, let's get the image digest and set it to a variable called `DIGEST` using the following commands:

```
$ DIGEST=$(docker pull docker.io/<your_dockerhub_user>\
/flask-app-secret:1 | grep Digest | awk {'print $2'})
```

Now, let's redeploy the image using the digest with the following command:

```
$ kubectl run flask-app-secret \
--image docker.io/<your_dockerhub_user>\
/flask-app-secret@${DIGEST} \
--port 5000
Error from server (VIOLATES_POLICY): admission webhook
"imagepolicywebhook.image-policy.k8s.io" denied the request:
Image docker.io/<your_dockerhub_user>/flask-app-secret@<DIGEST>
denied by binary authorization default admission rule.
Image docker.io/<your_dockerhub_user>/flask-app-secret@<DIGEST>
denied by attestor projects/<project_id>/
attestors/default-attestor: No attestations found that were
valid and signed by a key trusted by the attestor
```

And this time, it was denied for a valid reason! Now, let's look at how we can attest this image so that it can get deployed.

Attesting images

Use the following command to attest the image, using the attestor we created:

```
$ gcloud beta container binauthz attestations sign-and-create \
--artifact-url="docker.io/<your_docker_user>\
/flask-app-secret@${DIGEST}" \
--attestor="${ATTESTOR_NAME}" --attestor-\
project="${PROJECT_ID}" \
--keyversion-project="${PROJECT_ID}" --keyversion-\
location="${KMS_KEY_LOCATION}" \
--keyversion-keyring="${KMS_KEYRING_NAME}" \
--keyversion-key="${KMS_KEY_NAME}" \
--keyversion="${KMS_KEY_VERSION}"
```

Now, let's try to redeploy the pod again using the same image with the following command:

```
$ kubectl run flask-app-secret \
--image docker.io/<your_dockerhub_user>/\
flask-app-secret@${DIGEST} \
--port 5000
pod/flask-app-secret created
```

And it worked this time! Well, that's because we've attested this image, and the default binary authorization allows images certified by our attestor. That secures your Kubernetes cluster as of now, meaning no one can deploy unattested images in the cluster, and therefore you have complete control of your environment. If something breaks, it will not be because someone deployed an image that was not tested or scanned for vulnerabilities.

Security of modern DevOps pipelines

Tooling is not the only thing that will help you in your DevSecOps journey. Here are some helpful tips that can help you address security risks and have a more secure culture within your organization.

Adopt a DevSecOps culture

Adopting a DevSecOps approach is critical in implementing modern DevOps. Therefore, it is vital to embed security within an organization's culture. You can achieve that by implementing effective communication and collaboration between the *development*, *operations*, and *security* teams. While most organizations have a security policy, it mustn't be followed just to comply with rules and regulations. Instead, employees should cross-skill and upskill themselves to adopt a DevSecOps approach and embed security early on during development. Security teams need to learn to write code and work with APIs, while developers need to understand security and use automation to achieve this.

Establish access control

You might have heard about the **principle of least privilege** (**PoLP**) several times in this book. Well, that is what you need to implement for a better security posture, which means you should make all attempts to grant only the required privileges to people to do their job, and nothing more. Reduce the just-in-case syndrome by making the process of giving access easier so that people don't feel hindered, and as a result, they do not seek more privileges than they require.

Implement shift left

Shifting left means embedding security into software at the earlier stages of software development. This means security experts need to work closely with developers to enable them to build secure software right from the start. The security function should not be review-only but should actively work with developers and architects to develop a security-hardened design and code.

Manage security risks consistently

You should accept risks, which are inevitable, and should have a **standard operating procedure (SOP)** should an attack occur. You should have straightforward and easy-to-understand policies and practices from a security standpoint in all aspects of software development and infrastructure management, such as **configuration management**, **access controls**, **vulnerability testing**, **code review**, and **firewalls**.

Implement vulnerability scanning

Open source software today is snowballing, and most software implementations rely on ready-made open source frameworks, software libraries, and third-party software that don't come with a guarantee or liability of any kind. While the open source ecosystem is building the technological world like never before, it does have its own share of vulnerabilities that you don't want to insert within your software through no fault of your own. Vulnerability scanning is crucial, as scans can discover any third-party dependency with vulnerabilities and alert you at the initial stage.

Automate security

Security should not hinder the speed of your DevOps teams, and therefore to keep up with the fast pace of DevOps, you should look at embedding security within your CI/CD processes. You can do code analysis, vulnerability scanning, configuration management, and infrastructure scanning with policy as code and binary authorization to allow only tested and secure software to be deployed. Automation helps identify potential vulnerabilities early on in the software development life cycle, thereby bringing down the cost of software development and rework.

These best practices will help in managing security risks effectively.

Summary

This chapter has covered CI/CD pipeline security, and we have understood various tools, techniques, and best practices surrounding it. We looked at a secure CI/CD workflow for reference. We then understood, using hands-on exercises, the aspects that made it secure, such as secret management, container vulnerability scanning, and binary authorization.

Using the skills learned in this chapter, you can now appropriately secure your CI/CD pipelines and make your application more secure.

In the next chapter, we will explore an alternative method of doing DevOps—GitOps.

Questions

1. Which of these is the recommended place for storing secrets?

    a. Private Git repository

    b. Public Git repository

    c. Docker image

    d. Secret management system

2. Which one of the following is an open source secret management system?

    a. Cloud KMS

    b. HashiCorp Vault

    c. Anchore Grype

3. Is it a good practice to download a secret within your CD pipeline's filesystem?

4. Which base image is generally considered more secure and consists of the fewest vulnerabilities?

    a. Alpine

    b. Slim

    c. Buster

    d. Default

5. Which of the following answers are true about binary authorization? (Multiple answers are possible.)

    a. It scans your images for vulnerabilities.

    b. It allows only attested images to be deployed.

    c. It prevents people from bypassing your CI/CD pipeline.

Answers

1. d
2. b
3. No
4. d
5. b and c

Section 3: Modern DevOps with GitOps

This section will look at an alternative approach of DevOps – GitOps – and explore why it is growing in popularity. We will learn about the concepts, tools, and techniques needed to implement GitOps effectively by building a complete CI/CD pipeline using the GitOps approach.

This section comprises the following chapters:

- *Chapter 13, Understanding DevOps with GitOps*
- *Chapter 14, CI/CD Pipeline with GitOps*

13

Understanding DevOps with GitOps

In the previous chapters, we looked at the core concepts of modern DevOps, **Continuous Integration (CI)**, and **Continuous Deployment/Delivery (CD)**. We also looked at various tools and techniques that can help us to enable a mature and secure DevOps channel across our organization. In this chapter, we'll look at an alternate concept that enables DevOps with **GitOps**. In this scenario, GitOps uses Git as the central tooling to enable DevOps, and Git becomes a single source of truth.

In this chapter, we're going to cover the following main topics:

- What is GitOps?
- The principles of GitOps
- Why GitOps?
- The branching strategy and GitOps workflow
- Declarative infrastructure and config management

Technical requirements

In this chapter, we will spin up a cloud-based Kubernetes cluster – **Google Kubernetes Engine** – for our exercises. Currently, Google Cloud Platform provides a free $300 trial for 90 days, so you can go ahead and sign up for one at `https://console.cloud.google.com/`.

You will also need to clone the following GitHub repository for some of the exercises: `https://github.com/PacktPublishing/Modern-DevOps-Practices`.

You can use the cloud shell that is available on Google Cloud to follow this chapter. Navigate to the cloud shell and start a new session. Run the following command to clone the repository inside your home directory, and `cd` into the `ch13` directory to access the required resources:

```
$ git clone https://github.com/PacktPublishing/Modern-DevOps-\
Practices.git modern-devops
$ cd modern-devops/ch13
```

Now, in the next section, let's take a look at what is GitOps.

What is GitOps?

GitOps is a method that involves the implementation of DevOps such that Git forms the single source of truth. Instead of maintaining a long list of scripts and tooling to support this, GitOps focuses on writing declarative code for everything, including the infrastructure, configuration, and application code. That means you can spin anything out of thin air by simply using the Git repository. The idea is that you declare what you need in your Git repository, and there is tooling behind the scenes that ensures the desired state is always maintained in the running application and infrastructure surrounding it. The code to spin up the tooling also resides in Git, and you don't have anything outside of Git. That means everything, including the tooling, is automated in this process.

While GitOps also enables DevOps within the organization, its primary focus is on using Git to manage infrastructure provisioning and application software deployments. DevOps is a broad term that contains a set of principles, processes, and tools to enable developers and operations teams to work in a seamless fashion and shorten the development life cycle, with an end goal to deliver better software more quickly using a CI/CD cycle. While GitOps relies heavily on Git and its features and always looks to Git for versioning, finding configuration drift, and only applying deltas, DevOps is, as such, agnostic of any type of tool and focuses more on the concepts and processes. Therefore, you can implement DevOps without using Git, but you cannot implement GitOps without Git. Put simply, GitOps implements DevOps, but the other way round may not always be true.

The principles of GitOps

GitOps has the following key principles:

- **It describes the entire system declaratively**: Having declarative code forms the first principle of GitOps. This means that instead of providing instructions on how to build your infrastructure, applying the relevant configuration, and deploying your application, we declare the end state of what we need. This means that your Git repository always maintains a single source of truth. As declarative changes are idempotent, you don't need to worry about the state of your system, as this will eventually become consistent with the code in Git.

- **Version desired system state using Git**: As Git forms an excellent version control system, you don't need to worry too much about how to roll out and roll back your deployments. A simple Git commit means a new deployment, and a Git revert means a rollback. That means you do not need to worry about anything apart from ensuring that the Git repository reflects what you need.

- **It uses tooling to automatically apply approved changes**: As you've stored everything within Git, you can then use tooling that looks for changes within the repository and automatically applies them to your environment. You can also have several branches which apply changes to different environments along with a pull request-based approval and gating process so that only approved changes end up in your environment.

- **It uses self-healing agents to alert and correct any divergence**: We do have the tooling to automatically apply any changes in Git to the environment. However, we will also require self-healing agents that can alert us of any divergence from the repository. For example, let's suppose that someone deletes a container manually from the environment but doesn't remove it from the Git repository. In that scenario, the agent should alert the team and recreate the container to correct the divergence. That means there is no way to bypass GitOps, and Git remains the single source of truth.

Implementing and living by these principles is simple with modern DevOps tools and techniques, and we will look at how to implement them later in this chapter. However, first, let's examine why we want to use GitOps in the first place.

Why GitOps?

GitOps provides us with the following benefits:

- **It deploys better software more quickly**: Well, we discussed this benefit when we talked about CI/CD pipelines. But what does GitOps offer in addition to this? The answer is simplicity. You don't have to worry about what tool you need to use for what type of deployment. Instead, you need to commit your changes in Git, and the tooling behind the scenes automatically takes care of deploying it.

- **There is faster recovery from errors**: If you happen to make an error in deployment (for example, a wrong commit), you can easily roll it back by using `git revert` and restore your environment. The idea is that you don't need to learn anything else apart from Git to do a rollout or a rollback.

- **It offers better credential management**: With GitOps, you don't need to store your credentials in different places for your deployments to work. You simply need to provide the tooling access to your Git repository, and the image repository and GitOps will take care of the rest. You can keep your environment completely secure by restricting your developers' access to it and providing them access to Git instead.

- **Deployments are self-documenting**: Because everything is kept within Git, which records all commits, the deployments are automatically self-documenting. You can know exactly who deployed what at what time by simply looking at the commit history.

- **It promotes shared ownership and knowledge**: As Git forms the single source of truth for all code and configurations within the organization, teams have a single place in which to understand how things are implemented without any ambiguity and dependency toward other team members. This helps in promoting the shared ownership of the code and knowledge within the team.

Now that we know about the principles and benefits of GitOps, let's take a look at how to implement them by using a branching strategy and GitOps workflow.

The branching strategy and GitOps workflow

GitOps requires at least two kinds of Git repositories to function: the *application repository* from where your builds are triggered and the *environment repository* that contains all of the infrastructure and configuration as code. All deployments are driven from the environment repository, and the changes to the code repository drive the deployments. GitOps follows two primary kinds of deployment models: the **push model** and the **pull model**. Let's discuss each of them.

The push model

The push model pushes any changes that occur within your Git repository to the environment. The following diagram explains the process in detail:

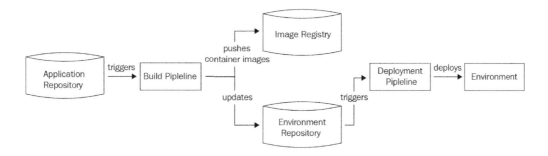

Figure 13.1 – The push model

The push model is inherently unaware of the existing configuration and reacts only to changes made to your Git repositories. Therefore, you will need to set up some form of monitoring to understand whether there are any deviations. Additionally, the push model needs to store all environment credentials within the tools. The reason for this is that it interacts with the environment and has to manage the deployments. Typically, we use **Jenkins**, **CircleCI**, or **Travis CI** to implement the push model. While the push model is not recommended, it becomes inevitable in cloud provisioning with **Terraform**, or config management with **Ansible**, as they are both push-based models. Now, let's take a closer look at the pull model.

The pull model

The pull model is an **agent-based deployment model** (which is also known as an **operator-based deployment model**). An **agent** (or **operator**) within your environment monitors the Git repository for changes and applies them as and when needed. The operator constantly compares the existing configuration with the configuration in the environment repository and applies changes if required. The following diagram shows the process in detail:

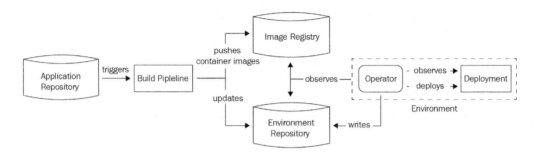

Figure 13.2 – The pull model

The advantage of the pull model is that it monitors and reacts to environment changes alongside repository changes. This ensures that any changes that do not match the Git repository are reverted from the environment. It also alerts the operations team about anything that it could not fix using mail notifications, ticketing tools, or Slack notifications. Because the operator lives within the same environment where the code is deployed, we do not need to store credentials within the tools. Instead, they live securely within the environment. You can also live without storing any credentials at all with tools such as Kubernetes, where you can employ **Role-Based Access Control** (**RBAC**) and service accounts for the operator managing the environment.

> **Tip**
>
> When choosing a GitOps model, the best practice is to check whether you can implement a pull-based model instead of a push-based model. Implement a push-based model only if the pull-based model is not possible. It is also a good idea to implement polling in the push-based model by scheduling something, such as a `cron` job, that will run the push periodically to ensure there is no configuration drift.

We cannot solely live with one model or the other, so most organizations employ a hybrid model to run GitOps. The hybrid model combines both of the push and pull models and focuses on using the pull model. It uses the push model when it cannot use the pull model. We'll do the same in this chapter. Before we move on to a hands-on example, let's gain an understanding of how to structure our Git repository to implement GitOps.

Structuring the Git repository

To implement GitOps, we require at least two repositories: the *application repository* and the *environment repository*. This does not mean that you cannot combine the two, but for the sake of simplicity, let's take a look at each of them separately.

The application repository

The **application repository** stores the application code. It is a repository in which your developers can actively develop the product that you run for your business. Typically, your builds result from this application code, and they end up as containers (if we use a container-based approach). Your application repository may or may not have environment-specific branches. Most organizations keep the application repository independent to the environment and focus on building semantic versions of code using a branching strategy. Now, there are multiple branching strategies available to manage your code, such as **Gitflow**, **GitHub flow**, and any other branching strategy that suits your needs.

Gitflow is one of the most popular branching strategies that organizations use. That said, it is also one of the most complicated ones, as it requires several kinds of branches (for instance, master branches, hotfixes, release branches, develop, and feature branches) and has a rigid structure. The structure of Gitflow is shown in the following diagram:

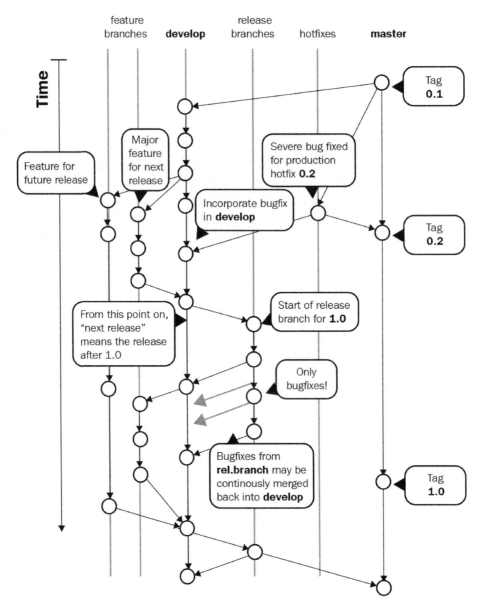

Figure 13.3 – Gitflow structure

A simplified way of doing things is the GitHub flow. The GitHub flow employs fewer branches and is easier to maintain. Typically, it contains a single master branch and many feature branches that eventually merge with the master branch. The master branch always has software that is ready to be deployed to the environments. You tag and version the code in the master branch, pick and deploy it, test it, and then promote it to higher environments. The following diagram shows the GitHub flow in detail:

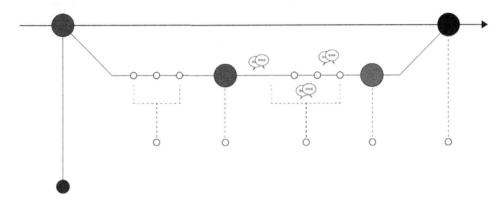

Figure 13.4 – The GitHub flow

Note that you are free to create your branching strategy according to your needs and what works for you.

> **Tip**
> Choose Gitflow if you have a large team, a vast monolithic repository, and multiple releases running in parallel. Choose GitHub flow if you are working for a fast-paced organization that releases updates several times a week and doesn't use the concept of parallel releases. GitHub flow also typically works for microservices where changes are minor and quick.

Typically, application repositories do not have to worry too much about environments; they can focus more on creating deployable versions of the software.

The environment repository

The environment repository stores the environment-specific configurations that are needed to run the application code. Therefore, they will typically have **Infrastructure as Code** in the form of Terraform scripts, **Configuration as Code** in the form of Ansible playbooks, or Kubernetes manifests that typically help deploy the code we've built from the application repository.

The environment repository should follow an environment-specific branching strategy where a branch represents a particular environment. You can have pull request-based **gating** for these kinds of scenarios. Typically, you build your *development environments* from a development branch and then raise a pull request to merge the changes to a staging branch. From the staging branch to production, your code progresses with environments. If you have 10 environments, you might end up with 10 different branches in the environment repository. The following diagram showcases the branching strategy you might want to follow for your environment repository:

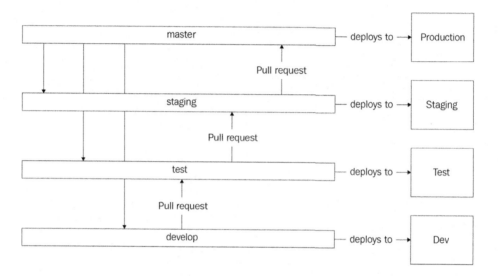

Figure 13.5 – The environment repository

The aim of the environment repository is to act as the single source of truth for your environments. Whatever configuration you add to the repository, it is applied directly to your environments.

> **Tip**
>
> While you can combine the environment and application repository into one, the best practice is to keep them separate. GitOps offers a clear separation between the CI and CD processes using the application and environment repositories, respectively.

Now, let's take a look at an example where we will create an environment repository and use Terraform to create a Kubernetes cluster.

Declarative infrastructure and config management

We've already looked at the chapters on Terraform and Ansible regarding declarative infrastructure and config management principles. In this chapter, we will use GitHub actions and Terraform to spin up a Google Kubernetes Engine instance. So far, we've been using `gcloud` commands to do this; however, because `gcloud` commands are not declarative, using them is not possible when implementing GitOps. Instead, we'll use Terraform to create the Kubernetes cluster for us. In the next chapter, we will also use the same cluster to understand other nuances of GitOps in more detail. For now, let's go ahead and create an environment repository.

Navigate to `https://github.com` and create a repository using a name of your choice. For this exercise, we will use `gitops-environments`. Once you have done that, navigate to Google Cloud Shell and clone the repository using the following command:

```
$ cd ~
$ git clone https://github.com/<your_account>\
/gitops-environments.git
$ cd gitops-environments
```

Now we can start writing the Terraform configuration within this directory. The configuration is available in `~/modern-devops/ch13/gitops-environments`. Simply copy everything from that directory to the current directory using the following command:

```
$ cp -r ~/modern-devops/terraform .
$ cp -r ~/modern-devops/.github .
```

Within the `terraform` directory, there are several Terraform files.

The `main.tf` file contains the configuration needed to create the Kubernetes cluster. It looks similar to the following:

```
resource "google_service_account" "main" {
  account_id   = "gke-cluster1-sa"
  display_name = "GKE Cluster 1 Service Account"
}

resource "google_container_cluster" "main" {
  name                = "cluster1"
  location            = "us-central1-a"
```

```
    initial_node_count = 3
    node_config {
      service_account = google_service_account.main.email
      oauth_scopes = [
        "https://www.googleapis.com/auth/cloud-platform"
      ]
    }
    timeouts {
      create = "30m"
      update = "40m"
    }
}
```

It creates two resources – a service account and a three-node Google Kubernetes Engine instance that uses the service account with the `cloud platform` **OAuth scope**.

We have a `provider.tf` file that contains the `provider` and `backend` configuration. We're using a remote backend here, as we want to persist the Terraform state remotely. In this scenario, we will use a **Google Cloud Storage (GCS) bucket**. The `provider.tf` file looks like the following:

```
provider "google" {
  project      = var.project_id
  region       = "us-central1"
  zone         = "us-central1-c"
}
terraform {
  backend "gcs" {
    bucket  = "tf-state-gitops-terraform"
    prefix  = "gitops-terraform"
  }
}
```

Here, we've specified our default `region` and `zone` within the `provider` config. Additionally, we've declared the `gcs` bucket as `tf-state-gitops-terraform` and `prefix` as `gitops-terraform`. We can separate configurations using the prefixes if we want to store multiple Terraform states in a single bucket.

> **Important note**
>
> As GCS buckets should have a globally unique name, you need to change the bucket name to something more unique. A good way is to use something such as `tf-state-gitops-terraform-<PROJECT_ID>`, as the project ID is globally unique.

We also have the `variables.tf` file that declares the `project_id` variable, as follows:

```
variable project_id {}
```

Now that we have the Terraform configuration ready, we need a workflow file that can apply it to our GCP project. For that, we've created the following GitHub Actions workflow file, that is, `.github/workflows/create-cluster.yml`:

```yaml
name: Create Kubernetes Cluster
on:
  push:
    branches: [ master ]
  pull_request:
    branches: [ master ]
jobs:
  deploy-terraform:
    runs-on: ubuntu-latest
    defaults:
      run:
        working-directory: ./terraform
    steps:
    - uses: actions/checkout@v2
    - name: Install Terraform
      id: install-terraform
      run: wget -O terraform.zip https://releases.hashicorp.com/terraform/0.15.3/terraform_0.15.3_linux_amd64.zip && unzip terraform.zip && chmod +x terraform && sudo mv terraform /usr/local/bin
    - name: Apply Terraform
      id: apply-terraform
      run: terraform init && terraform apply -auto-approve -var="project_id=${{ secrets.PROJECT_ID }}"
      env:
        GOOGLE_CREDENTIALS: ${{ secrets.GCP_CREDENTIALS }}
```

This is a two-step build file. The first step installs Terraform, and the second step applies the Terraform configuration. Apart from that, we've specified `./terraform` as the working directory at the global level. Additionally, we're using a few secrets in this file, including `GCP_CREDENTIALS`, which is the key file of the service account that Terraform uses to authenticate and authorize the GCP API and Google Cloud `PROJECT_ID`.

From the Terraform and workflow configuration, we can deduce that we will need the following:

- A service account for Terraform to authenticate and authorize the GCP API along with a JSON key file that we need to add as a GitHub secret.
- The project ID that we'll configure as a GitHub secret.
- A GCS bucket that we'll use as a backend for Terraform.

So, let's go ahead and create a service account within GCP so that Terraform can use it to authenticate and authorize the Google APIs. Use the following commands to create the service account, provide relevant **Identity and Access Management (IAM)** permissions, and download the credentials file:

```
$ PROJECT_ID=<project_id>
$ gcloud iam service-accounts create gitops-terraform \
--description="Service Account for GitOps terraform" \
--display-name="GitOps Terraform"
$ gcloud projects add-iam-policy-binding $PROJECT_ID \
--member="serviceAccount:gitops-terraform@$PROJECT_ID\
.iam.gserviceaccount.com" \
--role="roles/editor"
$ gcloud iam service-accounts keys create key-file \
--iam-account=gitops-terraform@$PROJECT_ID.iam\
.gserviceaccount.com
```

You will see that there is a file called `key-file` that has been created within your working directory. Now, navigate to `https://github.com/<your_github_user>/gitops-environments/settings/secrets/actions/new` and create a secret with the name of `GCP_CREDENTIALS`. For the value, print the `key-file` file, copy its contents, and paste it into the **values** field of the GitHub secret.

Next, create another secret, called `PROJECT_ID`, and specify your GCP project ID within the **values** field.

The next thing we need to do is create a GCS bucket for Terraform to use as a remote backend. To do this, run the following commands:

```
$ gsutil mb gs://tf-state-gitops-terraform
```

Additionally, we need to enable the GCP APIs that Terraform is going to use to create the resources. To do this, run the following command:

```
$ gcloud services enable iam.googleapis.com \
container.googleapis.com
```

So, now that all of the prerequisites are met, we can push our code to the repository. Run the following commands to do this:

```
$ git add --all
$ git commit -m 'Initial commit'
$ git push
```

As soon as we push the code, we'll see that the GitHub Actions workflow has been triggered. Soon, the workflow will apply the configuration and create the Kubernetes cluster. This should appear as follows:

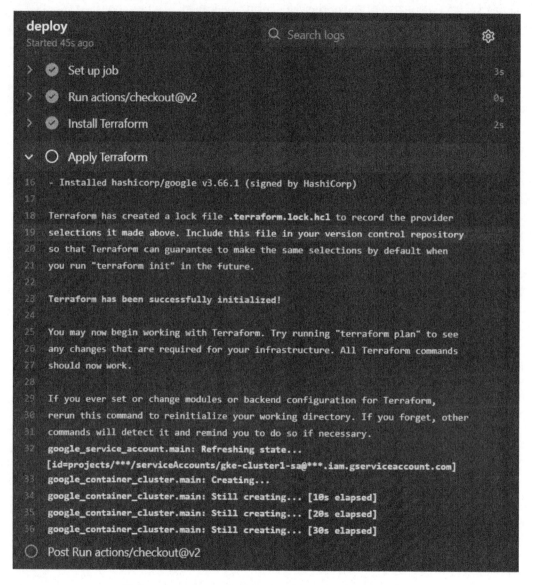

Figure 13.6 – GitOps with GitHub Actions and Terraform

To verify whether the cluster has been created successfully, run the following command:

```
$ gcloud container clusters list
NAME          LOCATION        MASTER_VERSION      MASTER_IP
MACHINE_TYPE  NODE_VERSION        NUM_NODES   STATUS
cluster1  us-central1-a  1.18.16-gke.2100  35.226.82.191
e2-medium       1.18.16-gke.2100  3           RUNNING
```

As you can see, the cluster named `cluster-1` is running successfully in the environment. If we make any changes to the Terraform configuration, the changes will automatically be applied to the environment. That is the *push model GitOps* in action for you.

Summary

This chapter covered GitOps, why we need it, its principles, and various GitOps deployments. We also looked at different kinds of repositories that we can create to implement GitOps along with the branching strategy choices for each of them. We then looked at a hands-on example of GitOps with declarative infrastructure and config management where we used Terraform to create a Kubernetes cluster using GitOps.

In the next chapter, we will deep dive into GitOps and look at application management with pull model GitOps and the end-to-end GitOps life cycle.

Questions

1. In GitOps, what forms a single source of truth?

    a. The Git repository

    b. The configuration stored in a datastore

    c. The secret management system

    d. The artifact repository

2. Which of the following options are deployment models for GitOps?

    a. The push model

    b. The pull model

    c. The staggering model

3. Should you use GitFlow for your environment repository?

4. For monolithic applications with multiple parallel developments in numerous releases, what is the most suitable Git branching strategy?

    a. Gitflow

    b. GitHub flow

    c. Hybrid GitHub flow

5. Which is the recommended deployment model for GitOps?

    a. The push model

    b. The pull model

    c. The staggering model

Answers

1. a

2. a, b

3. No

4. a

5. b

14
CI/CD Pipelines with GitOps

In the last chapter, we introduced GitOps, why we need it, its principles, and various types of GitOps deployments. We also looked at different kinds of repositories we would create to implement GitOps and the branching strategy choices for each of them. We then looked at a hands-on example of GitOps with declarative infrastructure and config management, where we used Terraform to create a Kubernetes cluster using GitOps. Now, we will deep dive into GitOps and look at application management and the end-to-end GitOps life cycle using CI/CD pipelines.

In this chapter, we're going to cover the following main topics:

- Continuous integration with GitHub Actions
- Release gating with pull requests
- Continuous deployment with Flux CD
- Managing sensitive configuration and Secrets

Technical requirements

For this chapter, we will spin up a cloud-based Kubernetes cluster – **Google Kubernetes Engine (GKE)** – for the exercises. Currently, **Google Cloud Platform (GCP)** provides a free $300 trial for 90 days, so you can go ahead and sign up for one at https://console.cloud.google.com/.

You will also need to clone the following GitHub repository for some of the exercises: https://github.com/PacktPublishing/Modern-DevOps-Practices.

You can use the cloud shell available on Google Cloud to follow this chapter. Go to the cloud shell and start a new session. Run the following command to clone the repository into your home directory, and cd into the ch14 directory to access the required resources:

```
$ git clone https://github.com/PacktPublishing/Modern-DevOps-\
Practices.git modern-devops
$ cd modern-devops/ch14
```

Now, let's look at **Continuous Integration (CI)** with GitHub Actions in the next section.

Continuous integration with GitHub Actions

While we've already discussed GitHub Actions in detail in *Chapter 10, Continuous Integration*, and used it in the last chapter – *Chapter 13, Understanding DevOps with GitOps* – we will use GitHub Actions to build our code in the application repository. In this chapter, we will take a simple Flask application that returns The Secret is <secret_name> when we hit the home page. The secret is sourced from an environment variable called SECRET, and if it's not present, the application will return Secret not found. It will return a The page <page> does not exist. response for all other pages. We will deploy it in a Kubernetes environment (GKE). In the previous chapter, we created a GKE cluster using the *push model* of GitOps. We will leverage that in this chapter as well. We will use the GitHub flow for the application repository as we have an elementary example here, and as it is a microservice, it suits us well. The application repository should have a master branch that should contain code that is ready to be deployed, and we will create feature branches for every feature we're working on. In our scenario, we will automatically raise a pull request for the code to be merged with the master if the tests run fine. Someone manually reviews the code and approves it, and then we merge the code to the master branch (that is the only manual check in this process). The process is illustrated in detail in the following diagram:

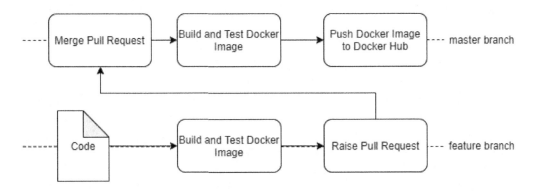

Figure 14.1 – CI process

So, let's start with the Flask application first. To access the resources for this section, cd into the following:

```
$ cd ~/modern-devops/ch14/ci/flask-app
```

The app.py file consists of the following:

```
from flask import Flask
from flask import make_response
import os
app = Flask(__name__)
@app.route('/')
def index():
  secret = os.environ.get('SECRET')
  if secret is not None:
    return "The secret is "+secret
  else:
    return "Secret not found"

@app.route('/<page>')
def default(page):
  response = make_response('The page %s does not exist.' %
page, 404)
  return response

if __name__ == '__main__':
  app.run(debug=True)
```

We will also write a test for this in the following `app.test.py` file:

```
import unittest
from app import app
class AppTestCase(unittest.TestCase):
  def test_index(self):
    tester = app.test_client(self)
    response = tester.get('/', content_type='html/text')
    self.assertEqual(response.status_code, 200)
    self.assertEqual(response.data, b'Secret not found')
  def test_default(self):
    tester = app.test_client(self)
    response = tester.get('xyz', content_type='html/text')
    self.assertEqual(response.status_code, 404)
    self.assertTrue(b'does not exist' in response.data)
if __name__ == '__main__':
  unittest.main()
```

It defines two tests in the test case. The first test checks whether the Flask application returns a `Secret not found` message with `HTTP 200` in the response when we hit the home page. The second test checks whether the application returns `does not exist` in the response with a `404 HTTP` code when we hit the `/xyz` page in the application.

Now, as we're all aware that Docker is inherently CI-compliant, we can run the tests using the `Dockerfile` itself. We create the following `Dockerfile`:

```
FROM python:3.7-alpine
ENV FLASK_APP=app.py
ENV FLASK_RUN_HOST=0.0.0.0
RUN apk add --no-cache gcc musl-dev linux-headers
COPY requirements.txt requirements.txt
RUN pip install -r requirements.txt
EXPOSE 5000
COPY . .
RUN python3 app.test.py
CMD ["flask", "run"]
```

That is all standard stuff that we've seen before. The next step would be creating an application repository on GitHub.

Creating an application repository on GitHub

To create an application repository, go to `https://github.com/new` and create a new repository. Give an appropriate name to it. For this exercise, I am going to use `flask-app-gitops`.

Once you've created it, clone the repository by using the following commands:

```
$ git clone https://github.com/PacktPublishing/Modern-DevOps-\
Practices.git modern-devops
$ cd flask-app-gitops
```

The next step would be to check in a `.gitignore` file into the directory. The `.gitignore` file lists all files that Git should ignore from commits, and is specially useful when you don't want people to accidentally check in files that are not desired in a Git repo, such as secrets. Copy the file to the directory and add, commit, and push changes using the following command:

```
$ cp ~/modern-devops/ch14/ci/flask-app/.gitignore .
$ git add --all
$ git commit -m 'Initial commit'
$ git push origin master
```

As we need to work on a feature branch, let's create a feature branch called `feature/flask` from the master and check that out using the following command:

```
$ git branch feature/flask && git checkout feature/flask
```

Copy `app.py`, `app.test.py`, `requirements.txt`, and `Dockerfile` into the repository directory using the following command:

```
$ cp ~/modern-devops/ch14/ci/flask-app/* .
```

Now, we need to create a GitHub Actions workflow file. Let's look at that in the next section.

Creating a GitHub Actions workflow

To start working with the workflow, create the `.github/workflows` directory within the repository. Let's do that using the following command:

```
$ mkdir -p .github/workflows
```

We will create two workflow files, one for our feature branches and one for the master branch. The `build.yaml` file takes care of building the code in the feature branches, testing them, and then raising a pull request to merge with the master branch. The `push.yaml` file takes care of rebuilding the code, testing it, and then pushing it to the Docker registry.

The `build.yaml` looks like the following:

```
name: Build, Test, and Raise Pull Request
on:
  push:
    branches: [ feature/* ]
jobs:
  build:
    runs-on: ubuntu-latest
    steps:
    - uses: actions/checkout@v2
    - name: Build the Docker image
      id: build
      run: docker build . --file Dockerfile --tag ${{ secrets.
DOCKER_USER }}/flask-app-gitops
    - name: Raise a Pull Request
      id: pull-request
      uses: repo-sync/pull-request@v2
      with:
        destination_branch: master
        github_token: ${{ secrets.GH_TOKEN }}
```

The YAML file does the following:

1. Checks out the code from the repository

2. Builds and tests the Docker image

3. Raises a pull request to merge with the master branch using the GH_TOKEN secret

The `push.yaml` file looks like the following:

```
name: Build, Test, and Push container image
on:
  push:
    branches: [ master ]
jobs:
  build:
    runs-on: ubuntu-latest
```

```
    steps:
    - uses: actions/checkout@v2
    - name: Login to Docker Hub
      id: login
      run: docker login -u ${{ secrets.DOCKER_USER  }} -p ${{
secrets.DOCKER_PASSWORD }}
    - name: Build the Docker image
      id: build
      run: docker build . --file Dockerfile --tag ${{ secrets.
DOCKER_USER  }}/flask-app-gitops:$(git rev-parse --short
"$GITHUB_SHA")
    - name: Push the Docker image
      id: push
      run: docker push ${{ secrets.DOCKER_USER  }}/flask-app-
gitops:$(git rev-parse --short "$GITHUB_SHA")
```

The YAML file does the following:

1. Checks out the code from the repository.

2. Logs in to Docker Hub using the DOCKER_USER and DOCKER_PASSWORD secrets.

3. Builds and tests the Docker image and tags the image with the Git commit SHA. That relates the build with the commit and therefore makes Git the single source of truth.

4. Pushes the image to Docker Hub.

There are a few things that are necessary for the workflows to function. First, we need to define a GitHub token so that the workflow can act as the current user while creating the pull request. For that, go to https://github.com/settings/tokens and create a new token with the repo scope. Once you've created the token, copy it and keep it handy.

We also need to define three secrets within our repository by going to https://github.com/<your_user>/flask-app-gitops/settings/secrets/actions.

Define three secrets within the repository:

```
DOCKER_USER=<Your DockerHub username>
DOCKER_PASSWORD=<Your DockerHub password>
GH_TOKEN=<Your GitHub token>
```

Now, let's copy the `build.yaml` and `push.yaml` files to the `workflows` directory by using the following commands:

```
$ cp ~/modern-devops/ch14/ci/build.yaml .github/workflows/
$ cp ~/modern-devops/ch14/ci/push.yaml .github/workflows/
```

We're ready to push this code to GitHub. Run the following commands to commit and push the changes to your GitHub repository:

```
$ git add --all
$ git commit -m 'Initial commit'
$ git push -u origin feature/flask
```

Now, go to the **workflows** tab of your GitHub repository by visiting `https://github.com/<your_user>/flask-app-gitops/actions`, and you should see something like the following:

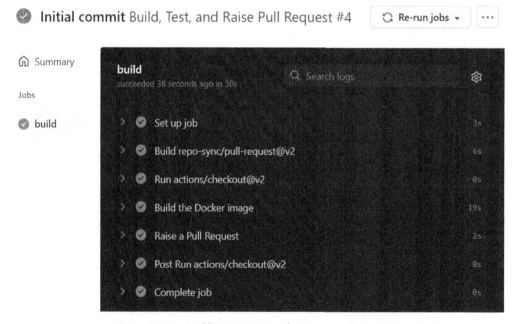

Figure 14.2 – Building, testing, and raising a pull request

As we see, GitHub has run a build using our workflow file, and it has built the code and created a pull request to merge the code with the master branch. The CI pipeline is running as expected. Now let's look at release gating with pull requests.

Release gating with pull requests

As we saw in the previous section, the CI pipeline built the code, did a test, ran a container, and verified that everything is OK. It then automatically raised a pull request to merge the code with the master branch. Now, we're in the **release gating** process. We want someone to manually verify whether the code is good and ready to be merged with the master branch or not. Apart from the CI workflow, we'll also use release gating in the **Continuous Deployment (CD)** workflow. As we know that the pull request is raised, let's go ahead and inspect the pull request and approve it.

Go to `https://github.com/<your_user>/flask-app-gitops/pulls` and you will see a pull request. Click on the pull request, and you will see the following:

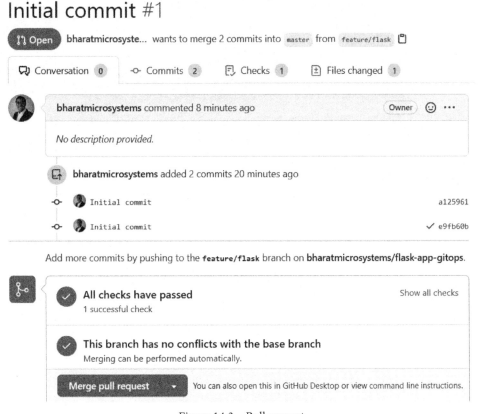

Figure 14.3 – Pull request

We see that the pull request is ready to merge. Click on **Merge pull request**, and you will see that the changes will reflect onto the master branch.

If you then go to `https://github.com/<your_user>/flask-app-gitops/actions`, you'll see the `Build`, `Test`, and `Push container image` workflow triggered. When you click on the workflow, you will see a workflow run like the following:

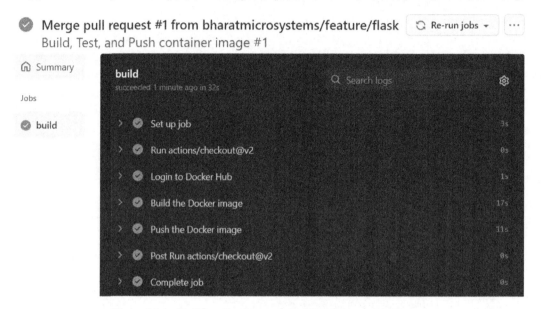

Figure 14.4 – Building, testing, and pushing the container image

When we merged the pull request, it automatically triggered the `push.yaml` workflow as it would react to any new changes in the master branch. The workflow did its job by building the code, testing it, building the container, and pushing the container to Docker Hub. If you go to Docker Hub, you will see a new image in the `flask-app-gitops` repository that will contain a tag with the commit SHA:

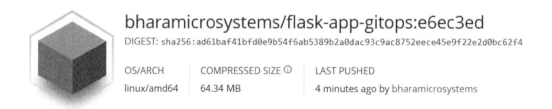

Figure 14.5 – Container image in Docker Hub

That was release gating in action for you. In the next section, let's look at the CD workflow with GitOps.

Continuous deployment with Flux CD

In the CI section, we created an application repository for building and testing the core application. In the case of CD, we would need to create an environment repository as that is what we will use for doing all deployments. We already have a repository that we created in *Chapter 13*, *Understanding DevOps with GitOps*, where we created a GKE instance on GCP using the GitOps push deployment model. We will reuse that and add configuration for deploying the Flask application using the GitOps pull deployment model.

We will have two branches within the environment repository – **dev** and **prod**. All configuration in the **dev** branch would apply to the **development environment**, and that on **prod** will apply to the **production environment**. The following diagram illustrates the approach in detail:

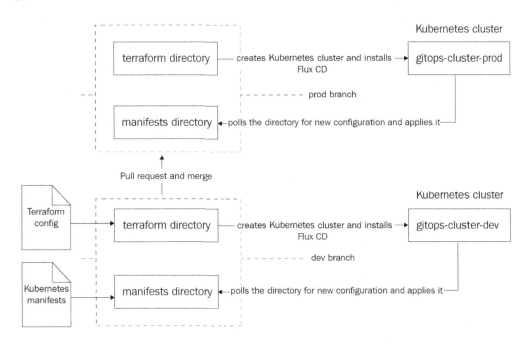

Figure 14.6 – CD process

The existing repository has a single branch called master. However, since we will be managing multiple environments in this repository, it would be good to rename the master branch to prod.

Go to https://github.com/<your_user>/gitops-environments/ branches and click on the pencil icon beside **master**. Type the name prod and click on **Rename Branch**.

Now, let's clone the repository using the following commands:

```
$ cd ~
$ git clone \
  https://github.com/<your_account>/gitops-environments.git
$ cd gitops-environments
```

We want to start with the dev environment, so it will be good to create a branch called dev from the prod branch. Run the following command to do so:

```
$ git branch dev && git checkout dev
```

Then, we can create a directory to hold our application manifests using the following command:

```
$ mkdir manifests && cd manifests
```

We then need to create Kubernetes Deployment and Service resource manifests that will deploy the Flask application and expose it externally.

The deployment.yaml file looks the following:

```
apiVersion: apps/v1
kind: Deployment
metadata:
  name: flask-app
spec:
  selector:
    matchLabels:
      app: flask-app
  replicas: 1
  template:
    metadata:
      labels:
        app: flask-app
    spec:
```

```
    containers:
    - name: flask-app
      image: <your_dockerhub_user>/flask-app-gitops:<your_
gitcommit_sha>
      ports:
      - containerPort: 5000
```

As you may have noticed here, you'll have to substitute the <your_dockerhub_user> placeholder with your DockerHub user and the <your_gitcommit_sha> placeholder with the tag created during the CI stage which correlates to the SHA of the Git commit that triggered it. Now let's look at the service.yaml file:

```
apiVersion: v1
kind: Service
metadata:
  name: flask-app
spec:
  selector:
    app: flask-app
  ports:
    - port: 80
      targetPort: 5000
  type: LoadBalancer
```

The service.yaml file exposes the flask-app Pods over a load balancer on port 80 and forwards connection from the load balancer to container port 5000. This is pretty much standard stuff. Now, let's copy these files to the gitops-environment repository using the following command:

```
$ cp -a ~/modern-devops/ch14/cd/manifests/flask-app\
/deployment.yaml manifests/
$ cp -a ~/modern-devops/ch14/cd/manifests/flask-app\
/service.yaml manifests/
```

Right, so as our manifests are now ready, we need a CD tool for doing the pull-based GitOps. We will be using Flux CD for this. Let's talk a bit about Flux CD in the next section.

Introduction to Flux CD

Flux CD is an open source CD tool initially developed by **Weaveworks**, and it works on the pull-based GitOps deployment model. It is a prevalent tool, and since it is a part of the **Cloud Native Computing Foundation** (**CNCF**), it is very much suited for applications running on containers and Kubernetes.

It polls the Git repository for changes periodically and syncs the Kubernetes cluster with changes in the repo. This ensures that we never have deviation with the code and configuration stored in the Git repository, and all changes eventually get applied to the cluster.

Flux CD has the following elements that make it work:

- **Flux CD operators**: They continuously poll the Git repository and/or the container registry for new changes. They are also aware of all objects present within Kubernetes and react when they detect any deviation from the current state in the cluster.

- **Memcached**: This is a key-value store where Flux CD stores the desired state of the cluster. If Flux CD notices any deviation from the desired state, it will make relevant changes using the Kubernetes API. Suppose the Flux CD operators notice changes within the Git repo or the container registry. In that case, it will apply/delete the delta configuration within the cluster and, once that is done, will store the new desired state in Memcached.

- The high-level components and the process is shown in the following diagram:

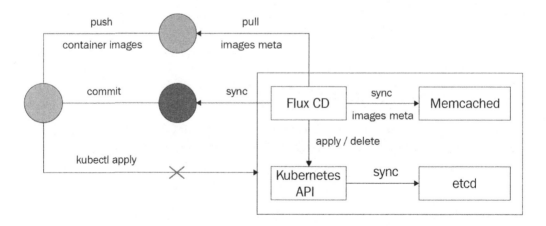

Figure 14.7 – Flux CD

Setting up Flux CD is also easy. While you have the native `fluxctl` and the manual way of setting it up, as GitOps requires everything as declarative code, we can alternatively set up Flux CD using Terraform, which we will use in this case.

Installing Flux CD

So, we will make some changes to the existing Terraform configuration to launch the cluster and install and set up Flux CD. The `main.tf` file will have multiple resources – let's look at each one by one.

We have a service account that the cluster will use and are naming it with a combination of the `cluster_name` and `branch` variables. That is necessary as we need to distinguish clusters from the environments. So, if the cluster name is `gitops-cluster` and the Git branch is `dev`, we will have a service account called `gke-gitops-cluster-dev-sa`.

We will also create a GKE cluster with the same naming convention as we did for the service account. In this scenario from the preceding example, we will have a cluster called `gitops-cluster-dev`. The following block shows the resources we'll create:

```
resource "google_service_account" "main" {
  account_id   = "gke-${var.cluster_name}-${var.branch}-sa"
  . . .
}
resource "google_container_cluster" "main" {
  name                = "${var.cluster_name}-${var.branch}"
  . . .
  node_config {
    service_account = google_service_account.main.email
  . . .
}
```

The next part will be some data sources that will help generate Kubernetes manifests that we will apply to install Flux CD. We will provide the `target_path` attribute where we want to generate the manifests within the environment repository (`manifests` in our case):

```
data "flux_install" "main" {
  target_path = var.target_path
}
data "flux_sync" "main" {
  target_path = var.target_path
```

```
  url          = "ssh://git@github.com/${var.github_
owner}/${var.repository_name}.git"
  branch       = var.branch
}
```

The next step would be to sleep for 30 seconds as we don't want to apply any configuration to the Kubernetes cluster until it is ready. To do so, we use the following `time_sleep` resource with an explicit dependency on the `google_container_cluster` resource. It will sleep for 30 seconds after the cluster is created so that it is ready to serve requests:

```
resource "time_sleep" "wait_30_seconds" {
  depends_on = [google_container_cluster.main]
  create_duration = "30s"
}
```

To connect with GKE, we will make use of the `gke_auth` module provided by `terraform-google-modules/kubernetes-engine/google//modules/auth`. We will add an explicit dependency on the `time_sleep` module so that the authentication happens 30 seconds after the cluster is created:

```
module "gke_auth" {
  depends_on            = [time_sleep.wait_30_seconds]
  source                = "terraform-google-modules/kubernetes-
engine/google//modules/auth"
  project_id            = var.project_id
  cluster_name          = google_container_cluster.main.name
  location              = var.location
  use_private_endpoint  = false
}
```

Once authenticated, we will initialize the `kubernetes` and `kubectl` providers with the `cluster_ca_certificate`, `host`, and `token` attributes obtained from the `gke_auth` module:

```
provider "kubernetes" {
  cluster_ca_certificate = module.gke_auth.cluster_ca_
certificate
  host                   = module.gke_auth.host
  token                  = module.gke_auth.token
}
```

```
provider "kubectl" {
  cluster_ca_certificate = module.gke_auth.cluster_ca_
certificate
  host                   = module.gke_auth.host
  token                  = module.gke_auth.token
  load_config_file       = false
}
```

We then start defining Kubernetes resources. We first create a namespace called `flux_system` using the following declaration:

```
resource "kubernetes_namespace" "flux_system" {
  ...
}
```

We then define a few data sources that can get the manifest files for installing Flux CD:

```
data "kubectl_file_documents" "install" {
  content = data.flux_install.main.content
}
data "kubectl_file_documents" "sync" {
  content = data.flux_sync.main.content
}
locals {
  install = [for v in data.kubectl_file_documents.install.
documents : {
    data : yamldecode(v)
    content : v
    }
  ]
  sync = [for v in data.kubectl_file_documents.sync.documents :
{
    data : yamldecode(v)
    content : v
    }
  ]
}
```

Finally, we start applying the Kubernetes resources using the data sources to the `flux_system` namespace:

```
resource "kubectl_manifest" "install" {
  depends_on = [kubernetes_namespace.flux_system]
  for_each   = { for v in local.install : lower(join("/",
compact([v.data.apiVersion, v.data.kind, lookup(v.data.
metadata, "namespace", ""), v.data.metadata.name]))) =>
v.content }
  yaml_body  = each.value
}
resource "kubectl_manifest" "sync" {
  depends_on = [kubectl_manifest.install, kubernetes_namespace.
flux_system]
  for_each   = { for v in local.sync : lower(join("/",
compact([v.data.apiVersion, v.data.kind, lookup(v.data.
metadata, "namespace", ""), v.data.metadata.name]))) =>
v.content }
  yaml_body  = each.value
}
```

We then generate a TLS key pair called `github_deploy_key` that Flux CD will use to interact with GitHub via SSH and create a Kubernetes Secret with it. That is the Secret that the Flux CD operator will use while polling the GitHub repository for new content:

```
resource "tls_private_key" "github_deploy_key" {
  algorithm = "RSA"
  rsa_bits  = 4096
}
resource "kubernetes_secret" "main" {
  depends_on = [kubectl_manifest.install]
  metadata {
    name      = data.flux_sync.main.secret
    namespace = data.flux_sync.main.namespace
  }
  data = {
    known_hosts     = local.known_hosts
    identity        = tls_private_key.github_deploy_key.private_
key_pem
    "identity.pub"  = tls_private_key.github_deploy_key.public_
key_openssh
  }
}
```

We then initialize the `github` provider with the `github_token` and `github_owner` attributes that we will supply as variables:

```
provider "github" {
  token         = var.github_token
  owner         = var.github_owner
}
```

We then define `github_repository` as a data source so that we can use it in the subsequent steps:

```
data "github_repository" "main" {
  full_name = "${var.github_owner}/${var.repository_name}"
}
```

We would then push the generated Flux CD manifest files to our GitHub repository using the following resources:

```
resource "github_repository_file" "install" {
  repository          = data.github_repository.main.name
  file                = data.flux_install.main.path
  content             = data.flux_install.main.content
  branch              = var.branch
  overwrite_on_create = true
}
resource "github_repository_file" "sync" {
  repository          = var.repository_name
  file                = data.flux_sync.main.path
  content             = data.flux_sync.main.content
  branch              = var.branch
  overwrite_on_create = true
}
resource "github_repository_file" "kustomize" {
  repository          = var.repository_name
  file                = data.flux_sync.main.kustomize_path
  content             = data.flux_sync.main.kustomize_content
  branch              = var.branch
  overwrite_on_create = true
}
```

Finally, we create the `github_repository_deploy_key` resource that Flux CD will use to interact with GitHub with the public key that we generated in the previous steps:

```
resource "github_repository_deploy_key" "flux" {
  title      = var.github_deploy_key_title
  repository = data.github_repository.main.name
  key        = tls_private_key.github_deploy_key.public_key_
openssh
  read_only  = true
}
```

Let's look at the `variables.tf` file to understand how we're managing the variables.

We first declare the `project_id` variable. As you can see, there is no default value for this, so we need to provide the value during runtime:

```
variable "project_id" {...}
```

The `branch` variable contains the name of the branch where we're running the plan. We will set this to the current working branch:

```
variable "branch" {...}
```

The following is the `cluster_name` variable, which is the prefix of the actual cluster name, which would be `${var.cluster_name}-${var.branch}` as we saw in `main.tf`:

```
variable "cluster_name" {...
  default   = "gitops-cluster"
}
```

The following is the cluster location that we default to `us-central1-a`:

```
variable "location" {...
  default     = "us-central1-a"
}
```

We use the `github_token` variable to allow Terraform to interact with GitHub to check in the Flux CD manifests. You can use the same GitHub token that we generated in the CI section:

```
variable "github_token" {...}
```

The `github_owner` variable specifies the owner of your environment repository. In this case, it will be your GitHub user:

```
variable "github_owner" {...}
```

The `repository_name` variable specifies your GitHub environment repository name:

```
variable "repository_name" {...
  default     = "gitops-environments"
}
```

The following `github_deploy_key_title` variable holds the title for `github_deploy_key`:

```
variable "github_deploy_key_title" {...
  default     = "gitops-deploy-key"
}
```

The `target_path` variable defines the relative path to the Git repository root where the manifests are present. We will use the `manifests` directory as default for that:

```
variable "target_path" {...
  default     = "manifests"
}
```

Now, let's look at the `provider.tf` file. It starts with the `google` provider as before:

```
provider "google" {...
  project = var.project_id
}
```

It then contains the `terraform` block with a `required_version` constraint of `>= 0.13`. It also defines a number of providers in the `required_providers` block that we've used in `main.tf`:

```
terraform {
  required_version = ">= 0.13"
```

```
required_providers {
  github = {...}
  kubernetes = {...}
  kubectl = {...}
  flux = {...}
  tls = {...}
}
```

It then defines the `backend` configuration. We will be using the **Google Cloud Storage** (**GCS**) bucket for this. Make sure the bucket name is globally unique:

```
backend "gcs" {
  bucket = "tf-state-gitops-terraform-a"
  prefix = "gitops-terraform"
}
}
```

We then finally define the flux provider:

```
provider "flux" {}
```

Now, there are several things that we require before we push the configuration to Git.

Let's start by creating the Terraform service account, giving it the appropriate permissions and creating the GCS bucket for storing our state using the following commands:

```
$ PROJECT_ID=<Your GCP Project ID>
$ gcloud iam service-accounts create gitops-terraform \
--description="Service Account for GitOps terraform" \
--display-name="GitOps Terraform"
$ gcloud projects add-iam-policy-binding $PROJECT_ID \
--member="serviceAccount:gitops-terraform@$PROJECT_ID.\
iam.gserviceaccount.com" \
--role="roles/container.admin"
$ gcloud projects add-iam-policy-binding $PROJECT_ID \
--member="serviceAccount:gitops-terraform@$PROJECT_ID.\
iam.gserviceaccount.com" \
--role="roles/editor"
$ gcloud iam service-accounts keys create key-file \
--iam-account=gitops-terraform@$PROJECT_ID.\
iam.gserviceaccount.com
$ mv key-file ~/
$ gsutil mb gs://tf-state-gitops-terraform-a
```

```
$ gcloud services enable iam.googleapis.com \
container.googleapis.com
```

You will see that there is a file called `key-file` that is created within your home directory. Now, go to `https://github.com/<your_github_user>/gitops-environments/settings/secrets/actions/new` and create a secret with the name `GCP_CREDENTIALS`. For the value, print the `key-file` file, copy its contents, and paste it into the **values** field of the GitHub secret.

Next, create another secret called `PROJECT_ID` and specify your GCP project ID within the **values** field.

Then, create a secret called `GH_TOKEN` and paste the GitHub token that you generated in the CI section.

Now, to run the Terraform workflow, we would need a GitHub Actions workflow file. The GitHub Actions `create-cluster.yaml` workflow file looks like the following:

```yaml
name: Create Kubernetes Cluster
on: push
jobs:
  deploy-terraform:
    runs-on: ubuntu-latest
    defaults:
      run:
        working-directory: ./terraform
    steps:
    - uses: actions/checkout@v2
    - name: Install Terraform
      id: install-terraform
      run: wget -O terraform.zip https://releases.hashicorp.
com/terraform/0.15.3/terraform_0.15.3_linux_amd64.zip && unzip
terraform.zip && chmod +x terraform && sudo mv terraform /usr/
local/bin
    - name: Apply Terraform
      id: apply-terraform
      run: terraform init && terraform workspace select
${GITHUB_REF##*/} || terraform workspace new ${GITHUB_
REF##*/} && terraform apply -auto-approve -var="project_id=${{
secrets.PROJECT_ID }}" -var="repository_name=${GITHUB_
REPOSITORY##*/}" -var="github_token=${{ secrets.GH_TOKEN }}"
-var="branch=${GITHUB_REF##*/}" -var="github_owner=${GITHUB_
REPOSITORY%/*}"
      env:
        GOOGLE_CREDENTIALS: ${{ secrets.GCP_CREDENTIALS }}
```

The workflow file gets triggered on a push action on any branch and runs a job with the following steps:

1. Checks out the current working branch

2. Installs Terraform

3. Applies Terraform configuration using the following:

   a. Initializes Terraform.

   b. Either selects an existing Terraform workspace with the branch name or creates a new one. Workspaces are important here as we want to use the same configuration with different variable values for different environments. The workspaces correspond to environments, and environments correspond to the branch. So, as we have the dev and prod environments, we have the corresponding workspaces and branches.

   c. It then applies the Terraform configuration and passes a few variable values as arguments. They include project_id, repository_name, github_token, branch, and github_owner.

As we've created all the variables and secrets required to run this configuration, we can go ahead and copy all files to the gitops-environments repository using the following commands:

```
$ cp -a ~/modern-devops/ch14/cd/terraform/* terraform/
$ cp -a ~/modern-devops/ch14/cd/workflows/* .github/workflows/
```

Now, commit and push the files to GitHub using the following commands:

```
$ git add --all
$ git commit -m 'Initial comit'
$ git push --set-upstream origin dev
```

As we've pushed the code to GitHub, we will see that the push has triggered the deploy-terraform workflow, and you should see something like the following:

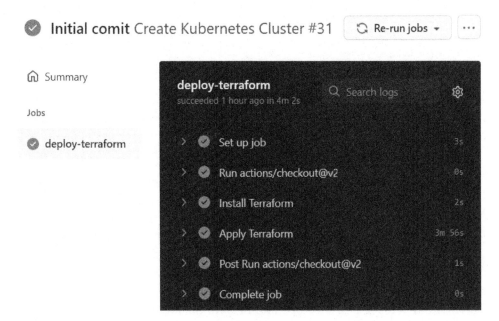

Figure 14.8 – Creating a Kubernetes cluster and installing Flux CD

So, as the workflow completes successfully, we can check whether Flux CD is working as expected.

> **Tip**
>
> If a Kubernetes resource takes a long time to create and Terraform times out, it might be because it depends on another Kubernetes resource (such as a service account) that Terraform hasn't created yet. So, wait for the workflow to time out and retry if it fails.

Once the workflow completes, you can fetch credentials from your Kubernetes cluster and check whether the required resources are created or not.

Run the following command to get the credentials:

```
$ gcloud container clusters get-credentials \
gitops-cluster-dev --zone us-central1-a \
--project $PROJECT_ID
```

Now run the following to see whether all resources are created successfully or not:

```
$ kubectl get all --template '{{range .items}}\
{{.kind}}{{.metadata.name}}{{"\n"}}{{end}}'
```

```
Pod flask-app-574fd65b8f-cflpg
Service flask-app
Deployment flask-app
ReplicaSet flask-app-574fd65b8f
```

We see that we have a `flask-app` Service, a `Deployment`, a corresponding `ReplicaSet`, and a `Pod` created. That means Flux CD is working fine and syncing up data from the repository.

Now, let's modify `deployment.yaml` and create two replicas of `flask-app`. Go to `~/gitops-environments/manifests/flask-app/` and change `replicas` in `deployment.yaml` from 1 to 2:

```
. . .
  replicas: 2
. . .
```

Once you've done it, commit and push the code to GitHub. Wait for 5 minutes and you should see two replicas of `flask-app` running. Run the following command to verify it:

```
$ kubectl get pod
NAME                          READY    STATUS     RESTARTS    AGE
flask-app-574fd65b8f-cflpg    1/1      Running    0           82m
flask-app-574fd65b8f-z8ldz    1/1      Running    0           29s
```

As we see, Flux CD automatically detects any changes on the repository and applies that. Let's try to manually scale up the replicas to 3 within the Kubernetes cluster and see how it reacts:

```
$ kubectl scale deployment flask-app --replicas 3
```

Now, let's see how many pods are running using the following command:

```
$ kubectl get pod
NAME                          READY    STATUS     RESTARTS    AGE
flask-app-574fd65b8f-cflpg    1/1      Running    0           85m
flask-app-574fd65b8f-kbpp4    1/1      Running    0           10s
flask-app-574fd65b8f-z8ldz    1/1      Running    0           3m
```

As we see, three replicas are running. Let's wait for 5 minutes for Flux CD to poll the Git repo and rerun the command:

```
$ kubectl get pod
NAME                            READY   STATUS        RESTARTS    AGE
flask-app-574fd65b8f-cflpg      1/1     Running       0           90m
flask-app-574fd65b8f-kbpp4      1/1     Terminating   0           4m41s
flask-app-574fd65b8f-z8ldz      1/1     Running       0           8m6s
```

As we see, in just around 5 minutes, Flux CD detected the deviation and corrected it by terminating the extra pod.

Now, let's try to trigger the `flask-app` service and see what we get. To get the External IP of the service, run the following command:

```
$ kubectl get service flask-app
NAME        TYPE          CLUSTER-IP      EXTERNAL-IP     PORT(S)
flask-app   LoadBalancer  10.43.255.182   34.71.167.225   80:30377
```

Now, let's go ahead and use `curl` to trigger the `EXTERNAL-IP`:

```
$ curl 34.71.167.225
Secret not found
```

As we can see, we get `Secret not found` in the response. That's expected because we haven't injected any secret into the pod's environment. Well, you might be tempted to create one manually, but that is not something we do in GitOps. What can we do then? Shall we create a manifest for the secret and check it in source control? No! Because secrets only contain a Base64 equivalent of the plaintext secret, and it is not secure. So, the general rule is to never check in Kubernetes Secret manifests to source control.

But GitOps uses Git for everything, right? What do we do for Secrets? Well, for that, we will look at another tool called Sealed Secrets in the next section.

Managing sensitive configuration and Secrets

Sealed Secrets solves the problem of *I can manage all my Kubernetes config in Git, except Secrets*. Created by *Bitnami Labs* and open sourced, they help you encrypt your Kubernetes Secrets into Sealed Secrets using asymmetric cryptography that only the Sealed Secrets controller running on the cluster can decrypt. That means you can store the Sealed Secrets in Git and use GitOps to set up everything, including Secrets.

Sealed Secrets comprise two components:

- A client-side utility called `kubeseal` helps us generate Sealed Secrets out of standard Kubernetes Secret YAML.

- A cluster-side Kubernetes controller/operator unseals your secrets and provides the key certificate to the client-side utility.

The typical workflow when using Sealed Secrets is illustrated in the following diagram:

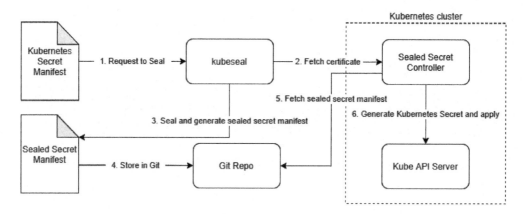

Figure 14.9 – Sealed Secrets workflow

Now, let's go ahead and install the Sealed Secret operator in the next section.

Installing the Sealed Secrets operator

To install the **Sealed Secrets operator**, all you need to do is to download the controller manifest from the latest release on `https://github.com/bitnami-labs/sealed-secrets/releases`. At the time of writing this book, `https://github.com/bitnami-labs/sealed-secrets/releases/download/v0.16.0/controller.yaml` is the latest controller manifest.

Create a new directory called `sealed-secrets` within the `manifest` directory and download `controller.yaml` there using the following commands:

```
$ cd ~/gitops-environments/manifests & mkdir sealed-secrets
$ cd sealed-secrets
$ wget https://github.com/bitnami-labs/sealed-secrets/releases\
/download/v0.16.0/controller.yaml
```

Then, commit and push the changes to the remote repository, and you should see that after about 5 minutes, the `sealed-secrets` controller will be visible in the `kube-system` namespace. Run the following command to check:

```
$ kubectl get deployment -n kube-system \
sealed-secrets-controller
NAME                          READY   UP-TO-DATE   AVAILABLE   AGE
sealed-secrets-controller 1/1     1            1           105s
```

So, as we see, the controller is running and ready, we can install the client-side utility – `kubeseal`.

Installing kubeseal

To install the client-side utility, you can go to `https://github.com/bitnami-labs/sealed-secrets/releases` and get the `kubeseal` installation binary link from the page. The following commands will install `kubeseal 0.16.0` on your system:

```
$ wget https://github.com/bitnami-labs/sealed-secrets/\
releases/download/v0.16.0/kubeseal-linux-amd64 -O kubeseal
$ sudo install -m 755 kubeseal /usr/local/bin/kubeseal
```

To check whether `kubeseal` is installed successfully, run the following command:

```
$ kubeseal --version
kubeseal version: v0.16.0
```

As we see that `kubeseal` is successfully installed, let's go ahead and create a Sealed Secret for `flask-app`.

Creating Sealed Secrets

To create the Sealed Secret, we would first have to define the Kubernetes `Secret resource`. The Secret called `flask-app-secret` should contain a key-value pair with the key called `SECRET` and the value `GitOps`.

First, let's go ahead and create the Kubernetes secret manifest called `flask-app-secret.yaml` using the following command:

```
$ kubectl create secret generic flask-app-secret \
--from-literal SECRET=GitOps \
--dry-run=client -o yaml > flask-app-secret.yaml
```

The `flask-app-secret.yaml` file is a simple Kubernetes Secret YAML manifest that contains the Base64-encoded value of the Secret. Do not check this in source control. We will have to use `kubeseal` to seal this Secret and generate the Sealed Secret to store in the Git repository. To seal the Secret and generate the Sealed Secret YAML file, run the following command:

```
$ kubeseal -o yaml < flask-app-secret.yaml > \
flask-app-secret-sealed.yaml
```

It generates the `flask-app-secret-sealed.yaml` Sealed Secret, which looks like the following:

```
apiVersion: bitnami.com/v1alpha1
kind: SealedSecret
metadata:
  name: flask-app-secret
spec:
  encryptedData:
    SECRET: AgBhhbWFAG98nSDKI5DoTJjEea…
  template:
    metadata:
      name: flask-app-secret
```

As you can see, the Sealed Secret is very similar to the `Secret` manifest. Still, instead of containing a Base64-encoded secret value, it has encrypted it so that only `sealed-secrets-controller` can decrypt it. You can easily check this file into source control. Let's go ahead and do that. Move the Sealed Secret YAML file to `manifests/flask-app` using the following command:

```
$ mv flask-app-secret-sealed.yaml ~/gitops-\
environments/manifests/flask-app/
```

Now, as we've created the Sealed Secret, we also need to change the `flask-app` deployment to inject the Secret as an environment variable in the `flask-app` pod. Modify `manifest/flask-app/deployment.yaml` to include the following:

```
...
        image: <your_dockerhub_user>/flask-app-gitops:<your_
gitcommit_sha>
        env:
        - name: SECRET
          valueFrom:
```

```
        secretKeyRef:
            name: flask-app-secret
            key: SECRET
    ports:
...
```

To make things simple, you can also copy the `deployment-from-secret.yaml` file from the `ch14/cd/flask-app/` directory to the `manifests/flask-app` directory. Remember that you'll have to substitute the <your_dockerhub_user> and the <your_gitcommit_sha> placeholders appropriately, and then run the following command:

```
$ cp ~/modern-devops/ch14/cd/deployment-with-\
secret.yaml ~/gitops-environments/manifests\
/flask-app/deployment.yaml
```

Now, commit and push the changes to the `gitops-environments` repository.

As soon as you push the changes, you should notice that the `flask-app` pods will get recreated in 5 minutes. Run the following command to check:

```
$ kubectl get pod
NAME                          READY   STATUS    RESTARTS   AGE
flask-app-65bcc94f5-7ffgc     1/1     Running   0          34s
flask-app-65bcc94f5-wgdk8     1/1     Running   0          37s
```

You will see it has created two new pods and terminated the old pods. Now, let's hit the external IP of the service again using the following command:

```
$ curl 34.71.167.225
The Secret is GitOps
```

As we see, now we get `The Secret is GitOps` in the response. That means the Sealed Secret is working perfectly fine.

As we're happy with the application, we can raise a pull request from the `dev` branch to the `prod` branch. Once you merge the pull request, you will see that similar services will come up in the production environment. You can use pull request-based gating for CD as well. That ensures that your environments remain independent of each other while being sourced from the same repository, albeit from different branches.

Summary

And we've come to the end of an eventful chapter and also the end of the book. We deep-dived into GitOps and looked at application management and the end-to-end GitOps life cycle using CI/CD pipelines. We started with the CI of a simple Flask application with GitHub Actions. We then discussed release gating with pull requests and then learned about CD in GitOps with a hands-on exercise with Flux CD. We then covered managing sensitive configuration and Secrets with Sealed Secrets. Throughout the chapter, we created all services, including the CI/CD pipelines, with code, and therefore implemented pure GitOps.

GitOps is a fantastic way of implementing modern DevOps. It is always fruitful in the long run as it is easy to implement, requires very little documentation, and the best part is that you have working code for every bit of infrastructure and software you're running. So, if you lose your entire estate but have your code and data, you can spin up everything from scratch – a great power indeed.

As we've come to the end of a fantastic journey, I would like to thank you for selecting the book and reading it through and hope you've enjoyed every bit of it. This book should give you all the skills you need to upskill yourself in the discipline of modern DevOps, and I hope you've found it valuable. I wish you all the best for your current and future endeavors.

Questions

1. What branch names should you prefer for your environment repository?

   a. `dev`, `staging`, and `prod`

   b. `feature`, `develop`, and `master`

   c. `release` and `main`

2. Which one of the following deployment models does Flux CD use?

   a. Push model

   b. Pull model

   c. Staggering model

3. True or false: You should use Terraform to install Flux CD, as you can store all configurations in Git.

4. Flux CD can sync resources from which of the following sources? (Choose two)

   a. Git repository

   b. Container Registry

c. JFrog Artifactory's raw repository

5. What would Flux CD do if you manually changed a resource outside Git?

    a. Flux CD will change the resource to match the Git configuration.

    b. Flux CD will notify you that a resource has changed outside Git.

    c. Flux CD will do nothing.

6. You can check in Sealed Secrets to a Git repository. (True or False)

    Answer:

Answers

1. a
2. b
3. True
4. a, b
5. a
6. True

Other Books You May Enjoy

If you enjoyed this book, you may be interested in these other books by Packt:

Google Cloud for DevOps Engineers

Sandeep Madamanchi

ISBN: 978-1-83921-801-9

- Categorize user journeys and explore different ways to measure SLIs
- Explore the four golden signals for monitoring a user-facing system
- Understand psychological safety along with other SRE cultural practices
- Create containers with build triggers and manual invocations
- Delve into Kubernetes workloads and potential deployment strategies
- Secure GKE clusters via private clusters, Binary Authorization, and shielded GKE nodes
- Get to grips with monitoring, Metrics Explorer, uptime checks, and alerting
- Discover how logs are ingested via the Cloud Logging API

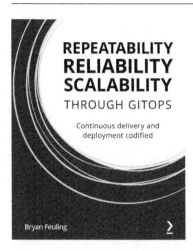

Repeatability, Reliability, and Scalability through GitOps

Bryan Feuling

ISBN: 978-1-80107-779-8

- Explore a variety of common industry tools for GitOps
- Understand continuous deployment, continuous delivery, and why they are important
- Gain a practical understanding of using GitOps as an engineering organization
- Become well-versed with using GitOps and Kubernetes together
- Leverage Git events for automated deployments
- Implement GitOps best practices and find out how to avoid GitOps pitfalls

Packt is searching for authors like you

If you're interested in becoming an author for Packt, please visit `authors.packtpub.com` and apply today. We have worked with thousands of developers and tech professionals, just like you, to help them share their insight with the global tech community. You can make a general application, apply for a specific hot topic that we are recruiting an author for, or submit your own idea.

Share your thoughts

Now you've finished *Modern DevOps Practices*, we'd love to hear your thoughts! Scan the QR code below to go straight to the Amazon review page for this book and share your feedback or leave a review on the site that you purchased it from.

https://packt.link/r/1-800-56238-1

Your review is important to us and the tech community and will help us make sure we're delivering excellent quality content.

Index

B

Oracle Cloud Infrastructure Registry 100

P

Packer
  image prerequisites 288, 290
  used, for creating Apache and
      MySQL images 288
Packer configuration
  defining 290-297
path-based routing 180-182
persistent volumes
  dynamic provisioning 194-199
  managing 189
  static provisioning 189-194
pod multi-container design patterns
  about 127
  adapter pattern 144-147
  ambassador pattern 131
  init container 128-131
  secrets 140
  secrets, example flask
      application 141-144
  sidecar pattern 139, 140
pods 312
Pretty Good Privacy (PGP) 420
principle of least privilege (PoLP) 435
private Docker registry
  hosting 97-99
production environment 469
Prometheus
  configuring, to scrape metrics 50
  installing 49, 50
  used, for monitoring Docker 48
Prometheus query language (PromQL) 48
public Docker registry 100
public key infrastructure (PKI) 430
pull model 446, 447

pull requests
  release gating 467-469
Puppet 283
push model 445
Python Flask app
  about 346
  building 336, 337
  deploying, on Knative 336-340
  using 422

Q

quality assurance (QA) 430

R

Ramped slow rollout 164-166
Recreate strategy 160-162
Red/Black deployment 388
release gating
  about 467
  with pull requests 467, 469
ReplicaSet resource 153
resource group, terraform
  creating, with Azure resource
      group 219, 220
return on investment (ROI) 23
Role-Based Access Control (RBAC) 446
Rolling Update strategy 160-164
RUN directives 71-73

S

Saltstack 283
sample container application
  launching 51-53
Scalable Jenkins
  on Kubernetes, with Kaniko 356-358

T

W